I Arise! 2025

A devotional book for women

Day by day, from one heart to another

I am so grateful and honoured to have had the opportunity to share in this project previously!

What a wonderful and on time resource. It is definitely for all women, but also anyone needing encouragement and reinforcements from the Lord, through the varied seasons of life. The reflections are intimate yet universal.

"I Arise!" devotional, so appropriately named, will definitely allow you to become aware of God's daily activity in your life; it will motivate you to rise, stand up, and move upward, as you ascend into His presence.

Sister Allison Todd
Canada

Before we begin:

"This is the day which the LORD hath made; we will rejoice and be glad in it" (Psalm 118:24).

The fingerprint of God is in our everyday lives, *"This I recall to my mind, therefore have I hope"* (Lamentations 3:21). I invite you to take a moment and bring to your mind the unending and overwhelming goodness and faithfulness of God in your life. Inexplicably, God is in the details, and He is working all things out for your good.

It was just another ordinary day – or so I thought! We had only one vehicle to transport us, the Datsun 8210. Our daily routine was to take our two-year-old daughter to the babysitter, and then Marcus and I would both go to work. I worked in downtown Baltimore, and Marcus worked almost polar opposite in Uptown Baltimore, in Westview Mall. After work, I picked up our little girl, went home and waited for Marcus to finish work after the store closed at 9pm.

It was now around 7pm-ish when the telephone rang:

"It's Jenny", she said. *"Marcus has been hurt"!*

"Hurt, hurt how?" I exclaimed!

"The ambulance is taking him to the hospital". Hearing my voice, Jenny voluntarily tried to assure me that Marcus was going to be okay. And then she blurted out, *"His leg - it's broken! The paramedics, they had to reset it"!*

Shaken, my dad drove me to St. Agnes. The X-rays had already meted out the sentence that his right femur (the thigh bone, the biggest bone in the human body) was broken. How does a broken thigh bone, which will require surgery with an approximate six-month recuperation period in a cast, sound like the goodness of God? Well, I realise that to some, it may not. But, let's put a pin in it, right here! I want to encourage us to rely on the truth of God's Word, rather than the facts of our circumstances, *"I will say of the LORD, He is my refuge and my fortress"* (Psalm 91:2). The truth is that God was indeed a refuge, a protection from danger that day. The fact that our precious little darling daughter didn't get to go into the back of the stockroom to her daddy that evening gives way to a litany of thanksgiving.

The truth is that God was a mighty fortress for Marcus to be able to withstand that sudden unsuspecting assault of the enemy. I'm reminded of the conversation God had with Satan, when Satan came into heaven's boardroom meeting that day. God explicitly told Satan, you can touch Job's body, but you cannot, take his life (Job 1:12). You see, the 2,400lbs of sheetrock laid up against the stockroom wall didn't discriminate who it would fall on that day. It was poorly stocked which means that our daughter's tiny frame could very easily have been its intended victim - or even me!

Father, thank you for this another day that you have given us in the land of the living. We will rejoice and be glad because we know that you have made this day. And because you made it, you have given us everything we need in this day, for this day. Father, we know that you have the ultimate authority; it belongs to you despite the difficulties we may face. Our circumstances don't have the final say! I see the evidence of your goodness all over my life.

Ralph Waldo Emerson once told us, *"The years teach much which the days never knew"*. Marcus' one surgery on his right femur that day turned into nine major surgeries over a course of seven years. **That one day!**

Reminiscent of the many hats that I have worn over those seven years, this fit and look seemed so much different than any hat I had worn previously. The hat that I wore as a young wife, married five years now, was such a great look and fit. Like a fascinator which gives a complimentary and overall balanced look. A brim and no crown were of the right proportion. You see, I was married to the love of my life, we had a happy home, and we were expecting our first child.

Three years into married life, and 22 years old, this hat I wore as a young mother was quite different, but another great look and fit - like the pillbox hat which gives a conservative look. A somewhat flat crown and no brim were of the right size and shape. I enjoyed motherhood, especially as we got past the stage of constant crying (both baby and me), cleaning bottles, changing tons of diapers/pampers, and sleepless nights. I was quite proud that I was getting this mother thing 'down pat'.

And now, life had fashioned another hat for me - it was thrust upon my head - one that I did not choose and, quite frankly, one that I did not feel that I deserved! We were serving God with all our heart, mind and soul. But, even still, this hat felt and looked drastically different. It had a crown and the height of it made it heavier than my pillbox hat! The brim extended far out from the crown, unlike the fascinator, which made it harder at times for me to see my way. Picture one of those Kentucky Derby fashions; this hat looked way too mature for me to wear 24/7. I was only 24!

Sometimes we quote that, *"God will not put more on you than you can bear"* (that's not scripture by the way, even though we quote it like it is). That quote actually comes from 1 Corinthians 10:13, which says: *"No test or temptation that comes your way is beyond the course of what others have had to face. All you need to remember is that God will never let you down; He'll never let you be pushed past your limit; He'll always be there to help you come through it"* (MSV).

The truth of God's Word also lets us know that, *"Many are the afflictions of the righteous: but the LORD delivereth him out of them all"* (Psalm 34:19). That's the Word! For nine years, I was Marcus' wife and caregiver. They are not always one-and-the-same. Yes, sometimes he had nurses that came to the house around the clock, but after I worked all day, I still had to come home and take care of an ailing husband. Those responsibilities and duties included some of the activities of daily life like: bathing him, preparing meals, transporting him or arranging transport to various doctors' appointments, helping to dispense medications in which case some were narcotics, and to ensure that he was in a clean and safe environment.

Now when I consider our wedding vows, *"...To love in sickness and in health..."*, although we said those words without reservation, no one is expecting at age 24 and 26 to be a caregiver for what was once a healthy, energetic spouse! Even so, my testimony is that God gave me, with each new day, the strength for **that day**. Not for tomorrow, but for **that day**. His mercies are new every morning; great is thy faithfulness!

Needless to say, Marcus had many hospital stays over those seven years, sometimes weeks at a time. During that time period, I also had to advocate for him. Being there when the doctors came in with updates and treatment plans. I was there to ask the right questions which, in some cases, were hard questions, then getting those answers we didn't want to hear. I remember during one of his hospital stays, his doctor came in and said, *"I don't know what else to do for you Marcus. There is a specialist in Buffalo, NY that I have read about. I want you to go and see him"*.

So, his discharge was literally from his hospital bed directly to the airport to board a flight on a cold, wintry November morning to Buffalo, NY. It was so cold that the flight was delayed for the wings to be de-iced. Did I mention that this was my first flight on an airplane? I was travelling with my sick husband who had received priority boarding because he was wheelchair-bound. He was slid into his aisle seat and I sat next to him at the window. I was scared! Scared to fly! Scared we were doing this all by ourselves! Scared we were chartering into unknown territory, but I did it!

Fear, yes you can let it paralyse you, and stop you, or **you can let it propel you!** As the plane ascended, I white-knuckled my way to Buffalo. I had to grab the barf (throw up) bag from the seat in front of me, but again, I did it!

I know assuredly, that our God will not leave us without hope! If you are reading this and are a caregiver, please know that my heart's prayer for caregivers, is 2 Corinthians 1:3-4, *"Blessed be God, even the Father of our Lord Jesus Christ, the Father of mercies and the God of all comfort; Who comforteth us in all our tribulation, that we may be able to comfort them which are in any trouble by the comfort wherewith we ourselves are comforted of God"*.

For those of you who know, and those who do not know, Satan did not win in all his feeble attempts against my husband's life.

"And they overcame him, by the blood of the Lamb and the word of their testimony" (Revelation 12:11).

Lady Ronae A. Johnson
USA

This writing is intended for the BNWC "I Arise!" 2025 devotional book for women only. It should not be used for any other purpose without the express consent of the writer

Published by: Bethel National Women's Council

Category: Christianity
Copyright: Bethel National Women's Council 2024
ISBN: 9798342989978
Cover design by: Inspirational Journals
Graphic design by: Ashani Allen

Edited by: Jackie Jacobs

Proofreading Team:
Carol Lord-Paul
Cheryl Lowe
Rose Morrison
Deveen Smith
Vera Walters

CONTENTS:

Introduction & Acknowledgements   6

Monthly Writings:

January	All Things New	7
February	Love Stories of the Bible	51
March	Not Named & Hardly Mentioned Women in the Bible	99
April	The Fruit of the Spirit	149
May	Time to Pray	187
June	Family Life in the Bible	229
July	31 Days in the Psalms	277
August	Women of Purpose	321
September	Fearfully & Wonderfully Made	367
October	Parables of Jesus	413
November	The Goodness of God	463
December	Salt & Light	507

They said...   553
Support Directory   554
Contact Us   558

All Scripture references are from the King James Version unless otherwise stated

Themed days are correct at the time of printing

INTRODUCTION & ACKNOWLEDGEMENTS

Thanks be to God which giveth us the victory through our Lord Jesus Christ.

Welcome to *"I Arise!" 2025*, the 4th edition in this series. Look where God has brought us!

It's really wonderful to see how He has connected women from seven countries (Antigua & Barbuda, Guyana, Jamaica, Nevis, UK, USA, Zimbabwe) to fulfil this divine purpose. Although we differ in age, background and status, we do not differ in our faith.

The writings for 2025 are rich, a true outpouring of encouragement day by day from one heart to another.

Writers, proofreaders, readers, everybody, God bless you all!

Bethel National Women's Council

January
All Things New

*WEDNESDAY 1ˢᵗ

In the beginning God created the heaven and the earth...And the Spirit of God moved upon the face of the waters
Genesis 1:1-2

A NEW BEGINNING - Reading: Genesis 1:1-31

There are many clichés that are used at the beginning of a new year to motivate us to do something different or something new. Looking back is useful only as a way of assessing the past to forge a new strategy for future success.

At times things go wrong, at times the intended vision is interrupted by unforeseen circumstances such as a lack of resources, or a lack of planning.

While we have become proficient at making things, it is only God that can create. In Him there is no shadow of turning; God never repents or makes a mistake, so whatever He allows is His will for our lives.

At the beginning of this new year, we pause, as we always should, to give God thanks that we have lived to see another year. We turn the page, as it were, and start afresh. We have all made new year resolutions in the past to accomplish things or change certain behaviours, and by the end of the January we are no closer to our desired goals.

This year will be different! This year must be different, because with God all things are possible. God is both past, present and future. He is the "I am..." God, the God that knows the end from the beginning.

Genesis 1:2 suggests that what God had created has turned into chaos, but God started again and made all things beautiful in His own time.

Sandra Tayborn's song is such a blessing, no matter what time of year we are in...:

"I will do a new thing in you, I will do a new thing in you, whatever you've asked for, whatever you've prayed for, nothing shall be denied, says the Lord" (Sandra Tayborn 1989).

January 2025
Theme: All Things New

Be blessed, be bold, be beautiful, it's a new year in which incredible things can and will happen!

**Dexter E. Edmund, Presiding Bishop
& First Lady Yolanda Edmund
BUCJC Apostolic UK & Europe**

*New Year's Day

THURSDAY 2ⁿᵈ

O sing unto the LORD a new song; for he hath done marvellous things: his right hand, and his holy arm, hath gotten him the victory
Psalm 98:1

SING A NEW SONG - Reading: Psalm 98:1-9

As we embark upon a new year, with new ideas, a fresh start, let us raise our faith and expectations for 2025. Embracing the call to sing a new song to the LORD, symbolises our commitment to continually renew our hearts, minds and wills, recognising and celebrating the transformative power of God's salvation.

Celebrating the Lord's salvation through joyous praise not only honours His mighty deeds, but also serves as a spiritual practice that fortifies, strengthens our faith, and encourages unity within the body of Christ. The marvellous things which God has done, and is doing, are a testimony to His strength and faithfulness, challenging us to trust in His redemptive work and inspire others with the hope we have in Christ.

God's use of His right hand and holy arm to work salvation, is an invitation for us to submit to His sovereignty and participate in His redemptive plan of restoration for humankind. By acknowledging the salvation and marvellous deeds of the Lord, as described in Psalm 98:1, we are challenged to live abundantly and joyfully in Him.

True joy in the Christian life really springs forth from the acknowledgement of God's continuous love, His mercy, grace and marvellous deeds.

O sing unto the LORD with a new song. I pray a victorious and blessed year.

Evangelist Paula Clarke

FRIDAY 3rd

And I will give them one heart, and I will put a new spirit within you; and I will take the stony heart out of their flesh, and will give them a heart of flesh
Ezekiel 11:19

ARE WE INCLUDED IN THE NEW? - Reading: Ezekiel 11:1-25

What a promise! The prophecy came specifically to Israel with the promise of a new spirit and an undivided heart. One without stone, a heart of flesh.

The question is – are you and me in this prophecy? I am learning that the rebellious heart, which could not keep the commandments of God, would be a thing of the past. A promise of a turn in the right direction: repentance (Acts 2:37-38). Awesome! Finally, a heart with the ability and desire to love God wholeheartedly.

What a promise! So, are we included? The promise would be realised under the New Covenant or Testament. Though specifically made to Israel, and finding its complete fulfilment at Christ's Millennium reign, here's where we come in: *"...Any man be in Christ is a new creature...all things are become new"* (2 Corinthians 5:17).

This promise is therefore applicable to all because repentance towards God, and saving faith in Jesus Christ, is the pre-requisite under the New (Acts 2:37,38; 20:21). It's by faith! So, whosoever receives the infilling of the Holy Spirit with the pre-requisite, is a recipient of the New Covenant.

How is life in the Spirit without the stony, rebellious heart? What's new about you since you have become a recipient?

Pastor Josephine

SATURDAY 4th

...we don't know what to do: but our eyes are upon thee
2 Chronicles 20:12

OUR EYES ARE ON YOU - Reading: 2 Chronicles 20:1-30

It is important to understand that we are living in the days of the prophetic. Throughout the New Testament we are warned of entering such a period in our history prior to Jesus' second coming. This time is referred to by the Apostle Paul to Timothy as, *"perilous times"* (2 Timothy 3: 1:13).

However, amidst the challenges, the people of God are encouraged to stand and having done all to stand. In other words, what Paul was saying to the Ephesian brethren is that they must stand their ground, being prepared as a warrior is prepared for battle (Ephesians 6:13).

In 2 Chronicles 20:7-13, we read of the threats from Ammon, Moab and their allies to the nation of Judah, which left Jehoshaphat, the King of Judah, fearfully overwhelmed. The King was wise enough to seek the help of God. We too, despite our status, will at some time come to that place in our lives when we feel afraid, and uncertain how to deal with the challenges that daily confront us; but like Jehoshaphat, our relationship with God gives us access to Him.

Although a national leader, King Jehoshaphat was not embarrassed, neither was he ashamed to call the congregation of Judah together with him to seek help from God. There he stood, amid his people, and openly confessed to God that he didn't know what to do! Neither he nor Judah had the power to victoriously war against the armies of Ammon, Moab, and Mount Seir, **"but our eyes are on you"**, he told God.

It's important to know who to look to, and where to look to, in moments when it seems as if the enemy is closing in on us. Too many of us look to people who we consider to be our friends, only to be left disappointed and hurt.

We are encouraged by the writer of Hebrews who said, *"Looking unto Jesus the author and finisher of our faith..."* (Hebrews 12:2). If we are to

January 2025
Theme: All Things New

be victorious against the evil missiles which the enemy is launching at us, we must be intentional in spiritual warfare, while keeping our eyes fixed on Christ.

"Not by might, nor by power, but by my spirit, saith the LORD of hosts" (Zechariah 4:6).

Dr Una Davis

SUNDAY 5th

...put off all these...and...put on the new man, which is renewed in knowledge after the image of him that created him
Colossians 3:8-10

FROM DAMSEL TO DEFENDER OF THE FAITH
Reading: Colossians 3 1-17

You may recall the glorious step into a brand-new life in Jesus. If you haven't yet, there will never be a more life changing advance for a human than to see the love of one's maker through a cross and His resurrection.

You'd be forgiven for likening this to a superhero rescue scene where the precious damsel (us, the lost) is saved by love. But as believers, we must be reminded that this is where the similarity ends!

This hero, Jesus, didn't just save us and leave us as damsels. He empowered us by His Spirit to live with the same level of authority over the enemy by our own choices. We are no longer helpless damsels but empowered ambassadors to DO our part! Colossians 3 reflects this well. The enemy who fights against us is the old nature, controlled by Satan himself. But when the powerful spirit of God fills us, He calls us to action with two phrases: *"Put to death"* and *"Put on"* Colossians 3:8-10.

Now you and I are engaged in the battle, destroying with daily powerful intention the deeds of the flesh. Avid movie-follower, let's revisit that idea of the attacks soaring across the screen of your life: lust, impurity, greed, anger, rage, slander, idolatry. Do you imagine that a well-dressed damsel should just sit as if it's an ordinary day, whilst the flesh desires to destroy the spirit-man?

We, as the children of God, have to take action. We have DO something. We will not defeat attacks just by quoting our salvation (hero) story alone, No! Every day we have to cause the old sinful flesh to die! Put to death! What an aggressive and callous statement that cannot be achieved simply by attending church, singing songs, and looking the part. If we do battle with our flesh, we will know! If we rid ourselves and take off this raging enemy from our back, we will feel the advance.

Equally important is the affirmative: to *"Put on"*. An every day choice to adorn hearts with something. To determine our identity and decide daily who we are going to serve by picking our new wardrobe from the closet of the Spirit, measuring not by ourselves, but by the image of its Creator.

We will never be Christlike-beings waiting like a Damsel in Distress to be saved time and time again. Though God Himself is the victor within us, we have to want Him enough to do the work!

It's time to do battle.

Joy Lear-Bernard

MONDAY 6th

(Saul) is a chosen vessel unto me, to bear my name before the Gentiles, and kings, and the children of Israel
Acts 9:15

CHANGED! - Reading: Acts 9:1-19

Do you know that the power of God can change anybody? Yes, it can!

In our minds we may have unconsciously put a restriction on the types of people who can have a 180-degree turn when they have a divine encounter with Christ Jesus. But there is nobody walking the streets, or in the prisons of our country, who cannot be transformed.

We admire Paul the apostle, an inspired and anointed man of God, writer of so many of the New Testament epistles, and one who testified that he had seen the Lord (1 Corinthians 15:8). Yet when known by his Jewish name of Saul, we read of him in Acts 7 and 8 consenting to the stoning to death of Stephen, persecuting and causing havoc among believers, having Christian men and women arrested and dragged away to be imprisoned!

Such was Saul's infamy that, when God instructed disciple Ananias to go and lay hands on Saul, Ananias' response was, *"Lord, I have heard by many of this man, how much evil he has done to thy saints at Jerusalem: and he has authority from the chief priests to bind all that call on thy name" (Acts 9:13-14).* In other words, *"Lord, please send me to pray for somebody else or send someone else"*!

Let's thank God for the obedience of Ananias, who laid aside his fear and prejudice and went to the street called Straight, laid his hand upon Saul and Saul received his sight and the Holy Ghost. What would the New Testament of our Bibles look like today if God had not known the great potential in Saul for the Kingdom before his conversion? Imagine Acts of the apostles without Paul as one of the leading characters, without his testimony before King Agrippa, *"Having obtained help of God I continue unto this day" (Acts 26:22).* And the New Testament would be less than half its size without the Pauline epistles from Romans through to Philemon.

Paul, after his new beginning, so rightly said: *"For by grace are you saved through faith; and that not of yourselves: it is the gift of God: not of works, lest any man should boast. For we are His workmanship, created in Christ Jesus unto good works, which God hath before ordained…"* (Ephesians 2:8-10).

What about you, Dear Reader? What was your life story before you met with Christ? You are listed somewhere in 1 Corinthians 6:9-10, even if it's under the catch-all category of *"unrighteous"*! But thank God, *"We are washed, we are sanctified, we are justified in the name of our Lord Jesus, and by the Spirit of our God" (1 Corinthians 6:11).*

JEJ

TUESDAY 7th

And though your beginning was small, your latter days will be very great
Job 8:7 (ESV)

THE LOST COAT - Reading: John 12:20-37

Nobody can tell by looking at a seed just how many flowers or fruits it will produce. With the naked eye, one can hardly see a seed and, if dropped, you'd struggle to find it. Yet when sown in the right soil, and exposed to favourable conditions, that seed soon loses any semblance of its original form.

'Favourable' conditions for a seed to grow begin with it being buried deep into a dark place, where it will not be disturbed by what's happening on the ground's surface. But although nothing of the seed is yet visible to the gardener or farmer, something is definitely going on and a new beginning is happening underground.

The seed is absorbing nutrition from the soil and warmth from the heat of the sun as the sun's rays penetrate the earth. The seed's coat is lost as germination takes place. Roots are formed and now a shoot is pushing itself up towards the light of the sun. The next time that we see what was sown/buried, it is no longer called a seed - it has become something else! And, it will continue to become something else! The seed, now a shoot, will eventually be called a pumpkin, an apple tree, a rose.

Dear Reader, when God wants to do something new in us, He buries us for a while. We are incubated out of sight, in a lonely place, deep so that new roots can form, usually in God's favourable place – a place where we don't want to be – in soil which is also sometimes called dirt!

Nevertheless, who knows what you will start to be after your divine burial! To others, and even to yourself, right now you may seem insignificant and of no value, just like the single seed mentioned in my first paragraph. But what will you become, where in the world will God take you once, like the seed, you lose your coat?

JEJ

WEDNESDAY 8th

Blessed is the (one) who passing through the valley of Baca make it a well...
Psalm 84:5-6

THE VALE OF WEEPING - Reading: Psalm 84:1-12:

There's a peace that comes with knowing the source of our strength. It means that, even at our weakest point, we can still say that we are strong because of our strength's place of origin.

The Valley of Baca is situated near to Jerusalem; its name means *"weeping"*. Consolation from today's verse is that the Valley of Baca is not where we stay forever, we pass through it en route to somewhere else, and whilst there we make it a well. Rain doesn't fall often but when it does, it can be caught by, with expectation, having dug a hole or setting a cistern because rain will fall sometime.

There's a saying that, *"When life gives you lemons, make lemonade!"*. It is true that something positive can come out of the worst of circumstances, it may only be to share your experience of how you survived with someone else who will go through the same thing later on.

God knows how to irrigate us when we're in a dry place. The antediluvian world, i.e., before the flood, had no rain. God would send a mist upon the earth to water the dry ground (Genesis 2:6-7). Likewise, when in a personal drought, God still provides refreshing, we are not left to wilt and die although it may appear that all hope is gone. We learn that God sustains in every climate, and spiritual growth can take place. When we look back afterwards, we will give only God the glory.

In every condition, in sickness, in health
In poverty's vale, or abounding in wealth,
At home, and abroad, on the land, on the sea
The Lord, the Almighty, your strength e'er shall be.

Fear not, I am with you, O be not dismayed,
For I am your God and will still give you aid;

*I'll strengthen you, help you, and cause you to stand,
Upheld by my righteous, omnipotent hand.
(How Firm a Foundation – J Rippon)*

God is always faithful, even in Baca.

JEJ

THURSDAY 9th

He restoreth my soul
Psalm 23:3

RESTORED - Reading: Isaiah 61:1-11

Years ago, I bought a small clay pot. It was simple in design but to me it was beautiful. The pot was moved from room to room, serving different purposes, until it finally settled in our kitchen.

Unfortunately, one day it broke; it split down the middle. My initial thought was to throw the pot away and buy a new one, but my second thought was that there was nothing wrong with it other than it being broken! Why throw it away, why not mend it? I therefore put the pieces in a safe place until it would be repaired.

Sometime later, I laid out the fragments and started the work of making the pot whole again. It was an easy thing to do and the repair process conveyed so many messages to me. I'll share with you a few:

- Although sometimes we feel or are broken by life-events, it does not mean that we are finished
- In order to make the pieces into a pot, I had to apply some pressure whilst steadily holding both sides together with my hands
- After the pressing and sealing, I had to put the pot aside, just for a little while, for the glue to dry before it could be used
- The breakage and reset left a faint mark which indicated where the original break had been but, despite the scar, the pot was definitely useable

You may be wondering whether God can or will ever use you again as in former days because you broke. You may have decided that because of your circumstance you will have to live the rest of your life being less than God had intended, e.g., as a servant instead of a son (St Luke 15:19). What does God say?

It is a fact that at times, like Jacob, our experiences leave us with a limp or mark as a reminder of what has taken place (Genesis 32:24-25, 31). But when we look at our limp or scar, we should say: *"O give thanks unto the LORD for He is good: for His mercy endureth forever"* (Psalm 136:1). Why say that? Because God did not throw us away on account of our being broken! He did not replace us with another vessel, He knew that we were worth keeping! A songwriter said: *"Please be patient with me, God is not through with me yet"*! Paul to the Romans said: *"...we glory in tribulations...knowing that tribulation worketh (accomplishes or produces) patience; and patience experience; and experience hope"* (Romans 5:3-4).

If you have been broken by a previous or your present test, fret not. Even during such seasons: *"Yet His blessings fall on me, sweeter than all..."*. If you're in the process of being reset, although you're feeling sore from the pressing and squeezing, it is God holding you and your pieces together with His hands for restoration. He keeps on restoring my soul (Psalm 23:3) since surely after one trouble ends, there will always come another! Thank God for ongoing restoration:

"The Spirit of the Lord God is upon me; because... He hath sent me to bind up the brokenhearted...to comfort all that mourn; to appoint unto them that mourn in Zion, to give unto them beauty for ashes, the oil of joy for mourning, the garment of praise for the spirit of heaviness; ... that He might be glorified" (Isaiah 61:1-3).

JEJ

FRIDAY 10th

... if anyone is in (Christ), he is a new creation. Old things have disappeared, and – look! – all things have become new!
2 Corinthians 5:17 (ISV)

NEW CREATIONS IN CHRIST - Reading: Acts 9:1-19

"If anyone...". This is noteworthy; its appeal does not discriminate, it is a clarion call to equal opportunity in Jesus Christ for all humankind, regardless of nationality, language, education, male, female, middle class, working class, or upper class. God sees all humankind as His children. There is no barrier to anyone becoming a new creature in Jesus Christ.

We cannot become a new creature in ourselves, it is only in Christ Jesus. Once we acknowledge our wretched condition, hopeless and desperate sinful situation, He draws us to His precious bleeding side. When we come to Christ, He changes our nature into a new creation by a process known as regeneration. Paul reminds believers that it is by faith we put off the old man, i.e., the old Adamic nature, and put on Christ.

Consider: what do you think was easier for God to accomplish - the work of creating the world, or the work of the new creation? Yes, I hear someone saying there is nothing that God cannot do, and there is nothing too hard for Him. But the work of creating the world, I would say, was easier. I say this because, in the beginning there was nothing and God started the work of creating the world with nothing to oppose Him. In the work of creation there was nothing to help, neither did God need any help. However, humankind had a disobedient and stubborn will to oppose the will of God. Therefore, I believe that this was more challenging than the rest of creation.

God desires to do a new thing in all our lives (Revelation 21:5). This is not to repair His creation, but to recreate it over again. We become God's workmanship which He gives a 10/10 mark with the words, *"very good"* (Genesis 1:31).

Missionary Audrey Simpson

SATURDAY 11th

...though our outer self is wasting away, our inner self is being renewed day by day
2 Corinthians 4:16 (ESV)

DAILY RENEWAL - Reading: 2 Corinthians 4:1-18

I left school many years ago, but can still remember being advised by my teachers before taking any exam to look at which questions would give the highest marks, and spend most of my time answering those. If the paper had to be completed within two hours, it'd be absolutely pointless labouring for 90 minutes over questions that would give only one or two points!

As we read today's focus verse, Paul alerts us that our outer (physical) case, i.e., our body, is progressively decaying. We sometimes find this fact hard to accept, and do our best to slow down what is a natural process for us all. With cosmetics, good nutrition, etc., we may succeed in delaying but not cancelling the inevitable.

Paul did not give us bad news with no good news! The good news is that our inner self, the part which cannot be seen and is often forgotten, does not age and is renewed by God every day. As women, many of us adhere to a strict morning and evening daily routine for our face: cleanse, tone, moisturise. Once or twice a week we may (should) also exfoliate and relax with a face mask to further remove dead skin cells to brighten our complexion.

Although Paul said that our spirit is renewed day by day, this is not without effort on our part. Of more importance than our skin care, or any other beauty routine, we must have a strict course that we follow with the Lord - daily prayer, reading and application of the Word, meditating thereon. Set aside time each week to fast and pray to keep our innate Adamic nature under control. It is also Paul who said, *"I die daily"* (1 Corinthians 15:31). He said, *"Put to death your worldly impulses…"* (Colossians 3:5 - ISV). Paul said, *"Put on the whole armour of God…for we wrestle not against flesh and blood…"* (Ephesians 6:11-12). He said, *"… I keep on disciplining my body…so that after I have preached to others, I myself will not somehow be disqualified"* (1 Corinthians 9:27 - ISV).

Inner daily renewal is **not** a passive occurrence, it isn't automatic, and needs more attention than what can be seen!

JEJ

SUNDAY 12th

Remember ye not the former things, neither consider the things of old. Behold, I will do a new thing...
Isaiah 43:18-19

NEW BEGINNINGS: Reading: 2 Corinthians 5:11-21

As we prepare candidates for baptism on their baptism day, we remind them of the Word of God that St. Paul spoke to the brethren in Corinth:

"Therefore, if any man be in Christ, he is a new creature: old things are passed away; behold, all things are become new" (2 Corinthians 5:17).

The old things are in the past, and with the symbolic washing in the blood of Jesus through water baptism, the new has come. The new has come to stay because our God makes all things new. Just like He did for the children of Israel, who too underwent a symbolic baptism as they walked through the Red Sea as if on dry land.

Isaiah 43:18-19 KJV states: *"Remember ye not the former things, neither consider the things of old. Behold, I will do a new thing; now it shall spring forth; shall ye not know it? I will even make a way in the wilderness, and rivers in the desert".*

After baptism in the name of Jesus Christ, infilling of the Holy Spirit, and walking in covenant relationship with our God, we experience what 'new' looks like and feels like. He causes new fountains of water to spring forth in dry places in our lives, and He forges new ways ahead, even when there seems to be no way!

So, as we step into this new day, let us thank Him for newness of life, and that He is the God, who despite our sinful past, makes all things new.

Min Jo Earle

MONDAY 13th

...this one thing I do, forgetting those things which are behind...
Philippians 3:13

HAVE A GOOD STRETCH - Reading: Philippians 3:12-21

Do you know this hymn, "I Want to Love Him Better"?

I want to love Him better for He died for me
I want to love Him better for He set me free
I want to love Him better as the moments fly
I want to love Him better as the days go by.

These words of Johnson Oatman could be echoed by each reader of this page. The start of another year is a time when we naturally do reflections and set new goals. Hopefully, we will accomplish some, even if not all. However, there are certain things which are like a moving goal post. By this I mean, cannot be exhausted or completed (I guess housework would fit well into this category, i.e., always more to do!).

Loving Jesus is also like this, even when I love Him better, I could still love Him better and more for all the things He's done for me and for who He is. Working for Him and serving Him, I can always do more and better as my faith and relationship with Him develops.

Paul the Apostle recognises that God called him for a particular purpose, and although Paul has accomplished so much, he acknowledges that there is more. Although Paul is holy, there's another level in Christ which he has not yet attained. Though he has received extraordinary revelations, and even speaks in code of being caught up into the third heaven and seeing things which are not lawful to be uttered (2 Corinthians 12:2-4), Paul still exclaims in today's chapter, *"That I may know Him..."* and admits that he has not yet fully taken hold of the purpose for which he was divinely seized and taken hold of by God.

How many of us with the anointing of Paul would have realised that there's yet more? Paul passionately, and even surprisingly, states that he is going to forget those things that are behind which he's already done, good or bad, and focus only on what is ahead. *"I press (stretch and strain) towards…",* because he knows that the goal post which he or others had set for him has been moved to a further place by God. Stretch because of the struggle to get there with fightings and fears within and without. Yes, for many, the main purpose for which we were captured has not yet been found (apprehended).

Let go of, and forget the sins and mistakes of yesteryear and beyond. Even lay aside feelings of being satisfied with what you've already gained; they will only slow you down so that you never apprehend! Now press, strain, stretch to get to where you're destined. Greater than your past is your future!

JEJ

TUESDAY 14th

I waited patiently for the LORD...and he hath put a new song in my mouth
Psalm 40:1-3

UNANSWERED (YET!) -: Reading: Psalm 40:1-17

Is there anybody reading this page that loves to wait?

All over the world, helpdesk staff deal with customers who become more agitated the longer that they have to wait for a solution to their question(s). Then there are customers who give up chasing for an answer because of the length of time which has lapsed since first logging their complaint.

God doesn't keep us waiting because He has forgotten what we asked Him; it's all about His timing. It was when Elisabeth and Zacharias were in their senior years, 'past it' we would say, that here came Gabriel to announce that God had heard their prayers and they would soon become parents!

You would understand that Zacharias may have struggled to comprehend what Gabriel was on about – surely to become a parent had not been a recent prayer! This would have been an appeal made while Zacharias was not *"an old man"* and before Elisabeth became *"well stricken in years"* (Luke 1:18), not now...

I'm sure that I am not the only one who has a file with my name on it in heaven marked, *"Unanswered Yet"*. Here is what FG Burroughs had to say:

Unanswered yet? The prayer your heart has pleaded
In agony of heart these many years?
Does faith begin to fail, is hope departing,
And think you all in vain those falling tears?
Say not the Father has not heard your prayer;
You shall have your heart's desire, sometime, somewhere.

Unanswered yet? No, do not say ungranted;
Perhaps your part is not yet wholly done;
The work began when first your prayer was uttered,
And God will finish what He has begun.
If you will keep the incense burning there,
His glory you shall see, sometime, somewhere.

Unanswered yet? Faith cannot be unanswered;
Her feet were firmly planted on the Rock;
Amid the wildest storm prayer stands undaunted,
Nor quails before the loudest thunder shock.
She knows Omnipotence has heard her prayer,
And cries, "It shall be done", sometime, somewhere!

JEJ

WEDNESDAY 15th

When the LORD restored the fortunes of Zion, we were like those who dream
Psalm 126:1 (ESV)

STEP BY STEP - Reading: Psalm 126:1-6

"When I look back over my life and I think things over...I can truly say that I've been blessed I have a testimony!" (Unknown)

We often sing the words of this song with joy in our heart, as we think about the end result and the victories accomplished. But there is so much more to our stories. Recognising God's hand as we move from season to season, through each phase of our lives, should cause us to lift our hands in thanksgiving!

Passing through different seasons or life changes is not always comfortable, even when it's something we are excited about, or something our heart desired. However, being able to trust God in these moments can be a powerful experience. Seeing God's hand revealed is a wonderful opportunity to stand in awe of Him and consider what He has done, is doing and is able to do.

Today, take a few moments to reflect on what God has brought you through and where He's brought you from. In doing so, you will realise that your testimony is even greater than you realised!

Let your heart offer up praises knowing that without God, the outcome would not have been the same! Rejoice in the knowledge that you are not alone and give Him praise! We are victorious only because of the grace of God.

CDK

THURSDAY 16ᵗʰ

God makes everything happen at the right time. Yet none of us can ever fully understand all He has done...
Ecclesiastes 3:11

A CLEAN SLATE – Reading: Psalm 72:1-20

We all retired happily to our beds contemplating an exciting trip. My visitors from overseas had their minds set on travelling to Zambia.

In the early hours of the morning, the Lord urged me awake. As I listened and prayed, I got the distinct impression that we were not to go to Zambia. Heavy with this revelation, I waited eagerly to share it.

To make the news more palatable, I spread out a huge map of Zimbabwe on the floor, offering instead to take my guests anywhere within its borders. Visibly disappointed, they kept urging me to go on.

Knowing that I had definitely heard from God, but against my better judgment, I relented. I solicited prayer along the way from everyone whom we encountered in an effort to quell the growing knots in my stomach, i.e., that uneasy feeling one experiences when the right course of action is evident yet one ignores it!

All was well until, when climbing the winding roads of the Escarpment, we encountered, to my horror, an 18-wheeler bearing down upon us, straddling the road! There was only a split-second to make a decision, i.e., meet the lorry head-on or swerve off the road into a ditch of unknown depth. As we veered off the road, the most eloquent prayer I could form was simply to call on the beautiful name of Jesus! Helper to the helpless, very present help in time of trouble (Psalm 46:1; 72:12)!

The car seemed, as if in slow motion, to float like an autumn leaf to the bottom of the crevasse. One occupant only awoke on landing, and the other appeared engulfed in peace. Truly, the hand of God held us that day!

It was clear why we were not to travel. I felt great sorrow and condemnation for choosing to ignore God's warning; others readily agreed that it was disobedient and foolish. All true accusations, but how they stung! I cried out to the Lord - squirming in shame, repentant. It was then that I heard these liberating words, *"I AM bigger than your mistakes"!*

He truly makes all things beautiful in His time! Merciful in our mistakes, ready to dust us off, comfort us, help us up to live again in newness of life (Romans 6:4)! It's never too late to admit our errors, God awaits with beauty as we hand over the ashes (Isaiah 61:3)!

Gudrun Witt
Zimbabwe

FRIDAY 17th

...one thing I know, that, whereas I was blind, now I see
John 9:25

GRATITUDE – Reading: John 9:13-25

When a need is met, gratitude must be expressed.

Those who are in dire straits, suffering loss and hardship, rarely look at the means by which help arrives with a critical eye; neither do they refuse such help in disdain. Occasionally, there may be some fear that it is not real, or that it will not last, but rarely would it be rejected out of hand.

For the one who has never suffered lack, the messenger may not be acceptable. He will spend excessive amounts of time looking for ulterior motives, faults, and failures, because the need was not severe. For the one who has been longing for relief, there will be no hesitation in accepting that relief when offered.

Particular attention will be paid to the 'saviour' who will never be forgotten. Even though he may never get an opportunity to express thanks in person, he will never allow that one to be evil spoken of in his presence. That is a spirit of gratitude. Accepting the gift, and not condemning the giver.

This type of acceptance and gratitude will only be expressed by one who has determined so to do. This is the same type of spirit that is necessary within the body of Christ. In learning not to look at the outward appearance of the messenger, or to judge their motives, we learn more how to show the love of God and be free with our expressions of gratitude. We learn to believe that the packaging is a true representation of the contents, i.e., that there is no deception.

Pastor Londy Esdaille
Nevis

SATURDAY 18th

After that you have suffered a little while, the God of all grace will...himself restore, confirm, strengthen, and establish you
1 Peter 5:10 (ESV)

NEW AGAIN – Reading: 1 Peter 5:1-11

When God created the heavens and the earth, He created all things new. He created the trees, birds, animals, and His last creation was humankind. Just as He breathed life into man, He can breathe life and make everything new out of pain and chaos. Sometimes it takes the testing and trials in life to get us to that place where the newness begins.

Years ago in 2013, I lost my son to knife crime. In fact, I not only lost one son but two sons and a grandson that God had blessed me with, I lost them by the hands of violent men. My life changed suddenly as I started a journey that I had not experienced before.

Firstly, my body didn't feel like mine, I didn't understand what was going on inside. I felt different, my entire being didn't feel right. My mind and my whole body felt disconnected, to the point that I couldn't return to work. As I reflect back, it wasn't because I didn't want to return, it was because my whole being was numb with grief. It was a turbulent time but now I am going through the healing process. I have forgiven the perpetrators and God has helped me from being bitter. By no means has it been an easy road but with God – I can do valiantly. As the saying goes, *"If there is no cross, there will be no crown"*.

Despite the storms and difficulties, I have seen God's goodness and favour toward me and my family. He is good all the time and we must give Him the praise. God has proven Himself faithful in all my circumstances. He made them new again. He's given me new sons, new family. New beginning - new hope!

Jennifer Beckford

SUNDAY 19th

...I will take away the stony heart out of your flesh, and I will give you a heart of flesh
Ezekiel 36:26

I NEED A NEW HEART – Reading: Ezekiel 36:1-38

The children of Israel, a people scorned and maligned. A nation who once knew God but had now become a laughing stock for their famine, experiencing the fulfilment of God's unshakable Word.

They defiled the holy name, carrying it in vain; God righteously regards His name. His people shrivelled their own honour of carrying God's name, becoming focused on self and made barren and fruitless.

But with a promise that in the future the land and families would flourish again, God shared another distinctive prophecy. In order for true repentance and new life to be complete, God said, *"I will put in you a new heart"*. Your past conduct was reflective of a heart that had become stony. But to prosper in me, you need from my own hand a fleshy heart fit for my blessing; tender, soft, pliable, humble and repentant.

Today, we may have become hardened by scorn we've experienced, or by a bad run in life that causes us to look hopeless and broken. We may have hardened hearts by our own sinful desire, pride and rebellion. At this moment, what we need more than anything is a new heart. Not manufactured by man, mechanically doing good, but a new heart held by the holy hand of God, placed on the inside of us after the purging and replacing of our hearts diseased by sin.

Lord, give me a clean heart. I surrender my trust and will for yours. Cut, purge, cleanse and heal.

Give me a heart like yours.

Joy Lear-Bernard

MONDAY 20th

But for you that honour my name, victory will shine like the sun with healing in its rays, and you will jump around like calves at play
Malachi 4:2 (CEV)

NEW SEASON IN CHRIST – Reading: Malachi 4:1-6

The book of Malachi is a rebuke to the Israelites for their failure to trust God, their unfaithfulness and their sin; it's also a warning of judgment to come. However, Malachi 4:2 is assurance for the righteous; in spite of the judgment that will befall the wicked, Malachi reminds the faithful of God's deliverance and restoration. **This is God's glorious promise for believers at all times.**

Facing life's challenges, we sometimes grow weary, our endless prayers seem to go unheard - we may wonder if God hears, if God cares, if God really is…We need deliverance from doubt and the sin that accompanies it. We also need restoration – to trust and have faith in God - and to the joy of our salvation.

Regardless of our failings and our sins, we can return to a place of reverence for God and humbly ask His forgiveness. He welcomes us and delivers us from judgment. He frees us from the weight of our sins and fully restores our joy. Truly, we can begin a new season in Christ, a season of peace and surety, whatever our external situation may be.

Take joy in God's unfailing love! Bask in His presence, and go forth joyfully into each day with which the Lord has blessed you. May your thoughts, words and actions reflect a new season of godliness every day.

Kat Lowry
USA

TUESDAY 21st

Be renewed in the spirit of your mind
Ephesians 4:23

A NEW MIND - Reading: Ephesians 4:17-32

A feature of living is looking forward to new things.

At the very least, we look forward to a new day. We desire to have items replaced by new things after using them for a while. Frequently, updated technology sparks the desire for new gadgets with every model released. Something happens in the brain that makes one feel good when something new is experienced. Indeed, new things can spark ideas. New experiences can breed greater creativity and, according to scientists, are also linked to greater happiness. New things can have positive effects. Who then does not want new things?

It is no wonder that the scriptures admonish one to desire a new mind. Romans 12:2 further teaches that it is with a renewed mind, a mind that does not approach things and situations according to customs and traditions, but one that is based on godly principles and values, that is going to lead to the goodliest outcome. In other words, one needs to operate with a changed mind, a new mind, a mind that is Godward, to ultimately know God's will which is proper, pleasing, and perfect.

You are encouraged to ask God for a renewed mind as you face situations and tasks in your day. Seek for God's mind in each matter to ensure that you are not leaning onto your own understanding. Having God's perspective on matters is essential to ensure the best possible outcomes. And who does not want good, pleasant, or perfect things?

Seek God for a new mind on the matter.

Keshawna Salmon-Ferguson
Jamaica

WEDNESDAY 22nd

And I will bless her, and give thee a son also of her...then Abraham fell upon his face, and laughed...
Genesis 17:16-17

WHY ARE YOU LAUGHING? – Reading: Genesis 17:1-19

One of the most common limits that we place on God to use us, or bless us in a particular way, is our age. We're either too young, or too old. What is the 'right' age for God to fulfil His purpose in us, anyway?

Age was the problem with Sarah when she overheard a conversation between Abraham and three heaven-sent guests who were talking outside Abraham's and her tent. They could not be serious when they said that she would be a mother this time next year. It was impossible! She was post-menopausal! In fact, just the thought made Sarah have a good laugh to herself – wouldn't you?

Before we condemn Sarah for her lack of faith, if you are an 89-year-old woman reading this page, what would your response have been? Or, if you have an elderly mother or aunt, or a grandmother of a similar age, and at family dinner on Sunday, Granny announced, *"I'm pregnant!"*, who would not laugh (or choke)?! And let's not overlook that Abraham also laughed in Genesis 17:16-17 when he heard that Sarah would still one day become not just a mother but, *"a mother of nations;..."*.

There are promises attached to the lives of some of the readers of this page, and as they unfold, you may first have a nervous laugh, or a hysterical laugh, or a laugh of unbelief. People who think nothing like that could ever happen to you will have a laugh of scorn. But whatever kind of laugh it is, the promise will still come to pass. You may be old. You may not be known. You may feel forgotten. Or really the prophecy simply sounds farfetched. Even so, don't write it off, and don't get comfortable with 'Ishmael' (Genesis 17:18), he's not the promise God has in mind. Dear Reader, God has got some brand new things in store for you this year, and not just new, but extraordinary!

By faith, start to laugh with God!

JEJ

THURSDAY 23rd

For a just (person) falleth seven times, and riseth up again…
Proverbs 24:16

DOWN BUT NOT OUT – Reading: Proverbs 24:15-20

Have you ever received a blow from which you thought you would never recover? It may have been sickness, bankruptcy, scandal or betrayal of some description, a broken relationship, a loss. You wept sore at the force with which you were hit.

The sons of Korah wrote in Psalm 42:3, *"My tears have been my meat day and night, while they continually say unto me, Where is thy God?"*. During such seasons, you may be surprised to observe that not everyone around you really wants you to get back up again. The psalmists of Psalm 42 allude to this suggesting that they are being jeered rather than comforted by those around them, *"Where is your God?"*.

This also happened to our Lord Jesus Christ as He hung on the cross at Calvary, i.e., nobody said a kind word to Him, the onlookers taunted and mocked Him and said that if He really was the Son of God, He should come down from the cross and save Himself and others also (Mark 15:29-34).

Already bleeding, already exhausted, hungry and thirsty from the intense heat of the day, yet here came another nail, and another nail, and another one to tear Jesus' flesh! No compassion was shown to our Saviour. Likewise, we may continue to receive blows whilst we are down and trying to get up.

Nevertheless, we have confidence that the worst of trials will not be our end. Resilience to fight on must emerge from the core of our being as we recognise that down does not mean out! So Micah 7:8 says, *"Rejoice not against me, O mine enemy: when I fall, I shall arise; when I sit in darkness, the LORD shall be a light unto me"*.

With God's help, get up with more power than when you went down!

JEJ

FRIDAY 24th

And God saw everything that he had made, and, behold, it was very good
Genesis 1:31

VERY GOOD - Reading: Genesis 1:29-31

By the sixth day of creation, God's manifold works are unfolded including foods fitting for every life form to propagate, populate, and reproduce new life perpetually.

God's evaluation and approval of all things new, with ability to replicate itself, was *"awesome"*, *"thumbs up"*, a *"like"* or *"very good"*. But new things did not cease as a new day dawned, Sabbath was born and instituted on the seventh day. A day of rest from servile work, to rest in the presence and beauty of the Creator of all things new. For God Himself rested, not from being tired by all that He had done, but as an example for us to teach us new ways to worship.

In order to worship in truth, God further promised to do a new thing. He created within us a new heart and new Spirit so we could have a new and living way. And although David's new cart ended tragically, still new wine, new songs, new names are favourable to the God of new beginnings. Yet we hope for a new heaven and a new earth.

So the reason why there is no new thing under the sun is because God made all things new before the foundation of the world.

Sis Jx

SATURDAY 25th

And the rib, which the LORD GOD had taken from man, made He a woman, and brought her unto the man
Genesis 2:21-22

GOD BROUGHT THE WOMAN TO THE MAN - Reading: Genesis 2:18-25

In today's reading we see a simple truth that has been forgotten in the 21st century. Scripture reads, *"...made he a woman, and brought her unto the man"*. God brought the woman to the man. I'll repeat this again, God brought the woman to the man.

I've read this scripture numerous times but it's only recently that this truth has struck a chord as it were. Adam didn't wake up and find Eve lying next to him, God brought her to him. God instituted the first relationship by taking the rib from the man, creating a woman, and bringing her to the man.

God saw Adam's need for companionship (Genesis 2:18) despite Him having fellowship with Adam. This is not to say that every person needs to be married. God has called some to remain single (1 Corinthians 7:7-9). However, when a man longs for companionship, God's answer is a woman. It wasn't in the animals that God brought for Adam to name as we read in the previous verses (Gen 1:18-20). A dog may be 'man's best friend', but a dog could not satisfy Adam's need for companionship. Only a woman could. God did not create a father, mother, nor a child, not another man but a woman.

Think about it, sisters. You are a treasure, a gift. I encourage my single sisters to stop looking for a man, a godly man will know you are the one. Allow the Lord to bring you to the man. Blessed is the man who says, *"My wife is a gift from God"*. I pray that the man will be led by God to find you (Proverbs 18:22).

CP

SUNDAY 26th

For, behold, I create new heavens and a new earth: and the former shall not be remembered, nor come into mind
Isaiah 65:17

REMEMBERED NO MORE – Reading: Isaiah 65:1-25

The grief and loss
The taunt and isolation
The weeping of infant silence
Or old men who do not live out their days.
The hustle and bustle
The endless sowing and no reaping
The infirmity, injustice, inequality,
Silent cries
And intolerable threats.

Cold, pain, danger, anguish
Poverty, doubt, darkness
Highs hit by lows
Cycles of good and bad.
They will be forgotten
And remembered no more.

These very present 'things'
Prominent and important 'things'
At the fore of our mind 'things'
At the centre of our focus 'things'
That weigh heavily in the fibre of our being, 'things'.

They will become 'former things'
And will never again come to mind.
The barricades of our mortality bursting
Invisible
Giving way to the new thing
The new heaven
And a new earth.

And those former things will be remembered no more!

Joy Lear-Bernard

January 2025
Theme: All Things New

MONDAY 27th

And God spake unto Noah, saying, Go forth of the ark, thou, and thy wife, and thy sons, and thy sons' wives with thee
Genesis 8:15-16

GOD'S LAW IN OUR HEART - Reading: Genesis 8:1-22

Noah and his family had been in the ark for just over a year, this was at the end of the second dispensation, i.e., the dispensation of Conscience (Genesis 3:22 - 8:14). This was followed by the third dispensation, called Human Government (Genesis 8:15 - 11:32).

In a biblical context, a dispensation refers to a period in history during which God deals with humankind by a particular method.

The dispensation of Conscience was a time when a person's conscience was used to help them distinguish the difference between right and wrong, to guide them how to behave. Since man now had knowledge of good and evil, God's purpose was to guide them how to correctly use their conscience, teaching them to do the right thing and refuse evil. However, Genesis 6:1-7 tells us that, *"God saw the magnitude of the wickedness of man. Their imaginative thoughts that centred from their heart was continually evil".* This resulted in the flood, judgment came to all who refused to repent, and Noah and his family were saved only because Noah found grace in the eyes of the LORD (Genesis 6:8).

The dispensation of Human Government speaks of legislative laws and governmental leadership to bring order upon the earth. There were moral laws for sins such as murder or theft, and civil laws which dealt with issues pertaining to how we as individuals should live with one another. There were consequences for disobeying the law, alongside promises and benefits for obedience.

God was doing a new thing upon the earth, and the purpose was to help us better understand right from wrong by way of the ten commandments (which was written on stone), a new standard of conduct for the preservation of life. We are now under the dispensation of Grace which came following the death, burial and resurrection of Jesus Christ. We are saved through the grace of God, not because of any works that we have done (Ephesians 2:8-9). Salvation comes through Jesus Christ and we have redemption through His blood that forgives us of (and removes) our sins, enabling us to have a relationship with God and a hope of eternal life.

God continues to do a new thing because His laws are now written in our heart through the power of the Holy Ghost, *"...so that our own conscience and thoughts either accuse us or tell us we are doing the right thing"* (Romans 2:15). Therefore, *"Let us draw near with a true heart in full assurance of faith, having our hearts sprinkled from an evil conscience, and our bodies washed with pure water"* (Hebrews 10:22).

Rachel Lewin

TUESDAY 28th

...we are buried with him by baptism into death: that like as Christ was raised up...even so we also should walk in newness of life
Romans 6:4

EMBRACE NEW LIFE – Reading: Romans 6:1-14

Death, the end of life as we know it, is not a subject that many like to think or talk about, although it is an important reality. It is however worth giving thought to death as the destruction or permanent end of something. While many desire to live a long life, and understandably so, there are other things that should die or be put to death, the sooner the better.

There are things that need to die in one's life for one to fully live, or take on new life. For example, the desire to be liked needs to die in order to be at peace with oneself. The penchant for focusing on negative things needs to die to facilitate a more positive and uplifting approach that focuses on things that are true, lovely, honest, virtuous, and praiseworthy as instructed in Philippians 4:8. Likewise, the desire to always be in control needs to die, to give way to the all-powerful God taking control of the situations and circumstances in one's life.

Today's scripture points to new life to be found after death of the old man through the salvation process. Indeed, there are some ways of thinking and being that do not serve us well that should be put to death to gain a new life, where the things that matter flourish.

Seek for God's wisdom and help to understand what might need to die for you to experience new life in some aspect of your being.

Embrace new life today.

Keshawna Salmon-Ferguson
Jamaica

WEDNESDAY 29th

And God shall wipe away all tears from their eyes; and there shall be no more death, neither sorrow, nor crying, neither shall there be any more pain: for the former things are passed away
Revelation 21:4

NOTHING TO CRY ABOUT - Reading: Revelation 21:1-7

It's fair to say that some people are more emotional than others. Some people shed tears easily, others struggle to shed one or shed theirs in private. But the 'hardest' of us, will break because of something sometime!

John the apostle has done a good job capturing in one verse the main causes for tears. We shed tears because of *"death", "sorrow", "crying out unheard"* or mental, emotional or physical *"pain".* Since none of the above have access into heaven John, from his elevated and spiritual perspective, confidently says that tears will be a thing of the past because the former things, i.e., the cause of death, the cause of sorrow, the cause of crying, the cause of every type of pain, will be left behind on earth.

How disappointing it would be to get to heaven and still weep and sob because of… Thanks be to God that:

"Tears will never stain the streets of that city
No wreaths of death on my mansion door
Teardrops aren't welcome beyond the gates of glory
Because the heart will never break anymore" (D Rambo)

JEJ

THURSDAY 30th

And they shall be mine, saith the LORD of hosts, in that day when I make up my jewels…
Malachi 3:17

THE GROOMING OF A VESSEL – Reading: Jeremiah 18:1-6

Every season of our lives has its purpose, its beauty, and its glory. Yet they intermingle and pass so subtly from one to the other, it is sometimes difficult to realise where one ends and another begins.

Spring with its new life, innocence, and beauty slowly glides into Summer with its strength and passion. Summer's warmth and vigour gently allows Autumn to display a sudden burst of colour and zest. As Fall fades into Winter, life seems to be coming to a close. We begin to reminisce and to be thankful for moments and reminders of seasons gone by. What is more beautiful than a new birth, a budding plant, a lovely garden, a dashing ocean wave, a spectacular display of Autumn's foliage, or a gorgeous and serene snowfall?

And so it is with one's life, both, naturally and spiritually. Enjoy each phase to the fullest and to the glory of God. Being obedient to His will, as we travel through the seasons of our lives. With faith that God's love, His grace, and His mercy will take us through. Allow His peace and contentment to sustain you during each special time - be it joy or pain. Give thanks and praise to God for His goodness that leadeth to repentance. With longsuffering and patience, He will shape us. Through His spirit comes humility and meekness. By His Word He will create in us a clean heart and renew a right spirit within us. So, we offer up a praise unto His name just because He's God. We continue praising Him as He makes something beautiful of our lives.

As we reflect upon our walk, we can see God's hand from beginning to end and beyond. From the time He puts us on the potter's wheel until we are fully made - meet for the Master's use - a vessel of honour – well-groomed and ready to be presented to our Lord and Saviour.

Where are you? Where am I? Is it Springtime with new beginnings? Summer with growth and production? Fall (Autumn) with a display of energy, strength and beauty? Or is it Winter, a time for rest, tranquility and reflection with much to share of God's love and wisdom?

There will be Winter days and some Summer days during our Spring seasons. There will be Spring days and Fall days during our Summers. Spring, Summer, and Winter may present themselves in the Fall of our lives. And in the Winter of our lives, the time when we are most aware that life is coming to a close, our days will be brightened and softened by moments of Spring, and warmed by the bright rays of the sun to remind us of our Summers.

We may even experience some crisp and vigorous days to spark the energy we once had. The leaves are gone now, the flowers no longer bloom; the grass has ceased to grow. Winter sometimes seems long and hard, cold and indifferent. It seems to immobilise then suddenly lose its grip. Now it's over. We can say, *"We've fought a good fight"*. We've come full circle. We are vessels of honour. There's peace and joy; the strength of our contentment, hope for all we do. No more pain, no more struggles, but everlasting peace.

It's Jesus, and He's been there all the time, as we passed through the seasons of our lives working out our soul's salvation, God was there. He was the potter and we were the clay. He knew that we were diamonds in-the-rough. He looked beyond the external and began to remove all that marred our vessels. His workmanship revealed such precious gems - the souls of His people. God is using these gems paid for with His life, and perfected by His love, to make up His jewels. For He has said, *"These shall be mine" (Malachi 3:17), "and for their inheritance I will give them a crown of Life"*.

We're free. What a blessing! Such joy!

To God be glory! Amen.

Evangelist Edith P. Penn
USA

FRIDAY 31st

For I know the thoughts that I think toward you, saith the Lord, thoughts of peace, and not of evil, to give you an expected end
Jeremiah 29:11

CALL TO HOPE – Reading: Jeremiah 29:1-14

Today's reading is one of hope in the midst of chaos.

I once read a story where a doctor called one of his patients to tell him that he had bad news and some really bad news. He asked the patient which one he wanted to hear first. The patient asked him what was the bad news. The doctor said that his test results came back and that the patient only had 24 hours to live. The patient then asked what was the really bad news. The doctor answered and said that he should have called him yesterday! Sometimes news just goes from bad to worse. We are living in perilous times, but as bad as things may feel or may get, we must never lose sight of hope.

Jeremiah 29:11 is a hopeful verse in the midst of chaos. The people of Israel had strayed from the covenant they had made with God, time and time again. Now the time had come for judgment but, in the midst, there is call to hope. This scripture is great news in a bad situation. We see the mercy of God and the love He has for His people. God has a plan and if you submit to Him it will come to fruition.

Despite the condition in our trial, if we want hope, the expected end, it is in the next verse, *"...seek me with all your heart and you will find me"* (Jeremiah 29:12-13). God is calling you to Himself. Hope is the treasure in your trial, joyful expectation of the future, because God is the God of all hope as you connect to Him.

CP

February
Love Stories of the Bible

SATURDAY 1st

The LORD hath appeared of old unto me saying yea I have loved thee: therefore, with loving kindness have I drawn thee
Jeremiah 31:3

CONFRONTING THE LOVE OF GOD – Reading: Jeremiah 31:1-40

Sometimes we may wonder why certain situations happen; our expectations of the love of God raises personal questions. Some may ask, *"Why doesn't everything fall into place as soon as we ask, after all, we believe that God is love?".*

The truth is that we don't see the whole picture, we only know in part; we live in current times, with hindsight of the past.

Reflecting on the prophet Jeremiah (Hebrew meaning: God hurls/God exalts). He was born into a priestly family in Anathoth. He was a young man (about 17 or 20yrs old) when God called him to be a prophet unto the nations (Jeremiah 1:5). He was called The Weeping Prophet, because of the emotional distress and anguish he experienced while he ministered to the people. He would have identified with the heartbreak of God, for the love felt for His people (Jer. 9:1-3).

It was a time of political upheaval across the known world. The main 'powers' were Assyria, Egypt, and Babylon.

Against the background of Gentile uprising, God was and is in total control over the affairs of nations; He can lift a nation and put down another (Daniel 2:21).

God is love, light, a consuming fire; He is goodness, pure power, supreme excellence, highest level of righteousness, highest wisdom, and knowledge, divine and royal. The love of God is His pure character of holiness and glory. It is the pulse of His purpose. Sin will always trigger the righteous justice of God; it will be consumed by His manifest presence (Deuteronomy 4:24; Hebrews 12:29).

The mercy of God delays immediate destruction, it pauses His wrath upon sin. We see His warnings through Jeremiah to His people, interjected the appeal and amnesty of His love, but when the expiration date of His warnings is ignored, and time and purpose are exhausted to bring about change, then judgment appears swift.

Judah had not paid attention to the fall of their Northern tribes (captured by Assyria 721 or 722 B.C). The destruction on the land and captivity all happened to God's covenanted people because they had forsaken the living God (Jer. 30:15).

Jeremiah despaired over Judah's backslidden ways! The turmoil of preaching for 40 years (626 or 627-587 B.C.) with not one convert would have been soul-breaking. Such was the condition of Judah that God told him not to marry (Jer. 16:2). He witnessed the fall and captivity of his people, about 586 BC, by Nebuchadnezzar King of Babylon.

Through the complexities of life, entanglements, and problems, the Lord will find you wherever you are, for He knows those who are His. No matter how grave the situation, His love will search for you, wherever you are.

Our consolation is Jesus can be touched with the feelings of our infirmities. His love is our confidence.

The presence of our Lord God, and His love, will bring peace in knowing that He is in absolute control.

CDP

SUNDAY 2nd

But God commendeth his love toward us, in that, while we were yet sinners, Christ died for us
Romans 5:8

PERFECT LOVE – Reading: Romans 5:1-11

As I mused upon this powerful, inspiring scripture I was reminded of the renowned song, *"There is no greater love   There is no greater love, no love nowhere, no greater love; than a man would lay down His life for a friend, no love nowhere, I've searched all over".*

This sacrificial, unconditional love of God, demonstrated over 2,000 years ago, was exemplified through His Son, Jesus Christ, revealing to us that this divine love of God is not contingent upon our moral perfection, but is freely given even to those in a state of sin…

The psalmist asks the question in Psalm 8:4, *"What is man that thou art so mindful of him"*? We are constantly on the mind of God. What a reassurance, what a hope humankind has been given, that God's love for us goes beyond our faults, our imperfections, our insecurities and inhibitions, our struggles, and is demonstrated by His willingness to forgive us despite our sinful state.

The cross of Christ not only reconciles us with God but serves as the ultimate model of selfless love, beckoning us to a life transformed by grace, and committed to loving as Jesus loved.

God's gift of salvation through Christ is a testament to His immeasurable love for us, inviting us to enter into a transformative relationship with Him.

Evangelist Paula Clarke

MONDAY 3ʳᵈ

And Abraham said of Sarah his wife, she is my sister: and Abimelech king of Gerar sent and took Sarah.
Genesis 20:2

ATTEMPTED DESTINY SABOTAGE – Reading: Genesis 20:1-18

Sarah, who is already marked by divine destiny in terms of a carrier of the Messianic lineage; found herself in a dilemma, nothing short of a lose-lose: but for God. Yet we see this special couple, who has a God-appointed time in their lives got rescued, as God protected His eternal Word they were carrying.

Sarah prophetically carried a promise of God; she also personally carried flare, was fair and attracted princes as well as kings; and Abraham had the privilege of calling her his wife. To paraphrase, here comes Abraham: *"Sarah you are so beautiful my love, be kind to me now and say you are my sister. Do it for my sake, for down in Egypt they will kill me to get you. Oh yes… remember you are my father's daughter so yeah sister, please spare my life".*

So, sister of convenience is less of a liability but as wife, a very high risk of Abraham being killed. Abimelech saw, desired and had the power as king to take Sarah, so he made his move and what an attempted destiny sabotage! However, watch God move in to protect His destiny! Abimelech, you are a dead man! He was not just messing with a fair lady but with the mother of nations!

Avoid that which encourages destiny-sabotage; we are of God and He will move in according to His Sovereignty and name's sake!

Pastor Josephine

TUESDAY 4th

You did not choose me, but I chose you and appointed you that you should go and bear fruit and that your fruit should abide…
John 15:16 (ESV)

THE GREATEST RELATIONSHIP OF ALL – Reading: John 15:1-16

What a privilege to be chosen by God! Not as a last-minute whim, but a totally well-thought-through, before the foundation of the world, choice.

You are God's special choice. Chosen because He loved you even when you were a thought, not yet brought into existence. It's the greatest love story ever told: *"For God so loved the world, that he gave his only begotten Son, that whosoever believeth in him should not perish, but have everlasting life"* (St John 3:16).

There is a responsibility of being chosen. We must know who chose us, and our great responsibility to choose God back in return. It is only when the choosing is reciprocal (it goes both ways), when we stand firm in our identity, that we can then bear not just fruit, but fruit that remains, that is, good fruit, fruit that is not rotten.

Now the fruit we bear is primarily to feed others although, according to 2 Timothy 2:6, *"The husbandman that laboureth must be first partaker of the fruits"*. The fruit benefits everyone, and is evidence that you are aligned with the will of God.

So, chin up! Put a pep in your step! You are chosen, you are valued, and you are loved!

Min Jo Earle

WEDNESDAY 5th

...I will make him an help meet for him
Genesis 2:18

ANOTHER LOVE STORY – Reading: Genesis 2: 18-25

Today I am drawn to a love story, not between a man and his wife, but between God and humans.

The coming together of man and woman as husband and wife was built firstly upon God's love. In Genesis 2:18, *"the LORD God said, It is not good that the man should be alone; I will make him an help meet for him"*. God was moved by His loving concern for man's situation and provided a loving solution. Man was alone and God provided a helper just right for him, even without man asking.

Oh, what a love that provides for socio-emotional needs through marriage, the need to procreate through birth, and nutritional needs from plant and animal sources. God's love is seen in the many ways He acts on our behalf to respond to spoken and unspoken desires. Matthew 6:8 reminds us that God knows what we need **even before we ask**. And, out of the bounty of his love, God will supply all our needs from his glorious riches (Philippians 4:19). Yes, God who is love, is moved by love, and acts in love to provide and care for His people.

What an assurance today of God's love. It is great to know that the loving God who created us, has the means to sustain us and will in His love provide what we need, sometimes even before we ask. As we look at the things in our lives, let us see the love of God and the God of love who carefully makes provisions to take care of our needs, whether or not we are conscious of what those needs might be. See your spouse, your child, your job, your home, your academic achievements, your possessions, and anything else you might have some claim to, or lack thereof, as God's love for you as He makes provision to take care of your needs.

Rejoice today knowing that God's love can respond to your needs in any situation. Yes, God has both the resources and the loving intention to do you good. You are a part of a beautiful love story.

**Keshawna Salmon-Ferguson
Jamaica**

THURSDAY 6th

For God so loved the world, that he gave his only Son, that whoever believes in him should not perish but have eternal life
St John 3:16 (ESV)

THE NEVER-ENDING LOVE – Reading: St John 3:1-21

Often when we think of the greatest love story, we think of characters in films, books and even in animation. Over the last half a century, each decade has featured love stories that fill the mind with thoughts and memories that can evoke an array of emotions.

My personal reflection and experience of the greatest love story, can only be the love of God. His unfailing, unwavering love gives me hope and reminds me that as long as I am near to the Father, I can rest in His complete peace, God's true and perfect love. The love for His people, that He gave us through, *"...His only begotten Son! That whoever believes in him should not perish but have everlasting life. For God did not send His Son into the world to condemn the world, but that the world through Him might be saved"* (John 3:16-17 NKJV).

A love story so awesome and magnanimous, telling how the God of heaven and earth came in the form of man - a son to a mortal woman, fully divine and equally fully flesh, into a calamitous world to be the living sacrifice for us to have life! That's a Father who never abandons His children.

Can it be that the world has saturated our senses to the extent that we fail to recognise the importance of God's love, to be such an overwhelming love, through the embodiment of Jesus Christ, that this **is** the Greatest Love Story ever to told?

Through Christ Jesus we are now heirs to the throne, we're in the most esteemed Royal Priesthood, with the promise of eternal life when we walk in relationship with Him.

A line from a song says, *"I'll never know how much it cost to see my sin upon the cross!"*. We will never be able to comprehend the full love of God. Jeremiah 29:11 (NIV) states, *"For I know the plans I have for you, declares the Lord, plans to prosper you and not to harm you, plans to give you hope and a future".* Take comfort and peace in the Word that became flesh, that His love for you is the greatest love you will ever experience.

Georgina Walker

FRIDAY 7th

Many waters cannot quench love, neither can floods drown it...
Song of Songs 8:7

THE POWER OF LOVE – Reading: Esther 2:1-23; Song of Songs 8:1-14

We know that there is no greater love than God himself, and He demonstrated His love in such unique and powerful ways (John 3:16). His very nature and character are LOVE, and the Lord wants us to manifest His love to each other (1 John 4: 7-10).

The love story in the book of Esther draws us to this beautiful young girl, her Jewish name was Hadassah. She was an orphan raised by her cousin, Mordecai (Esther 2:15). They were in the group that stayed behind in Persia after the 70 years of captivity was over. We can see how the plan of God unfolds as Esther is chosen to be the Queen of Persia, as a replacement for Queen Vashti.

There were criteria that had to be met, *"Let there be fair young virgins sought for the king"* (Esther 2:2). The king (Ahasuerus) also had to approve (v4).

Esther's qualities for her to be considered to become queen included her being beautiful, a virgin, pure, untouched by a man. Esther, along with other maidens, was chosen to go to the palace in Shushan, under the custody of Hegai, who was the keeper of the women. Esther was treated favourably by Hegai (vs 8-10).

In her preparations, she had to wait for 12 months before she could be presented to King Ahasuerus, that is how long the purifying process was (v12). Esther's preparation and waiting were not in vain as the king fell in love with her immediately; he showed her grace and favour above all the other virgins, and made her his Queen. His love for Esther was so powerful that it extended to her being able to approach him, unannounced, and not be killed for doing so (Esther 5:2-3)!

The Lord has chosen us for such a time as this. However, we have to go through our purification process regardless of how long that might be, and wait patiently on Him.

Esther was in the right place and made herself available as part of God's plan. Esther was a Jewish girl, but became a Persian Queen because of the power of love. We are the bride of Christ; we are chosen and loved unconditionally despite our backgrounds.

Single sisters, you are beautiful chosen vessels, well-loved by our Heavenly Father. Keep availing yourself to the work of the ministry to your maximum capacity. Be sanctified vessels for the Lord, allow the will of God to blossom in your life and bask in the power of love, God's unconditional love. He will do the rest!

Minister/Lady Genevieve Dinnall

SATURDAY 8th

But a certain Samaritan, as he journeyed, came where he was: and when he saw him, he had compassion
Luke 10:33

THE INN-KEEPER'S JOB – Reading: Luke 10:25-37

"Thou shalt love thy neighbour as thyself" - *"Who is my neighbour?"*

That was a profound question; and Jesus in His usual pragmatic way, doesn't waste time remonstrating with what might seem obvious to most people. He simply tells a story that will answer this question with force and clarity, so that no one leaves the discussion confused or uncertain.

This story has resonated across cultures, age, class and ability. It has been told and retold without losing its relevance or impact. So what is it that makes it such a good story? It deals with the basic principle of love of which the foundation is God's agapé love. You shall love as I love, Jesus said. *"Love your neighbour as yourself"* (Leviticus 19:18), and, *"By this shall all men know that ye are my disciples"* (John 13:35). Consequently, Christ becomes the focal point because what people see in His disciples, is what they see in the way Christ treated people. Unconditional love.

Generally, the approach in interpreting this story is to examine the various characters and then to explain the possible intent. One such explanation suggests that Jesus is the Good Samaritan, the attacked man - anyone in need of help, the Levite and the Priest - leaders in the church and the inn keeper, those whom Jesus has left in charge of His work to do as He did until He returns.

However, the intrinsic quality of what Jesus intended us to gain from this story is that we are our brother's and sister's keeper. Once we become aware of needs, we address it without considering the cost to ourselves. Whether we have one little mite or millions of denarius, one hour or years, we must be interested in giving to alleviate the needs of our fellow person.

You may or may not know that Jews and Samaritans were sworn enemies. For a Samaritan to assist a Jew was unheard of! Jesus talks in other places in the Bible about loving our enemies, and doing good to those who despitefully use us. He expects His disciples to get rid of all bigotry and prejudice. God is love, God is compassionate, God is merciful. This is not metaphor, this is fact. Christ's parting message to the lawyer that initiated the question was, *"Go thou and do likewise".*

That commission is for all who would be His disciples.

Cheryl Lowe
Guyana

SUNDAY 9th

My daughter, shall I not seek rest for thee, that it may be well with thee?
Ruth 3:1

WOMEN WHO LOVE – Reading: Ruth 3:1-2; John 13:34-38

God's Word is so relevant in addressing our relationships.

We can learn something of this from Naomi's care for her daughter-in-law, Ruth. There are some relational and practical tips in Ruth 3 that may help our modern-day relationships.

Naomi was without a husband, and now a son, but she craved for Ruth what she no longer had for herself. What deep love! Her desire to have Ruth cared for was one so deep that it became her own mission, and so Naomi discussed this with Ruth.

Naomi could vouch for the character and consistency of Boaz, i.e., *"This is who he is and he will be found at a certain place working"*. Here was more than a strategy, this spoke of the character of Boaz. He was a doer and a man of consistency and trust. Naomi's word, *"He will be..."*! In today's world of politics, agendas and (dare I say) even media ambiguity in the church, here was a man who would be where he said, be working where he could, and showing up enough for Ruth to lean on his integrity. Naomi didn't mention Boaz's status right here, or even his wealth. but she regarded that he was an honest and hardworking man. Let's consider that - can I lean on you?

In just two verses we see this, trust and truth, between women who are invested in one another and whose love wants the best for them.

Powerful!

Joy Lear-Bernard

MONDAY 10th

To appoint unto them that mourn in Zion, to give unto them beauty for ashes, the oil of joy for mourning…
Isaiah 61:3

WHAT BEAUTY! – Reading: Isaiah 61:1-11

O what beauty, Lord!
A broken life restored and made anew
A different picture now
From how it once had been
Only You could do this Lord
Your purpose to fulfil.

For you took this broken life
And let it really live
You brought glory where once
There had been shame
Rivers of healing, You took my pain
In its place love, joy and peace
Like I'd never known
To me, dear Lord, Your great love You have shown.

Oh, what beauty, Lord!
My broken life restored, completely made anew
A different picture now
From the life I once knew, only you could do this, Lord
Your purpose to fulfil
For you took my broken life, Lord, and really let me live.

Rena P Grzeszczyk

TUESDAY 11th

Husbands, love your wives, as Christ loved the church and gave himself up for her
Ephesians 5:25 (ESV)

LOVE ONE ANOTHER AS CHRIST LOVES YOU
Reading: Ephesians 5:21-33

"*H*usbands, love your wives, as Christ loved the church
Sanctified and cleansed, through the water of the Word,
A love so deep and boundless, in every act inferred
Presented without blemish, holy and pure and bright,
In robes of righteousness, in garments of pure light".

This scripture reflects the deep and selfless love Christ has for the church.

God's love is unconditional and we must love each other that way. This is a selfless commitment to the well-being of one's spouse. Just as Christ gave Himself up for us, this is the same love and sacrifice we must give for our husbands/wives. A marriage chosen by God must involve nurturing spiritual and personal growth, creating an environment where both can thrive in purity and righteousness.

When two are married they become one, and grow a deep connection. This godly relationship provides emotional support, physical care, and spiritual guidance. I encourage you to practice selfless love, and have honest conversations about your goals and your spiritual journey. Pray with others and strengthen your spiritual bond through activities.

Treat your partner with care and make decisions together, simple words of affirmation and gratitude can significantly enhance the emotional bond between you and your spouse. Express your love through actions and words, and let God be the centre of it all as He is the foundation of your relationship.

Name withheld

WEDNESDAY 12th

For this cause shall a man leave his father and mother, and shall be joined unto his wife, and they two shall be one flesh. This is a great mystery...
Ephesians 5:31-32

AS ONE THROUGH CHRIST – Reading: Genesis 2:24-25; Ephesians 5:31-33; 1 Peter 3:1-9

The mystery profound, yet clear as day,
As Christ and church, in love's divine display.
So let each husband love his wife as he
Loves himself, with deep humility.

Husbands, love your wives as Christ the King,
Loved His church, the heavens echoing.
He gave Himself, a sacrifice so grand,
To sanctify, to cleanse, with a hold hand.

And wives, respect your husbands with pure grace,
Together, in his sacred, holy space.
For in this, a greater love is shown,
The love of Christ, through marriage made known.

For we are members of His loving image,
Gods' beautiful creation, set apart,
Our covenant with Him shall we not depart,
God and His people, a bond nothing can diminish.

So let each heart with fervour seek,
In humble acts, in words we speak.
To honour, love, and deeply care,
In this, our sacred love affair.

In the Book of Ephesians, a truth is clear,
A call to love and honour, dear.
In love and respect, day and night
As Christ loves His church, in holy light.

A heavenly bond, adjoined as one,
Forever matched, together belonged.
Loving through the love of God so strong,
A marriage never wavering, to forever prolong.

Name withheld

THURSDAY 13th

...My well-beloved has a vineyard in a very fruitful hill... What could have been done more to my vineyard, that I have not done in it?
Isaiah 5:1,4

UNREQUITED LOVE – Reading: Isaiah 5:1-30

Isaiah 5:1-4 speaks of God's agapé love for His church.

The text is a lament, a sad love song, full of pathos and longing. It reminds me of when Jesus rode into Jerusalem on a donkey, and wept over Jerusalem: *"Oh Jerusalem, Jerusalem, how often would I have gathered thy children together, even as a hen gathers her chickens under her wings and ye would not"* (Matthew 23:37-39). This imagery is full of gentleness, protective care, nurturing, affection, concern for the well-being of His people that might be compared to a mother's love.

The text speaks of unrequited love, for although God is doing all that He can to win the heart of His people they (Israel) are motivated by self-interest and worldliness. They are not interested in His advances. God then, as it were, appeals to a third unidentified party that they might tell Him where He went wrong, *"What more could I Have done"*? This is a rhetorical question for He has already said that He has done everything that could be done, except force His church, for love cannot be coerced.

God's desire for His people was that they should choose Him and through them reveal His plan of salvation and love for the world. John 3:16 says, *"For God so loved the world..."*. His love is unfathomable and takes in everyone. His enduring mercy never fails. The Bible tells us that God's love is unconditional. He first loved us and revealed the extent of His love by His condescension and willingness to give Himself a ransom for us all (1 John 4:19). Christ's coming to this earth was to show us the mercy of our Father and the extent to which He was willing to go to redeem the human race even though it was undeserved.

When God talks about His vineyard, He is referring to us, His people, His church. Grapes, the fruit of the vine, symbolises that which is good and righteous, reflecting God's intention. The vineyard is the place in which His truth is kept and conveyed to the world. When He says that the vine brought forth wild grapes, though, it suggests that sin is present, the false has taken the place of the true.

God's longing for His people is no less today than it was back then, in the days of Israel. The Messiah has come and is about to return again. It is important that we so familiarise ourselves with His Word, that we recognise Him when He speaks to us. Jesus said my sheep know my voice (John 10:4b). Let us not fill our lives with wild grapes that we block out the truth of God, and miss out when he returns.

Cheryl Lowe
Guyana

FRIDAY 14th

Therefore, shall a man leave his father and his mother, and shall cleave unto his wife: and they shall be one flesh. And they were both naked, the man and his wife, and were not ashamed
Genesis 2:24-25

TWO BECOMING ONE – Reading: Genesis 2:24-26; Ephesians 5:25-33

Two hearts now beat as one (Unknown).

The union between a man and a woman is a journey full of adventures, lots of sacrifice, compromise, love and hard work. In the sight of God, marriage is *"honourable in all"* (Hebrews 13:4a).

This unbreakable, lifelong union will take a journey of a lifetime to be accomplished. A journey often filled with tears, struggles, conflicts, joy, apologies, laughter, humility, moments of sadness, brokenness, ups and downs. It is therefore important that, when considering marriage, much time is given to seek God's guidance and direction before making this lifelong commitment.

Every successful marriage is often built on the fundamental building blocks of love, respect, purpose, trust, communication, and a mutual support for each other. The union then between a man and woman, has got to go far beyond the faith/belief of the couple, but is directly linked to the individual's destiny and purpose. This mystery of the two becoming one, is beyond human comprehension This fusion of souls clearly paints the perfect picture of the unity that is reflected in the relationship between Christ and the church, as described in Ephesians 5:31-32.

The scripture in John 17:21 clearly expresses the deep desire of the Father's heart as it pertains to the two becoming one: *"That they all may be one; as thou, Father, art in me, and I in thee, that they also may be one in us: that the world may believe that thou hast sent me".*

Two hearts now beat as one.

Name withheld

SATURDAY 15th

Love never ends
1 Corinthians 13:8 (ESV)

FOR MOMS *(adapted from 1 Corinthians 13:1-13)*

I can read bedtime stories till 'the cows jump over the moon' and sing *"Ten Little Monkies"* until I want to call the doctor, *but if I don't have love*, I'm as annoying as a ringing phone.

I can chase a naked toddler through the house while cooking dinner and listening to voicemail, and tell a child's temperature with one touch of a finger, but if I don't have love, I am nothing.

Love is patient while watching and praying by the front window when it's 30 minutes past curfew. It does not envy the neighbours' swimming pool, or their brand new mini van, but trusts the Lord to provide for their every need.

Love does not brag when other parents share their insecurities and disappointments, and love rejoices when other families succeed. It is not easily angered even when my 15-year-old acts like the world revolves around her.

It does not delight in evil (is not self-righteous) when I remind my 19-year-old that he is going 83 in a 55-mph zone, but rejoices in the truth. Love does not give up hope. It always protects our children's spirits, even while doling out discipline. It always trusts God to protect our children when we cannot. It perseveres through rolled eyes, crossed arms, messy rooms and slammed doors. Love never fails.

But where there are memories of thousands of diaper changes and painful labour(s), they will fade away. When there is talking back, it will eventually cease (*Please Lord*). Where there is a teenager who thinks she knows everything, there will be an adult who knows you did your best.

When we were children, we needed a parent to love and protect us. Now that we're parents ourselves, we have a Heavenly Father who shelters us and holds us when we need to cry.

And now these three remain, hope, faith and love. But the greatest of these is love.

Unknown author

SUNDAY 16th

...But while he was yet a great way off, his father saw him, and had compassion, and ran, and fell on his neck, and kissed him
Luke 15:20

LOVE OF THE PRODIGAL'S FATHER – Reading: Ezekiel 16:6-10; Luke 15:11-32

Jesus shared the parable of the prodigal son who demanded a legacy he had not yet earned, being the younger of the two.

The father's longsuffering for this unworthy son demonstrates the greatness of God's love. We as outsiders have been nurtured into the longing for a good Father's heart. Reckless and not yet entitled still the father allowed his son's journey to bring him to a place of seeing himself and His need for His Father.

Our God knows that our demands are just a sign that we may not fully comprehend who He is. How can we - we're sons exploring a world too big for us to go alone. He is patient with our revellings and questions because ultimately, it does not only show our weakness but also convicts us of our great need for His strength.

He waited. This father did not use his riches and influence to seek out his wandering son. He did not try to force back in body a son who had not been reconciled in heart. He waited. With pain and sacrifice, he allowed the course of experience and freewill to unction the son back to Him of his own volition. God is merciful towards our repented hearts, yes, but He too is patient with our uncertain ways, our humanity, our wandering.

Why did he not drag that son back to safety? Would that not be true love? No. He knew that his son would be home but his mind still be elsewhere. This loving father endured the absence of his son, and the shame, in order to allow his son's mind and heart to mature. Such was the care for his son's wellbeing, that he allowed the humiliating process to work for his son's good.

What is most beautiful is that he faced towards His son. God's love faces us. It looks beyond our faults and sees our need. Upon the son's return we see that the Father's love had been anticipating a comeback. That calf was already being prepared for a great celebration. Hear this, the calf was being fattened whilst the son was still eating animal food in a pig pen. Such is the Father's heart towards you and I – while we were yet sinners, He loved us.

His Love desires to be loved back. The Father loves when we choose Him. He loves when we run back to Him and acknowledge Him as Sovereign. He loves when life's lessons bring us back to Him. Our Father is Love.

Joy Lear- Bernard

MONDAY 17th

MICHAL: THE COMPLEXITIES OF LOVE – Reading: 1 Samuel 18:17-30; 19:11-17; 25:44; 2 Samuel 6:17-23

Rarely do we see a woman in the Bible openly fall in love and get her heart's desire. Michal was one of those few. Though her father, Saul, intended to use her as a trap for David, he underestimated the power of a woman's love.

Michal risked everything for David, going as far as betraying her father to help him escape. This was a very bold action, especially during a time when women had little say in their lives or marriages. She was loyal, unhesitatingly showing her love and devotion to David, taking courageous steps to protect him and do the unthinkable - defy the King.

This brazen act of marital loyalty would lead to her father again using her to hurt David. Saul simply gave her to another man after David fled. This forced marriage, combined with years apart from David, possibly changed her. When she finally reunited with David, he was now King, with other wives and children. Michal, once so full of love for him, had grown distant. In 2 Samuel 6, her bitterness showed when she watched disdainfully as David danced and worshipped God. The passionate Michal we initially met had become hardened by her circumstances. So much so, that her story simply closed on the note that she bore no children up to her death.

Michal's story is one of love and courage, but also a warning of how life's circumstances can change us. The political and personal forces beyond her control led her to lose the attractive spark she initially had. Perhaps if Michal had drawn closer to David's God, she could have found the strength to rise above the bitterness and disappointment that eventually altered her.

Shani Oliphant
Jamaica

TUESDAY 18th

...make not thyself known unto the man, until he shall have done eating and drinking
Ruth 3:3

WOMEN WITH WISDOM – Reading: Ruth 3:3-18

In seeking a husband, trusting the intention and wisdom of Naomi, Ruth did not say, *"I have been here before, I know what to do"*. She was able to lean into the wisdom of this older woman, she saw in her that there was something of value to still learn. She trusted her. They had shared life together and cared for one another.

Now, can we be brave in collecting this goldy mother's wisdom? Here it is!

Wash. Use perfume. Get dressed in your best clothes. There we have it! Long gone are the days of apology for the beauty of a woman, where meekness and modesty are confused, and at times replaced by fleshy expressions or degradation of our beauty with shame and belittling. Rather, the inward real beauty of a meek and quiet spirit of a woman can then, and only then, safely be adorned with beauty on the outside. Ruth, this potentially soon to be married woman, relied first on character and godliness, with a little perfume and good presentation!

Here too were early practical types of communication between a man and a woman. We can be guilty of speaking too soon, or at ill appropriate moments. Knowing this, here was Naomi's suggestion, *"Don't distract him while he's working, but once he's rested and has eaten, then approach him"* (Ruth 3:3). The following verses say that when Boaz was *'in good spirits',* Ruth approached him. Could it be true, the adage, *"The way to a man's heart is through his stomach"*?

With the instruction to uncover his feet and lie down, it was a potential indication of a request to wed. Boaz follows and 'tells...what to do'. Somewhere in this ritual, Ruth is clear on her part and Boaz shows the quality of assertiveness and leading. Naomi, woman of wisdom, knew how much to instigate and instruct and then to leave the rest for them to follow through.

Let's pause and consider, am I or do I have a woman whose judgment and wisdom allows these words, *"I will do whatever you say"*? What a testament to them both; one of humility, one of trust in the greater plan between these two women. Note that from verse one, Naomi did not coerce Ruth, she simply made her suggestion clear.

These women do not seem apologetic in their desire for Ruth to be wed, nor timid in their pursuits. They are meek with strength, coupled with guidance with good intention, sealed with respect for each other. We see an intertwining of purpose and pursuit.

Joy Lear-Bernard

WEDNESDAY 19th

I will heal their backsliding, I will love them freely
Hosea 14:4

LOVE IS PATIENT – Reading: Hosea 14:1-9

The book of Hosea is an amazing account of the prophet Hosea's marriage and God's love. God directed Hosea to marry a lady by the name of Gomer; she was as God said, a wife of whoredoms.

The Israelites were of a comparable state, i.e., they had been unfaithful to God. Such was the condition that they found themselves in, God wanted to demonstrate to them their actions by means of the relationship between Hosea and his wife. God wanted to show them the pain that their unfaithfulness caused Him. Using Hosea to represent God, the sorry situation unfolds.

All is not lost though; there is still hope as they have time to repent and return to God. They have been worshipping idols and forgetting how much God loves them, but God still has a heart full of love for them. Hosea 2:19-20 says, *"And I will betroth thee unto me for ever; I will betroth thee unto me in righteousness, and in judgment, and in lovingkindness, and in mercies. I will even betroth thee unto me in faithfulness; and thou shalt know the LORD".*

There is a call to repentance because God's faithfulness outweighs their sin! Hosea 6:1 says, *"Come and let us return unto the LORD; for he hath torn, and he will heal us; he hath smitten, and he will bind us up".* Then finally in Hosea 14:1 *"O Israel return unto the LORD thy God; for thou hast fallen by thine iniquity'.* Then verse 4, *"I will heal their backsliding, I will love them freely: for mine anger is turned away from him".*

Love is patient.

BVG

THURSDAY 20th

And Laban had two daughters: the name of the elder was Leah, and the name of the younger was Rachel...And Jacob loved Rachel... Genesis 29:16-18

JACOB'S LOVE STORY – Reading: Genesis 29: 14-35

Everyone loves a good love story, especially if it ends happily ever after. In today's world, when we hear the term love, we instantly think of 'boy meets girl, fall in love, get married, raise a family and live happily ever after', at least that's how we used to think. However, the Bible enlightens us that there are different kinds of love of which agapé love is superior, for that relates to God's unconditional love.

In studying the Bible, one thing becomes clear - sin takes no unconscious prisoners. This is clearly exemplified in the tale of Jacob's life. Talk about dysfunctional! Now how did Jacob become the soft, malleable person he turned out to be before God rescued him? Well, it became noticeable after he practiced to deceive his father and his brother (Genesis 25:27-34;27:1-46). Oh, what a tangled web his life turned out to be after that. First, we yield to the temptation, because it seems like a good idea at the time; then, we start to feel guilty as the consequences of our sin begin to kick in.

For Jacob, that meant leaving his home prematurely and actually never seeing his mother alive again. The agapé of God's love followed him all the way and never left him. From time-to-time, God stepped in to encourage him because He does not like us to believe that our punishment is more than we can bear (Genesis 4:13). He repeats His promises so that we accept that His Word will not return unto Him void (Isaiah 55:11).

But how did Jacob turn out to be so easy to manipulate? Like David, he got to the place where he realised that when you do wrong, it is very difficult to rebuke sin in others, whether it be those who are clearly taking unfair advantage, or children who harboured jealousy, malice and hatred in their hearts until they could commit murder (2 Samuel 13:22-39). The results? A guilt-ridden Jacob, who ends up with two wives (not his original plan) who became warring sisters; four mothers of his children; twelve sons who found it difficult to get on, etc.

What has all this got to do with women today? There are many lessons in Jacob's love story. He fell in love with one woman, Rachel, and ended up being passed around between Rachel and her sister, Leah, and their handmaids, like a football in an unholy competition. Jacob's eldest son, Reuben, disrespected him by sleeping with one of Jacob's concubines, Bilhah, the mother of two of Jacob's sons, i.e., the mother of two of Reuben's younger brothers. Jacob's daughter, Dinah, was seduced and raped by Shechem, son of Hamor, a Hivite, whilst exploring the land of Shechem. This led to her brothers, Simeon and Levi, taking revenge on the men of the city of Shechem.

Newton's law says that, *"For every action in nature there is an equal and opposite reaction"*. Hosea puts it like this… *"sow the wind, reap the whirlwind"* (Hosea 8:7).

The tragedy of Jacob's story does not end there though. God's promises came through for him. When he began to realise his need of God, then God was able to act for him. After years of labouring exploitation, he had no wealth of his own to care for his family. God stepped in with a plan, and he became one of the wealthiest men in Padanaram, before returning with his wives and children to Canaan. He was protected from harm even though his father-in-law, Laban, pursued him with intent to hurt him. He was victorious in a battle with the Lord in the wilderness and experienced a name change - from Jacob to Israel - because he hung on to the Lord for His blessing. Jacob was amicably reunited with his brother and joined with him to bury their father. He was also reunited with his favourite son, Joseph, after thinking for many years that he was dead.

Jacob died a happy man, blessing each of his sons and two grandsons. Whilst God may not intervene in the consequences for sin, He promises overcoming power for anyone that requires it. In John 3:16, God throws out an invitation to 'whosoever will'. His agapé love is sent out to the world, that includes you and me, guilty or not guilty. If he could forgive Jacob and turn his life around, he can do the same for you and me.

"...He is faithful and just to forgive us our sins, and to cleanse us from all unrighteousness" (1 John 1:9).

Cheryl Lowe
Guyana

FRIDAY 21st

And we know that all things work together for good to them that love God, to them who are the called according to his purpose
Romans 8:28

GOOD ALWAYS COMES OUT – Reading: Romans 8:18-28

No matter what the problem is
Good will come out of it.
The lady sprained her ankle
But good came out of it.

There was no one for her to call
People had plans and were busy
As she prayed to her God
But in a way she was glad
For she had to depend on Him.

Good will come out of it
She realised
She could enjoy
Just her and God's company.

She realised
There are times
She can't always
Rely on others
Or on herself.

As she reflected
She can't naturally walk
Without Christ
But she has to rely on him.

Though it was difficult
Walking was a pain
It caused her to keep talking

To communicate
With the Saviour again.

Good will always come out
This lady believed it to be so
And through her mishap
She could see
What her God had to achieve.

Praise God.

Sister Jennifer Henry

SATURDAY 22nd

And she went down unto the floor, and did according to all that her mother in law bade her And when Boaz had eaten and drunk, and his heart was merry, he went to lie down at the end of the heap of corn: and she came softly, and uncovered his feet
Ruth 3:6-7

AND SHE MOVED SOFTLY – Reading: Ruth 3:6-7; Galatians 5:22-23

Oh, what beauty to trust a mother so implicitly that every word spoken in instruction can be followed without variation. Such a delicate obedience that comes from deep trust.

How does one arrive at such a relationship? I believe that throughout this emerging love story between Ruth and Boaz, there was already a love story of two women - mother and daughter - who had proven over time that they had one another's best interest at heart. They had shared family and tribesmen but, deeper than this, was that Naomi's God was now also Ruth's God. They shared faith that guided their character and their connection.

To-the-letter, Ruth did as Naomi said and uncovered Boaz's feet; they even knew that this man would be easily approached after a good dinner! Note to women! But note too, one gentle adjective added to the text depicting Ruth's approach, *"she came softly, and uncovered his feet".*

Well, of course she did, she didn't want to disturb him! That seems obvious, doesn't it? But some metaphoric handling of a mother's instruction influenced this daughter to motion with sweet respect and gentleness. A wonderful quality.

Could we take from this that, when a mother passes on her wisdom with grace and poise, it shares the very approach for her daughter; it teaches her how to move powerfully as a woman.

Daughters who feel safe simply begin to deck themselves with godly character, and softness, because it has been modelled to them just how beautiful godly womanhood is. And indeed rather than rebuke, a reminder of this daughter's purpose and regard caused Ruth to move more gracefully into her own purpose, **from the inside out**.

Perhaps what is to be developed amongst mothers, daughters and sisters is not just a list of instructions, but a love that moves softly with power and purpose, and a heart for one another, because we love the same God and crave the best in God for one another.

Joy Lear-Bernard

SUNDAY 23rd

It came to pass, that as (Jesus) was come nigh to Jericho, a certain blind man sat by the way side begging
Luke 18:35

THE HOMELESS PEOPLE – Reading: Luke 18:35-43

As I was walking in Leeds Town Centre
I came to a hotspot. Just one spot.
Where homeless men and women
Are always found.

Folded up tables were outstretched
And they were happily surrounded
By the strangers that stood around them.

Smiling volunteers
They listened
And gave out food
With cups of soup
Or was it tea?
As the hits from the radio played relentlessly.

As I write this
I know if it was not
For God's mercy
One homeless person
I have no doubt could have been me.

Nowhere to go
No parents or family
Friends or acquaintances
To help and to say, I love you so
Come off this street
And come home and follow me.

To show you kindness
With a roof for one night
Or several nights
To be introduced to a lovely warm bed
With a hearty breakfast
Of toast, sausage, eggs and beans
So you're fed.

The victims of homelessness
Some, it was an accident
And some it was not
Many did not get there overnight
A loss of job
A house eviction
Some drug or alcohol addiction.

A mental breakdown
A sudden sickness
These are only a few
That I have mentioned
Families that fight.

Or being abused
And needing to leave
To avoid
More abuse and strife.

But homelessness
Can be fixed
Society tries to take full control
And tries to alleviate all of this.

But homeless ones
Need more than a home
And android telephone.

They need a Saviour
And they can now say
Though once I was homeless
Jesus Christ has saved me
And I have truly come home.

Jesus will provide
A spiritual family
He will do the work
And provide all blessings
And His sweet Shalom.

Sister Jennifer Henry

MONDAY 24th

And it came to pass at midnight, that the man was afraid, and turned himself: and behold, a woman lay at his feet
Ruth 3:8

A WORTHY COVERING – Reading: Ruth 3:8-11; Proverbs 31:9-12

Truly unexpected, Boaz is startled by this woman and again sees her - maybe even more so than before. Instantly, just because of their positions in the family and their ages, there is insight of how they regard one another.

"You", Ruth says, *"are the guardian and redeemer of our family"*. This means it's only right that he should cover her safely and honour the order of his position. He, being older, and seeing the younger (potentially richer men) as competition, sees her as kind in considering him. Boaz sees her as someone to be admired and immediately promises safety, protection and honour. He entreats her to this point as a daughter. She is a potential wife though a much younger woman, but her asking of his covering, to him, also indicates her safety as he describes her as a woman of renown *"noble character"*.

Boaz's honesty compels him to explain that there are more suited, or better matched men, one more in line. Even in an age where traditions were so unlike those of our Western World, we still have a peek of the notable character of Boaz in just a few words. His first being, *"The LORD bless you…"*. Can a man pronounce God's blessing over you such sincerity unless you are noble? Can my reputation of honesty honour me even before I am known, and can a future suitor see and speak similar things over you, *"As surely as the LORD lives I shall…."*?

This man of God's words were sure and committed. As sisters, wives, mothers and grandmothers, let's pray for the strong conviction and covering of brothers, husbands, sons and grandsons for such a time as this. *"Lie here till morning"*. The tender care of a man of God showed her the quality of his character. and safely she followed.

Joy Lear-Bernard

TUESDAY 25th

And Boaz said…Ye are witnesses this day that I have bought all that was Elimelech's, and all that was Chilion's, and Mahlon's, of the hand of Naomi
Ruth 4:9

GOD'S IMPERFECT RIGHT MAN – Reading: Ruth 4:1-9

Boaz was much older than Ruth, hardworking but slower. He may not have been as alluring as younger men, even in his own eyes.

He was not sinful, or insincere. He was not lazy or dishonest. But he, like every man, was imperfect. Perfection: meaning without fault or room for betterment, flawless. By this definition of perfection, we can assume that Boaz was like every other man, or woman, for that matter.

But I think that what made Boaz appealing to Naomi and Ruth was his consistent commitment to apply himself, his desire to work and to graft. He showed himself to be a kind man and honest in his integrity - honest about himself and honest about his intentions. Boaz was not perfect but he was right! Right standing as a man, rightly positioned in his heart and rightly ready to become a leader and protector for Ruth.

When we observe our brothers, leaders, husbands and sons, it can take some bravery and grace to not only see their flaws, and to honour the integrity behind that man. Oh, I know that the world would love for us to tear down men amongst women and women amongst men. Yet when we engage with such rhetoric, we tear down the very idea for men and women to move in harmony together as God has intended!

In our homes and churches, we are always to be counter worldly culture. We must always raise the bar, lifted from the Word of God. We move to a different beat which is the one of heaven.

'Right' men can see their own flaws and admit them too, as Boaz did. Their internal desire to do their best reflects something of the very nature of God. And righteous men implore and nurture this in their sons, because life is imperfect and sometimes men need a hub of godly men and women to speak into their imperfections, knowing that their desire is only to be right before God.

So what do we pray for in men, what do we observe in men who are right? Maybe not so much their age/years or status that can shift and wane. But his character, his integrity, his ability to repent if he needs to change, his burden to work and serve. Maybe we should listen more keenly to how solidly he lives with character in his home and community, how gently he responds to the vulnerable around him and how deeply he trusts God.

An imperfect man can be right when he entrusts himself into the hands of the God that we as women trust.

Joy Lear-Bernard

WEDNESDAY 26th

Husbands love your wives as, as Christ also loved the church...
Ephesians 5:25

ARE YOU CLEAVING? – Reading: Genesis 2:21-25

When God created man, He created him as an extension and a portrait of Himself. From the earth, God formed a compliment to Himself. An earthen creation with whom He would have relationship. He breathed into the man's nostrils and brought to life a creature from the dust of the earth who becomes a living soul. A relational component is central to God's creative act. Relationship of God to man, and man to God. Yet equally important is the human-to-human relationship.

Then the Lord said, *"it is not good for man, to be alone"* (Genesis 2:18). God caused a deep sleep to fall upon Adam, and as he slept, he took one of his ribs, and he made a help meet called woman because she was taken out of man.

As bone of Adam's bone, and flesh of his flesh, God said, *"a man shall leave his father and mother, and shall cleave to his wife, and they shall be one flesh"* (Genesis 2:24).

The word *"cleave"* means to cling, stick, stay close, join to, bond. The Hebrew word *'dabag'* means to solder or weld. We can see how divorce is so painful as it literally tears the persons apart. To cleave to your mate means we are to be completely blended as one, but still, we are not to lose our own identity.

So often there is trouble in marriages because we leave but we do not cleave. Where there is no cleaving, we leave space for things to creep in and divide a bond that should be unbreakable. Marriage is to be a spiritual union, a sexual union, and a purposeful union. That union with your spouse and Christ is that three-stranded chord that cannot be easily broken.

The marriage union is so precious in the sight of God that He calls the church His bride. Husbands are admonished to love their wives as Christ loves the church, and gave Himself for it. There is nothing/nobody that is supposed to be more important than your spouse. Not your parents, your job, your children, or outside interest. What a beautiful example for us to have for the lover of our souls. There should be nothing between our souls, and our Saviour.

"Who shall separate us from the love of God?" Romans 8:35-39 tells us that if we cleave to our Saviour, as a man should cleave to his wife, we will be more than conquerors through Him that loved us! Are you cleaving?

Lady Winsome Saunders
USA

THURSDAY 27th

Let not mercy and truth forsake thee: bind them about thy neck; write them upon the table of thine heart
Proverbs 3:3

TAKE IT STEADY – Reading: Proverbs 3:1-35

Take it steady
Take it slow
For in this day
There are many seen and unseen
Things that will make you grow.

Take it easy
Be gentle on you
To thy own self
Be honest and true.

Take time out
And let go
Remember Jesus
Stole away to the mountain
And took time
To revive his soul.

I know you love others
It's commendable of you
But pour all your love
Into Christ your Saviour.
So no matter what comes
Jesus, your dearest friend
He will anchor you.

Take it steady
Worry no more
Remember you are blessed
And Jesus will open

Every shut door.

Take it steady
Always find time for Him
For with His love and power
You can live victoriously
For the Saviour always wins.

Praise God!

Sister Jennifer Henry

FRIDAY 28th

May the LORD make the woman who is coming into your home like Rachel and Leah, who together built up the family of Israel. May you have standing in Ephrathah and be famous in Bethlehem
Ruth 4:11 (NIV)

GREAT GRACE, GREAT INFLUENCE – Reading: Ruth 4:10-11; Titus 2:3-5

Ceremonies of the times in this text were not really acts of romance and new love, as such, but almost transactional arrangements of honouring, generational regard and financial stability. Boaz's announcement introducing Ruth does feature something though, that has withstood the change of time: *"You are witnesses"* (Ruth 4:9).

Looking beyond this ceremonial declaration, let's see what witnesses of marriage deem as their responsibility. Is it an obligatory piece of cake, or an invite to after celebrations? No, simply. Say a powerful and meaningful prayer, a blessing, an accountability of the woman entering into her new home, *"May she be like Rachel and Leah who together built up the family of Israel"* (Ruth 4:11). What high expectations of a bride, of the influence of a woman in her home and in her community! Note to us as believers: pray for godly marriages.

Women, we are blessed to influence by our godliness, giftings and grace. The power of a godly woman can cause generational change. O that in choosing a new bridal gown, a new home, a new job, we would rather believe the declarations over us that our fame will be one that speaks of our Great GOD in our lives.

Joy Lear-Bernard

March

Not Named & Hardly Mentioned Women of the Bible

SATURDAY 1st

...about three months after, it was told Judah, saying, Tamar thy daughter-in-law hath played the harlot...
Genesis 38:24

TAMAR – WHAT ABOUT HER? Reading: Genesis 38: 1-30

Tamar found her destiny in a family that was divinely mantled; in a twist. She was the daughter-in-law of Judah, son of Jacob, a carrier of the Messianic prophecy, *"The sceptre shall not depart from Judah....until Shiloh comes and unto Him shall the gathering of the people be"* (Genesis 49:10). This means that leadership would remain and be maintained in Judah's lineage; *"unto Him"* is in reference to Jesus Christ the ultimate Leader.

Trauma and tragedy would seem to mark Tamar's fate. She married Judah's son, eldest of the three, who was killed. Married again to the second son, who also was killed, and a promise for the third son after he was grown. So, in the family, Tamar was a daughter-in law-twice, widowed twice, and sent back to her father to wait for Judah's third son. This promise was by 'defraud' through fear (Genesis 38:1) and Tamar would realise after a while that she was conned (Genesis 38:14). How do we feel about that?

Tamar finally conceived twins, but her conception was by way of deception. She made her father-in-law pay! What about Tamar? She ended up a part of the messianic genealogy of Jesus Christ, through one of the twins, Pharez, and Mathew 1:3 would have us to know this.

The plan was surely bigger than Tamar. So, what about us? The same is true for us; the focus is never on our unacceptable, clever, crafty, messy dramas and behaviour, which only hurt ourselves. But here's the shift not to be missed; it is about the divine salvation plan of God reaching earth. Judah was tagged! His purpose is to save us from ourselves (Genesis 3:15); yes, from our sins as promised (Matthew 1:21). Salvation has come! By faith, with godly fear and some trembling; work out your salvation, remaining in Christ.

Pastor Josephine

SUNDAY 2nd

And her adversary (Peninnah) also provoked (Hannah) sore, for to make her fret...
1 Samuel 1:6

PENINNAH – Reading: 1 Samuel 1:1-20

Have you ever experienced bullying, which has become all too common in society in general: the home, the workplace, schools, online, and also in the Church?

Until we have a spirit-filled heart, behaviours which are not Christlike will present in the Church. The definition of the name bully is a form of aggressive behaviour in which someone intentionally and repeatedly causes another person injury or discomfort. This type of behaviour can be physical contact, words or understated actions. This type of behaviour, in my opinion, is an exercise of power and control over an individual which can lead to destroying that individual.

God heard the cry of Hannah's heart and saw her tears when she first petitioned Him to open her womb so that she could become a mother. However, she had to get to a place of brokenness which came about when she was accused of being drunk in the temple. Hannah made a Nazarite vow to give the child back to the Lord all the days of his life, if God blessed her with a son.

Our Sovereign King used the tactics of a bully to root up sin in His house. Idolatry/compromise was the norm for that time, Eli the High Priest and his sons knew the Shema and had disregarded the King. His sons did what was right in their sight, and Eli disregarded his first duty to God and became complicit with his sons' sins.

God used Peninnah, who had children, to taunt Hannah who was barren. I can imagine the constant jeering – *"Hannah - what do you know about raising a child? You will never know!"*. Bullying Hannah made Peninnah feel good for, despite having children, Peninnah always felt second best as she was Elkanah's second wife (1 Samuel 1:2). She would rejoice at Hannah's misfortune because she had children that

March 2025
Theme: Not Named & Hardly Mentioned Women in the Bible

Hannah was desperate to have, and this was the power which Peninnah had.

We have to smile at the awesomeness of God's plan to shine His light back into His temple, and Israel as a whole, with the birth of Samuel who was to become God's faithful High Priest.

Leadership power struggles are also not excluded from adopting bullying behaviours. How often do we hear about Church splits? In Exodus 15:20, this is the first time that Miriam is mentioned by name, the sister of Aaron and Moses (Exodus 4:14). She witnesses the greatness of God and rejoices by leading the women in worship by dancing and singing to the Lord, making a joyful noise with her tambourine.

But despite having such leadership qualities, she used these in an ungodly way to challenge the authority of God's appointed leader. The Church of the living God must not tolerate a child of God who adopts this ungodly behaviour.

We are all created in God's image; therefore, we should not belittle or abuse/bully anyone. I encourage one and all to, *"Let no corrupting talk come out of our mouths, but only such as is good for building up, as fits the occasion, that it may give grace to those who hear"* (Ephesians 4:29).

Missionary Audrey Simpson

MONDAY 3rd

Tabitha… was rich in acts of kindness and charity which she continually did
Acts 9:36 (AMP)

A GREAT WORK – Reading Act 9:36 – 42

Here we have a woman, Tabitha by name, who may have appeared to be so insignificant to some, but to others she was a great woman of God. Why was this?

The Bible tells us that she was FULL of good works. Her works were so highly regarded that when she died, the brethren refused to accept it!

Sisters, what are your God-given gifts and talents? Shine! Press through in spite of adversity!

It is only then that we can join with Nehemiah and say, *"We are doing a great work and we cannot come down"* (Nehemiah 6:3).

Deveen Smith

TUESDAY 4th

I'm reminded of how sincere your faith is. That faith first lived in your grandmother Lois and your mother Eunice. I'm convinced that it also lives in you
2 Timothy 1:5 (GW)

A FAITH THAT IS GENUINE – Reading: 2 Timothy 1:1-18

Soon after birth, we were given a name, an identity. Our name captures our uniqueness and individuality of who we are.

There are certain women in the Bible whose names are not mentioned. There are others whose names are rarely mentioned; two such women are Lois and Eunice.

Luke refers to Eunice in Acts 16:1, but does not mention her name. We first learned of her name when Paul named Eunice and her mother, Lois, in his second letter to Timothy, *"I am reminded of your sincere faith which was first lived in your grandmother Lois and your mother Eunice and I am persuaded now lives in you"* (2 Timothy 1.5).

Eunice and Lois go silent in the New Testament after this mention. Still, we continue to be impacted by their faithful training of Timothy. Eunice may have been mentioned only briefly but we learned a lot from the few words written in scriptures about her. She was a devoted mother and daughter. She dedicated time and effort to educate her son Timothy about the scriptures and trained him to live according to God's will. Eunice is a Jewess and her name means, *"Conquering well"* or *"A good victory"*.

Lois' name means, *"Superior"* and *"Most beautiful"*. A fine Christian lady and the only grandmother mentioned in the scriptures! Both Eunice and Lois followed Christ Jesus and their lives illustrated their faithfulness (ref: Christianity.com).

Both Eunice and Lois taught Timothy the scriptures from childhood (2 Timothy 3:14-15). Eunice's faithful teaching laid the foundation for Timothy to have become Paul's trusted and beloved fellow worker (Romans 16:21).

Ladies, some of us may not have children and grandchildren who are Christians, but keep praying, mentoring and teaching the scriptures. When children learn the Word of God, it could be argued that they will have received a faithful foundation that can help to guide them throughout their lifetime.

Minister ML Fraser

WEDNESDAY 5th

...the woman came and told her husband, saying, A man of God came unto me...
Judges 13:6

PURPOSE ABOVE NAME – Reading: Judges 13:1-25

Manoah's wife had a name but was not named in this text, yet she carried purpose on the inside.

It was customary for names to depict an event, experience, or one's mission, therefore purpose gave significance to a name. Since a name carries purpose, then purpose must be greater: *"Thou shall call His name Jesus"*; and the purpose… *"He shall save His people from their sins"* (Matthew 1:21). You will find that, *"God magnified His word above all His name"* (Psalm 138:2).

Of the rarely mentioned women of the Bible, and on top of that, not named; in today's world, one would have something to say about that! The pride of life would certainly ensure a frown. Yet, this is insignificant from God's perspective and plan, as accomplishing His own will is what really matters. Here is Manoah's wife, unnamed, who obeyed God's plan and became a carrier of one of the deliverers of Israel.

Women, your value is not found in the frequency of the mention of your name, or even whether it is called; but in your loving obedience to **whose** you are. Have you been living a surrendered life unto Him? You can carry His burden and birth His purpose as you make the LORD your Lord and say like a certain woman, *"…be it unto me according to thy word"* (Luke 1:38).

You are authentically you but it is all about God's divine purpose fulfilling in your surrendered lives for His glory.

Pastor Josephine

THURSDAY 6th

Then took Mary a pound of ointment of spikenard, very costly, and anointed the feet of Jesus, and wiped his feet with her hair: and the house was filled with the odour...
John 12:3

PERSONAL WORSHIP – Reading: John 12:1-11

Today's lesson proves that, although we should not forsake the assembling of ourselves together in a central place of worship (Hebrews 10:25), worship can take place anywhere. The text shows just how personal and intimate true worship is; it's between you and Jesus - you can't worship Him for me, and I can't worship Him for you.

Before we reach to John 12, we've already met this Mary on a few occasions. One of these was when Jesus came for a visit to the house where Mary lived with her sister, Martha, and their brother, Lazarus (Luke 10:38-42). Another is in St John 11 where her brother, Lazarus, became sick and soon died but was later resurrected by Jesus. To me, Mary always comes across as very calm and gracious. I might even say that she was a bit reserved (if compared with her bold sister Martha). What is clear though is the love that Mary had for Jesus, she adored Him, and loved His company.

If you've ever really loved someone, you will understand that you often wonder what you can give to them to express your depth of feeling. Love is not really, *"I love you",* although that's nice to hear. But even without the *"I love you",* you will know if you're loved by actions.

Mary was so full of love for Jesus, and overwhelmed with the miracle of her brother being raised from the dead that, whilst dinner was being served that day, she made a decision that she wanted to start her own worship service! This feeling was so strong that she couldn't wait until after dinner. No, she couldn't wait until Jesus was on His own, and she was not going to over-think this urge to worship now and talk herself out of it!

The conversation within herself may have been, *"Heads may turn when they see what I'm going to do, but I've got to let out my worship - now!*

I've got some spikenard ointment; its ingredients are from the Himalayan mountains. I wasn't sure when I would use it, it's in a precious Alabaster Box. It's costly - worth a year's salary. The timing may be a bit off for Martha – I might upset her, she's serving dinner – but I'm going to interrupt this dinner party without apology. I will not withhold any of the ointment and keep back for myself. I will bow and soak Jesus' feet with every drop of it. He deserves it! And, since I'm 'breaking with convention', I'm going to let my hair down as well and use it as a towel to dry my Lord's feet".

Mary had to have a made-up mind to do all of that - a room filled with male guests looking on would have been intimidating otherwise! A woman letting her hair down like that in public in Jewish custom would be seen as out of order! Did someone maybe recognise the fragrance of spikenard as it was poured out? While some were criticising Mary's lavish expression saying, *"What a waste!",* Mary was probably thinking, *"It's not enough!".* What on earth had got into 'reserved' Mary? Perhaps, *"You don't know, like I know, what He's done for me!"* had got into her. The other question has to be, *"What did what Mary was doing have to do with anybody else?"!*

But whatever it was that happened to Mary, is what needs to happen to us all. A songwriter says, *"Let's forget about ourselves, concentrate on Him, and worship Him…".* We will never give true worship whilst conscious of our surroundings, what we look like, what people may or will say. We will always put off anointing Jesus with real worship for another day.

"But the hour cometh, and now is…" (John 4:23).

JEJ

FRIDAY 7th

Zipporah circumcised her son...
Exodus 4:25

ZIPPORAH: A SUPPORTIVE WIFE – Reading: Exodus 2:21; 4:20-26; 18:1-6

In the Book of Exodus, we are introduced to a woman, Zipporah by name, who despite her limited mention in scripture played a critical part in the life of Moses, Israel's deliverer, and consequently one would say in Israel's history. Despite the pivotal role she had in a moment of immense crisis for Israel, during their sojourn in Egypt and in Moses' life in general, there are only three passages in Exodus that actually make mention of her.

Zipporah, was the daughter of a Midianite priest named Jethro. She met Moses in the desert as he sought to escape from Pharaoh, following an altercation with an Egyptian which resulted in Moses taking the Egyptian's life. Whilst fleeing from the scene of the crime, Moses comes across Zipporah and her sisters in the desert being harassed by shepherds. Moses responded yet again in the face of injustice by coming to the rescue of the sisters.

As a result of Moses stepping in to prevent the continued harassment of Jethro's daughters, Zipporah, the eldest of the girls was offered to him by her father. The chance meeting in the desert resulted in Moses meeting and marrying his wife. It is suggested by Clarke that there are similarities between their encounter and subsequent nuptials with Jacob and Rachel. Both rendered services for their wives.

To their union was born two sons; Gershom and Eliezar. At the birth of Gershom, Moses said, *"I have been an alien (foreigner) in a strange land"* (Exodus 2:22), referring to the 40 years spent in Midian. With the birth of Eliezar, Moses declared, *"the God of my father was mine help and delivered me from the sword of Pharoah"* (Exodus 18:4). Both of Moses' sons were later mentioned in 1 Chronicles 23:14-17 as part of the Levites. So, this barely mentioned woman had sons who gave their father hope, and also formed part of the tribe that ministered to God, the tribe which were musicians, gatekeepers, guards, Temple officials, judges and craftsmen. In a society that is obsessed by social media 'likes', and 'pseudo fame', it's important to recognise that we can have Kingdom impact and influence, even if our names aren't on everyone's lips!

Ironically, the meaning of the name Zipporah is *'little bird'* which, perhaps added to the idea of her insignificance, in fact, this barely known woman, some scholars would say, was responsible for saving Moses' life, when he neglected to circumcise his sons. Zipporah took on the task, thus appeasing the Lord's anger.

There are times when the best of us are plagued with feelings of insignificance, but in times of introspection and reflection, we need to remember women like Zipporah, who ensured that Moses' life was better because she was in it. She, like so many spouses we know, was in the background ensuring that her husband, the leader, the deliverer could shine!

Lady Shirley Hamilton

*World Day of Prayer

*SATURDAY 8th

Lay not up for yourselves treasures upon earth, where moth and rust doth corrupt, and where thieves break through and steal
Matthew 6:19

WORTHY OF IT ALL – Reading: Matthew 6:19-34

February 9, 2023, my father passed away in Maryland, USA, at the age of eighty-six.

Many years ago, my mother gave me a china dinner set with matching crystal stemware. My father had bought the china set for his mother whilst stationed in Germany when he was in his twenties.

His mother gave the china dinner set to my mother in 1962, when my parents got married, stating, *"Give it to your daughter!"*. My mother did that twenty years ago.

Last year, I shared with our then 29-year-old daughter, *"The china dinner set will one day be yours"*. *"Of course; I would want the heirloom of my grandfather"*, she said.

When our 'forever' home in the United States was sold, items to be kept were placed in storage, including the china dinnerware. The china remained in storage until June 2024, when we decided to end the rental agreement after five years of paying rent.

When we went in person to the rental office to 'close-out', we discovered that the storage unit had been broken into, with no sign of our box of German-bought bone china dinner set!

But to God be the glory: HE's WORTHY OF IT ALL!

It was my cross You bore
So I could live in the freedom You died for
And now my life is Yours
And I will sing of Your goodness forevermore.

Worthy is Your name, Jesus
You deserve the praise
Worthy is Your name

*Worthy is Your name, Jesus
You deserve the praise
Worthy is Your name.*

*And now my shame is gone
I stand amazed in Your love undeniable
Your grace goes on and on
And I will sing of Your goodness forevermore.*

*Worthy is Your name, Jesus
You deserve the praise
Worthy is Your name
Worthy is Your name, Jesus
You deserve the praise
Worthy is your name.*

*Worthy is Your name, Jesus
You deserve the praise
Worthy is Your name
Worthy is Your name, Jesus
You deserve the praise
Worthy is Your name.*

(Worthy - Song by CeCe Winans)

First Lady Yolanda Edmund

*International Women's Day

SUNDAY 9th

Now the Syrians on one of their raids had carried off a little girl from the land of Israel, and she worked in the service of Naaman's wife
2 Kings 5:2 (ESV)

HE KNOWS YOUR NAME – Reading: 2 Kings 5:1-27

There are times in our lives when we are made to feel rejected, insignificant and invisible. While it comes with unbearable emotional turmoil, it seems to be the springboard from which God catapults His most significant Bible characters. They often have no name, no significant genealogy, no pedigree.

In this lesson, we are introduced to a young girl who served the wife of Naaman, the commander of Aram's (Syria's) army. 2 Kings 5:2 tells us that she was an Israelite slave who got captured by Aramean raiders. This means she was not only working for her enemy, but also serving the household of the very person who commanded those that enslaved her. It's hard to imagine how much resentment she bore towards her masters. However, when she saw how Naaman suffered as a result of his leprosy, she had compassion and told his wife about what she believed Elisha could do: *"If only my master would see the prophet who is in Samaria! He would cure him of his leprosy"* (2 Kings 5:3).
As a result, Naaman was healed and developed a new-found belief in the God of Israel, the only true God!

Who'd have thought that this (seemingly) insignificant slave girl would have the answers to her master's physical and spiritual plight? Just one encounter with our God can make us completely whole. All that God needs is an available vessel to accomplish His divine will on earth.

Today you may be saying, *"I'm not as smart, or as gifted, or as beautiful as the sister in the pew"* Or, *"I'm not the most seen on my job"*. Take heart, because God is getting ready to use you to display His love and compassion to those in your sphere of influence. He knows your name!

F Garrick
USA

MONDAY 10th

And they took them wives of the women of Moab; the name of the one was Orpah...
Ruth 1:4

HER NAME WAS ORPAH – Reading: Ruth 1:1-15

At least we are told her name: Orpah. Some women in the Bible, despite their greatness, have remained nameless.

Who was Orpah? Good question. Not many people know who Orpah was. Orpah was the daughter-in-law that returned to her family after her husband, one of Naomi's sons, had died. She is the one who turned back to her people and to her gods.

How about Ruth? Do you know that name? Again, she was Naomi's daughter-in-law, but she didn't return to her people or to her gods. Ruth saw something in Naomi that was special - something in her God worth clinging to.

Orpah went back, and was never heard of again. Ruth went forward and is mentioned in the lineage of Jesus Christ in Matthew 1:5; she will forever be remembered in the chronology of great women who serve a Great God!

Message of today: Never go back! Never give up! Go forward and fulfil your purpose in God!

Min Jo Earle

TUESDAY 11th

When (Pilate) was set down on the judgment seat, his wife sent unto him saying...
Matthew 27:19

AN URGENT MESSAGE – Reading: Matthew 27:15-26

The wife of Pontius Pilate is mentioned only once in scripture but her part is noteworthy.

She sends a warning to her husband during Jesus' trial before His crucifixion to warn him to leave Jesus alone, not only because He is a righteous man, but because of a disturbing dream which she'd had concerning Him. The timing of her message added to the inner struggle which Pilate was already having with his conscience. He wanted to release Jesus whom he knew was innocent, but at the same time wanted to avert a riot by pleasing those who were calling for Jesus to be crucified and the release of Barabbas, a murderer.

There is a serious danger in being a people-pleaser, knowing the right thing to do but doing the opposite to be popular and for your own personal advantage. In his position of Roman governor, it is unlikely that many people would be brave enough to challenge any decision Pilate made. It is also unlikely that his wife ever tried to interfere with any of the cases which he tried, but this time she could not hold her peace. At the most inconvenient of times, just as he sat on his bench at court to start work and pass a verdict, here came his dear wife's message, *"Have thou nothing to do with this righteous man, I have had a very disturbing dream about him"* (Matthew 27:19).

You may be in a similar situation as Pilate's wife, having a message or warning to give to someone which you know will not be received well. It may be a message for a family member, or someone in a high position of authority, and you've been delaying saying what you need to say. The details of Pilate's wife's dream are not recorded but we can sense that she said just enough to try and influence the verdict.

Why not release yourself and speak up today? The timing may not be 'convenient' - someone may be just about to leave the country, just about to marry the wrong person, just about to make a rash decision on a matter. Even if they do not heed your warning, you will at least have delivered your soul, and not have to live or die with an urgent message undelivered.

JEJ

WEDNESDAY 12th

Then came two women, that were harlots, unto the king, and stood before him
1 Kings 3:16

THE SWAP – Reading: 1 Kings 3:1-28

The first test of the extraordinary wisdom of Solomon, King of Israel, was to solve a distressing case involving the death of a young baby.

Two young harlots lived in the same house and both gave birth to baby boys. I've seen that, when women are pregnant, even if they do not know each other they easily bond because they are in the same life stage. They willingly share how they're feeling - their fears and excitement - general commonalities. This would have all been true for the women in today's lesson.

Sadly, one night one of the mothers overlay her son whilst he was in the bed asleep with her. What a terrible moment when she awoke and saw what had happened! In shock and disbelief, she made a snap decision to swap her dead child for the live child of the other woman.

She could have got away with the switch, had it not been for the mother of the live child knowing her son. The mother would have gazed on him after his birth and absorbed every detail of his features whilst she nursed him at her breast. I've heard it said that all babies look the same but of course that is not true.

We certainly sympathise with the woman's tragic loss, but cannot endorse her course of action, not only to take what was not hers but to later agree that Solomon should cut the remaining child in half and kill it. Do you know anyone like that, or are you like that, i.e., *"If I can't have it, neither should anybody else"*? It is a spirit of covetousness.

The friendship which had been easily formed between these two women came to an abrupt end, as do many relationships when you were once both on the same level and one is now excelling, suddenly things are not the same. Rather than celebrating your success, the preference would be that your gift would die also. You may have resolved to keep climbing higher in Christ, but someone is trying to pull you from behind and say that anointing can't be yours.

But the mother of the child who lived said, *"...when I looked at him closely in the morning, behold, he was not the child that I had borne"* (1 Kings 3:21). Can you recognise what is yours differently to what someone is trying to put on you? Do you know when it is you speaking compared to when someone has sown a negative seed into your spirit which starts to manifest? *"Look closely"* at yourself, query any changes in your behaviour. That loss of spiritual vigour and enthusiasm for the Lord, where did it come from? Why are you suddenly always complaining and murmuring? Has a swap taken place to try and stop your progress? After inspection you need to 'take it to the top', i.e., to God, and say like the rightful mother, *"It's not mine"*!

JEJ

THURSDAY 13th

...and this woman (Anna) was a widow of about eighty-four years, who did not depart from the temple, but served God with fastings and prayers night and day
Luke 2:37

AND SHE SPOKE OF HIM – Reading: Psalm 116:1-14; Luke 2:36-38

There are many women in the Bible where extraordinarily little is said about them. However, in comparison to others, we learn a lot about this woman.

Name: Anna which means – grace
Father: Phanuel
Tribe: Asher
Marital status: Married 7 years, widowed for 84 years
Occupation: Prophetess
Duties: Fastings and prayers
Place of work: Temple
Hours: Day and night

I can just imagine the excitement Anna may have had as a young lady who was about to be married; the hopes and dreams for the future, the plans for a family and business and where her new life may her take her. Imagine the conversations with her friends and peers about the man in her life – her husband-to-be, her fiancé. Perhaps she'd describe him by his physical appearance and character traits, the family he's from and so on.

However, tragedy struck in her young life. She only had her husband for seven years when he died. From that moment on, she dedicated her life to the service of the Lord in the temple, joyously and hopefully awaiting a new man to arrive on the scene. The wait took Anna into her early nineties. This man, though currently a baby, was going to change the course of history for the entire world! Anna rejoiced and was so grateful that she had seen our redemption and spoke of Him to all who believed and had the same hope.

Oh, the joy of being able to speak of HIM, the Redeemer, the deliverer of the entire world. Jesus Christ is worth talking about! He is our reason for living even when life is throwing us unexpected curve balls.

Keep talking about Jesus!

MinK/ Minister Kay

FRIDAY 14th

...Talitha cumi; which is being interpreted, Damsel, I say unto thee, arise
Mark 5:41

JAIRUS' DAUGHTER – Reading: Mark 5:21-24, 35-43

Good fathers will do anything to help their children, and Jairus was no different. He approached Jesus and *"begged him earnestly"* to save his little daughter who was at the point of death. Jairus' faith propelled him to the Master as he believed with all his heart that just by laying His hands on her, his daughter would be healed. His relief when Jesus started to follow him home was short-lived as word came that the child is dead.

Her name was not significant enough to warrant a mention by any of the authors of the gospels. The daughter of a ruler meant that she would have been held in high regard by others, simply because of who her father was. No particular ambitions for the future. Just a little girl enjoying life, playing in the sand and being comfortable in her father's house...until the cold hands of death grabbed a hold of her.

For those saved for many years, do you remember that initial feeling of joy knowing that Daddy Jesus is in full control? For those newly saved, you are likely basking in that level of joy right now. Yet in the shadows, the hands of the enemy wait to snatch us, but just like that little girl, our purpose cannot die before the appointed time, nor will our ministry be aborted. Even when we feel we are dead, buried and *"stinketh"* (John 11:39), the God of miracles will extend his hand to us and say, *"Daughter...ARISE"*.

ZAHRA H. OLIPHANT

SATURDAY 15th

And (Potiphar) saw that the LORD was with him. And it came to pass after these things, that his master's wife cast her eyes upon Joseph; and she said, Lie with me
Genesis 39:3 & 7

POTIPHAR & HIS WIFE: TWO PERSPECTIVES
Reading: Genesis 39:1-23

There are times in life when we find ourselves betwixt and between.

There are two choices, two paths, two different directions and you don't know which to choose. However, imagine being between the gaze of two individuals, but these two individuals see two different things when looking at you: two different motives, two different plans.

This is what happened to Joseph. He was favoured by God and also found favour with almost everyone he encountered. Potiphar was so pleased with Joseph and entrusted so much to him because he was found to be a faithful steward with great character. Potiphar didn't even know the extent of his own wealth because of his trust in Joseph as an honest, upstanding man who took good care of his estate.

Potiphar saw the great man that Joseph was because of the great God in him; however, Mrs. Potiphar saw a man, a hardworking man who she 'fancied'.

I can just imagine the hours that she spent watching Jospeh going and coming, giving instructions to the other staff, busying himself with his daily duties. Joseph was second in command to Potiphar her husband, but now she intended to make Joseph her second lover.

What would make a woman in her position want to do such a thing? Why would she want to start an illicit affair with a Hebrew servant as the wife of the Officer of Pharoah, Captain of the Guard? One of many probable answers is, the anointing of God is attractive; and you never know who will be attracted by the God in you, and what their motives are. Mrs. Potiphar fixed her gaze on Joseph and started an intense pursuit of him to seduce him. I can imagine that she used all her feminine charms and wiles to get him to "lie with" her, all to no avail.

Joseph's response to Mrs. Potiphar teaches us how to *"flee fornication"* according to 1 Corinthians 6 v 18a. It's quite simply put, "SAY NO & GO!"

Joseph's underpinning principle for "no and go" is based on what he stated in Genesis 39 v 9 *"There is none greater in this house than I; neither has he kept back anything from me but you, because you are his wife: how then can I do this great wickedness, and sin against God?"*. Joseph made it very clear to Mrs. Potiphar that he had authority and knew his position as number two to Potiphar, however this sin would not be against Potiphar but against God Himself. We must understand that sin is firstly committed against God and then after that, sin can be committed against each other. Joseph lived with the constant awareness that I am always seen by God, and how I live for Him directly affects my interactions with others.

Therefore, it doesn't matter who is watching and the motives behind their gaze, even if it's the devil himself who is prowling and keeping you under surveillance, God sees us.

Never forget that you are not good or great without God.

Remember the anointing of God is attractive – beware of their stares, and if you have to, *"SAY NO & GO!"*

MinK / Minister Kay Dawkins

SUNDAY 16th

...when King Xerxes was in high spirits ... he told the seven eunuchs ... to bring Queen Vashti to him with the royal crown on her head. He wanted the nobles and all the other men to gaze on her beauty, for she was a very beautiful woman. But when they conveyed the king's order to Queen Vashti, she refused to come

Esther 1:10-12 (NLT)

AN END AND A BEGINNING - Reading: Esther 1:8-12 (NLT); 3:1-15; 4:14

It is said that the Book of Esther, while it never mentions the name of God, it's *"one of the fullest illustrations of God's providence, in His use of a young woman to protect His people"* (Unknown).

So, how did this young girl Esther, happen to be in a position to advocate for God's people in a time of crisis? In a time when their lives were under great threat, in a time that Mordecai terms to be *"a time such as this?"* Esther 4:14c.

In Esther 1, perhaps in keeping with the theme of 'Hardly Mentioned Women', we are told at great length of the riches, greatness, power and influence of the King of Persia. We are also told in great detail the lavishness of his Kingdom, and the extravagant banquets that he made available to the dignitaries in and around his 127 provinces for a full 180 days to display his great wealth. We are further told that the King followed up this banqueting with a seven-day feast for all his subjects. At this juncture, we are told that during those seven days, Queen Vashti also entertained the women.

At the height of this opulence, revelling, drunkenness, where the King ensured that everyone received their heart's desire, the King himself, being "merry with wine", instructed his servants to bring Queen Vashti to be paraded in front of his drunken quests in her royal crown. According to one rabbinical tradition, it is suggested that the queen would have been required to wear only her crown. Although this is not a view supported biblically, it is a view that is held by a range of Bible scholars.

Vashti's refusal to obey the King's command, set in motion the chain of events that would culminate with the crowning of Queen Esther, a Jewish girl, whose assignment was to be the conduit through which deliverance would come to the Jews.

What can we learn from the above and the significance of Queen Vashti? We learn that God is clearly in control with a panoramic view of our lives and our circumstances. We are assured that no enemy, in fact no one can block our deliverance, no matter what God has to do, to move or shift, He will do it, move it, shift it, in order that we will be victorious.

We also learn that what might appear to be a negative situation, can result in positive outcomes. Joseph was sold into slavery, he languished in prison in order that Israel could be saved from famine. Queen Vashti's banishment, made room for Queen Esther, who was commissioned to bring enlargement and deliverance to the Jews (Esther 4:16a)!

Lady Shirley Hamilton

MONDAY 17th

Thine handmaid has not anything in the house, save a pot of oil
2 Kings 4:2

LITTLE THINGS DO COUNT – Reading: 2 Kings 4:1-7

Just because one is not known by name does not mean that one is insignificant to God.

You are special and known to God, He hears the cry of your heart. Something about the widow in today's lesson touched God; she is recorded in His Word for perpetuity and we, thousands of years later, are still blessed by her.

God chooses seemingly weak and foolish things to accomplish much (1Corinthians 1:26-29)! Never underestimate your ability to positively impact the Kingdom, howbeit, it is often those most unlikely things we do that do so!

I was once asked to preach at a church's commissioning of a new ablution facility in Zambia. It was a grand affair with at least a thousand in attendance. Unfortunately, I had broken my foot badly prior to the event and was hobbling around on crutches. I remember thinking how much more effective I could be, were I able-bodied.

En route to the airport, a dear brother shared with me, *"The preaching was fine but what really spoke to us was that God cares so much. Despite your injury, God's grace still brought you here; we are overwhelmed by God's demonstration of His love for us".* Wow! I was somewhat humbled... the very thing that I despised, God had used for His glory!

How that unnamed widow must have felt when she declared that a tiny bit of oil was all she had. Little did she know that her testimony would encourage millions!

Gudrun Witt
Zimbabwe

TUESDAY 18th

...behold your sister in law has gone back unto her people, and unto her gods
Ruth 1:15

ORPAH: A DIFFERENT PERSPECTIVE – Reading: Ruth 1:1-15

The story of Ruth is familiar to many of us reading today's page. A lot is said concerning Ruth and her mother-in-law, Naomi. They are the two main characters throughout the book of Ruth.

Orpah is the sister-in-law of Ruth and daughter-in-law of Naomi. Like Ruth, Orpah is from Moab, a heathen nation which was birthed from an incestuous relationship between Lot and his eldest daughter. Orpah was a Gentile. She too had been widowed as had Naomi and Ruth.

Much is not said concerning Orpah other than she did not choose to return to Bethlehem with Naomi. We know that she started the journey, but then on second thoughts went back to Moab. She went back to her gods and her people. I don't think that returning to Moab was an easy decision for Orpah to make. She would have formed a close bond with these other two women before their husbands died, and probably even more so after their husbands' deaths.

I believe that Orpah loved Naomi and loved Ruth, but maybe her love was just not enough to leave everything behind. She lifted up her voice and wept when she had to say goodbye. What did that sound like? Have you ever wanted to do two different things, to stay and to go, to say yes and to say no? What did that feel like for you? It can be painful. Even after making a decision, you may still always wonder if it was the right choice.

You might be reading this whilst struggling with the idea of carrying on with Jesus, or even making a start with Him. As much as Naomi loved Orpah, she did not try to persuade her to follow her back to her homeland; Naomi even encouraged Orpah to go back! Was that the right thing for Naomi to do and say – sending Orpah back to her gods (Ruth 1:15)? Possibly Naomi thought that Orpah would have been in

Bethlehem but pining for Moab, just as one can be in the church yet longing for what you left in the world.

But listen to cries at the altar calls during our church services, seek to discern the cause behind the sound. Why is 'Orpah' crying like that? Do you need to give her a follow-up call to ask about her tears, or if she backslides, will we say, *"She was never really in it anyway!"*? Orpah went back home, but perhaps with the right counsel and patience, she could have had a change of heart. Of course, following Jesus is a personal decision. Still, think about Orpah and her tears.

A different perspective on Orpah.

JEJ

WEDNESDAY 19th

And Miriam...took a timbrel in her hand; and all the women went out after her with timbrels and dances
Exodus 15:20

ONLY BECAUSE – Reading: Exodus 15:1-27

In today's lesson, we read of Miriam, sister of Moses and Aaron, leading a praise service with many women. Not only did they play their timbrels, but also danced before the LORD in celebration of their deliverance from the bondage of Egypt.

They recount the amazing destruction of their tormentors who tried to abort their escape from Egypt, pursuing them on horseback right into the Red Sea. These women probably remembered the fear that was in their heart as they heard the hooves of the horses coming up behind them, and their terror as they saw the wide, deep sea in front. LORD, we're trapped! And suddenly, He made a way! Isn't that true for us too? We sing, *"You made a way, when our backs were against the wall and it looked as if it was over...and we're standing here, only because you made a way"*.

I wish that I could hear some of the testimonies of the readers of today's page – maybe, or especially, the ones that you've never been brave enough to share, or you're embarrassed to talk about. We may tell of times when it felt like God was doing lastminute.com in answering our prayers. O, each of us has a different story, but the conclusion is clearly the same, *"...And we're standing here, only because you made a way"*.

Travis Greene's lyrics continue with, *"You move mountains, you cause walls to fall, with your power perform miracles. There is nothing that's impossible! And we're standing here **only because** you made a way!"*

Acknowledge and praise the real Way Maker. Not your bank manager, doctor, lawyer, counsellor or best friend. *"I don't know how, but **you** did it!"*. Bless His name.

JEJ

THURSDAY 20th

Jehoshabeath, the daughter of King Jehoram, the wife of Jehoiada the priest...hid (Joash) from Athaliah, so that she slew him not
2 Chronicles 22:11

JEHOSHABEATH – Reading: 2 Kings 11:1-3; 2 Chronicles 22:1-12

Worldwide, we celebrate Mother's Day and Father's Day with pomp and flair. However, oftentimes, the actions of the aunties and uncles go unnoticed and, in the case of Jehoshabeath, her exploits were briefly recorded in 2 Kings 11 and only one verse in 2 Chronicles 22.

Jehoshabeath was a princess in Judah and after her brother King Ahaziah died, she witnessed the terrible actions of Ahaziah's mother Athalia, who killed 'all' the seed royal. The *"But"* in 2 Chronicles 22:11 was a critical conjunction however – *"But Jehoshabeath, the daughter of the king, took Joash the son of Ahaziah, and stole him from among the king's sons that were slain, and put him and his nurse in a bedchamber".*

The Bible interestingly says that she stole him from among those that were killed. This presents the possibility that an attempt on his life was made, and the child perhaps laid amongst his dead brothers!

Jehoshabeath would have needed courage, stealth and tenacity to rescue that child; she had all these traits because she succeeded in doing just that and hiding him from Athalia so that he would not be destroyed.

Jehoshabeath was married to Jehoiada the priest. In the remaining chapters, the Chronicler speaks of all that Jehoiada accomplished in returning the throne to Joash, while there is no further mention of Jehoshabeath. Yet, her bravery secured the Davidic lineage; Joash as the seed of David, was preserved by the actions of one woman. She only had a fleeting mention, but her historical impact cannot be quantified.

Zahra H. Oliphant
Jamaica

FRIDAY 21st

I beseech Euodias, and beseech Syntyche, that they be of the same mind in the Lord
Philippians 4:2

THE MIND OF CHRIST UNIFIES HIS BODY
Reading: Philippians 4:1-9

Euodias was one of the women Paul beseeched in his letter about unity.

But as with any disagreement, it takes two to solve the matter. Syntyche was her co-worker in ministry with whom such disagreement was in play. Euodias was of Greek origin whose name means, *"Fragrance"* (ref: Bible study tools.com). Syntyche was also of Greek origin whose name means *"Fortunate"* (ref: Bible studytools.com). Paul pleaded with both women to lay aside their differences and unify their minds in the Lord (Philippians 4:2.)

The scriptures only give two verses that specifically refer to Euodias but we can still gather certain details from the context. We know that Euodias and Syntyche were Christians who played active roles in spreading the gospel to the Philippians. They had a disagreement which they allowed to develop to the point of affecting the church. These two women had worked with Paul who loved the church and wanted its members to remain strong in their faith and unified in the body of Christ.

Paul knew that for this to happen, believers must strive to be of one mind. He therefore exhorted Euodias and Syntyche to lay aside their disagreements as it was causing a rift, not only in personal relationships but also in the church. Much of Paul's letter is devoted to teaching on humility and showing the church the importance of unity within the body of Christ.

When believers experience discord with each other, it is the will of God that we quickly reconcile our differences for Christ's sake, *"Be ye angry and sin not, let not the sun go down upon your wrath"* (Ephesians 4:26). The scriptures encourage us on this wise, *"Till we all come in the unity of the faith and of the knowledge of the son of God"* (Ephesians 2:3).

Ladies, we should do this *"with all lowliness and meekness with long suffering forbearing one another in love, endeavouring to keep the unity of the spirit in the bond of peace"* (Ephesians 4:2-3).

Minister ML Fraser

SATURDAY 22nd

I perceive that this is an holy man of God, which passeth by us continually
2 Kings 4:9

──────── ◆●◆ ────────

A RELATIONSHIP UPGRADE – Reading: 2 Kings 4:8-17

Our focus passage today is taken from 2 Kings 4, a familiar scripture to many of us. It starts with an account regarding a poverty-stricken widow who thinks that she has nothing, but in fact has everything she needs to solve her financial problem. It's in the form of an overlooked pot of oil, already in her house.

This is immediately followed with us being in another woman's house – she's a stark contrast to the insolvent widow, this one is described as a *"great"* woman, i.e., a wealthy woman. She will later become known to us as the Shunammite Woman best remembered for her statement of faith, *"It is well"*.

I recently read 2 Kings 4 more slowly than in past times and took note of how we arrived at, *"It is well"*. Elisha would frequently pass through Shunem and this hospitable woman would constrain him to come and eat with her and her husband at their home, and stay overnight if necessary. They treated Elisha so well that, every time he was in Shunem, he would return there.

During these visits, the woman observed Elisha and identified that he was no ordinary man (v9). At this revelation, see a change in the relationship between Elisha and his Shunammite hosts. The woman suggested to her husband that they no longer accommodate Elisha in the way they had been doing, probably in a guest room used also by other visitors, but that they build a room on the roof of their house for Elisha's use only! A room set apart from the rest of the house with a bed, a desk, a lamp and a chair. A consecrated room. A room which demonstrated *"you are welcome – we want you to stay"*!

We will always treat God based upon our perception of Him. An ordinary room for Elisha was fine when they didn't know who he was – when he was just an 'ordinary' stranger passing by. But as the woman got to know him better it was impressed upon her to give Elisha more.

Are you giving God 'ordinary' treatment, i.e., less than He deserves? Is your relationship with Him only on a casual now-and-then basis? Do you share with someone else what should only be His? Is your heart crowded with all kinds of stuff that there's scarcely space left for Him to come in to stay?

It was after this woman made room, extended her property, and gave the man of God an 'upgrade', that Elisha asked her, *"What can I give you for the diligent care which you've given?"* (2 Kings 4:11-16). She didn't ask for anything, she was content (or so she said). She had not made room for Elisha to get a favour in return, she just wanted him to keep on coming back!

The woman was married to a man much older than her and they had no children. Noticing what she did not have, amidst all that she did have, Elisha spoke to her unspoken request, that this time next year she would be embracing her own son. Because of what she'd perceived which prompted her hospitality sacrifice, followed by the miracle of her son's birth exactly as Elisha had said (v17), the Shunammite Woman could say with confidence in the part of the lesson which we know, not only *"It shall be well",* (v23) but her faith quickly moved up another gear to say, *"It **is** well"* (v26)!

JEJ

SUNDAY 23rd

And the child grew, and she brought him unto Pharaoh's daughter, and he became her son. And she called his name Moses: and she said, Because I drew him out of the water
Exodus 2:10

DRAWN OUT & DRAWN IN – Reading: Exodus 2:1-10

There are circumstances in life that draw us from one place, moment, or action to another.

The draw of an invitation to the UK in order to rebuild the country after the 1st and 2nd world wars, with the chance to make a better life in the UK, was accepted by many of the Windrush generation from across the Caribbean.

Moses' mother, Jochebed, had a draw on her heart strings to preserve life amid male infanticide. She came up with a clever plan to hopefully ensure that her baby boy would live - her son had to be an Egyptian, and the safest place and best upbringing he could possibly receive to guarantee his identity as an Egyptian, was in the palace of the Pharoah who was issuing the death edict.

Pharoah's daughter was drawn to the water for daily ablutions with her maidens. Curiosity drew her to retrieve the ark from the water, but mercy and love drew her to adopt this Hebrew baby boy.

Amidst it all, God drew up the plans to ensure that the life of the Leader of His people would be preserved. God drew Pharaoh's daughter to fulfil His plans as was Jochebed.

Could it be that today God could be drawing on your heart of love and mercy to fulfil His purposes? Could it be that a simple everyday task is where you'll be drawn to fulfil the destiny of somebody great?

Whether we are drawn to make an ark of protection, or to the water, whether a heart of love or mercy, let us pray to be favoured to be participants in God's plan like Pharoah's daughter. Moses got his name because he was drawn from the water, not knowing he'd be drawn into the palace, and then later drawn into being one of Israel's greatest leaders. Let us be willing to be drawn out from the everyday and drawn into destiny!

MinK/ Minister Kay

MONDAY 24th

...the queen of Sheba...came to prove (Solomon) with hard questions
1 Kings 10:1

─────────── ◆•●•◆ ───────────

QUESTIONS! QUESTIONS! – Reading: 1 Kings 10:1-13

Today our focus Scripture is concerning the Queen of Sheba, an affluent business woman who heard of the wealth and success of King Solomon from where she lived in Sheba.

Stirred by curiosity, she made a journey across many miles to see if what she'd heard was true, and to have an audience with the king. Note that she followed protocol and did not go to visit the king empty-handed. She travelled to Jerusalem bearing gold, spices and precious stones. In all of Solomon's reign, it's written, no other visitor ever brought him as much spices as the Queen of Sheba (v10)! She could have said, *"Well, Solomon is already rich, he doesn't need anything"*, but no, her presentation was to acknowledge who he was, spices needed or not.

The queen came not just with gifts but we read that she had some *"hard questions"* for Solomon (1 Kings 10:2), to interrogate his exceptional wisdom. It's even possible that the questions were the real reason or motivation for her trip! I also imagine that when the time came for her to quiz Solomon, they both went into a private room away from the servants, and shut the door. Although she was so impressed with the splendour of the palace and all that she saw, she did not want to return to Sheba with unanswered questions. It seems like there was nobody that the queen could confide in and empty her heart of its questions in Sheba. Ladies, it's a fact that, sometimes in order for our heart to get a full release and find a solution to our woes, we have to pack a bag and get alone somewhere with God!

It's not reported that she was invited to Jerusalem, or that Solomon had any prior knowledge of her. Yet he welcomed her and at the end of the visit, despite her hard questions, he surprised her by going beyond the 'Honorarium Policy' of the day, i.e., a standard gift from his royal bounty.

See that Solomon said to this woman (who too was rich in her own right), if you have seen anything in this palace that you'd like for yourself, you can have it (v13)! Nothing that you've told me, nothing that you have asked me, has changed my perception of you! For beyond the queen's display of wealth and appearance of 'having it altogether', there was a vulnerable woman who simply needed reassurance, in a safe place, about some crucial matters from somebody greater than her!

Somebody greater than all of us is inviting us to ask Him our *"hard questions"*! What is it that you'd really like to ask God today?

"Let us therefore come boldly to the throne of grace, that we may obtain mercy, and find grace to help in time of need" (Hebrews 4:16).

JEJ

TUESDAY 25th

...she came trembling, and falling down before him...
Luke 8:47

DESPERATE FOR A CHANGE – Reading: Luke 8:43-48

Have you ever been so desperate for change that you would do almost anything to see an end to your struggle? That's where the woman in Luke 8:43-48 found herself. Though unnamed, her brief but powerful encounter with Jesus continues to inspire us today.

This woman had suffered from a bleeding issue for twelve years. Aside from the physical toll of this condition, the emotional impact would be equivalent to daily turmoil. She had tried everything - visited doctors, spent all her money - yet it persisted.

She would have been considered unclean according to Jewish law and should be in isolation, far from the crowd and high-ranking men like Jairus. Yet, despite everything pointing toward hopelessness, she heard about Jesus. Sometimes we feel far from God during challenging times. It seems like He's blessing and helping others while we remain isolated in the shadows. But if we can just push for one touch like this woman did, everything can change!

She pushed through the crowd, risking public humiliation and harm. Her mustard seed faith was sufficient; she believed enough such that only briefly touching the hem of Jesus' garment undid what seemed unchangeable.

Can we be desperate enough to push through the obstacles that seem permanent in our lives? To reach out to God in faith - even when everything tells us to give up?

If we can push through the enemy's whispering lies and touch God, by the faith that pleases Him, like this woman, we will find the healing, change and transformation we desperately need.

Shani Oliphant
Jamaica

WEDNESDAY 26th

And Jeroboam said to his wife, Arise..., and disguise thyself...
1 Kings 14:2

JEROBOAM'S WIFE: AN UNDERSTATED WOMAN
Reading: 1 Kings 14:1-18

She was considered insignificant; neither her name or words were recorded. Her thoughts didn't matter. Her position as the king's wife was inconsequential, that is, until there was a job he dare not do himself. Nevertheless, he would have things done his way. He would obtain the truth by deception.

From the beginning to the end of this story, she remains a vehicle through which messages are conveyed between parties. Jeroboam's treatment of his wife is heartless. He knows he has sinned and caused Israel to sin too. He is convinced that the cost will be severe. Presumably his wife knows too, there is no doubt that she shares his anxiety about the verdict, but there is a calmness and serenity about her as she follows her husband's dictates and receives the news.

The punishment decreed on the house of Jeroboam feels like the devouring thrust of a two-edged sword! The language used is raw and explicit. How she must have flinched, how her sensibilities crushed! But God is a kind and merciful God. Whilst He will in no wise clear the guilty, His love endures forever (Psalm 107:1). The news that the child will die is a blow to Jeroboam's wife, but it is cushioned by God's acknowledgement that her son is the only one He sees as 'good' in Jeroboam's household; God seems to accredit this to her doing. His death is God's means of saving the child. He will not eat the sour grapes of his father (Exodus 34:7; Ezekiel 18:1-4).

Her silence spoke volumes and she prevailed with God (Genesis 32:28) in saving her son. This message is profound. Be encouraged. You may not be articulate or charismatic, but God sees and knows you, He loves you and has your best interest at heart.

Cheryl Lowe
Guyana

THURSDAY 27th

...they glorified God, saying, ... that God has visited his people
Luke 7:16

THE MIRACLE OF A WIDOW'S SON – Reading: LUKE 7:11-17

Nain was a small town outside of Nazareth. One day, Jesus accompanied by His disciples and a large crowd, visited there.

Entering Nain, Jesus encountered a funeral procession; it was that of a young man, the only son of a widow. Jesus saw this woman and observed what was happening.

Jesus, understanding that this was her only son, was filled with compassion; His heart bursting with love, He looked on her and said, *"Do not weep"* (v13). The procession was halted, the large crowd looked on in wonder! Jesus approached the coffin and with one touch spoke to the widow's dead son, *"Young man, I say to you arise!"* (v14).

The dead boy took on life, sat up and spoke! Jesus in loving kindness presented him alive to his mother. The crowd in amazement realised that they had been witnesses to a miracle, and they perceived this could only have been done by God. News spread of this miracle as people recognised that someone remarkable had been in their midst. Was it a prophet? Luke writes in verse 16 and tells us that the crowd expressed, *"God has visited his people"*!

An encounter with Jesus is an opportunity for great things. In this case, this hardly known woman of the New Testament (that is not named) was the recipient of an extraordinary, surprise interruption by Jesus whilst she was weeping over her loss. Now she had a miracle of life restored to her only son.

Let us embrace every meeting with Jesus as an avenue to new possibilities, blessings and open-door experiences. He is a miracle worker, promise keeper, way maker, and our light in dark places. Women, let's build our faith with anticipation that a brief encounter with Jesus will effect change.

Hedy C Edmund

FRIDAY 28th

...Saul said, Seek out for me a woman who is a medium...and his servants said...there is a medium at Endor
1 Samuel 28:7 (ESV)

IT'S MY LIFE & I'LL DO WHAT I WANT – Reading: 1 Samuel 28:1-25

Since records were kept, much of the human race has had a fascination with the occult. The origins of this preoccupation are out of this world and mother Eve, in some ways, is the first human victim in it. Wanting to know more stems from a curiosity to understand something never experienced before, but it looks mesmerisingly beautiful. There's a desire to be like God, knowing what He knows, understanding what He understands, and thinking you can handle it (Genesis 3:1-4).

In the 1900s, Aleister Crowley, a well-known occultist, wrote The Book of the Law. The essence of its contents is encapsulated in one extract, *"Do what thou wilt shall be the whole of the Law"*. This modern philosophy of life presumes that you are in control of you, and does not acknowledge that when we meddle with sin, we are everything but in control (Genesis 3:5-6)!

The witch of Endor, like Eve, concluded that in spite of the consequences, she wanted to engage in the activity of communicating with 'the other side'. Did she do this for economic gain, or fame? It couldn't be the latter, because she had gone underground with her activity. So what was the attraction? There is something seductive about sin. Eve, once she had disobeyed, enticed her husband to participate. Strange how easy it is to share when we entangle ourselves in sin, but God has to remind us that we are His witnesses (Isaiah 43:10).

This lady remains incognito/concealed and is known only by her profession. This way, she can continue in her nefarious/wicked endeavours, with little focus on her. However, we can't hide from God. It has to be noted too, that she didn't actually say that she saw Samuel; that was Saul's doing (1 Samuel 28:13-14). She just said that she saw gods ascending up out of the earth, not coming down from heaven. This in itself should have been a warning sign. We know Samuel is dead. The text makes clear from Saul's own admission, that neither God, nor His prophets were communicating with him.

God had declared that a witch is an abomination and should not be allowed to live (Exodus 22:18). So who was Saul actually conversing with? This story is full of anomalies and warnings. This woman is a slave to her craft, sold on deception, she lives in fear of her life. Saul is rebuked by the apparition; *"if God is not dealing with you, why are you coming to me"* (1 Samuel 28:16)? Why indeed?

The Bible makes it clear that we can only serve one master (Matthew 6:24). So choose you this day whom you will serve (Joshua 24:15). Saul chose to go on enchanted ground. He refused the love of the truth, so he was sent a strong delusion to believe a lie (2 Thessalonians 2:11).

Be a vessel through which God works, not Satan. Jesus said, *"I am the resurrection and the life"* (John 11:25). He is our only hope for the future.

Cheryl Lowe
Guyana

SATURDAY 29th

(Jesus') mother saith unto the servants, Whatsoever he saith unto you, do it
John 2:5

YOUR VOICE CAN MAKE A DIFFERENCE - Reading: John 2:1-5

As parents, we know that our children will not always do what we desire. Jesus Christ our Savior was not exempt.

Once, when Jesus was 12 years old, His family went on a far journey to worship in Jerusalem. His parents expected that He was in the group of children on the return trip, only to find after about a day that he was not with them. Jesus had stayed behind to listen to and ask questions of the religious teachers. It took His parents three days to find Him. Jesus' intention was good, but His parents were not amused by this behaviour (Luke 2:41-48).

Fortunately, however, His mother Mary was able to look beyond Jesus' undesired behaviour and see the good and God in Him. Like any mother, there were things that Mary observed, knew, and admired about her son, which she might not have articulated. Indeed, she pondered many things about Him in her heart (Luke 2:19, 51).

When the opportune time came, Mary showed approval of her child's ability when she asked Jesus to help a family friend out of an embarrassing situation at a wedding - they ran out of wine. She knew Jesus had the power to sort things out somehow. She told the people, *"Whatsoever he tells you to do, do it"*. What assurance, what positive affirmation, what a vote of confidence from His mother!

One lesson that women can learn from Mary is to find ways to affirm our children and the youth in our care. We can often get caught up with observing and dealing with their undesirable behaviours, that we fail to acknowledge and praise the good in them. We can pay so much attention to the negative that we even fail to see the positive.

It is prudent to remember that what we feed grows. Mary's vote of confidence in her son was the breeding ground for a miracle. Pray today that as a woman, as a mother, God will give you the wisdom and grace to encourage the good in some child. Lend your voice to make a positive difference in someone's life today.

Keshawna Salmon-Ferguson
Jamaica

*SUNDAY 30th

Her children arise up, and call her blessed…
Proverbs 31:28

ON BEING A MOTHER – Reading: Proverbs 31:26-28; Matthew 19:13-15

Being a Mother is more than giving birth

It's preparing a soul for God before it leaves this earth
It's caring, guiding, helping, whenever it is needed
It's giving, sharing, loving, after long you have pleaded.

It's praying, fasting, crying, for more wisdom to understand
It's patience, forgiving, and faith in God's helping hand
It's mercy, long suffering and compassion as in God's Word is spoken
It's using them to the fullest when your heart is sad and broken.

It's strength to stand firm and to say "wait " or to warn of the dangers you know
It's knowing when to explain or just to simply say, "No".
As I hold my little baby, what a tremendous job I see
But the joy comes when I realise God is helping me.

Motherhood is wonderful with all its joy and pain
If we can do it God's way, some soul Heaven may gain.
Yes being a Mother is one of the greatest blessings on earth
It's helping a soul back to God and not just giving birth.

Evangelist Edith P Penn
USA

*Mother's Day (UK)

March 2025
Theme: Not Named & Hardly Mentioned Women in the Bible

MONDAY 31st

And Elijah said unto her, Fear not; go and do as thou hast said: but make me thereof a little cake first, and bring it unto me, and after make for thee and for thy son
1 Kings 17:13

OBEDIENCE IS BETTER THAN SACRIFICE
Reading: 1 Samuel 15:22; 1 Kings 17:8-16;

Today we look at another woman whose identity is concealed in anonymity, an obscure widow, living under the rule of King Ahab who *"did more evil in the eyes of the LORD than any of those before him"* (1 King 16:30).

We meet this widow at the city gates gathering sticks to make a fire for her last meal. Imagine what it must have been like for this mother, her husband was dead and together she and son were starving to death! They were victims of a widespread famine. Her plan was to take her handful of flour, last bit of oil, make a little cake, and prepare to die. How could life get any worse?

A stranger approaches this widow and asks for a drink of water. As she is about to get it, he takes his request a step further by asking her (who is at the end of her resources) for some bread. What she did not know was that God had already made a way.

God had chosen this weak and broken mother to be a part of something that would influence people of faith down through the ages. Her life was about to drastically change. In fact, Jesus specifically mentions this widow in Luke 4:25-26.

What is often overlooked in this story is that the Word of the Lord did not come only to Elijah, but in the same verse God said, *"I have commanded a widow there to feed you"* (1 Kings 17:9)! God had prepared this unnamed woman to obey the request of the prophet, and blessings followed. We can see here that obedience is better than sacrifice (1 Samuel 15:22).

Like the widow of Zarephath, we too may live quietly, occupied with the daily work of making a living and caring for our households. We too may be unnamed and ordinary, poor or of an ethnic minority, yet when the Word of the Lord comes to us, no matter the sacrifice, obey.

CP

April

The Fruit of the Spirit

TUESDAY 1st

...if when you do well, and suffer for it, you take it patiently, this is acceptable with God
1 Peter 2:20

CULTIVATE VIRTUE – Reading: 1 Peter 2:11-25

God spoke creation into physical existence by the word of His power (Hebrews 1:1-3). All classifications of life were commanded to bring forth fruit and God saw it was good (Genesis 1:22, 27,28).

Throughout the holy scriptures believers are encouraged to be fruitful. If we consider that fruit is produced from what is planted, the seed contains all that the plant is.

The manner of our living is to pattern the life of Christ; by cultivating virtue, we allow the grace of God to permeate our life. Virtue is excellence or valour, a "moral excellence". It's also power, strength, or courage. It is only by the power of God that a believer can live in an increasingly anti-Christ world.

Peter the Apostle wrote this first letter (about A.D.63) to the community of believers across the Roman provinces of Asia minor (1 Peter 1:1}. Trouble was imminent, the mood of the Roman Empire had shifted. Unrest and suspicion were prelude to persecution of the saints.

Yet in Sovereignty of His divine will, Almighty God had already elected and chosen those whom He loved as 'Elect'. Realising that suffering is varied in experience, the work of the Spirit by patience, ripens the virtue of divine nature within.

The fruit of the Spirit is love, by the grace of God, we produce of His Spirit (Galatians 5:22-23). Suffering for well doing, and taking it patiently, requires maturity of a surrendered life (1 Peter 1:20).

We are to bear the peaceable fruits of righteousness (Hebrews 12:11). Only then can we bring forth fruit in season. There is a fellowship in suffering with Christ, identifying with His life.

If we suffer with Him, we will reign with Him.

CDP

WEDNESDAY 2ⁿᵈ

Knowing this, that the trying of your faith worketh patience. But let patience have her perfect work, that ye may be perfect and entire, wanting nothing
James 1:3-4

LET THE GOLD COME FORTH – Reading: James 1:1-27

Why do failures come? Why do trials arise? Could not every day be fun and laughter? Would not the sun shine always and the Summer remain? I ask the question, "why?". And there are so many 'whys?'.

But the heaven and earth have already declared the story. If we win every day, where will the joy be in trying? Without trials, where is the testimony?

We have heard reports of man how gold is tried in the hot furnace until it reaches 99.99 percent for it to be pure gold. What says the report of God when we face trials? Many of us, I am sure, have walked into stores desiring and lusting at a piece of gold to call our own but forgetting it is the visible mark of victory through a process of burning and great beating. In Matthew 5, Jesus did not say, blessed are they that laugh, but He declared that, *"Blessed are they that mourn: for they shall be comforted. Blessed are they which are persecuted for righteousness' sake: for theirs is the kingdom of heaven"*.

Arise out of doubts, stop holding your head down; the God of Creation, our Lord Jesus is with you. Now, your duty is to not only have faith in the high seasons but also during the low ones. Be reminded that without faith it is impossible to please God. If you have faith, you will be able to get through your wilderness and arrive surely to the promised destination God has in His divine plan for you.

Shanique Graham

THURSDAY 3rd

...for this day is holy unto our LORD: neither be sorry; for the joy of the LORD is your strength
Nehemiah 8:10

THE FRUIT OF JOY – Reading: Nehemiah 8:1-18

The Word of God came to bring hopeful conviction. All too often we see believers' response to the Word as one of rejection and even mourning. This is so different from conviction to change, and in fact indicates that we may still be enthroning (rather than just observing or experiencing) our own will or limitations instead of the potential of the Word of God to take root and grow joy on the inside of us, the hearers.

The Levites in Nehemiah, upon revealing the words of God's laws, stirred a sombreness in the people as if they were grieving. But the Word, though sobering and reverential, was meant to bring about joy. The same is true today. When we are faced with calamity, it can easily erode our joy. It is as if the reality of life and law shows us our state, like a mirror reflecting what is, and that can feel hopeless.

But Nehemiah harnessed their mournful state back towards a higher spiritual response, reminding them that it is the Joy of the Lord that needs our attention during calamity because it is synonymous with strength.

Paul too pointed to another law. Not an earthly one that constrains us to sadness and hopelessness, but the law that develops the fruit of God's Spirit which surpasses happiness or sadness. It is a deep-seated hope and assurance that the Bible calls Joy. How do I restore that joy in myself when I feel real sadness?

Just as in Nehemiah, we grow the joy of the LORD by assimilating to the His Word, and not just our own thinking. Being filled with His Spirit we begin to bear the fruit of deep joy.

Joy Lear-Bernard

FRIDAY 4th

He that loveth not, knoweth not God; for God is love
1 John 4:8

LOVED NONETHELESS – Reading: 1 John 4:7-21

Love, a small word that holds so much power! Love in its truest form, i.e., God's love, defies understanding. That God would love us in the way that He does will never be fully understood. The more that we look at who our God is, we see real and pure love in action.

The example of love displayed by God is oh so powerful and at times even overwhelming! It can move mountains in our lives, restore what has been broken and gives us a reason to keep moving forward.

True love does not wait for reciprocation to reveal itself. Romans 5:8 declares that while we were yet sinners, Christ died for you and for me. He willingly went to Calvary to take away our sins (John 1:29) and the penalty of death, and replaced it with the gift of eternal life (John 3:16).

I do believe that there are no simpler or more meaningful three words than, *"God is love"*. He gave His only begotten Son to declare this message. To know God is to know His love. We should appreciate God's love and never take it for granted. It is our source of life, redemption, and deliverance. Hallelujah!

The love of God underlines everything about Him. This love is strong enough to offer peace in the midst of rebuke or during a period of correction; His chastising of us is always mixed with grace, compassion and mercy.

As we enjoy the expression of God's love towards us, let's remember that we should share the love of God with those around us, also with the same grace and compassion as we received.

Love Him because He first loved you.

CDK

SATURDAY 5th

...let us run with patience the race that is set before us
Hebrews 12:1

THE FALL – Reading: Hebrews 12:1-29

She was rushing along
Her hands laden down with bags
The phone was in her hands
As she suddenly fell.

Their conversation was interrupted
Her and the caller's words instantly changed
Reassurance was given by the caller on the line again and again
As she recognised she had fallen.

Miraculously, her hands were intact
No evidence of a scratch
No spilt shopping
No broken phone.

God was on hand
As she was getting up on her own
No lingering pains
She did not catch the bus
But she continued to walk and did not fuss
She walked even further
Then when she was sat
The pain came on suddenly
She couldn't walk.

In agony
For a time
Then as the gel and tablets
Started to work
She would be able to walk again.

She asked God for help
As the pain increased
So many things were going on in her head
But God is good - she can still walk
In God we can have our falls, but always God gets us up again.

God never stops you from walking in Him
You can stop
But continue
You can stagger
But continue.

Hold on and continue
Never stop
Though your heart may have been broken
Never stop.

Remember our Great Saviour
Though sometimes weary
He continued
And never stopped.

Sister Jennifer Henry

SUNDAY 6th

Rejoice in the Lord always: and again I say, Rejoice
Philippians 4:4

REJOICE! – Reading: Philippians 4:1-9

Rejoice: to feel or show great joy!

Apostle Paul penned this verse while in prison for preaching the gospel. He was a man who could take a negative situation and turn it into a positive. He was one of those people who could turn his frown upside down, take life's lemons and make lemonade! Yet he was still in prison! How did he do it?

He was a scholar who had sat at the feet of Gamaliel searching the scriptures. When he finally met the Lord whom he thought he had been helping, it all fell into place! Now his life had true meaning; he had a goal, a purpose!

The Word of God with which he was so familiar was now an arsenal of weaponry that he could apply to each and every situation. Now that his spiritual blindness had cleared, he could see God's hand at work.

Looking into the Word we see Psalm 126:6, *"He that goeth forth and weepeth, bearing precious seed, shall doubtless come again with rejoicing, bringing his sheaves with him"*.

Isaiah 25:9 says, *"And it shall be said in that day, Lo, this is our God; we have waited for Him; and he will save us; this is the LORD; we have waited for him, we will be glad and rejoice in his salvation"*.

So women of God, let us consider that we have the same Spirit at work in us to bear the same fruit.

"Weeping may endure for a night, but joy cometh in the morning" (Psalm 30:5).

BVG

MONDAY 7th

He hath showed thee, O man, what is good: and what doth the LORD require of thee, but to do justly, and to love mercy, and to walk humbly with thy God?
Micah 6:8

MAYBE WE ALREADY KNOW, DON'T WE? – Reading: Micah 6:1-16

Micah's word to the children of Israel was a prophecy imploring them to revisit a place of relationship with God.

I came across this scripture in new light some 30 years ago and during countless times of feeling lost and adrift I've prayed these exact words *"Lord, what do you require of me?"*

Here, Micah offers us a 'go to' for those times by prophesying essential and unwavering foundations that God has principled for us. Imagine if you are struck by a relentless storm with just one unperturbed deep-rooted tree. Wouldn't you grab at it to harness you back to safety from certain destruction? Well, this was the state of Israel and here was that prophetic tree.

(Phrased for our own self-reflection)

* Am I just before God? Am I at a place of standard and right standing before the Holy God?

* Do I love His mercy? To do so I must see that I am in constant need of it, which shifts my composure and decisions. How would I be speaking, thinking and living, if I was in grateful receipt of His mercy?

* And as a result, the proof is my actions. A heart that has embraced justice and mercy 'walks' humbly with our God. Do I, by my actions, show humility to the Sovereignty of God? What in my 'walk' shows respect and surrender to Him?

The definitive question mark at the end of Micah 6:8 clearly indicates that they already knew what to do! With almost a bemused weariness or rebuke at times, God sees us crying out for answers yet we have not applied ourselves to His truth.

For us it should be an anthemic repeat that when I stray, when I am lost and unsure whether by life circumstances or by being wayward, I already have a deep seated 'go to' in the secret place with God and that will be the catalyst for my next steps as I walk humbly before Him.

Simply put, when you feel adrift from God, and don't know what to do, we already have a safe and reassuring invitation to consider what we actually already know and may have abandoned. We need to begin again there. We may not have a clear vision of afar, but His truth will stop us from going adrift in the storm.

Joy Lear-Bernard

TUESDAY 8th

The God of hope fill you with all joy and peace in believing
Romans 15:13

LIVE IN HOPE – Reading: Romans 15:7-13

A child who is hopeful of a gift from its parents, is excited, happy (joyful) and contented (peaceful) because they truly believe that they will receive something wonderful. They have faith in their parents that they will provide. If it doesn't happen then the child is disillusioned and becomes unhappy and possibly angry.

Faith in God is hope and the hope that God provides is not wishy-washy or ambiguous, but firm, unmoveable assurance that what we are hopeful for will come to pass. To have faith is to have hope. When we have hope we should have joy and peace; both joy and peace are key characteristics of the fruit of the Spirit.

Joy is not happy today and sad tomorrow, but always joyful. Peace is not about having alone time to relax, but it's a perfect peace deep within during good and bad times. This type of joy and peace is given to those that trust the Lord. Paul's prayer and blessing here is not just that we have joy and peace, but that it *overflows* in our lives.

Having received the hope of eternal life through salvation by Jesus' death on Calvary, we should now live in the assurances of that hope. When we remain 'hopeful' we will experience joy and peace

If you have not/are not experiencing this joy and peace, then today it's your time to seek the Lord and surrender your life to Him.

Lady Pam Lewin

WEDNESDAY 9th

Looking unto Jesus the author and finisher of our faith; who for the joy that was set before him endured the cross, despising the shame, and is set down at the right hand of the throne of God
Hebrews 12:2

THE IMPORTANCE OF VISION – Reading: Hebrews 12:1-13

There are happenings in our lives that give us the opportunity to exercise the Fruit of the Spirit and to be exercised by them! James encourages us to *"count it all joy"* when difficulties arise knowing that when our faith is tried, patience results. And when patience has completed her work we shall be *"perfect and entire, wanting nothing"* (James 1:2-4). Peter exhorts us to embrace the *"fiery trials"* (1 Peter 4:12 & 13).

It is the knowledge of certain reward that keeps us going. Consider an Olympian, hours of disciplined, grueling training. With eyes firmly on the prize, the effort, pain even, becomes worth it. No wonder the Bible tells us in Proverbs 29:18 that without a vision the people perish. Vision inspires us, ignites our faith and gives rise to joy that strengthens us!

When Peter's eyes were on Jesus, he conquered the waves and overcame the laws of gravity. Transcending all his limitations, he stepped out into the miraculous! (Matthew 14:29)

When we concentrate on circumstances around us, it is so easy to get bogged down, to sink into an abyss of despondency. When we examine the minutiae of everyday difficulties, we are overwhelmed. But when we look up in faith to the *"joy set before us"*, to our Wonderful Saviour and His Reward, we are strengthened to continue running this race to its glorious end!

Gudrun Witt
Zimbabwe

THURSDAY 10th

Blessed are the peacemakers: for they shall be called the children of God
Matthew 5:9

SWEET PEACE - Reading: Matthew 5:1-12

The fruit of the Spirit is often likened in the natural to an orange which has many segments. In Christendom, this refers to the fruits of the Holy Spirit. Galatians 5:22-23 lists nine attributes; the segment which I will focus on for today is Peace.

Today we live in a dark world where the cry from humanity is for peace, which is only obtainable from Jehovah God in the Old Testament and, today, Jesus Christ in the New Testament. The peace that God gives to His children is not only when things are calm and settled. This peace, even in times of battle and strife, only comes from God and is beyond our comprehension (Philippians 4:7). To have this divine peace, which is filled with blessings and goodness, we must experience the new birth in two parts (John 3:5). This comes when we repent of our sins; note, we all were born with an inherent sinful nature. Baptism, in the name of Jesus Christ, is a process of burying our sinful nature, and the infilling of the Holy Spirit. Only then can we truly experience the Peace of God.

The Bible affirms that there is a special blessing bestowed upon a peacemaker. We live in a world of social and political confusion. God knows the heart of humankind is deceitful and desperately wicked, that is why we should not be astonished to hear of wars and rumours of wars.

We, the children of God, must stand firm on the word of God. A peacemaker is blessed by God although often ill-treated by man as they share God's passion for peace and reconciliation by actively removing barriers.

It is not peace at any price; however, we must actively seek to produce peace. To achieve peace, we must first start with a self-examination. I must ask the Lord to deliver me from myself. I must ask the Lord for a renewal of my mind and to view situations according to the Word of God.

First, search the scriptures to see what the Bible says on the matter. Seek to engender peace, even if you have to stand in the middle and be hit from both sides when resolving a conflict! As a peacemaker, we are truly a child of God.

Missionary Audrey Simpson

FRIDAY 11th

With all lowliness and meekness, with longsuffering, forbearing one another in love
Ephesians 4:2

WE ARE ONE – Reading: Ephesians 4:1-16

Lowliness speaks of having a humble opinion of one's self, humility of mind, modesty. Philippians 2:3 says, *"Let nothing be done through strife or vainglory; but in lowliness of mind let each esteem others better than themselves"*.

Meekness means submission, and longsuffering means forbearance and patience. In the epistle to the Ephesians, Paul talks to Jews and Gentiles telling them that the church is one body, and that Gentiles can become Christians without conforming to Jewish traditions. There was strife within this church because the Jews esteemed themselves as being greater than the Gentiles, but Paul preached against their prejudices. He also demonstrated lowliness and meekness when he said that he was *"less than the least of all saints"* (Ephesians 3:8). He encouraged the saints to *'be rooted and grounded in love'* (Ephesians 3:17). Only when we become rooted and grounded in the love of God can we forbear, i.e., be tolerant, accept one another. This is longsuffering because we learn to be patient with each other, and restrain from behaviours that cause divisions within the church.

Paul emphasises the importance of unity, and speaking the truth in love because there will be times when we won't agree, but it's how we deal with disagreements that makes the difference! The Jews and Gentiles were two different nations, with different traditions and cultures, and they struggled to come together in unity because of these variances.

We continue to see this in many churches today, where attendance is dominated by a particular culture and ethnic group. We are still struggling to embrace diversity, struggling with, *"being likeminded, having the same love, and being of one accord…",* rather than being like Jesus who made Himself of no reputation (Ephesians 2:1-7).

Rachel Lewin

SATURDAY 12th

A soft answer turneth away wrath; but grievous words stir up anger
Proverbs 15:1

A SOFT ANSWER – Reading: Proverbs 15:1-33

The fruit of the Spirit comes from God, so its manifestation is like Him.

A soft answer is loving, a soft answer is joyous
A soft answer is peaceful, a soft answer is longsuffering
A soft answer is gentle, a soft answer is good
A soft answer is faithful, a soft answer is meek
A soft answer is temperate.

The fruit is not divided - you cannot have one attribute without the others. It's a fruit not fruits (Galatians 5:22-23).

There is something about putting God first that causes us to be victorious without being argumentative or angry. We maintain our love for others if we take a moment before we answer. Try to see the funny side of a situation and share your joy! Use some of God's peace to stop a spark being fanned into a flame. Take your time; respond rather than react. Use that gentle Spirit rather than a hasty answer. Staying calm is good for us – let's not raise our blood pressure! Aim high, be good. Keep the faith. Meek does not mean weak. Exercise self-control and keep spiritually fit.

Loving words will cost but little
Journeying up the hill of life
But they make the weak and weary
Stronger, braver for the strife.

Do you count them only trifles
Trifles then are sun and rain
Never was a kind word wasted
Never was one said in vain.
(Old English Hymn by John Zundel)

BVG

SUNDAY 13th

Take my yoke upon you, and learn of me; for I am meek and lowly in heart: and ye shall find rest unto your souls
Matthew 11:29

AN EASY YOKE – Reading: Matthew 11: 20-30

A yoke is a heavy wooden harness that is fitted over the shoulders of certain animals, typically oxen. It is attached to a piece of farming equipment that they must pull together.

In the spiritual, with Jesus' yoke, He walks alongside us to take the weight of our heavy burdens, we cannot bear our burdens alone. In Matthew 11:28, Jesus encourages those who are weary and carry heavy burdens to come to Him and He will give us rest.

The Pharisees had instituted additional laws which were intolerable yokes for the people to carry (Matthew 23:4). Jesus came to free us from the many rituals instituted under the Mosaic Law, bringing a new and better covenant for us all. Although Israel is God's chosen nation, salvation is for everyone who believes (Romans 1:16).

The Fruit of the Spirit in this scripture is meekness which means to submit, humility, and *"God will beautify the meek with salvation"* (Psalm 149:4). A person who is lowly makes themselves of no reputation, e.g., Jesus, who was not like the Pharisees who did things out of selfish motivations and a need for recognition.

Jesus is speaking to sinners too - they carry the weight of sin, and also to the saints of God who carry the pressures of life. If we repent and take up our cross and follow Jesus, He will share our heavy burdens because although the righteous will suffer, God will never give us more than we can handle (1 Corinthians 10:13).

When we take up our cross and follow Christ, only then will we find rest unto our souls. That's because He carries us through our tests and trials enabling us to rest in Him through the storms of life.

Rachel Lewin

MONDAY 14th

Put on therefore, as the elect of God, holy beloved, bowels of mercies, kindness, humbleness of mind, meekness, longsuffering
Colossians 3:12

REPRESENTING CHRIST – Reading: Colossians 3: 8-17

Throughout scripture, Paul encourages us as children of God, to put on the nature of Christ. It comes from the realisation that failure to do so will make us unable to fulfil our mandate to present Christ as the Savior of humankind.

When the world looks at us, Christ must be seen in us. This reminds me of the words to a song, *"Let the beauty of Jesus be seen in me…"*. In this particular scripture, Paul is telling us to don positive characteristics in order for others to be drawn to Christ, and, ultimately, be saved.

Sin must no longer have the rule over us. *"But now ye also put off all these; anger, wrath, malice, blasphemy, filthy communication out of your mouth"* (Colossians. 3:8). Instead, the fruit of the Spirit must be on full display. The traits that were demonstrated by Jesus Christ must also be present in His followers, but the Spirit has to be in us so that the fruit can be seen. Without the Spirit, there can be no fruit.

As we journey through life, we encounter persons whose needs we can minister to simply by demonstrating the fruit of the Spirit. The characteristics, as outlined in this verse, include mercy, kindness, humility and meekness. As God's representatives, we know that it is the Holy Spirit that produces these traits in us. We cannot get them on our own. These are part of the *'new man'* mentioned in verse 8. When present, they cannot be hidden as Christ's nature will shine through us. Our attitudes, our behaviours, our deeds will all point to the one who died to save us all.

As representatives of Christ, may His beauty be seen in us as evidenced by the Fruit of the Spirit.

Sister Barbara Hendrickson
Nevis

TUESDAY 15th

For his anger endures but a moment; in his favour is life: weeping may endure for a night, but joy comes in the morning
Psalm 30:5

J.O.Y. JOY! – Reading: Psalm 30:1-12

"J.O.Y. joy! Joy in the Holy Ghost". Do you remember this chorus? I do! Every time I heard this song, I saw the joy on the faces of the saints as they sang about a joy that originates from the Holy Spirit, and the warning was not to allow anyone (including the Devil) to steal this joy.

So, what exactly is Biblical joy? I like to define it as a stabilising factor which grounds and settles an individual, regardless of positive or negative circumstances, therefore giving the feeling of great delight, gladness, or pleasure.

The joy that God gives surpasses human comprehension. It's the kind of joy that allows you to smile even when, by all accounts, you have absolutely nothing to smile about.

This joy that you have acts as a reminder that although it may currently be a dark night of weeping, joy is still there. The sun never disappears because it's night, it stays exactly where it is in its position at the centre of our solar system. Planet earth rotates away from it, and as we do, the sun appears to move from an elevated position in the sky and sets behind the horizon. Therefore, this joy stabilises us because it never disappears on our darkest day. Be encouraged move closer to God and experience even more of His joy.

Remember, it might be night where you are but it's daytime somewhere in the world. So fret not, your morning will come, and with it God will flood you with the daylight of His joy.

MinK / Minister Kay Dawkins

WEDNESDAY 16th

...beside this, giving all diligence, add to your faith virtue...
2 Peter 1:5

THE DIVINE NATURE OF GOD – Reading: 2 Peter 1:1-11

Peter encourages us to take on the divine nature of God of which there are several characteristics.

The first is faith, it's paramount before you can even come to God. This initial ingredient of acceptance that *"God is"* (Hebrews 11:6), is the number one element of all attributes, to which God has so graciously given every man a measure. Faith enough to be able to build upon for spiritual development. If we're ever going to possess His divine nature of holiness, we need to be diligent and steadfast to multiply our faith.

We have been cleansed, saved and sanctified from former desires, and now have access to all of God's bountiful promises and fullness that come only from Him. Each element is acquired through the Holy Ghost to shape Christian character. Therefore, you must never think that you have 'arrived' and become satisfied - there should always be spiritual aspirations to increase to another level in God. Reflecting and obtaining the image of Christ.

These are fruits and proof that transformation is taking place with evidence such as virtue which is power and knowledge. Power to change, power to endure and power to obtain knowledge. Here knowledge is at multi levels. Knowledge is understanding and mental ability. Knowledge speaks of intimacy and close relationship with Him. Also, knowledge is a living experience of God.

Peter states that when evidence of spiritual maturity is manifested in your life, there will be no spiritual lack but you'll continue to grow and be fruitful. You will produce good substance, not only beneficial to yourself, but will impact and teach others also, to the glory of God.

Sis Jx

THURSDAY 17th

But the meek shall inherit the earth; and shall delight themselves in the abundance of peace
Psalm 37:11

STRENGTH IN MEEKNESS – Reading: Psalm 37:1-40

What does it mean to be meek? It is to possess a gentle, quiet and humble spirit that easily submits. Submits to anything? NO. Meekness will always submit to the truth of God's word. It is not weak, but strong in faith and has total confidence in God. It refuses to boast, or esteem itself; it knows in whom it believes and will always give the glory to God.

The Word of God teaches that Moses was meek *"above all men that were upon the face of the earth"* (Numbers 12:3). Although he was opposed and his leadership was constantly challenged, he remained grounded.

My mind is taken back to Abraham. In Genesis 22:2, God told him to take his only son Isaac *"whom thou loveth"*, and offer him as a burnt offering. In verse three of the same chapter, there were no arguments, no negotiations, no asking God why give me my son if you planned to take him from me. Abraham simply rose up early in the morning, saddled his donkey, made sure he had all that was required, to carry out what was expected of him and went to the place God had showed him. He was fully prepared to carry out the LORD's command.

In Psalm 37:11, it states that, *"The meek shall delight themselves in the abundance of peace"*. True meekness, when combined with humility and faith, brings peace.

So, let us remember that we don't have to allow the pressures of life to overtake us. Jesus said, *"Take my yoke upon you and learn from me, for I am gentle and lowly in heart, and you will find rest for your souls. For my yoke is easy and my burden is light"* (Matthew 11:29-30 NKJV).

Evangelist Deveen Smith

*FRIDAY 18th

Surely he scorneth the scorners: but he giveth grace unto the lowly Proverbs 3:34

───────◆●◆───────

LOWLY IN HEART IS A VIRTUE – Reading Proverbs 3:27-35

The Word of God is always true. It does not matter how hard we squeal and wail, or make a fuss against the Word, it is real and without it and His Spirit it is impossible to manifest the fruit of the Spirit in our lives, or even please God.

As we, the human race contends with the reality of our changing world, we need to understand fully that whatever solutions are presented, if it's not God driven, it will not work. The Holy Spirit will allow the fruit of the Spirit to manifest in our daily living, if we allow Him.

In decision-making, the fruit of the Spirit is very important as sometimes we can scoff at other people's ideas or suggestions. We may even scorn because of cultural differences such as their accent, their dress, or even how they eat due to their culture, e.g., eating with their hands and not a knife and fork.

Having the fruit of meekness, being lowly in spirit, will help us to conduct ourselves toward others in a godly way. The Word of God reminds us in Psalm 1:1-3, *"We must not stand in way of sinners nor sit in the seat of the scornful"*. We should not be a hindrance to other people because of our negative behaviour, prideful attitude and actions. May we find ourselves in a place where we can be among the lowly to exercise humility. We need to be humble and receive the grace of God in our lives.

Remember - you are fearfully and wonderfully made!

Be blessed.

Jennifer Beckford

*Good Friday

SATURDAY 19th

For the kingdom of God is not a matter of eating and drinking but of righteousness and peace and joy in the Holy Spirit
Romans 14:17

THAT'S THE KINGDOM! – Reading: Romans 14:1-23

Human customs, traditions and habits are not the cornerstones of God's Kingdom.

Many traditions can be wholesome fabrics to enhance the kingdom, but there are far greater eternal materials that evidence our Kingdom focus. Righteousness, peace and joy should be firm structures we walk by for eternal living.

In such a complicated time where each man seeks his own, we are reminded that simple ideas about food and drink should not cause divisions in the body of Christ. The characteristics of His spiritual fruit, displayed in us, show that we are citizens of the Kingdom because we look like the King. And, furthermore, we let the world see that we truly follow Him and not our own ideologies.

Paul, writing to the church in Rome, teaches that if we eat freely, and at will do the very thing that causes a stumbling block to another, we are no longer building the Kingdom. Food and drink do not build God's kingdom, but rather the heart with which we engage with Him and others.

The privilege and challenge are ours, i.e., to live right before God, to carry His love and share His joy. That's the Kingdom of God.

Joy Lear-Bernard

*SUNDAY 20th

We love him, because he first loved us
1 John 4:19

HE LOVES ME, HE LOVES ME! – Reading: 1 John 4:1-21

One of my favourite songs to sing when I was a toddler was, *"O, how I love Jesus, because He first loved me"*.

Love is such a powerful emotion that it is possible to love without having your love reciprocated. Who better to prove this than our Lord Jesus Christ who demonstrated His love towards us while we were yet sinners (Romans 5:8).

The apostle John, who has a repetitive theme of Love in all of his writings, so beautifully pens today's focus verse. John presents a fact which cannot be argued, i.e., the reason why we love God is because He loved us first. We were not even thinking of Him, much less loving Him, when He called our name.

Love is contagious and also persistent, especially God's love. Many of us can testify how, for years, we tried to resist the love in the voice that was evidently calling us to Him, but the hardest of hearts melted eventually.

God's unconditional love is the kind which we as His children are called to reflect to others. Not loving only those who love us in return, not only loving those who are not difficult, not waiting for someone to change and then we will love them. But since Christ loved and died for us while we were yet sinners, we choose to manifest the love with which He first loved us, because His love is shed abroad in our hearts by the Holy Ghost (Romans 5:5).

JEJ

*Easter Sunday

*MONDAY 21ˢᵗ

And above all these put on love, which binds everything together in perfect harmony
Colossians 3:14

BONDED TOGETHER – Reading: Colossians 3:1-17

Carefully examining a fruit will yield a multitude of revelations.

Most of us will look at a fruit to determine if it is suitable for consumption. Is it ripe? Is it tasty? Is it juicy? Is it sweet? Is it tangy? Is it sour? Is it firm? Is it soft? Is it seedless? Is it full of seeds? Is the skin edible? Are the seeds edible? The questions can go on and on. The answers will be quite varied. The purposes will be limitless. Our preferences will be distinct.

Very few of us look at a fruit and wonder what it would look like on the branch or the vine without a skin. All of us would raise our eyebrows in astonishment if we were to find a seedless mango hanging on the tree. We would all begin recording if we found a banana with a huge seed in the heart of it.

Just as we have certain expectations with our natural fruits, so too we must have certain expectations with our spiritual fruit. Just as we do not see what binds the skin to the flesh, or the flesh to the seed, but believe that it exists and serves a purpose, so too we must acknowledge the purpose of every part of the fruit of the Spirit.

In our verse today, we are encouraged to put on the *"bond of perfectness"*. A fruit cannot be peeled without some of the fruit adhering to the skin. The flesh cannot be removed from the seed without leaving some residue thereon. Likewise, we cannot be separated from our *"bond"* without losing a piece of ourselves.

The moment that any part of the fruit is removed, it has lost its perfection. Perfection did not rely on its appearance, but on the quality of being whole. Without charity, there is no one who is whole. In seeking to be whole individually, as a family unit, as a church body, it cannot be accomplished without charity.

Let us be *"bonded"* or clothed in charity, enhancing and protecting the best qualities of the fruit for the benefit of all consumers.

Pastor Londy Esdaille
Nevis

*Bank Holiday (UK)

TUESDAY 22nd

And let the peace of God rule in your hearts, to the which also ye are called in one body; and be ye thankful
Colossians 3:15

WHERE IS YOUR PEACE? – Reading: Ephesians 2:11-22

In today's scripture, Paul is encouraging us to let the peace of God rule in our heart since, as members of one body, we are called to peace. In other words when the circumstances of life overwhelm, we must allow the inner peace of God to be the controlling force in our lives by speaking and reacting in a way that would preserve it.

One day my eldest son (who was a teenager at the time) asked me a question: *"Where is your peace?"*

Profound words but words that would become a catalyst for future trials in this journey we call life. It was my lightbulb moment. I was losing my children to the world. Other influences had more of an attraction. We had relocated to England several years prior. *"Had we made the right decision in coming back? The children back in our home church seemed to be strong in the Lord. Where had we gone wrong?"!*

A whirlwind of emotions swirled around my head like angry wasps. It was during this season in my walk when my eldest son posed the question, *"Where is your peace?"* It seemed contradictory at the time, considering the hardness of his heart, but he knew deep down that Jesus should make a difference in your life. I can't remember my response, but I was jolted! *What fruit was I displaying to my children? What were they seeing?* Here I was worrying constantly about them, taking the whole situation personally, rather than realising that we are in a spiritual battle. Yes, I was praying, but my prayers were murmuring prayers, prayers that focused more on the problem than on God's faithfulness.

What my son was in effect saying was, where is the fruit of the Spirit? Over the years, those words have taken a hold of me. Jesus said in John 16:33, *"...in me ye might have peace"*. When worry and anxiety rears their head, I now know that my focus is not in the right direction.

April 2025
Theme: The Fruit of the Spirit

That was well over 20 years ago. This same son is now married with a family and living for God.

CP

WEDNESDAY 23ʳᵈ

...Blessed is the (one) that endureth temptation
James 1:12

THE CROWN OF LIFE – Reading: James 1:1-18

In today's scripture it is plain to see
Everything that my Father requires of me
To grow in His grace, mercy and love
With the strength He gives from above.

And when I finally reach eternity
Receive the crown of life promised to me
What a glorious day that will be.

His mercies are forever sure
So, we must strive to endure
In days of grief, heartache or strife
These seasons will come …for this is life!

But we are secure in His love and grace
As He wraps us in His warm embrace
Temptations each day will surely arise
But we must resist for us to win our prize.

This statement was made many years ago
That people don't care how much we know
Until they know how much we care
It's not by our suits but by the fruits we bare
A crown of life awaits us when we get home
For it's by the fruit of the Spirit that we are known.

So, cling to His promises, they are true
A crown of life awaits for me and you
What a wonderful reward no one else can give
Let us prove every day in Him we live.

Barbara Mason

THURSDAY 24th

...before honour is humility
Proverbs 18:12

HUMILITY FIRST – Reading: Proverbs 18:1-13

Take pride in yourself!

It's a phrase I used to hear often as I grew from a child to a teen. Clearly, I was being taught that my actions and how I treated myself was a priority. As I grew in my faith, the Holy Spirit revealed to me that self-respect is important, but showing the same grace to others is just as significant.

1 Peter 5:6 reminds us, *"Humble yourselves therefore under the mighty hand of God, that he may exalt you in due time".* A meek spirit is a prerequisite as we follow Christ's example, but we all know putting other's needs before our own can be a difficult assignment.

Reading through the gospels, Jesus sets the perfect precedent of humility throughout His ministry until death. The tiredness and weariness in His fleshly body when travelling far and wide, continually preaching and teaching, must have been unimaginable. Despite this, His purpose and focus were to reach lost souls and show love. He put others first showing servanthood.

In Psalm 131:1, David cried out, *"... LORD, my heart is not haughty, nor mine eyes lofty: neither do I exercise myself in great matters, or in things too high for me".*

Humility doesn't show weakness but love. It doesn't seek validation but other's wellbeing. It doesn't display a badge of righteousness but God's grace.

Empty us of self, Lord, so that we can honour you!

DR

FRIDAY 25th

Be not overcome of evil, but overcome evil with good
Romans 12:21

IT IS UNNATURAL – Reading: Romans 12:1-21

It's instructive, a command which carries an urgency for immediate action.

We must first remember that there is no good thing in our flesh (Romans 7:18). Furthermore, the human heart is desperately wicked (Jeremiah 17:9). It is therefore unnatural to accomplish this instruction. So how can it be? Here is the victory!

Our human spirit is born again; which after God is created in all righteousness and true holiness (Ephesians 4:24). We are born again of incorruptible seed by the Word of God (1 Peter 1:23). The Greek word *"sperma"* means *"seed"*. So, consider the God-quality and makeup of our second birth.

Have you ever seen an orange seed bearing raspberries? It must yield seed after its kind according to the divine order of creation. Therefore, having within us the seed of God's Word, i.e., good, godly characteristics and attributes, this manifestation of being cannot be overcome of evil.

With such power and divine ability growing into a lifestyle, we overcome evil with good. We manifest godly responses of love and longsuffering in the face of hate. For if we love those who love us, then sinners do the same naturally, and there's a big difference between nature and what is done by the Spirit of God!

The command given in today's focus verse is attainable, but only by the Spirit, as it's not a natural act but spiritual. Perhaps you prefer unnatural, or even supernatural.

Pastor Josephine

SATURDAY 26th

But if we say that we love God and don't love each other, we are liars. We cannot see God...
1 John 4:20 (CEV)

LOVE AGAIN – Reading: 1 John 4:7-21

God is love and those who love Him must not only say it, but show it in their deeds

The whole law can be summarised by the greatest commandment of all, *"Love the Lord your God with all your heart, and with all your soul, and with all your mind... And the second is like unto it, Thou shalt love your neighbour as yourself"* (Matthew 22:37-38).

How can we say that we love God, whom we haven't seen before, and hate those whom we see from day to day? The Bible calls such a person a liar!

Sisters, we must love everyone and anyone with the love of God, even our enemies. Jesus laid His life down for us while we were yet sinners, and He expects us to let love go beyond our hurt, by forgiving those who offend us four hundred and ninety times (Matthew 18:21-22)!

Keep praying, keep believing, keep trusting, as God continues to work within us on a daily basis.

Sis Esther Miller

SUNDAY 27th

And Jesus answering said unto them, Have faith in God
Mark 11:22

THE ATTRIBUTES OF A GODLY LIFE – Reading: Mark 11:11-26

Have faith in God! Jesus tells us in St Mark 11:22, because Jesus wants His people to understand that through Him, they too can do marvellous things, and obstacles can be removed if they truly believe.

Faith is described as a fruit of the spirit in Galatians 5:22. It means to have confidence or trust, belief in God or in the doctrines or teaching of religion (Ref Wikipedia).

Hebrews 11:1 also defines faith as, *"the substance of things hoped for, the evidence of things not seen"*. Peter was amazed when Jesus withered the fig tree by speaking to it.

As Christians we are not exempt from opposition, trials, burdens, mountains of all description whatever those maybe. Jesus wants us to be completely assured that whatever mountains we face, it will be removed if we trust the Lord's power. We should not allow doubt to hamper our faith in God.

In Paul's letter to the Romans, he explains that we are justified by faith in Jesus Christ and since we are justified, we have peace with God (Romans 5:1-2). Those who are in Christ are distinguished from unbelievers in that they have been gifted with the Holy Spirit enabling us to bear fruit. Jesus declared, *"My peace I leave with you, my peace I give unto you, not as the world gives..."* (St John 14:27).

The Word does not promise us that we will not have disruptions, fears, anxieties, or that we will live free from the storms of life. What we are promised is peace and God's divine protection (Isaiah 43:2; Philippians 4:11).

All of us are exposed to situations that can make us anxious or distressed, but always remember, *"My peace I leave with you..."*.

Because the peace that Jesus bequeathed us, is the peace that surpasses all understanding (Philippians 4:6-7).

When the fruit of the Spirit is produced within us by the Holy Spirit, we can live victoriously in harmony and tranquillity despite of our circumstances.

Minister ML Fraser

MONDAY 28th

Most important of all, continue to show deep love for each other, for love covers a multitude of sins
1 Peter 4:8 (NLT)

LOVING AT ALL TIMES – Reading: 1 Peter 4:7-19

The scripture in today's devotional gives the directive to continue to show love to others in spite of the wrong they may do. How can one do this? The natural human tendency is to rebuff, take vengeance, malice, distance oneself from. All these are the opposite of loving actions.

As humans we will encounter people who make loving hard. It might be a promiscuous wife like Gomer who Hosea kept taking back after she messed up, a prodigal son who one must embrace after wasting his life, or some other friend, relative, or close associate who has caused nothing but pain and disappointment. It is easy to love the lovely, but how does one love the unlovely?

One can only truly show love in such circumstances if empowered by some other force that is stronger than one's natural inclinations. This requires the work of the indwelling Holy Spirit. Such display of love under trying circumstances comes when one walks in the Spirit instead of yielding to the lust of the flesh (Galatians 5:16).

The encouragement today is to yield to the Holy Spirit in matters of love. May you surrender to the Holy Spirit's leading so that you can truly love at all times.

Let your prayer today be, *"Lord God please teach me and help me to love the unlovely so that I may truly love at all times".*

Keshawna Salmon-Ferguson
Jamaica

TUESDAY 29th

...without faith it is impossible to please him
Hebrews 11:6

FAITH SEEN IN ACTION! – Reading: Hebrews 11:1-6

It takes faith to serve God. It takes faith to hold onto hope. It takes faith to move the mountains in our lives.

When faced with what sometimes feel like impossible situations, there is a point where we must stand and declare to others, and sometimes to ourselves, where our hope and faith lie.

Faith requires action. Living out our purpose and operating in the gifts that God has given us takes 'boldness'. The early church prayed for boldness to operate and do the will of God (Acts 4:29-31).

By faith we trust God. Despite the situation we are facing, we see ourselves as conquerors and overcomers, because we believe that He is God and more than able to bring us through.

We pray in faith – there is no other way to pray. Why would we ask, if we do not have faith to believe that God is able to do just what He said He would do? In exercising our faith, we reach out and give thanks in advance, knowing that He has done it before and can do it again.

No matter what today holds, know that God is more than able to bring you through. By faith in God, victory is possible. Remember, faith does not mean that the answer will always be our desired outcome. So, allow your faith to walk in alignment with the Father's will and accept His plans for you.

CDK

WEDNESDAY 30th

For we walk by faith, not by sight
2 Corinthians 5:7

THE FAITH WALK – Reading: Matthew 14:22-33

We are used to working with facts, and are always seeking for factual information, *"What time will you be here?", "How will I get there?" "How long will it take?" "Do I need to bring anything with me?" "Who else will be there?" "How much will it cost?" "Will I get better?" "What's the prognosis?"* We also make full use of available technology and search online for anything that we need to know.

This is completely at odds with our feature verse for today. For many of us, we walk by sight and not by faith. We may even qualify our limited faith as 'using wisdom'! Faith does not depend on facts because quite often, facts contradict the call for faith. We sometimes become so overwhelmed with facts that our faith cannot rise.

Something simple that's worth remembering is God never sets us up to fail. The fear we sometimes have is, *"What if I take a step of faith and I end up looking like a fool"?* But a fool to who? Lack of faith speaks of a lack of or an immature relationship with God, we are therefore uncertain of His voice so will say things like, *"I was going to do it but I thought it was just my mind".* I do believe in getting confirmation for certain things but how many witnesses do you need, and for how long?

Peter was the only disciple who dared to step out of the boat, not on to dry land, but into real water! What made him do that? Relationship! Having wondered whether they were seeing a ghost walking on the sea in the storm, Jesus had already assured the disciples, *"It is I, be not afraid"* (Matthew 14:27). Peter then said, *"Lord, if it's you, bid me to come"* (v28). Jesus said to him, *"Come".* That was all Peter needed to hear. Jesus did not have to keep on repeating, *"Come",* He said it only once and that was enough for Peter. The other disciples stayed where they were, just watching.

The question for today is, how long will you stay in the safety and security of where you are, when Jesus is beckoning you to, *"Come"*?

Also, is your confidence in yourself, or is it in God? You will never get anywhere by staying where you are!

JEJ

May
Time to Pray

THURSDAY 1st

So (Jesus) prayed very hard in anguish. His sweat became as drops of blood, trickling to the ground
Luke 22:44 (GW)

CONSIDER JESUS & PRAY - Reading: Mark 14:32-42

Jesus has left us with the perfect example of how to behave under pressure: **pray**!

With His finishing works ahead, Jesus was fully aware what that meant; the lethal death by crucifixion; His cup of suffering.

Look at the contrast, His disciples fell asleep for sorrow, and exhaustion, being overwhelmed with sadness. Naturally, humankind tends to want to 'sleep away' their troubles and fears by cutting to numb the pain, or, more drastically, attempted or completed suicide, as a way of escape. Our circumstances can be frightening, where we want to bury our head in the sand of life.

Yet, Jesus felt all that sorrow and more, but prayed! When we consider Jesus in His humanity, the period leading up to His death was an agonising one for Him. The struggle was real! Conflict of the Father's will versus the will of His flesh for comfort and ease. However, in His prayer-attitude, He conquered the desires of the flesh by intensifying His prayer in the struggle. A wilful submission to God's plan; fulfilling the will of His Father.

It is not so much the overwhelming circumstance, but our attitude towards it. So, use that prayer life-line. He taught us to pray God's will be done and not ours. Therefore, let us consider Jesus whilst we're under the pressure, and earnestly pray - it is time!

Pastor Josephine

FRIDAY 2nd

And being in an agony he prayed more earnestly…
Luke 22:44

IT'S ALWAYS THE RIGHT TIME TO PRAY - Reading: Luke 22:39-46

The beauty of prayer is that, there's never a time not to pray.

Sometimes we say that we don't have time to pray, but that is doing ourselves a disservice because, *"(We) ought to always pray, and not faint"* (Luke 18:1). So, the time to pray is, always!

Always, because there are always situations that will come upon you. Always circumstances you have no control over. Always a time to ring Home, always a time for going into the throne room. Always a time to commune with the Father, to sup with Him, and tell Him all about your troubles.

So rather than fainting, rather than giving up, rather than being overtaken by the circumstances, pray about everything. Jesus said to, *"Pray that you don't enter into temptation"* (Luke 22:40), because temptation will come. Prayer helps to build up your spiritual muscles so that you're strong and not easily overcome by evil.

Pray earnestly when you're feeling the agony of a situation! Scripture says that when we run out of words, and know not what to say, when we can only groan, the Holy Ghost will step in, and stand in the gap (Romans 8:26-27). Because you're experiencing such turmoil, the Spirit intercedes with words that cannot be uttered, and prays the Will of God.

Sis Jx

SATURDAY 3rd

(Daniel) kneeled upon his knees three times a day, and prayed, and gave thanks…as he did aforetime
Daniel 6:10

PRAY AS YOU ALWAYS DO - Reading: Daniel 6:4-16

We often sing the song, *"I must tell Jesus all of my trials, … Jesus can help me, Jesus alone" (Elisha Hoffman).*

The pastor who penned this song, wrote it after visiting a distressed parishioner who didn't know what to do in her dire situation. He told her, *"You must tell it to Jesus"*. *"Yes"*, she said, *"Yes, I must tell Jesus"*. As the pastor left her home, all that he could hear was her voice saying, *"I must tell Jesus"*; hence the song.

We don't know if the parishioner had a prayer life, but in her distress, she forgot to speak to Jesus.

The odds were against Daniel; if he prayed to God, he would die. However, Daniel didn't care about dying, all that he wanted to do was to pray as he always did. Prayer was more important to Daniel than death!

Interestingly, Daniel didn't pray for deliverance, but he prayed a prayer of thanksgiving. He remembered what God had done for him, recognised who God was, and gave thanks.

In your hard times, it's important to take the time to pray and remember who God is, and what he has done for you. Give Him thanks at all times. This was nothing new for Daniel, he prayed as he always did.

The problem for some of us is that there is no prayer routine so, in times of hardship, we find it hard to pray. But if we develop a robust prayer life, when bad times come, we will be fearless like Daniel and, *"pray as you always do"*.

Lady Pam Lewin

SUNDAY 4th

If...I will hear from heaven, and will forgive their sin, and will heal their land

2 Chronicles 7:13-14

THE SOUND OF INTERCESSION – Reading: 2 Chronicles 7:11-22

The setting for this stirring passage of scripture, so frequently quoted, was after King Solomon had finished building the temple that his father, King David, had in his heart to build.

Solomon prayed and dedicated the temple, asking God to dwell there and honour those who seek Him in the temple. Solomon knew that Israel would sin and turn away from the true God, and come back and ask forgiveness, as they did so many times before. Solomon therefore asked the LORD, when you hear the people pray, forgive them, and bring them back to the land that you have promised them and their fathers.

After Solomon finished praying the prayer of dedication, fire came down from the heavens and consumed the burnt offerings. The glory of the Lord so filled the temple that even the priests could not enter the house! For seven days, they praised and feasted.

God then appeared to Solomon by night and confirmed that not only had He heard Solomon's prayer, but also His house was a house of prayer and a house of sacrifice.

God will allow circumstances in our lives to come to let us know that He alone is truly in charge. He said, *"If I shut up heaven that there be no rain, or if I command the locusts to devour the land, or if I send pestilence among my people; if my people who are called by my name shall humble themselves..."* (2 Chronicles 7:13-14). This is how we know that we can move the LORD by the sound of intercession. First, we must humble ourselves, pray, seek His face and turn from our wicked ways. Then the LORD said, *"I will hear from heaven, and will forgive their sin, and will heal their land"*.

The Lord knew Israel's tendencies to stray and wonder away to foreign gods. We too at times may find ourselves falling short. The song writer penned it this way, *"Prone to wander, Lord, I feel it… prone to leave the God I love. Take my heart, oh take and seal it …. with thy Spirit from above"*.

God is moved by the sound of intercession!

Lady Winsome Saunders
USA

*MONDAY 5th

And (Hannah) was in bitterness of soul, and prayed unto the LORD, and wept sore
1 Samuel 1:10

WHEN NO ONE UNDERSTANDS YOU – Reading:1 Samuel 1:1-20

It's always time to pray - after all, we are asked to pray without ceasing (1 Thessalonians 5:17).

Let us consider the situation of Hannah - she is happily married to Elkanah. He loves Hannah and is very generous towards her. They make an annual trip to sacrifice in Shiloh, but Hannah does not enjoy these experiences. There is one thing missing as far as Hannah is concerned, she just wants to have a child.

There is also another thing that pains her - the presence of Elkanah's other wife, Peninnah. Peninnah has several children. Peninnah provokes Hannah and makes her fret. Hannah weeps and cannot eat because she is so upset. Elkanah notices Hannah's distress and asks her if he is not better to her than ten sons. Nobody at home understood her pain so Hannah went to the house of God…

When Hannah reaches the house of God, she finds the priest, Eli, sitting on a seat by a post of the temple. Hannah was in bitterness of soul and prayed in her heart to God. Hannah made a vow unto God that if He gives her a son, she will give him back into the service of the Lord. She would raise this son according to the Nazarite vow, i.e., no haircuts, no alcohol, and no touching of dead bodies.

Now because Hannah was praying in her heart and only moving her lips, Eli thought that she was drunk - he did not understand her! So, she had to explain that she had a sorrowful spirit and had poured out her soul and grief to the Lord. It would not have been appropriate for Hannah to discuss her personal situation with the priest. Eli said to her, *"Go in peace and the God of Israel grant thee thy petition" (v17).*

God heard Hannah and a year later she had a son whom, when she had weaned him, she took to live with Eli in the temple. We know him as Samuel:

- the child to whom God spoke
- High priest unto the Lord
- Last of the Judges of Israel
- Anointer of King Saul and King David
- Prophet of the Lord
- Military leader

Hannah went on to have three more sons and two daughters with Elkanah.

When no one else understands…pray!

BVG

Early May Bank Holiday (UK)

TUESDAY 6th

And the prayer of faith shall save the sick, and the Lord shall raise him up; and if he have committed sins, they shall be forgiven him –
James 5:15

THE PRAYER OF FAITH – Reading: James 5:13-18

The prayer of faith shall save the sick is a loaded statement in James 5:15. It suggests that some prayers are not of faith and ultimately will not achieve desired results. When one considers the implications of this verse, an important question looms, *"What is the prayer of faith?"*

The prayer of faith is not a monumental task that can only be achieved by Christian stalwarts. It is simply offering prayer in faith. It is prayer that proceeds from faith, having unwavering confidence in God that He will do what's best, and completely committing the situation into His hands. It is more than saying a prayer or repeating words. It is truly meaning the words that are said and believing that God will, out of His bounty of love and grace, act to deal with the situation in the best way.

How many times in prayer have we said words but somehow still wonder if things will work out? That's not praying in faith. How many times have our prayers been merely crying as an emotional response to situations and more begging God to intervene than expressing faith in Him dealing with the situation? Like I have experienced, you might have sought God on some matter without seeing results. Could it be that crying, begging, repetition of cliché phrases, or offering formal prayer was not mixed with faith?

I am reminded about the Syrophoenician woman in Matthew 15: 22–28 who came to Jesus crying about her ailing daughter, but Jesus answered her not a word. Yes, it is true, Jesus gave her no reply although she cried. He later responded when she worshipped and addressed her concern when she demonstrated faith. I have come to realise that God does not respond to our tears, our mere words, or even our pain, He responds to our faith. It is not enough to say a prayer, we should pray in faith.

Make a decision to go beyond how you feel or think about the situations you bring to God, and believe that He will give you His best as you pray in faith today.

Keshawna Salmon-Ferguson
Jamaica

WEDNESDAY 7th

Hear, O LORD, when I cry with my voice: have mercy also upon me, and answer me
Psalm 27:7

HOW FAR IS FAR? - Reading: Psalm 27:7; Psalm 61:1-8

Prayer is an awesomely powerful tool, and by it we have access to God's answers.

The Bible declares that His ears are not heavy so that they cannot hear, neither His hands shortened that they cannot save (Isaiah 59:1).

Indeed, we are encouraged to let the Lord know our requests and there is an attendant peace that comes when we unburden ourselves before Him (Philippians 4:6&7).

What sometimes discourages us when we begin to pray is that often the opposite of what we've asked for seems to be happening! However, 2 Corinthians 4:18 tells us that what is unseen is eternal and everything that can be seen is temporary. When, for example, we pray for someone and many unseemly things start to manifest, we should rather rejoice for the very fact that they are revealed shows that the Lord has just stamped a big fat "sell by date" on them!

I remember once crying out to Jesus about a person I was praying for...they appeared to be going further and further in the opposite direction. My lament was, *"Oh Lord they are so far from you?"* Immediately, I felt Him say, *"How far is far?"*! Right then, God reminded me that the prodigal son at his lowest point, his furthest descent into depravity was NEAREST to his Salvation (Luke15:16-20)!

Be encouraged! Truly the Most High can reach into the deepest depths, His hands are not shortened and His ears are open to the faintest of our cries!

Gudrun Witt
Zimbabwe

THURSDAY 8th

If I had not confessed the sin in my heart, the Lord would not have listened
Psalm 66:18 (NLT)

A PRAYER FROM THE HEART, NOT THE LIPS – Reading: Psalm 66:1-20

Let us pray...

Father in the name of Jesus, our God, our Saviour, our Lord, our King, our Master, our everything.

We give all honour to you; you alone are worthy. We thank you Heavenly Father for you are our always accessible God. Father, Jesus, we come before you acknowledging that there is no one that understands us like you do. Lord, please purify our hearts that are prayers will not be hindered. Father, Jesus you see the struggles that we go through. Father, you see when we are hurt, you know who has caused us such pain and discomfort. Father Jesus sometimes they cause so much damage that we struggle to recover from it. Lord Jesus, our heart becomes heavy as we hold the individual as prisoner in our heart. We pour out the contents of our hearts before you Lord, because if we regard iniquity in our heart, you will not hear us.

Father, we need you to hear our prayers because only you can get to the core of the situation we face. Lord, sometimes our character and integrity are being attacked by the very ones that are closest to us. O Lord my God, we allow the spirit of jealousy and resentment to clog up the flow of brotherly love that should be flowing freely through our heart. Lord Jesus, we need a release to prevent spiritual heart attack.

Almighty God, give us the grace and strength to let go of the sins that so easily beset us. Help us to be willing to surrender iniquity into your hands, because you want to hear and act on the prayers that are issued from our hearts, not just our lips.

Lord, please create within us a clean heart, so that we can serve you and know how to love each other with the pure love of our Heavenly Father. Lord, help us not to let sin block the passage of our prayers, because we need to hear from you and we need you to hear our prayers, for you are the prayer-answering God, and we thank you for love, forgiveness, patience and compassion.

We are the result of prayers that have been prayed from pure hearts, and we have proof that those prayers have been heard.

Thank you, Heavenly Father, Jesus. Thank you.

Minister/Lady Genevieve Dinnall

FRIDAY 9th

Peter was kept in prison, but earnest prayer for him was made to God by the church
Acts 12:5 (ESV)

PRAYING FOR GOD TO DO THE MIRACULOUS – Reading: Acts 12:1-19

Time is very precious and once spent, it is gone forever. If we use the time given to us by God well, it will be profitable for His kingdom - especially time given in prayer. It is then that we truly see the almighty hand of God miraculously moving mountains and changing the impossible into the possible in the lives of those for whom we are interceding, and in our lives also.

Note, in our key verse from Acts 12:5, Peter was in prison. There was no way out. He was in chains and heavily guarded. It is evident as we read verse 6 that Peter was in an impossible situation; he truly needed a miracle.

Nevertheless, prayer was made for Peter without ceasing. The church was committed and created a continuous prayer chain all around. 1 Thessalonians 5:17 exhorts us to pray without ceasing. We are to pray continually, to pray intentionally, to prayer fervently, in other words we are to live a prayer-filled life.

It was the intentional, fervent, and continual prayers of the saints of God for Peter, that the Lord Jesus Christ heard and answered. He honoured their faith and wrought the miracle for which they had all prayed. Jesus did the impossible! Jesus did the miraculous! He sent an angel to the prison and Peter's chains were broken, the prison doors were opened and he was set free!

It is time to pray for the miraculous!

Rena Grzeszczyk

SATURDAY 10th

One lamb thou shalt offer in the morning; and the other lamb thou shalt offer at even
Exodus 29:39

A SACRIFICE OF PRAYER – Reading: Exodus 29:37-46

The prescription today is Prayer for our daily offering to the Lord.

Our most powerful resource is earnest prayer continually, i.e., in the good and bad times. Prayers of thanksgiving, protection, guidance and peace for all in authority (1 Timothy 2:1-2).

Daniel turned to prayer and fasting in the midst of adversity (Daniel 9:3-5). A lesson for us today is that, as Daniel confessed his sins and asked God for forgiveness, so let us examine ourselves first, and not be quick to blame others. Many people are blaming climate change for the deterioration of our environment, but we serve a God who is the Master/Creator of every climate and is in control (Genesis 1).

We can also see that through prayer Elijah announced that God would withhold rain for three-and-a-half years as His judgment on the disobedient people (1 Kings 17:1-3). Please note that through this period of drought, God would take care of His faithful servant as He led him, fed him, and enabled him to help others. When we walk by faith, our God will supply all of our needs (Philippians 4:19).

It is therefore important for us to trust the Provider, and not the provision. We serve a mighty God that never, never fails (Ephesians 3:20).

Evg. DG

SUNDAY 11th

...Lord, teach us to pray...Luke 11:1

START A CONVERSATION – Reading: Luke 11:1-13

Prayer is simply a conversation with God. Conversation is a dialogue, not a monologue; it involves one person speaking while the other is listening. Each person has a chance to say something.

Prayer is a means by which we demonstrate our relationship and connection with God. It is a moment of surrender and submission to Him, where we place our lives into His hands. We place our hopes, desires, challenges and our needs before God at the precious throne of grace. We pour out our hearts, trusting and depending on the grace of God to cover and hold us.

Prayer allows us to build a relationship with God as we take the time to listen for His voice. It's okay to not pray like someone else! We must talk with God in our own unique and special way that is peculiar to our personal relationship with Him.

Sometimes we look at the prayer lives of others and see how God moves and answers their prayers then, as a result, feel that we are not doing enough. We know we want more – more faith, more trust, more and greater testimonies. In the book *'Spiritual Letters'* by Dom John Chapman, it says, **"Pray as you can, not as you can't"!**. When I came across this quote, it caused me to stop and reflect. It reminded me of the need to build my own relationship with God, to learn to listen to His voice, to allow Him to guide me, to offer up my own thanks and praise, as I seek His presence.

Use your times of prayer to focus and recognise who God is. Listen to what He wants to say to you, reflect on all that God has done and can do, and give Him praise each and every day.

CDK

MONDAY 12th

And he prayed again and the heaven gave rain and the earth brought forth her fruit
James 5:18

PRAY AGAIN! Reading: 1 Kings 18:1-46

The word *"again"* means another time. In James 5:13-18 there is an emphasis regarding prayer mentioned seven times, once is not enough!

The remedy for the afflicted is pray! When we pray for the sick, they are healed. The passionate prayer of the righteous achieves much. Prayer leads to great results. Naaman was told to wash seven times in the dirty river; if he only washed once, he would not have received his complete healing.

Prayer is the language of breakthrough. Prayer will unlock the doors that have been closed. Prayer is God connecting to His people. Prayer is God answering His people. Prayer is where God listens. He understands and knows our heart's desire.

Consider the pianist practising for hours, the orchestra reaching a harmonious melody after continuous rehearsals. Just as they play on, we must keep praying.

I remember praying for a job, the interview did not go well. When I prayed again, God blessed me with the job of His choice, so bring your situation to the Lord. If your request is a desire to be married, for peace of mind, or revival for this nation, pray one more time! Your prayer will silence the enemy, give you hope, increase faith, it will result in victory.

Be fruitful in prayer, your prayer is like scattering seeds. We may not see the growth that takes place on the inside, but one day that seed will begin to sprout and the evidence of praying becomes visible. Hallelujah!

When we pray it is like the Lord waters the seed. Keep praying, there will be growth. The Lord will allow the seed to bring forth much fruit. Don't stop praying, remember your seed needs to be watered. Pray again.

Selina Grant

TUESDAY 13th

I exhort therefore that, first of all, supplications, prayers, intercessions, and giving of thanks, be made for all men; for kings, and for all that are in authority…
1 Timothy 2:1-2

AN EVERY DAY PRAYER - Reading: 1 Timothy 2:1-8

Paul in today's scripture reading, gives clear instructions to Timothy to make supplications, prayers, and intercessions for everyone. He makes a specific appeal for kings and all who are in authority that we may lead a quiet and peaceable life (1 Timothy 2:1-2).

I took note and wondered how often do I/we pray for world rulers and our government leaders? Do we only complain about them? Many of us have a set list of individuals for whom we pray every day. When was the last time that you prayed for your Prime Minister or President and their leadership cabinet? If we're honest, we mainly mention the Royal Family or our political leaders when there is a major unfortunate or tragic occurrence announced concerning them. We pray for our church leaders but not for world leaders as we should.

It's possible that Timothy would not have called their names to God either, hence why Paul gave him this important action point. Timothy needed no reminder to pray for his family, friends and brethren, but those who make laws and put their signature to endorse new legislations, Paul said *"I urge you…make specific requests, pray and intercede for them"* because their decisions will affect your daily life.

In our troubled End Times, as leaders rise and fall, may we respond to Paul's appeal to Timothy and every believer – devoted prayers are needed now more than ever. Let's each see it as our personal responsibility to extend our prayer lists beyond the familiar. The entire world is in crisis and needs the church's prayers, every day.

JEJ

WEDNESDAY 14th

Pray without ceasing
1 Thessalonians 5:17

NON-STOP PRAYER - Reading: 1 Thessalonians 5:12-28

I received a text recently which reminded me of the first cordless telephone.

This was not an iPhone or an Android mobile like a Samsung phone with all its impressive features. This mode of communication is called Prayer. It does not suffer from interference or poor signal, and it never has the setting switched to, *'Do not disturb'*, where you have to call repeatedly for the person to answer!

Prayer was created thousands of years ago. The manufacturers of Apple and Samsung can ever be a competitor or match to the first cordless telephone as the storage is never full and it is self-charging.

As I encourage myself, and other women reading this, may I say that nothing beats prayer, prayer beats everything. The Word of God encourages everyone to pray continuously. Why? Once you become a child of God you are in a relationship, therefore we must seek first the kingdom of God and everything else will be added to us.

The action of bowing our heads and closing our eyes is a custom of praying. However, prayer is communication with our heavenly father, it does not matter where we are, we can live every day in constant communication.

There are times when it is important to go into our closet, shut the door and share what is on our hearts with our sovereign Lord, even though He already knows our thoughts and what is in our hearts. The power of prayer cannot be underestimated, it is the tool God has divinely given to enter into his throne room.

Missionary Audrey Simpson

THURSDAY 15th

Pray for the peace of Jerusalem! May they be secure who love you
Psalm 122:6 (ESV)

PRAY FOR PEACE – Reading: Psalm 122:1-9; 1Timothy 2:1-3

Glory and honour to our Lord and King, Jesus Christ, who is, who was, and who is to come. Psalm 122: 6 commands us specifically to pray for the peace of Jerusalem.

Therefore, we gird our loins with truth, put on the breastplate of righteousness, and with our feet shod with the preparation of the gospel of peace, we take the shield of faith, the helmet of salvation, and the sword of the Spirit which is the Word of God that we may be able to stand against the wiles of the devil (Ephesians 6:11-15). It is time to pray without ceasing for the peace of Jerusalem, a city set on a hill, the city of the great King. It is the place where God chose to place His name, and the very place where our Lord Jesus Christ was crucified. Pray when all seems lost; pray when all is going well.

Peace be within your walls, and prosperity be within your palaces; Oh, Jerusalem and in all Israel. The LORD is your shield and buckler; and the rock of your salvation. He is your helper, a very present help in trouble; for He is a man of war and will fight your battles.

1 Timothy 2: 1-3 also requires us to pray for all men, and for all that are in authority, *"that we may lead a quiet and peaceable life"*. So, we cry out and shout for the inhabitants of Zion and for all in Israel, that *"the word of the Lord may have a free course, and be glorified"* (2 Thessalonians 3:1). Pray for wisdom for the Prime Minister and leaders of that nation. May the Lord lead and guide them in their decision-making at all times.

"The effectual fervent prayer of a righteous man availeth much" (James 5:16); so, **P**ray **U**ntil **S**omething **H**appens (PUSH!) in Jesus' name. Amen!

Dr Anna Crouch

FRIDAY 16th

Please listen, God, and answer my prayer!
Psalm 61:1 (CEV)

HEAR MY CRY, O GOD - Reading: Psalm 61:1-8

King David's cry to God at the beginning of this Psalm is heartfelt. He is in trouble, far from home and does not know what to do next, so he turns to the one who can help.

David encourages himself with God's promises, and repeats his allegiance to the God he knows. God is his rock, his shelter and his strong tower. Where do we go when we need help? We may not be in David's situation, but we serve the same God and we have access to the same help, no matter what.

God responds to prayer! We just need to cry out to Him.

Have you ever been lost? It's a very uncomfortable feeling. I can clearly recall being in Germany with a National Apostolic Choir for the Kirchentag. We were taking part in a Youth Festival, and sang at various churches and open-air services. Our timetable was strict to attend all the events. One day we were dropped off by our co-ordinator at a shopping mall to buy souvenirs; we were given our pickup time and told that the coach would be leaving promptly to reach our next event.

Two of us spent too long shopping and missed the coach; we were left stranded! We were able to speak a few words of German but not enough to explain ourselves, so we prayed standing in front of the shopping mall. It was one of those, *"Help Lord!"* prayers. We were lost in a strange country, had no means of communication (this was pre-mobile phones and satellite navigation). We were completely dependent on God.

Thankfully we had a copy of our itinerary, so agreed that the best thing to do would be to ask for help. We looked around and saw a couple that looked approachable, they spoke a little English and told us to go straight. We started to walk, then ran in the direction they had indicated.

May 2025
Theme: Time to Pray

We stopped at every junction and looked around us, but kept going straight. Finally, we saw a church and heard one of our choir songs. It sounded so good, and it was even better when we saw the faces of our choir members! We never missed the coach again. God heard our prayers!

So, no matter what your situation is today, He is the same God. Cry out; He will attend unto your prayer.

BVG

SATURDAY 17th

Then enquired (the nobleman) of them the hour when (his son) began to amend. And they said unto him, Yesterday, at the seventh hour the fever left him
John 4:52

BE SOMEBODY'S SOMEBODY - Reading: John 4:46-54

You may know this chorus:

Somebody prayed for me
They had me on their mind
They sacrificed their time and prayed for me
They must have known
That the Lord would see me through
I'm so glad somebody prayed for me.
(Unknown)

Each one of us at some stage in our lives has had to rely on the prayers of somebody else. That 'somebody' may never tell you that they were led to pray for you. They will have felt a burden within themselves to do a day of fasting and prayer because they could sense, through the Holy Spirit, that you were going through rough seas.

How grateful we are when we hear such a report of sensitivity within the body of Christ, that by our deeds we are living the Word which implores us to bear one another's burden and so fulfil the law of Christ (Galatians 6:2). During one of my dark seasons, I remember being at work and suddenly feeling a surge of spiritual strength. I didn't have to wonder if somebody was calling my name to God, and I didn't need to know who the somebody was either.

However, we too must be prepared to be so connected to the rest of the members of the body that, when prompted to pray for somebody, we will without hesitation also do our part. Somebody needs you to be their somebody to pray.

JEJ

SUNDAY 18th

But the prince of the kingdom of Persia withstood me twenty-one days: but, lo, Michael, one of the chief princes, came to help me; and I remained there with the kings of Persia
Daniel 10:13

YOUR HEART POSTURE FOR PRAYER - Reading: Daniel 10:1-21

I believe that verse 12 of Daniel 10 is an amazing verse of scripture that gives us great insight into prayer, how prayers should be made, and the efficacy of prayer.

How wonderful it is to know that when you set your heart to understand God's heart, His word, and His revelation that God is willing to go to war for your answer to prayer. None of your words are wasted when you pray and fast and afflict your soul in sincerity before God.

Thank God that He doesn't tune-out and daydream, which sometimes happens when in conversation with others! But every single word is accounted for, heard, kept, and acted on – what a mighty God we serve!

So, remember:

1) Set your heart to understand God's heart, let that be your motivation to pray, don't only pray to place your petitions at His feet.
2) Be willing to afflict and humble your soul with fasting as this is the spouse of prayer. Fasting with prayer shows that you are serious and dedicated to hearing from God.
3) Your words are heard and collected; oh, what a sweet aroma in the throne room of God they must be!
4) God will go to war to bring you your answer. When you are serious about God and His business, He will be serious about you and your business. Hallelujah!
5) Your heart-posture is as important as your prayer itself. May your heart bow in adoration lower than your knees before God.

MinK / Minister Kay Dawkins

MONDAY 19th

And the LORD said unto Moses...be ready in the morning, and come up in the morning unto mount Sinai, and present yourself there to me in the top of the mount.
Exodus 34:1-2

MORNING MOUNTAIN SUMMIT - Reading: Exodus 34:1-35

How do you begin your day? With your daily ablutions? By checking your phone for latest messages? Do you read, pray, and have your daily devotion with the Lord? Whatever you do, we see in this passage that God required a morning presentation of Moses at the top of Mount Sinai to receive the new tablets of stone with the ten commandments on them.

When God puts a meeting in your diary, you had better show up! Moses was given detailed instructions in preparation for the meeting with God.

We too have daily scheduled appointments with God. How privileged you are that He so longs to meet with you today to discuss His plans for your life; and just as Moses did, we need to:

1) Be Ready.

Be ready, make sure you are alert and prepared with everything you need. Check your heart posture, check that you've got your 'listening ears on', be ready not getting ready for your appointment with God. Have your pen and paper ready to record the revelations that God will give you with scribe-like diligence.

2) Come Up... To The Top.

Ascend above tiredness, distractions, trials, and all hinderances. You have to make a conscious decision to rise to the top just like oil on water. Why? I hear you cry. When you are at the top, in the quietness of the mountain summit you hear so clearly and see much further. A God-perspective will set you up perfectly for a brand-new day.

3) Present Yourself

Make a good presentation of yourself to meet with the King in His office which can be seen as your prayer closet and the throne of your heart. Engage and have a tête-á tête with the God of the morning summit.

Remember that when you have a morning mountain summit, as you meet with God to pray and bask in His presence, you spiritually enter a higher level. You take the higher ground and level-up in the Spirit, and you don't allow carnal things to keep you grounded. You spiritually replicate what the eagle does with its prey or predators. The eagle doesn't waste time wrestling and losing to the predator on the ground, it flies so high into the air that whatever is in its grip loses consciousness due to the change in altitude from being up so high.

So be ready! Come up… to the top! And present yourself; it's the best way to start any day. Anyone who kneels before God can stand before anyone.

Have a blessed and victorious day!

MinK/ Minister Kay Dawkins

TUESDAY 20th

When he had sent them away, he departed into a mountain to pray
Mark 6:46

ALONE TIME – Reading: Mark 6:45-52

Most of us like to be in the thick of things, in the middle of the excitement, in the heart of the matter.

We want to be where the action is happening, when it is happening, and generally want to feel indispensable. We want to be in a position to give a firsthand report rather than receiving one. We constantly remain on high alert, to ensure that we do not miss the latest happenings. In this state of hyper awareness and hyper vigilance, it is hard to hear the still small voice of God.

There comes a time when we need to shut down and shut out all of the noise, the chatter, the constant demands on our attention and focus only on God. Without these moments of solitude and quietness, we soon run out of power and die a silent death. These times are totally important to our survival; a time where we focus on 'praying' in an attitude of 'praising'.

In today's passage, we see Jesus leading by example. Whilst it is always a great idea to do good for others, to impart into our family and friends, to be available for those in need, there comes a time when we must consider ourselves to be also in need! In need of quiet moments with God. In need of restoration for our souls. In need of a renewed mind and spirit. In need of a little solitude to recharge.

We cannot afford to feel guilty in taking care of these needs when they arise. It is through these times that we are drawn closer to God. It is through these times that we receive the fortitude and the grace to carry on. It is through these times that we receive nourishment for our souls. It is from these times that we are able to pour out into others.

The next time you feel overwhelmed by the cares of this life, or under-appreciated by the people around you, actively seek some 'alone time' with God. **'Check out'** from being constantly on high alert for the world, and **'check in'** to being on high alert with God. You will stand amazed at how you will be refreshed and renewed by just taking *"time to pray"*.

Pastor Londy Esdaille
Nevis

WEDNESDAY 21st

Confess your faults one to another, and pray one for another, that ye may be healed. The effectual fervent prayer of a righteous man availeth much
James 5:16

LET US PRAY – Reading: James 5:1- 20

"*If my people, which are called by my name, shall humble themselves, and pray, and seek my face, and turn from their wicked ways; then will I hear from heaven, and will forgive their sin, and will heal their land*" (2 Chronicles 7:14).

Prayer takes humility, effort and faith. We are all commanded to pray and encouraged as the body of Christ in Hebrews 4:16, *"Let us therefore come boldly to the throne of grace, that we may obtain mercy and find grace to help in time of need".*

Often, we are literally called to stand in the gap for others, seeking for their forgiveness, peace and healing of their land. As the body of Christ, and individuals, the Lord is wanting us to be transparent with one another, striving to walk in integrity and uprightness of heart.

Psalm 66:18 *"If I regard iniquity in my heart, the Lord will not hear me"*

Psalm 133:1 *"Behold, how good and how pleasant it is for brethren to dwell together in unity!"*

As we enter the realm of unity, this creates such an assurance that we are in God's will and have obtained the liberty to command the blessings on the land.

Let's never stop praying as our healings and miracles, and revival, are just a prayer away.

Beverley Amaoade

THURSDAY 22nd

And Moses went up unto God...
Exodus 19:3

STAY IN TOUCH – Reading: Psalm 5:1-12

It's easy to lose touch with each other because of our busy lives, yet we are encouraged when we communicate with one another for, *"Iron sharpeneth iron"* (Proverbs 27:17).

Even more important is communication with God. Looking at the life of Moses today we see how often he went up to spend time with God. Moses was born to Amram and Jochebed (Exodus 6:20), who were of the tribe of Levi.

The children of Israel who were originally welcomed into Egypt were now used as slaves and had to make bricks and mortar and work in the fields. The King of Egypt even went so far as to tell the midwives to kill all the male babies who were born; he thought that there would be fewer Israelites to fight against him that way.

However, when Moses was born, his mother hid him for three months. When she could no longer hide him, she made an ark of bulrushes and put it in the river. Moses was found by Pharaoh's daughter and raised as a Prince in Egypt. Though Moses knew that he was an Israelite, he did not know his calling until the day when he saw a burning bush in the desert. God had positioned him to lead His people out of Egyptian slavery. This was not going to be an easy journey but as long as Moses kept in communication with God he would succeed.

He did not always get it right but he kept going back to God. The Israelites were now about 600,000 men, besides women and children and a mixed multitude.

God always has a plan, so no matter what our circumstances let us stay in touch with the One who calls us to come up to Him today.

BVG

FRIDAY 23rd

The LORD descended in the cloud, and stood with him there
Exodus 34:5

A TIME FOR RENEWAL – Reading: Exodus 34:1-5

God is gracious and patient, and gives us different opportunities for renewal, so do not quit.

Hold on to His everlasting arms and cry out for help from the Solid Rock (Psalm 61:1). Whenever you are going through challenging times, take stock and remember that God is available 24/7; He's never too busy to hear your cry. Worrying about your troubles will not change your circumstances, but when you present yourself before the Lord and ask for forgiveness, He will grant your petition. When you feel alone, take time out to pray. Let God lift you up and place you on the Rock that will never sink. God is kind and compassionate; He will restore your losses (Job 42:10).

Prayer changes things and people - starting with the one who does the praying! The benefits of praying will be evident. There are times in life when we reach a crossroad, and need to make a decision as what turn to take. It is always best to seek the Lord, and not to lean on our own understanding or feelings. When we trust Him fully, He will direct us (Proverbs 3:5-6).

We are reminded in Psalm 139 that wherever we go, we can never move beyond God's care, guidance and supporting strength, so when we pray for a new vision, we need to submit to God and to follow wherever He leads.

Our God can do much more than we can ask or desire in prayer; His ability exceeds anything that we can imagine (Ephesians 3:20). We can therefore take courage today that God has the ability to do anything. Pray and depend, remember that He is not limited to human times (Psalm 90:14). He is the great 'I AM' (Exodus 3:14) and on time in every situation!

Evg. D.G.

SATURDAY 24th

But I tell you, do not swear an oath at all: either by heaven, for it is God's throne; nor by earth; for it is his footstool...
Matthew 5:34-35

A TIME OF SWEET COMMUNICATION – Reading: Matthew 5:33-37

We often find ourselves in dire situations that require us to seek God's intervention desperately.

During those times, many of us swear an oath to God, promising to do something if He helps us. However, once the situation is resolved, we often forget our promises to God. If we make oaths, we must honor them. Making oaths shows weakness in our word, so it's better to let our *"Yes"* mean *"Yes"*, and our *"No"* mean *"No"*.

Prayer is a time of sweet communication where we speak to and listen to God. It's a daily relationship with God. 1 Thessalonians 5:16-18 says, *"Pray without ceasing..."* Does this mean that we should stop our daily activities and be always on our knees praying? No. It simply means that no matter where we are, or what activity we are engaged in, we can be in constant communion with God.

When we are in constant prayer with our Lord and Savior, there is no need to use empty phrases or swear an oath because our Father in heaven is already familiar with our situation, and stands ready to help us.

Marlene Hines
Jamaica

SUNDAY 25th

When thou saidst, Seek ye my face; my heart said unto thee, Thy face, LORD, will I seek

Psalm 27:8

THY WILL BE DONE – Reading: Psalm 27: 1-14

"Teach me from my heart to say, thy will be done!".

It's a line of verse that we commonly sing, but we can fail to realise its level of importance as a prayer.

As God instructs David to *"seek his face"*, a fervent and faithful pursuit of the LORD, must and should now take place, pacing throughout his entire lifetime.

While the face of God cannot be seen by man, due to our poignant, and sinful state, the obedient response of our *"broken and contrite heart"* (Psalm 51:17) allows us passage to embark upon actively seeking Him out, as He will not "despise" us for it. Hence, our hearts must commune with God and follow His will, His plan, and His agenda, as He desires relationship with us despite our negligence and initial rejection of Him.

The Lord still reminds us, no matter the situation or circumstance, to look for Him, and if God can ask for intimacy, how can we deny Him?

G~R

*MONDAY 26th

Praying always with all prayer and supplication in the Spirit, and watching thereunto with all perseverance and supplication for all saints
Ephesians 6:18

SUPPORT FOR EACH OTHER THROUGH PRAYER
Reading: Ephesians 6:10-24

Prayer is the uplifting of one's heart to God.

As far back as I can remember, my parents used to call our family together for prayer time. Everyone had to pray individually. My prayer was always, *"Gentle Jesus, meek and mild, look upon this little child. Pity my simplicity, suffer me to come to Thee".* I was about eight years old.

One morning, as we gathered and knelt by their bed, my mom said to me that she wants me to start saying my own prayer. I panicked because all I knew was, *"Gentle Jesus…".* I remember opening the Sacred Songs and Solos songbook, and quickly finding a song that sounded like a prayer. Wen it was my turn, I read it. After everyone had prayed and got up off our knees, my mom said to me that my prayer was good but, the next time, I should find something in my heart that I wanted to say to God - not from the hymn book or anything else that I had been reciting.

All day that day, I practiced saying what was in my heart and the next morning, in my own simple way, I asked God to bless my parents, my brother and sister and all the people in our church and all the people in the world. As I grew older and developed in prayer, I realised that according to God's Word, it was so important for us to make supplication (petition) for all Saints.

May we continue to make **supplication** for each other because our very existence and victory depends on it!

Evangelist Patricia Pierre

*Spring Bank Holiday (UK)

TUESDAY 27th

When my heart is overwhelmed: lead me to the rock that is higher than I
Psalm 61:2

YOU ARE MY SHELTER AND STRONG TOWER
Reading Psalm 61:1-8

The word *"overwhelmed"* is translated from the Hebrew word *"ataph"* which has a primitive root meaning a shroud, giving the sense of being covered – being in darkness. When we feel overwhelmed, there is a sense of losing perspective because we can't see direction or position with respect to everything else. We can feel stuck, hopeless, and fearful.

It is this feeling that David describes in Psalm 62. He perhaps felt at the end of his own human understanding, strength, and resources; he had reached the limit of his own wisdom, endurance, and ability. Sometimes this feeling of being overwhelmed comes from nowhere. It isn't brought on by a particular 'thing'; yet sometimes it's brought on by 'many things.'

Overwhelming feelings exist, but so does our God, who is our Shelter and our Perspective Adjuster. Job puts it this way: *"Look, I go forward, but He is not there, And backward, but I cannot perceive Him; When He works on the left hand, I cannot behold Him; When He turns to the right hand, I cannot see Him. But He knows the way that I take; When He has tested me, I shall come forth as gold"* (Job 23:8-10 NKJV).

Yes, there are times when we become overwhelmed, but He knows the way, He knows where we are. Prayer at these times is not just about warfare, it's about being still in His presence. Our joy, peace, restoration, healing, and clarity of mind lie there.

Carmen Hibbert

WEDNESDAY 28th

What, could ye not watch with me one hour? Watch and pray, that ye enter not into temptation`; the spirit is willing but the flesh is weak
Matthew 26:40-41

SLEEPING THROUGH THE STORM - Reading: Matthew 26:36-46

You are on the other end of the telephone, pouring your heart out to your best friend about an ugly experience that's left you traumatised, when you suddenly realise that your friend has fallen asleep and you have been speaking to yourself for the last 30 minutes of the conversation.

That can blow the wind out of your sails, so to speak. *"How can you sleep through something so important to me?"* Jesus directs His comment to Peter, particularly, since he was the first to insist that he would rather die than deny his Lord and here he is, just a few hours later, fast asleep when Jesus needed him most. This is the beginning of Peter's road to conversion. This is where he gets a glimpse of his humanness, his vulnerability and his need to trust self less, and God more.

At this point, Jesus knows there's worse to come. He knows that if Peter had remained awake, he would have gained a sense of the magnitude of the situation and the pressure Christ was under. We are told that Jesus' sweat became like drops of blood (Luke 22:44). If Peter had seen that, and heard the prayer of Christ pleading with His Father to take the cup away from him, he may have defended rather than denied him later on.

Throughout the Bible, and especially in the New Testament, we are encouraged to watch and pray. Jesus cites this as the means by which we overcome temptation. This is how we gain strength and power to resist the devil that he may flee from us.

In the final part of the text, Jesus observes that the spirit is willing but the flesh is weak. All his disciples swore they would stay by him and hours later the fact is recorded that: 'they all forsook him and fled. What an embarrassment, but how like us as humans; unreliable and disloyal. It takes a compassionate Saviour to note that although, *"the spirit is willing, the flesh is weak"* (Matthew 26:41).

There is no harsh accosting spirit in those words, just a statement of fact. Jesus is clear about where his success came from. He does nothing of Himself. Likewise, His disciples are to cultivate dependence on God to build resilience against the enemy of souls. After Christ's death and resurrection, the disciples begin to understand and then we see significant changes in the lives of each one as they realise their humanity and need of divinity.

As modern-day disciples, we are to apply the tried and tested formula: watch, pray and depend on God. It will create harmony between flesh and spirit.

Cheryl Lowe
Guyana

THURSDAY 29th

I want everyone everywhere to lift innocent hands towards heaven and pray, without being angry or arguing with each other
1 Timothy 2:8 (CEV)

HOLY HANDS - Reading: 1 Timothy 2:1-8

Paul writes to Timothy, his son in the Lord, to help him with ministry.

His charge to Timothy stands as solid instructions for everyone - after all, we too have a ministry.

Just because Paul was no longer persecuting Christians, it did not mean that challenges to the Christian faith were over. The early church had so much opposition that it would be tempting to respond with anger and doubt about God's plan for them.

When Paul instructs Timothy about prayer and worship, he is talking about prayer as a means of developing a relationship with God, not just giving God a list of our woes and needs! God already knows all about us. Instead, we need to know more about Him and His wonder-working ways.

Remember that Jesus said, *"Come unto me all ye that labour and are heavy laden, and I will give you rest"* (Matthew 11:28). We just need to get in step with God, walking with Him, accepting His offer of a yoke that will not wear us down but help us share the burdens of life with Him.

That is how we learn about Him, by walking through life yoked to Him, experiencing His meekness and lowly heart. So many people are broken by loneliness while God is standing with open arms to comfort them, *"Take my yoke upon you and learn of me; for I am meek and lowly in heart; and ye shall find rest unto your souls. For my yoke is easy and my burden is light"* (Matthew 11:29-30).

Raised hands are the international sign of surrender. Prayer has us surrendering to God and His will, rather than having our own way:

*All to Jesus I surrender
All to Him I freely give
I will ever love and trust Him
In His presence daily live.*

*All to Jesus I surrender
Humbly at His feet I bow
Worldly pleasures all forsaken
Take me Jesus, take me now.*

*All to Jesus I surrender
Lord, I give myself to thee
Fill me with thy love and power
Let thy blessings fall on me.*

Refrain
*I surrender all
I surrender all
All to thee my blessed Saviour
I surrender all
(I Surrender All - Judson W Van Deventer)*

Let us continue to serve the One that saved us, He is able to keep our hands Holy.

BVG

FRIDAY 30th

Hide not your face from me. Turn not your servant away in anger, O you who have been my help. Cast me not off, forsake me not, O God of my salvation
Psalm 27:9

DARK SEASON - Reading: Numbers 6:24; Psalm 38:3; Isaiah 50:10; Hosea 6:3

Today's reading is a heartfelt cry from David expressing a deep desire for God not to hide His face (favour and grace) from Him. He is expressing a fear of rejection, a fear of being turned away in anger. What a thought! To be rejected by God! It would appear that David understood that his sins and failures could justifiably provoke God's anger. Psalm 38:3 reflects his deep awareness of his own shortcomings and his reliance on God's mercy.

As believers we all desire for the face of God to be turned toward us, to bless and sustain us (Psalm 67:1). In fact, who doesn't desire for the face of God to shine upon them (Numbers 6:24)? But sometimes, however, we go through seasons *"when darkness veils His lovely face"* - a line from the hymn My Hope is Built On Nothing Else written by Eric Mote in 1934. Times when we feel God is hiding, when we don't feel His presence. All the challenges, doubts or hardships may be obscuring our perception of God's presence.

Despite these challenges, the hymn emphasises the constancy and reliability of God's grace as an 'anchor' that holds firm. David knew this, ending the verse, referring to God as his *"help"* and the *"God of His salvation"*.

So my prayer is that when you walk through such a season, you would do what Isaiah 50:10 says: *"Let him who walks in darkness and has no light trust in the name of the LORD and rely on his God"*. Because *"His going out is sure as the dawn; he will come to us as the showers, as the spring rains that water the earth."* (Hosea 6:3).

CP

SATURDAY 31ˢᵗ

(Peter) came to the house of Mary the mother of John, whose surname was Mark; where many were gathered together praying
Acts 12:12

PRAYERFUL FRIENDS - Reading: Acts 12:1-12

When Noah came out of the ark after the flood waters had abated, the first thing that he did was to build an altar where he could offer sacrifices unto the LORD (Genesis 8:20).

Apostle Peter's first stop after his miraculous escape from prison, was to the house of Mary, mother of John Mark. Peter had a close relationship with the Mark's family such that John Mark was his son in the Gospel, in the same way that Timothy was to Paul.

By observation and regular visits, Peter will have known that Mary as a praying woman would quite likely at that time of day be holding a prayer meeting in her home. Of all the places that Peter could have chosen to stop-by first, he chose to go to a house of prayer. He wanted to thank the saints for praying him through and praying him out.

"Show me your company and I'll tell you who you are" is a proverb which my mom used to recite. It is a fact that you can tell a lot about a person just by their close companions (Amos 3:3). No wonder Peter was such an anointed apostle, sometimes referred to as the disciples' spokesman, and the one who had 'the key'. That's because he surrounded himself with prayer warriors!

If you want to be impactful in ministry, take a look at your friends. This will not only tell you who you are, but also where you are going!

JEJ

June
Family Life in the Bible

SUNDAY 1st

And the angel of the LORD said unto her, Behold, thou art with child, and shalt bear a son, and shalt call his name Ishmael; because the LORD hath heard thy affliction
Genesis 16:11

---◆●◆---

SAY SOMETHING! – Reading: Genesis 16:1-16

What a family life drama of highs and lows! Context shows conflict, jealousy, insecurities, hurts, yet tagged with the covenant of Promise. Someone has crossed paths with God's divine plan for that family; accepting cultural custom above God's way: hence trouble! Hagar is on the run from an undermined first lady, Sarai.

This scripture is also written for our learning; God hears! We find ourselves at times in varying, sticky, complex situations. Instead of quitting, we can be hopeful and receive God's comfort.

Therefore, crying out to God is crucial; we must say something, *"...the LORD hath heard thy affliction"*. The word affliction emphasises the idea of being under immense pressure or experiencing great trouble. Whether self-inflicted or not; the fact is; Hagar was afflicted but she was heard. How? God heard her saying something: she cried out to God from a heart that was ready to receive God's answer.

God must be the object of our faith, in our highs or in our lows. God hears faith! So, whether a tear, mutter, whisper, moan or groan, express in faith; help is near. When we are unable to utter the deep things of the heart: what do we do then? The Holy Spirit takes the unvoiced and with groanings adds voice in making intercession for us. So, say something in faith!

Pastor Josephine

MONDAY 2ⁿᵈ

Grant that these my two sons may sit, one on thy right hand, and the other on the left, in thy kingdom
Matthew 20:21

BELIEF & THE SPOKEN WORD – Reading: Matthew 20:20-28

It is not easy to keep believing in someone who has disappointed us.

There comes a time when we feel that we have arrived at the end of our tether because of disappointment. We expect to see certain behaviour in our loved ones, and it is missing. We expect to be accepted despite our faults and we are disappointed.

If we are truly honest with ourselves and those around us, we will admit that we are the ones who failed to live up to the expectations of others. We may have allowed hurt and/or anger to get the better of us and said things in haste that we can never retrieve.

There are many families that are fractured and splintered today because of harsh words spoken hastily. Our example from this passage can be that spoken words are powerful and can have a lasting effect on the hearers.

What words have we uttered that have caused the death of many in the church? What mistakes have we condemned as being unpardonable?

By speaking negative words, many lives can be lost. Words of affirmation can lead to life. Words of condemnation can lead to death. If we speak words of condemnation with faith and conviction, how many trees are we effectively removing from the body of Christ?

One young man carries within him an entire nation. Are we condemning that nation to the depths of the sea? One young woman carries within her an entire empire. Are we banishing that empire to the barrenness of the desert?

The need to believe and speak positive words is implicit in the scripture. The condemnation of the tree was swift and immediate. The upliftment of a fallen brother or sister can be equally swift and immediate. In which direction will our spoken words flow?

Pastor Londy Esdaille
Nevis

TUESDAY 3rd

...the LORD called Samuel: and he answered, Here am I
1 Samuel 3:4

THE RISE OF SAMUEL – Reading: 1 Samuel 3:1-21:

This scripture shows a family in crisis at Shiloh, and its impact on all of Israel.

God calls for the child, Samuel, to speak because the leadership was out of touch and out of line. Hence God was angry with Eli and his household and therefore aimed to purge the entire lineage from His holy order.

You could say that they were adult members of the family who were responsible for their own behaviour, and accountable to the wider office which they held. Even so, they had no regard for God nor the priesthood. As a result, the whole Kingdom came into disrepute, as judgment fell upon Shiloh and particularly the house of Eli.

Because the sins of Hophni and Phinehas were left unchecked, God intervened for the honour of His house and His great name. The House of Eli was banished with ramifications for generations. The House of Samuel was erected and established to the glory of God for there was a dereliction of duty by God's spokesman, Eli, the head of the family.

This resulted in *"Ichabod"* being pronounced (1 Samuel 4:21-22) in a dispensation when families were chosen to be custodians to uphold the commandments and statues of God, according to birthright. But the light went out at Shiloh, the glory of the LORD left when the ark was taken, death came to Eli and his sons.

Yet the child Samuel became God's voice for the season. So, another family was chosen as overseer, prophet, priest and judge of his generation. This continued until Israel rejected God and demanded a king like other nations, not wanting God Almighty to be their King anymore.

Sis Jx

WEDNESDAY 4th

And thou shalt teach them diligently unto thy children, and shall talk of them when thou sittest in thine house, and when thou walkest by the way, and when thou liest down, and when thou risest up
Deuteronomy 6:7

TO LOVE GOD IS TO OBEY HIS WORD – Reading: Deut. 6:1-25

In today's devotion, we read Moses' instructions to the children of Israel before entering into the Promised Land. He exhorted them to keep God's commandments in their heart, and then gave explicit instructions on how to teach those commandments to their children.

Jesus says, *"...the words that I speak unto you they are spirit, and they are life"* (John 6:63). There is therefore a responsibility placed upon us as parents, and the family of God, to train up our children to know and love God and others. Do not take it lightly or for granted that they will find God for themselves. They will be lost forever if we don't do what God has commanded.

We are to teach them diligently (Deuteronomy 6:6-7). Be persistent, don't give up! Let the Word of God be a lamp unto their feet and a light unto their path (Psalm 119:105). Let the Word be hidden in their hearts that they might not sin against God (Psalm 119:11). Every opportunity we get, let us teach them. This training is precious (see Proverbs 22:6). What we put into our children will remain with them for the rest of their lives.

Remember that God's Word never returns to Him void (Isaiah 55:11). Also, lead them by example in love, in discipline, in obedience and in reverence to God and His Word. God's commandments are as important today as when they were first given to Israel. As women of God, we are constrained by the same words not only to live a life with the laws of God in our hearts (Jeremiah 31:33), and mind (Hebrew 10:16) but to communicate them diligently to the next generation.

Sister Urcenette Adoti

THURSDAY 5th

But continue thou in the things which thou hast learned…knowing of whom thou hast learned them
2 Timothy 3:14

THE WILL OF GOD IN THE FAMILY – Reading: 2 Timothy 3:1-15

Praise be to the One that is Most High,
God, a place of life and a place to thrive,
Without such we are lost to the snare of worldly pressures,
But, succumb not to the temptations of worldly pleasures.

For God's Word is final and God's Word is just,
God our anchor, in God we trust,
It is through God that the darkness of the world is revealed to us,
And through Him we find peace, without a tussle, without a fuss.

For many will become blasphemous, may tempt you, against God's will,
But stay true to the Word of God, hold fast and be still,
For there are two sides to this world concerning the Lord in this day,
You are either for God or against God, there are no shades of grey.

It is the fear of God that keeps us grounded, it's the fear of God that keeps us humble,
And in your selflessness profess the love of God, be bold, do not mumble,
So, Women of God, let both the fear of God and the love of God order your steps,
And let your commitment to God and His will, be impetuously kept.

Name withheld

FRIDAY 6th

Isaac loved Esau...but Rebekah loved Jacob
Genesis 25:28

GOD LOVES US ALL EQUALLY – Reading: Genesis 25:27-28; Jeremiah 31:1-10

Some of us may relate to this story because we have grown up in homes where one or both parents preferred a sibling(s) over us. Despite assurances from our parent(s) that there were no favourites, and all siblings were loved equally, the actions displayed didn't synchronise with what was being said or felt.

Here, it is written that Jacob preferred Esau and Rebekah preferred Jacob. It's not surprising that the children grew up disliking and competing against each other; don't underestimate the impact of favouritism in a family. We only have to read the story of Joseph and his brothers; the favouritism of their father, Jacob, to Joseph led to jealousy amongst the siblings which led to attempted murder.

Merriam-Webster dictionary defines favouritism as *"the unfair practice of treating some people better than others"*.

Scripture says in Acts 10:34, *"...God is no respecter of persons"*, meaning that everyone will be treated the same.

Thank God for His perfect love, which shows us the godly way of how to be with each other. Favouritism is destructive and is not a characteristic of God; it has no place in the church and no place in our homes.

Let us spend today searching ourselves whilst pondering the following and ask God to help us be more like Him:

- Am I consciously or unconsciously showing favouritism to someone or a particular group?
- Are my actions building or destroying my family life/the church?

Lady Pam Lewin

SATURDAY 7th

Jacob said, Swear to me this day; ...and (Esau) sold his birthright unto Jacob
Genesis 25:33

PRIORITISE LOVE - Reading: Genesis 25:29-34

Family life in the Bible is rich with lessons that resonate through generations. The story of Jacob and Esau in Genesis 25:29-34, offers insight into family dynamics and the lasting impact of decisions made within a family unit.

Esau, the firstborn, returned home weary and famished, only to find his brother Jacob cooking a pot of stew. In a moment of weakness, Esau traded his birthright, the inheritance and entitlement of the firstborn, for a simple meal. This exchange reveals the tension that can arise in families when immediate desires outweigh long-term blessings. Jacob's shrewdness and Esau's impulsiveness set the stage for future conflict, reminding us that family decisions can have lasting consequences.

This story encourages us to reflect on our own family relationships. Are we valuing temporary comforts over enduring spiritual inheritance? Do we, like Esau, sometimes lose sight of what truly matters? Or, like Jacob appeared to be, are we taking advantage of a loved one's vulnerability?

In our families today, we can learn from Jacob and Esau by prioritising love, patience, and understanding over selfish desires. Let's strengthen our family bonds, recognising the value of having each family member in our lives and all the blessings they bring. May we never trade our spiritual birthright for fleeting pleasures, but instead, nurture our families with compassion, wisdom and grace that comes only from God.

Latoya J. Foster

*SUNDAY 8th

Now Israel loved Joseph more than all his children, because he was the son of his old age: and he made him a coat of many colours
Genesis 37:3

BROTHERS IN ARMS - FATHER'S FAVOURITE
Reading: Genesis 37:1-36

Genesis, chapters 37-50; tracked the life of Joseph (Hebrew, Yosef, God shall add) from age of seventeen; a teenager sold into Egypt, served in the house of an official and eventual chief adviser next to Pharoah. Sent ahead as a preserver of life, seventy souls went down into Egypt with Jacob (Genesis 46:27.) The fulfilment of the dreams he received and the blessings and prophecy of Jacob upon the twelve sons.

Picture the scene; Joseph, was born in Paddan-Aram, Syria circa 1900 B.C. His biological mother, Rachel, had died in childbirth after her last child Benjamin, Joseph's full brother. Joseph was the son of Jacob's old age and preferred over his older brothers. His life was radically uprooted as a teenager; favouritism and the dreams which he shared with his family fuelled jealousy, hatred and bitterness from his older brothers to plot his downfall (Gen. 37:18-20).

The family history of deception by Jacob's Uncle Laban, who tricked Jacob to marry Leah (the older daughter) before he could marry Rachel the younger sister, resulted in a mix of unrequited love and rivalry for Jacob's attention. Delayed by the cunning of Uncle Laban, his mother's brother, Jacob had to work a further seven years (fourteen years in total) to marry Rachel, the one he truly loved (Gen.29:16-30). The thread of family trickery was already in the generation - Rebecca had tricked Isaac to bless Jacob instead of Esau (Gen. 27)

Joseph was identified by the coat his father, Jacob, made for him. In that culture of the time, it was mainly women who made/designed cloth. Yet Jacob is noted for being the maker of the garment. Such was his love and memory for Rachel. The coat of many colours: Hebrew meaning *"Haketonet Passim"* was a full-length garment, down to the ankle/foot.

Made of wool/silk - it was the coat of the Bekorah, or B'kohr; the first-born child. Consider the dynamics, there were two sons in Jacob's household; his biological first born, Reuben, and there was Joseph, known as the 'dreamer' by his brothers, but known by the family as the firstborn of Jacob's heart. The coat of colours spoke volumes. An indication of the birthright and blessing of a first born and only the firstborn could normally inherit the birthright.

Reuben lost his position as first-born son because he slept with his father's concubine, Bilhah (Gen. 35:22), who was servant to Rachel. She bore two of Jacob's sons; Dan and Napthali (Gen.35:25). Reuben committed this offence after the death of Rachel. Jacob had heard of Rueben's gross sin but did not openly reveal his knowledge of Reuben's adultery with the concubine until the time of blessings just before his death. Jacob knew the characters of his sons and prophesied their future generations.

So, Reuben's sin and misconduct disqualified him from leadership of the family. When Jacob on his deathbed gave final instructions to all of his sons, Rueben was condemned by his father, *"as unstable as water"*. It was prophesied that he would not excel (Gen.49:3-4). Although Reuben had not joined with his brothers' earlier conspiracy to kill Joseph and delivered him from their plot, he had committed an offence against his father by violating his father's bed. The Law of Moses was not established yet - had it been Reuben would be put to death (Leviticus 20:11). May we learn that no sin goes unpunished (Proverbs 11:21), we confess to God that He may pardon and lift the curse and deliver.

The ways of God are past finding out, His ways are not our ways, neither are His thoughts our thoughts (Rom.11:33-36). God can draw out His purpose from a dysfunction for His glory. We have seen how the exemplary life of Joseph revealed the purpose of God to deliver a chosen family and, despite their flaws, to make them a great nation, the children of Israel. Let us reflect that, even in dysfunction, with God all things work together for good. Whom He justifies, he also glorifies!

CDP
*Pentecost Sunday

MONDAY 9th

Train up a child in the way he should go: and when he is old, he will not depart from it
Proverbs 22:6

AS THE TWIG IS BENT, SO GROWS THE TREE (*Alexander Pope*) – Reading: Proverbs 22:1-6; 29:15

The words of wisdom from Solomon in Proverbs 22:6 are directed to parents, guardians or anyone who has responsibility for children.

To train, according to the Merriam Webster Dictionary, means, among other things, *"to teach so as to make fit, qualified or proficient".* It stands to reason, then, that training takes time. It is a process which includes continuous work, consistency and covers a period of time. To train a child means commitment to a task. Training is about telling, teaching and living what we want them to acquire.

As persons charged with the upbringing of children, we cannot force our own will on them – that's a recipe for disaster in the long run. Rather, children need to be directed in a way that will help them to make wise choices. Left up to themselves, the choices may not be as wise. If we call to mind Proverbs 29:15b, it says, *"But a child left to himself, bringeth shame to his mother".* Although they have a choice, with supervision and wise counselling, they can be taught how to discern right from wrong and be guided onto a path that leads to good decision-making.

This does not mean that children will not err, but we are encouraged that, with proper grounding in values and godliness, the hope remains they will return to foundational truths in their later years. Ultimately, once we do what we ought to do as parents, we rely on God to lead them home to Him, much as in the parable of The Prodigal Son. And God can do so without a doubt.

Prayer:
Father, God, we ask your help in training our children so that they would learn to love, obey and please you. If they move away from the path of righteousness, lead them back to you. Remind them that you love and care for them and that their well-being is always a priority for you.

Thank you, Lord.

Sister Barbara Hendrickson
Nevis

TUESDAY 10th

Honour thy father and thy mother: that thy days may be long upon the land which the LORD thy God giveth thee
Exodus 20:12

OBEY GOD & RESPECT PARENTS – Reading: Exodus 20:1-26

We should always put God first in every area of our lives. He is in total control and knows everything about us and truly cares (Psalm 139).

To obey God is more than lip service; your motive should be genuine love for Him. If you disobey, there will always be consequences. If we love God and obey Him, we should also love others and serve them (Matt.22:35-40).

To honour our parents is the fifth of the Ten Commandments, and is the first with a promise attached, i.e., a long, full life (Ephesians 6:1-3).

Our attitude and behaviour to our parents should be courteous, and also include acts of kindness with unconditional material and mental support. Obedience to one's parents, that are in line with God's laws, are pleasing to Him.

Please note that parents also have a responsibility to train and discipline their children to obey the laws of the land with godly principles (Proverbs 22:6).

This can be challenging sometimes and is not always achievable alone, so it can *"take a village' to train and grow children".* This is true even in the 21st century with its changing values. We all need each other, and we are all part of God's family.

Evg. D.G.

WEDNESDAY 11th

When Rachel saw that she wasn't having any children for Jacob, she became jealous of her sister. She pleaded with Jacob, 'Give me children, or I'll die!'
Genesis 30:1 (NLT)

THE LOVE SITUATION IN THE FAMILY – Reading: Genesis 30:1-8

Childlessness is one of many challenging situations that impact on the family, and was the trouble that Rachel faced.

Looking closely, one will however realise that the fact of not being able to have a child in and of itself was not the major issue. The root of the situation was issues with love. Jacob's partiality in demonstration of love for the women in his life had repercussions. The story behind Rachel's irrational demand was one of jealousy and unkindness.

Indeed, how we treat each other, and ourselves, matters. It is not a coincidence that the greatest commandment involves loving one's neighbour as oneself. Love is the foundation of healthy family relationships whether a nuclear or complex family. But what does it really mean to love? The answer can be found in 1 Corinthians 13. Let us review a few verses.

1 Corinthians 13:4-7 NLT, *"Love is patient and kind. Love is not jealous or boastful or proud or rude. It does not demand its own way. It is not irritable, and it keeps no record of being wronged. It does not rejoice about injustice but rejoices whenever the truth wins out. Love never gives up, never loses faith, is always hopeful, and endures through every circumstance"*.

What is the love situation in your family? What loving factors are missing or being challenged? What loving elements need to be strengthened to facilitate better family relationships or lead to greater peace? How could you show more love?

The truth is that loving unconditionally often requires more than human effort. We need help from God who is the embodiment of love. In your prayer today ask God to work on the love situation in your family, and to show you how to love.

**Keshawna Salmon-Ferguson
Jamaica**

THURSDAY 12th

...Lord, doth thou not care that my sister has left me to serve alone?
Luke 10:40

IT'S MORE THAN DNA – Reading: Luke 10:38-42

Families throughout scripture teach us so much. We see favouritism, commitment, jealousy, betrayal, deception, good parenting and not so good parenting – families of all types!

Being related does not mean that we are all the same. We generally look for similarities in facial features, mannerisms, traits, but we don't always see these on the surface.

Mary and Martha were sisters that shared the same passion for Jesus yet expressed it in different ways. Mary was happy to just sit and absorb all that Jesus had to say, while Martha needed to make sure His needs were met. They both loved Jesus but expressed their love in their own way.

The Household of Faith operates with comparable dynamics as seen with Mary and Martha. Some declare their praise from the mountain tops and dance around the church, while others are perhaps not as outwardly expressive but find peace and contentment getting lost and immersed in the Word.

We are all children of the Most High God, part of the family of God. Today let's revel in the knowledge that we have been chosen, adopted and loved by God. He calls all of us His own and we are loved equally by Him.

No matter how you choose to do it, the call is to serve Christ with ALL your heart, soul and mind. He knows you and knows what your all looks like! So, don't get trapped by the deception of comparison – He wants YOUR all.

CDK

FRIDAY 13th

But as for you, ye thought evil against me; but God meant it unto good, to bring to pass, as it is this day, to save much people alive
Genesis 50:20

A DIVINE CATALYST – Reading: Genesis 50:14-26

Sometimes it is good to slow right down and do deep reflections. Such thinking can really remind us of things which we have completely forgotten concerning the goodness of God. Circumstances which seemed (and were) so terrible at the time turned out to be a divine setup.

Joseph, through no fault of his own, was his father's favourite. Genesis says that Jacob's special love for Joseph was because he was the son of his old age. Jacob's open display of favour for Joseph caused severe friction in the family.

Friction can be a good thing, it's not always bad. It is irritation that causes an oyster or a mussel to produce a pearl. Being comfortable in a place, or repetitively doing a particular thing, does not stimulate growth or production. God will not get some of us to 'budge' so he excavates by sending trouble. The discomfort then stimulates a thought that perhaps we need to move or do something different.

I'm very cautious how I blame the devil for things. I think that Satan is accused of many things that are not his doing – sometimes it is actually God at work in a way which we don't understand. When our world is turned upside down by a sequence of unfortunate events, it may be God trying to get our attention. Bush fires were not uncommon in the heat of a Midian desert – the catalyst for Moses to draw near and *"turn aside to see"* was that the leaves on the bush were not being consumed (Exodus 3:3).

Is a 'fire' burning at your workplace, in your family, in your church, which prayer seems not to be helping? If yes, are you missing the message that God is speaking to you in the heat of the situation? Will you now turn aside to see? The dreams which Joseph rightly or wrongly shared with his family were the trigger for his brothers to hate him enough to start his journey to Egypt in a pit.

Joseph was absolutely right to say, *"you thought evil against me…"* – of course they did – *"but God meant it unto good"*. God chose the right pit and the right prison, aspects of Joseph's future not shown to him in his dreams. His dreams showed only the glorious outcome, not the painful process.

Today, let's try to think of some positive things which came out of sad things. We will surely agree with Joseph that *"God meant it unto good"*.

JEJ

SATURDAY 14th

And the cloud departed from off the tabernacle; and, behold, Miriam became leprous, white as snow: and Aaron looked upon Miriam, and, behold, she was leprous
Numbers 12:10

STRENGTHEN & GUARD YOUR FAMILY – Reading: Numbers 12:1-16

This scripture talks about the dangers of envy and discontentment. It shows how envy can cloud our judgment and harm our relationships. We are reminded that God hears and sees all; He understands and is always aware of our struggles and concerns. God knows our hearts and will address injustice.

Envy and jealousy can be extremely destructive within family and community relationships. They both destroy friendships and even turn you against your own family causing division. It is important to trust in God as only He can bring peace to these situations. As children of God, it is important to know that anyone who speaks against us in any negative manner is speaking against God and His child meaning they will face the consequences of their action, just like Miriam became leprous.

Just as God defended Moses, and revealed the truth behind Miriam and Aaron's criticism, He sees our struggles and stands as our protector and guide. When faced with misunderstandings or harsh words, we can find solace in knowing that God hears and understands our hearts.

Let us embrace humility, trust in God's perfect justice, and use our words to build up rather than tear down. In doing so, we create a foundation of love and support that strengthens our families and reflects the divine grace that God extends to each of us.

Name withheld

* SUNDAY 15th

O woman, great is thy faith: be it unto thee even as thou wilt
Matthew 15:28

A MOTHER'S CONSISTENT PLEA – Reading: Matthew 15:21-28

It must have taken a lot of courage and bravery for this Canaanite woman to ask Jesus, a Jew, for help. But she was a desperate mother and needed help for her sick child who was demon possessed. As a mother, I can relate with the severity of the Canaanite woman's worries about her daughter's poor health. But if it was left to Jesus' disciples, the woman would not have been able to get close to speak to Jesus; they asked Jesus to send the Canaanite woman away.

At first, Jesus ignored the woman. He later said, *"it is not meet to give the children's bread to dogs…"*. The Canaanite nation was described by Jews as unclean dogs and seen as an enemy of God. The woman did not deny the primacy of the Jews being served first, she humbled herself and didn't dismiss the possibility of eating the crumbs that fell from the master's table. She believed that Jesus would help her, although she was a Gentile so cried out even more for mercy for her daughter.

As a mother, her main concern was for her daughter, not about status. Through her struggles, which must have been many, the Canaanite woman overcame the obstacles presented without feeling angry or vengeful. Instead, she humbled herself and focused on the needs of her daughter. Jesus commended her faith as *"great faith"* and rewarded her faith by healing her daughter (Matthew 12:28).

Ladies, women of God, as mothers and matriarchs of our families, let's remember that Jesus showed great respect to women and included them in His ministry and family.

(Matriarch is a word that we use to describe women who have earned respect and gained the wisdom to enrich a family or group – ref. Jamiemetz.com)

Minister ML Fraser

*Father's Day

MONDAY 16th

...I will love thee, O LORD, my strength
Psalm 18:1

ARE YOU BUILDING ON ROCK OR SHIFTING SAND?
Reading: Psalm 18:1-19

You'll never know how solid your foundation is until the storms of life begin to rage, and your feet feel entrapped in a *"slough of despond" (The Pilgrim's Progress – John Bunyan).*

Life was challenging until those teenage years began to rise above the parapet of life, and then it seemed as though the formative years were not that bad after all. *"Lord, I'm not ready for this…"*! And the Spirit said, *"Pray on…My grace is sufficient for you".*

I questioned my parenting skills. Was I cut out for this? I was reminded, *"You are not alone. The battle is not yours, but mine; I will contend with those who contend with thee and I will save your children. Fight on".* Those words brought peace to my soul.

Then another confrontation, greater than the one before! All of my resolves were dissolving one by one. My 'achilles heel' was having the law at my door, endless fabrications, violent outbursts, wilful damage to property, vindictiveness. It began to feel like every day, every week there was a misdemeanour for me to deal with and finally the school announced that there was nothing more they could do for this youngster; take him somewhere else, and I did.

We flew to pastures green in search of a new start, but things got worse. Then I cried to the Lord in my trouble and He delivered me out of my distress. Nothing was as I expected. I had planned meticulously, prepared for every event of this journey, but it wasn't enough.

You see, God brought me face-to-face with experiences that I had really only heard about. Now I was living amongst the poverty stricken, the helpless, the hopeless. People, young people, were busy building their lives on shifting sand. Their only ambition was to obtain what they needed, to purchase a few moments of sweet oblivion. Could it be that in refocusing my attention on Him, on them, that I could alleviate my stresses in my home? Our world is fractured but nothing can separate us from the love of God (Romans 8:38).

I can see now that for every problem, God had provided a solution. My support came in the form of praying family, friends, helpful strangers. God's still small voice reminding me of the reliability and power of His Word. I knew that God was there - immoveable, solid as a rock! I had nothing to fear unless I forgot the way He led me. His plan for me and mine is solid as a rock. His support is solid as a rock. His love is solid as a rock. He is the Rock.

Things are calming down now. God has illuminated our way right to the end of the tunnel.

"The LORD is my rock and my fortress…my God, my strength, in whom I will trust" (Psalm 18:2).

Cheryl Lowe
Guyana

TUESDAY 17th

Jesus answered them, saying, Who is my mother, or my brethren?
Mark 3:33

GLOBALLY & INSEPERABLY CONNECTED – Reading: Mark 3:31-35

When we are born, we are born into a physical family. When we are born again, we are born into a spiritual family.

The spiritual family is not bound by ethnicity, gender or social standing. As Paul says, you are all sons of God through faith in Christ Jesus. The Church is made up of all people who call upon Jesus as Saviour. This is a family drawn from every nation, tribe, people and language (Revelation 7:9) and the defining character of this spiritual family is the love of God.

"A new commandment have I given unto you that you should love one another" (John 13:34). It could be argued that as Christians, we relate to other believers as members of one family, i.e., we relate to the church as family. The early church met together in the temple court and in homes where they were devoted to deep abiding relationships (Acts 2:42-43). They became spiritual families. Following the scripture, we see them exhibiting the characteristics of a family, sharing and eating food together, praying together hanging out together.

During Jesus' ministry, whilst talking to the crowd, someone told Him that His mother and brothers were outside wanting to speak to Him. Jesus asked, *"Who is my mother? And who are my brothers?"* Pointing to His disciples, Jesus said, *"Here is my mother and my brothers! For whosoever does the will of my father in heaven, is my brother, my sister and my mother"* (Matthew 12:46-50).

Jesus was not dismissing His physical family as not important, but making it clear that in the kingdom of heaven, the most important family is the spiritual, not the natural. The spiritual family is *"born not of physical descent, nor of human decision or the will of man, but of God"* (John 1:12-13).

Minister ML Fraser

WEDNESDAY 18th

...and (Jethro) gave Moses Zipporah his daughter
Exodus 2:21

THE POWER OF CUSTOMS & TRADITIONS: ZIPPORAH'S STORY
Reading: Exodus 2:21; 4:24-25; 18:2-6

Some customs and traditions, are hard to accept. In modern society, a woman might balk at surrendering her child to, in her view, 'unnecessary' trauma, e.g., a vaccination, or in Zipporah's case, circumcision. A mother's instinct is to nurture, protect and defend her offspring (Isaiah 49:15), any entity hindering her is likely to be 'in for a bruising'!

Zipporah presents as a strong, patient woman. Not much is written about her, but what we have, is significant. Bold in marrying a foreigner, she takes on his mores. She honours her father's choice in Moses for her.

This couple is close; she a skilled shepherdess, he, a shepherd in training. Zipporah gets to know Moses well. Moses is persuaded not to circumcise their sons. I guess that wasn't hard, since he was meek (Numbers 12:3). He just wanted an easy life.

Strong willed, Zipporah was confident in sharing her opinions. Before and after circumcising her son herself, she tells Moses that he is a *'bloody husband'*. In this, she questions God, yet remains obedient. She has come from spiritual stock; her father, a priest and advisor to Moses. Sometimes we question God too, when we don't understand or agree with His methods. At such times, we need to trust and obey Him (1 Samuel 15:22). Obedience saved her husband's life.

Patience is a virtue with which both Moses and Zipporah were blessed. Moses, in returning to Egypt, was gone a while. Wise Jethro considered it too long for his daughter and her children, so took them to meet Moses in the wilderness. After all, who prepares for forty years separation in a marriage!

We may see aspects of Zipporah's complexity in ourselves. God values and loves us all. He understands the things that affect and frustrate us

(Isaiah 1:18). Like Zipporah, some of us are called to keep the home fires burning and raise the children single-handedly. It takes a special kind of person to fulfil this duty. From the wife of an evangelist to a long-distance lorry driver, the job description is the same: *"Hold the fort"*. Through lonely nights and challenging days, remember, *"your help comes from the LORD"*. (Psalm 121:2).

Cheryl Lowe
Guyana

THURSDAY 19th

Fathers, do not provoke your children to anger, but bring them up in the discipline and instruction of the Lord
Ephesians 6:4 (ESV)

A FATHER'S LOVE - Reading: Ephesians 6:1-9

"*The true legacy of a father is the integrity, honesty, and kindness he instils in his children*" (Unknown).

This quote clearly captures the true essence of the impact of a father in the life of his children. It is not always about the gifts, treats or even the many trips and holidays they receive, but it's in the example and role he sets that shapes the life of his children.

We are living in a time where the family home is being redefined, the respect and regard for parental authority is slowly fading away. But the Apostle Paul encourages the Ephesian brethren of the importance of the father's role in the life of their children. The biblical principle of bringing up children in the Lord's instruction directly impacts the health and wellbeing of the home, it fosters a nurturing environment that supports familial growth.

The word, *"provoke"*, means to instigate, to stir up or cause a response. Paul clearly points out the importance of how to nurture children in such a godly way that will not cause or stir up frustration and anger, but he should ensure they feel the love, care and mercy of God. The love of God must be reflected in everything that we do.

Finally, I am reminded of Psalm 103:13: that states, *"As a father has compassion on his children, so the Lord has compassion on those who fear him".*

Name withheld

FRIDAY 20th

...Cain rose up against his brother, and slew him
Genesis 4:8

A SACRIFICE FROM THE HEART – Reading: Genesis 4:1-26

Today, society uses many names to describe the family - nuclear, extended and single-parent families are a few descriptions.

The first family in Genesis speaks of God enforcing an eviction order on Adam and Eve who breached the terms and conditions of their tenancy in the Garden of Eden. Breach of the Garden of Eden contract: Disobedience. Adam and Eve were therefore ordered to take up employment and produce children.

They had two sons, Cain and Abel, who were unique. Both sons followed their chosen career path. Cain was a farmer and Abel became a shepherd. The appointed time came when each had to present an offering unto the Lord. Each of the brothers gave the best of their livestock or vegetation.

I can hear the voices of some who would say that there is nothing wrong with either sacrifice – yes, you are right. However, a holy God requires humility, and our approach cannot be how we please, it must be with reverence. Our approach to our sovereign Lord is a heart-matter. God sees the condition of our hearts, while others see the outward appearance. Abel believed by faith in his heart that his sacrifice was pleasing unto the Almighty and it was so, just as God confirmed his acceptance at the dedication of the first temple built by Solomon (2 Chronicles 7:1-2).

Why would murder be in the heart of your brother, you may be asking? When we review the sacrifice offered by Cain, it had no blood, unlike Abel's offering. Cain offers his best organic vegetables. The spirit of pride, a feeling of self-satisfaction was in his heart. The Word of God clearly states that, *"pride goes before destruction and a haughty spirit before a fall"* (Proverbs 16:18). We must always remember, that God sees the condition of our hearts, therefore, we cannot make a sacrifice with a heart that is not pleasing to Him. Cain did not see fire come down from heaven to confirm acceptance of his sacrifice and, consumed by pride, the act to commit murder of his brother was conceived in his heart.

James 1:14 tells us that we can be enticed away from God by our inner desires. This is why believers need the indwelling of the Holy Spirit and must also build up on the Word of God in our hearts that we sin not against Him (Psalm 119:11).

Missionary Audrey Simpson

SATURDAY 21ˢᵗ

But they said, We will drink no wine: for Jonadab the son of Rechab our father commanded us, saying, Ye shall drink no wine, neither ye, nor your sons for ever
Jeremiah 35:6

WE WILL NOT – FOREVER! – Reading: Jeremiah 35:1-19

From our reading of today's scripture, it is clear that God is concerned with every aspect of our lives and, beyond that, the Bible uses that which resonates with us to teach us lessons where necessary. This will also give us insight into what God requires of us.

We see this with Hosea, when God tells him to marry a woman who is consistently unfaithful to him, and whose wanton infidelity causes Hosea to have to act as her Kinsman Redeemer to demonstrate how God viewed Israel as an adulterous wife who needed to be bought out of slavery.

Jeremiah tells the story of the Rechabites. They are descendants of the Kenites, and as a consequence family to the Midianites, Moses' in-laws, as recorded in the Book of Judges. This was a nomadic family who lived by extremely strict familial rules. Their ancestor, Jehonadab, had decreed that they refrain from:

1. wine
2. building permanent homes
3. sowing seed
4. planting vineyards

These regulations were passed down without deviation for generations. The Rechabites did not allow the changing times, nor peer pressure, nor the views of those around them to dissuade them from maintaining their family traditions. Even when they were invited to the temple, to one of the exclusive side rooms, and presented with wine, their steadfastness to their family mores remained intact. They were resolute in their refusal to disobey their family's instructions.

Jeremiah is told categorically that this is a lesson that my people Israel must learn from the Rechabites. Despite the fact that the directions were passed from generation to generation, despite the fact that times had changed, this tribe, in unison, held dear their family traditions. Judah, however, had a long history of disobedience. A succession of prophets, could not persuade God's people to remain faithful to His laws. Here, the 'weeping prophet' is once again commissioned by God to remind His people that, *"...obedience is better than sacrifice and to hearken than the fat of rams"* (1 Samuel 15:22b).

There is clearly much we can learn from the Rechabites' rigid adherence to their family's values. In the face of testing, they maintain their strict observance of their family lifestyle. Much like the Nazarites, who too were given stringent instructions to follow to retain their standing and, perhaps, one could say, their effectiveness in the sight of God.

If we are to keep our position in the family of God we must, even in the face of temptation, hold fast the laws of God.

Lady Shirley Hamilton

SUNDAY 22nd

And Laban had two daughters: the name of the elder was Leah, and the name of the younger was Rachel
Genesis 29:16

FAMILY TIES! – Reading: Genesis 29:14-30

Family Ties is a family relationship based on personal ties between persons. These are most commonly blood ties (Google definition). Another aspect of family ties is the connection of family members through marriage.

Laban was the father of two daughters, Leah the eldest, and Rachel the youngest. Laban made the dynamic of this 'Family Tie' very complicated when he through deception gave Leah to Jacob to be Jacob's wife, knowing very well that it was Rachel that caught Jacob's eye (Genesis 29:25)!

This family tie then becomes a 'Love Triangle' when Laban negotiates with Jacob to give Leah his attention for a week, then he could also have the love-of-his-life, Rachel, with the proviso that he will work for him seven more years (Genesis 29:27-28).

In those biblical days before the law, this kind of arrangement was acceptable! However, the structure of this family-tie puts Leah and Rachel in a very competitive relationship, and they are not only sisters to each other, but sisters-in-laws too!! We know about sibling rivalry in families, but this family had 'wives rivalry' at the same time too! Jacob certainly did not make the situation any easier, because he was madly in love with Rachel who was younger, beautiful and well favoured. Jacob was protective over Rachel (Genesis 33:2). He had no passion or affection for Leah, she was older, she was *"tender eyed"*, i.e., her eyes were weak and she was not desirous in Jacob's eyes or heart; he did not love her in the same way that he loved Rachel (Genesis 29:30), he just put up with her!

Leah must have felt that she was 'second best 'in her husband's eyes, she must have felt rejected, treated as the 'ugly duckling', but our God, he was gracious to Leah and opened up her womb. Leah was not favoured by her husband Jacob, but she was favoured by God (Genesis 29:31-35). Leah gave birth to six sons and one daughter. Leah perhaps thought that she had power over Rachel. Rachel struggled to have children and was barren for years. She envied Leah and became very competitive against her. Did Rachel feel less of a woman because she could not have children at the time or speed to which Leah was having children?? She gave Jacob her handmaid, Bilhah, to have children on her behalf (Genesis 30:1-8). Leah must had thought that she had the upper hand because she had conceived so many children for Jacob, and also competed to have children via her handmaid, Zilpah, which she gave to Jacob to wife (Genesis 30:9).

The rivalry of the two sisters is further shown when they barter with each other to spend time with Jacob, using mandrakes as payment for the opportunity (Genesis 30:14-17). Rachel, did eventually have children, Joseph (Genesis 30:22-24), and then Benjamin, which cost her her life (Genesis 35:16-18).

This family tie of Jacob and his two wives, plus the two handmaids, resulted in the birth of thirteen children. The twelve sons became known as the twelve tribes of Israel.

Leah, the unloved, gave birth to Judah, the lineage of David, through which our Saviour came, and gives salvation to all. Rachel, the loved, gave birth to Joseph who God used to preserve the lineage through which Jesus came. This shows that the sisters had a valuable role, regardless of their differences.

We are all brothers and sisters in Christ, there is no need for rivalry, resentment or jealousy. We are tied together in ONE BIG FAMILY, the Family of God. The Lord God is our Heavenly Father, He is not partial with His love towards any of us. He does not treat us differently because of our looks, skin tone, qualifications or social status. We are all loved, blessed and highly favoured. It is not what we are or look like, we are all the same in God's eyes.

I pray that we are all the same in each other's eyes and heart; there are no Leah or Rachel categories! We are connected together in this blessed family tie.

I love you, my sisters!

Minister/Lady Genevieve Dinnall

MONDAY 23rd

But there was none like unto Ahab, which did sell himself to work wickedness in the sight of the LORD, whom Jezebel his wife stirred up
1 Kings 21:25

JEZEBEL – Reading: 1 Kings 21:1-29

Jezebel, Jezebel, what is it about this Jezebel? Even the very name is frowned upon as an epitome of evil because of the horrible, historical, biblical family facts.

Within this infamous family's life, the leader of the home has already sold himself to do wickedness in the LORD's sight. Such covetous character attracts the manipulative, controlling and compromising spirit of Jezebel, stirred up as helpmeet. Consequently, she helped to meet the wickedness already in the heart, taking it to the next level of disaster!

Jezebel was an idol worshipper of the Canaanite god in Zidon, the princess-daughter of priest, King Ethbaal; one of influence. As a compromiser, she served both the LORD and her god, which infiltrated her husband, family and the people he ruled. Thus, attracting the curse (Deuteronomy 28:15-68); this meant divine judgment of 'a total family wipeout' (2 Kings 10:10-11).

This name appears again in Revelation 2:20, and Jesus has strong words for that woman Jezebel, who allowed herself to be used by that age-old spirit. Here, she had a teaching ministry allowed by leadership, with great influence and prominence. This spirit at work through Jezebel, seductively reassured the Christians that they could also partake in serving idols. Jesus named it fornication, (porneia in Greek), which is all kinds of gross immoral practices of ritualistic idol worship - the depth of Satan.

We can see the same predicted family fate, without bias, to root out such teachings wherever it is fed (Revelation 2:21-23). Jehu would ensure that God's justice was accomplished, and Jesus Himself would deal with this high-ranking spirit if there's no repentance.

A heart of covetousness attracts the nature of the spirit of Jezebel to help meet unentitled needs. So guard your hearts against greed and be thankful.

Pastor Josephine

TUESDAY 24th

And when Athaliah the mother of Ahaziah saw that her son was dead, she arose and destroyed all the seed royal
2 Kings 11:1

ATHALIAH – Reading: 2 Kings 11:1-3; 2 Chronicles 22:10-19; 23:1-15

The Bible has recorded some men and women notorious for their reign of terror.

The book of the Kings and Chronicles, tracks the history of various kings after the split of the nation of Israel. Violence and idolatry is the recurring theme. The reign of the House of Ahab and Jezebel ranks top for idolatrous worship. It seems more amplified when the violence was led by godless women.

Idolatry in Israel triggered the anger of God. The decline of Israel as a nation began with the multiple marriages of King Solomon to idolatrous women (1 Kings 11:1-13). Spiritual darkness had changed the landscape. In this setting, Israel had continued to deteriorate with the reign of King Ahab and Jezebel (although Elijah the prophet was in this period).

We come to Athaliah - her name means *"Jehovah is exalted"* ...

Now, Athaliah was of royal descent, the daughter of Jezebel and Ahab (some query her paternity; 2 Kings 8:25). She was the wife of King Jehoram of Judah. The marriage created an alliance between the two royal houses (Northern and Southern Kingdoms). Like her mother who influenced Ahab into idolatry, Athaliah influenced Jehoram to worship false gods. This lineage of evil, the strong influence of idolatry and witchcraft was passed down (2Kings 9:22). Her mother, Jezebel, daughter of King Ethbaal of Phoenicia (Tyre and Sidon) had introduced Baal worship into Israel when she married King Ahab of Israel (Northern Kingdom).

The judgment of God was by Jehu (see 2 Kings chapters 9 and 10), he wiped out the entire House of Ahab. When her husband (King Jehoram) and her son (Ahaziah) died, one would expect mourning and grief.

However, Athaliah seized power to the throne and massacred all her grandsons, the seed royal (2 Kings 11:1-3), all but Joash who was hidden by his aunt Jehosheba.

The unchecked wickedness of Athaliah had its roots in the family lineage, the level of witchcraft and sorcery was relentless. Like the spirit of Jezebel, a manipulative, controlling spirit that seeks attachment to rule through positions of power held by individuals; the spirit of Athaliah also seeks revenge. Except by the power of the Lord Jesus Christ, this spirit will annihilate any obstacle in its drive for power by violence which stems from uncontrolled pride-ambition.

This lust for power was to *"steal, kill and destroy"* (John 10:10) the potential of youth. This attack reflects of Pharoah's edict to kill the Hebrew baby boys (Exodus 1:15-22). Authority and evil power in the wrong hands results in sure death! *"To the froward God will be froward"* (Psalm.18:26).

All power is subject to the higher power. Jehovah God, our One and same LORD Jesus Christ, will be exalted!

CDP

WEDNESDAY 25th

...David sent and fetched (Bathsheba) to his house, and she became his wife, and bare him a son...but the thing that David had done displeased the LORD
2 Samuel 11:27

A ROYAL FAMILY IN CRISIS (Part 1) – Reading: 2 Samuel 11:1-27

God forgives us when we come to Him with humility, acknowledgement of our sins and repentance. Our God judges sin. He chooses and executes the consequences, even if it takes a lifetime.

God's servant David, was plucked from tending his father's sheep. After being equipped to look after sheep, God anointed and appointed him and he became the greatest King of Israel. Despite his high position, scripture confirms David as being a man after God's own heart (Acts 13:22).

Let us examine and consider a specific period in David's life when he was a mature middle-aged King. God had equipped him to be a great leader and warrior. However, he allowed his flesh to rule him. King David, a man of war, stayed home when it was the season to lead the army of Israel into battle. He sent his army to war without a God-ordained leader. The question that is on our lips, that is being asked today is, what good or credible excuse could he have given to remain in Jerusalem when he should have been on the battlefield?

Sisters, when we are not in the place where God ordained us to be, the devil will make work for our idol hands! I would suggest that David was struggling internally with his flesh which had been the norm for many years. Perhaps you missed it - you do not get yourself into a 'lust triangle' if you do not allow yourself to be drawn away by your lustful desires which cannot be satisfied.

This was about what David wanted and the fact that he was not satisfied with what God gave him. He did not heed the warning given that God in no way, shape or form approved of the practice of polygamy (many spouses at the same time) by any King of Israel, *"The King shall not multiply wives for himself, or else his heart will be turned away..."*

(Deuteronomy 17:17). My God gave the instruction and if we cannot hear, we will reap the consequences of our sinful actions.

God created Adam and Eve - one man, and one woman. King David started this trend in the family by having at least six wives while he ruled in Hebron. Solomon, his son, adopted this polygamous practice by having 700 wives and 300 concubines.

David was a man that was easily drawn away by temptation and enticed. In that moment of seeing this woman having a bath, he was not able to resist the alluring bait of pleasure. His sin was not on seeing a woman bathing, but keeping his eyes on her.

The Scripture tells us Bathsheba was the name of the woman bathing on the palace roof. She was a beautiful woman but it was not only her beauty, but the condition of David's heart and mind, that prepared him to take the bait. A strong desire for Bathsheba was conceived in David's heart which later birthed adultery.

Sisters, the flesh is carnal and base, and if we do not control its activity, it will lead us into sin. The act of adultery with Bathsheba was going to bring David's lack of romantic restraint into judgment. It was the apostle Paul who reminded us of the two natures that live within. He found a law in his members that when he wanted to do good evil was present (Romans 7:21).

The Word of God came to David through the prophet, Nathan. God promised to judge David's sin severely. Violence and bloodshed would happen in his family. The sins of David would be repeated in his children. Because of his actions of deceit, adultery and premeditated murder, Nathan confronted David with a story about himself, but he thought it was about someone else. His immediate reaction was to kill the man and to pay restitution four times. Then the prophet revealed to David that he was the guilty person. Psalm 51 is David's psalm of repentance. Notwithstanding, he paid heavily for his sins: his and Bathsheba's baby died, and his sons Amnon, Absalom and Adonijah died.

This tragic lust triangle had far-reaching consequences.

Missionary Audrey Simpson

THURSDAY 26th

Thus saith the LORD, Behold, I will raise up evil against thee out of thine own house...
2 Samuel 12:11

A ROYAL FAMILY IN CRISIS (Part 2) – Reading: 2 Samuel 12:1-31

We are continuing with yesterday's focus on King David's family.

Bathsheba, is now one of King David's many wives, and bitterness was brewing in her grandfather, Ahitophel, who was a counsellor to David.

Sisters, the consequences of sin are real. As the life of King David unfolds, we see that our Heavenly Father cannot be mocked by deception, whatsoever a man sows he will reap (Galatians 6:7). David's consequence for his sinful behaviour was enacted through his children and other family members.

Let us take a quick review of David's firstborn son Amnon, whose mother was Ahinoam (2 Samuel 3:2). He was first in line to the throne of Israel, today we would say he was the Crown Prince. Despite his position, his character was tainted. Amnon, like David, was driven by the desires of his flesh.

He had a lustful desire for his half-sister Tamar, He became so obsessed, to the point Amnon became lovesick and deluded by not recognising the desire he had was not love but lust. This part of David's family's story will be covered in tomorrow's reading. But sisters, be careful who you seek advice from. We must prayerfully ask God to show us who to approach for counsel.

Amnon shared what was in his heart with his friend, Jonadab, that he loved Tamar. He referred to Tamar as though she was not kin. This was his blood sister from another mother. He internalised the deception by referring to her only as his brother Absalom's sister. We see Satan, through Jonadab's counsel, using his cunning deceitful devices and planting the seed of treachery.

This was a major crisis within the family! It triggered Tamar's brother Absalom, from the same mother, to hate Amnon to the point where he plans the contract killing of his brother Amnon.

But, what is King David saying about his family which is in turmoil, despite being angry and upset? I suggest he was hearing the echoes of the Word of God that was spoken by the prophet, *"THE SWORD will not depart from your house..."* (2 Samuel 12:10). Despite this, I believe that King David still had a right to speak to his children, confess his past sinful behaviour, and admit the reason why the family was in crisis, which was a result of despising God's commandment.

I suggest King David was having a déjà vu experience. The death of Uriah was a means to an end. The death of Amnon ended his lineage to the throne. Both father David and son Absalom have blood on their hands - they give their servant an order to commit murder. King David's adulterous behaviour ends in murder. Amnon's incestuous behaviour became the catalyst that led to murder!

Our Heavenly Father forgives us of our sins when we acknowledge confess, repent and ask for forgiveness. However, God brings judgment on our sins. Yes! David felt the chastening rod because of the Father's love. Remember we too will feel the chastening rod if we wilfully sin.

Missionary Audrey Simpson

FRIDAY 27th

...Absalom the son of David had a fair sister, whose name was Tamar; and Amnon the son of David loved her
2 Samuel 13:1

LISTEN: A PLEA FROM TAMAR – Reading: 2 Samuel 13:1-22

Writings on the story of Tamar, sister of Absalom, need such respectful dissection of the text, that it would take a scholar to observe it duly, and with much more detail than a simple writing could ever do, to give theological justice.

Yet, simple and delicate is just how these words hope to leave the page. These words are the most powerful echo of the pleas of Tamar, the woman raped at the hands of her half brother, Amnon, who abused her trust by employing isolation and power.

"He refused to listen to her", although she pleaded and pleaded. He refused to listen, *"He was stronger than her"* (2 Samuel 13:14).

Dare we suggest that, concerning the cry of innocent and abused women, there is sometimes a deathly silence on our part, and we refuse to listen. The silence on matters of injustice, violence and abuse, speaks volumes. Yet, the voice of God still speaks for the broken and abused. Does our voice echo His? He still binds up the wounds. He still rescues the bound with liberty. God is not silent.

Worldwide, we must take seriously the hurts from within what should be safe walls, because God hurts when His children hurt. He hears the cries of young girls and boys, vulnerable children or adults, who have suffered assault because *"he was stronger"*. God's ear inclines to the hearts and minds disfigured by abuse, much as it did over Abel's cry (Genesis 4:10-11). God still walks amongst the most broken. He is not so much in the shouts as He is in the cries. He hears your cry.

There may be a thousand women who will read this story but for you, the one who was overpowered and silenced, God still sees. For the Tamar who has never shared her story, never been seen or heard, and never healed; you have never set foot into the places of agony again, you are loved enough to be seen today. And we are listening.

Speak in safety when you are ready, give permission to guard your own heart over that of a perpetrator, seek professional and godly help and know that you were never the problem. God will speak His love for you Himself.

Prayer:
Lord, please continue to grow safe spaces of listening ears and healing. Let us represent you well where someone has suffered at the hands of those who were stronger. Jesus, come into every broken heart and begin a good work. The work that held you to the cross for those you loved. Give water to the thirsty and barren hearts, and wisdom to walk through the tender paths of grief and healing to the justice and freedom that pleases You. Help us, Father, to minister to the agony of Tamar - teach us to listen to the broken. May we be touched with the feelings of her infirmity and be moved with compassion. And truly listen. In Jesus' name. Amen.

Joy Lear-Bernard

Please see the Support Directory at the back of this book if you have been affected by today's reading and need professional help

SATURDAY 28th

...and she poured out...
2 Kings 4:4

HOLD ON TO THE FAITH – Reading: 2 Kings 4:1-7

Remember, given unto us is the law of the land
To follow and take heed, obedient we must stay,
Even through trials, trust in God's just hand,
For there are things so much greater and miracles to display.

Even in the smallest of vessels, power can pour out,
For even in the mystery of God, you can expect a great work,
For we might not even see God's next move or what it is about,
The key to faith is patience so evident in His Word.

For God's provision is expected, God's provision is complete,
But without faith in God, God you cannot meet,
So, hold on to your faith, the wealth of a heavenly life,
Where you hold your ground in the midst of earthly strife.

Make known that this is the God you serve,
And you will find that God with your life He will preserve,
For there was a faithful widow and her oil,
And even in her worry, God did not make her toil.

For her faith was tested, and her patience tried,
She poured the oil, and God's divine action was supplied,
For we have to believe for ourselves, the great power God bestows,
Even empowered through the Holy Ghost, in us can flow.

Name withheld

SUNDAY 29th

And she conceived again and bore a son, and said, 'Now I will praise the Lord' Therefore, she called his name Judah. Then she stopped bearing
Genesis 29:35

BEGIN WITH GOD, END WITH PRAISE! – Reading: Gen. 29:31-35; Psalm 34:1-4

DEFINITION:

Family is a group of persons united by the ties of marriage, blood, or adoption, constituting one or more households, and interacting with each other in their respective social positions, usually those of spouses, parents, children, and siblings. Britannica.com

The family is one of God's most beautiful, and oldest institutions. He perfectly designed each role, each connection, and each interaction that takes place within it. The family unit isn't just designed to bring people together, but also to keep people together in the bond of love.

We see in Genesis 29:31-35 that Leah, although a big part of her family as a wife and mother, was missing a crucial component – love. She was married to Jacob, but not loved by Jacob, and God was acutely aware of this.

Be assured that God is seeing and listening, He's got you.

The Lord caused Leah to conceive, and she had three sons. Each meaning of their names represented the lovelessness she felt in her marriage, and the hope that each child would endear her to the heart of her husband. However, when she had her fourth son, she named him Judah meaning – *'now I will praise the LORD'*.

Leah learned from the birth of Judah, that praise will endear her to the heart of God and helped her to pursue the true love of her Heavenly Father. May we too, make a conscious decision to passionately pursue the heart of God and give up on futile attempts to gain love from the transient and fleeting things in life.

God opens the door to build and expand our families, and not just numerically by having children, but spiritually too by beginning with God and ending with praise. Praise seals the deal, signs off and closes-out whatever the issue may be. Whether it's lovelessness, rejection, sickness, anxiety, discouragement, strife, or anything else. As a family, whatever the problem, let us boldly declare: *"Now we will praise the LORD"*! Gather together and let praise be a permanent fixture in your schedule.

Begin with God, end with praise, and watch God positively affect the trajectory of your lives.

MinK/ Minister Kay

MONDAY 30th

That they may teach the young women to be sober, to love their husbands, to love their children. To be discreet, chaste keepers at home, good, obedient to their husbands, that the Word of God be not blasphemed
Titus 2:4-5

THE JOB DESCRIPTION - Reading: Matthew 5:16; Titus 2:3-5

As a young Christian, I used to attend a ladies Bible study group which comprised of women of all ages.

The Bible Study was so encouraging and I learned from the other ladies as they shared what God was doing in their lives. One lady said some wise words that I will never forget, *"How can you submit to God who you cannot see, and not submit to the husband who you can see?"* I thank God for this older woman who was teaching me, unknowingly, in such a way that the Word of God be not discredited.

Today's reading is a job description for older women. I encourage you reading this to look up the meaning of the above words: **discreet, chaste, keepers**, and ask God to help you in the areas that need changing. As Christian women we want to do as the Bible says, so our light will shine before men as Jesus said in Matthew 5:16.

J.B. Phillips, a well-known English Bible translator said, *"A woman's actions are a good advertisement for the Christian faith"*.

Older women teach by your words and your actions. Our younger women need you; they need your wisdom and experience. Let's be intergenerational.

CP

July

31 Days in the Psalms

TUESDAY 1ˢᵗ

O taste and see that the LORD is good: blessed is the man that trusteth in him
Psalm 34:8

THE DELIGHT OF HIS PRESENCE – Reading: Psalm 16:8-11; 34:6-8

On September 12, 2024, a close friend submitted her prayer list to friends in her weekly Bible study group. She noted that she would like these friends to pray for the next seven days that God would give her wisdom in her decision-makings, provide a flexible job that will allow her to stay in the presence of God and to receive the gift of the Holy Spirit with the evidence of speaking in another tongue. These were just some of the items on her list.

The Sunday following, whilst at church, she miraculously received the Holy Spirit with the evidence of speaking in another tongue. She testified of the unearthly feeling she had. It felt like something coming so deep out of her belly, she expressed. Of course, this was the Spirit of God, the well of living water.

His goodness is so unforgettable and experiencing Him for the first time is one of so indescribably good! I remember when I received the Holy Spirit, I felt like I was on cloud 9, as the saying goes. It was a joyous feeling. It is fitting to say, "O taste and see that the Lord is good" (Psalm 34:8).

God hears our cry and wants to be a part of our life. Do not withhold your requests from Him. Ask and you shall receive that which is according to His perfect will for your life. He is that good Father that loves you. Reflect on His goodness in your life.

Shanique Graham

WEDNESDAY 2ⁿᵈ

Unto thee, O LORD, do I lift up my soul. O my God, I trust in thee…
Psalm 25:1-2

CALL AND TRUST – Reading: Psalm 25:1-22

This psalm refers to calling on, and trusting, the LORD to protect us from our enemies.

Have you ever been in a situation where someone you thought was your friend turned out to be your enemy? A sister exhorted in church recently and referred to a new buzzword called, *"frenemy"*, meaning, *"a person who is or pretends to be a friend but who is also in some ways an enemy or rival"* (Merriam-Webster's online dictionary).

I can recall a situation where someone I thought was a friend turned out to be a frenemy! She was saying not-so-nice things and spreading untruths about me behind my back. It turned out that one day she said something to the wrong person who held her to account because they knew what was being said was not true. God did not let my enemy (frenemy) triumph over me; she ended up apologising and telling me she was ashamed of her actions. What a God!

When we find ourselves in situations beyond our control, whether it's with a friend, enemy, or frenemy, we need to do as David did and lift up our souls to God, call on Him, trust Him, and ask Him not to let our enemies triumph over us.

God will not fail to deliver you.

Lady Pam Lewin

THURSDAY 3rd

For I acknowledge my transgressions: and my sin is ever before me
Psalm 51:3

THE POWER OF ACKNOWLEDGEMENT – Reading: 2 Sam. 12:1-13

I have found the practice of identifying a word for focused reflection from my reading and other interactions to be instructive.

Today the word that stands out for me is *"acknowledge"*. King David in Psalm 51 was at the place where he acknowledged, i.e., admitted and accepted the truth of the situation he found himself in. This led to repentance and him finding grace in God's eyes, so much so that despite the evil he had done, God found David to be a man after His own heart. What a commendation!

There is power in acknowledging one's situation and by the same token it is detrimental to live in denial or ignore the realities of the situation. Healing and help come when one accepts and openly admits how things are, and moves in the direction that addresses the situation.

One is, however, often afraid to admit things considered to be too embarrassing or too big to deal with. Others have been so blinded by their own desires that they have dismissed the Nathan's who have been sent to point out where things have gone wrong, as they would rather not hear it. But not hearing, not admitting, and not dealing with it, will not make the situation or its effects go away. In fact, not acknowledging makes the situation worse.

As you seek to go forward in the various spheres of life, it is important to acknowledge where things need to be adjusted for health and growth. Ask God for His help and grace today to acknowledge how things are, and the courage and strength to take the steps towards positive change.

There is power in acknowledgement of your situation but, more so, the God of your situation.

Keshawna Salmon-Ferguson
Jamaica

FRIDAY 4th

...hope in God: for I shall yet praise him...
Psalm 43:5

YET PRAISE – Reading: Psalm 43:1-5

Sisters, if there was ever a time that we need God, it's now!

After all the recent happenings reported in the newspapers and on the internet, my soul is cast down with burdens and fear for the safety of friends and family. We can truly relate to the psalmists.

But the psalmist also encourages us by saying that we should put our hope in God's hands, and give Him our *"yet praise"*! Hallelujah! For He is not only our God, but also our Saviour.

No matter what happens or what is about to happen, God is in perfect control. Our emotions, fears and moods, should all be channelled through God. He is more than able to save and deliver. He is in perfect control. He will calm the storms. So let us continue to hide under the blood of Jesus Christ until our help comes from Him.

Keep trusting, keep praying, and don't stop praying. Give your *"yet praise"*!

Sis Esther Miller

SATURDAY 5th

God is in the midst of her, she shall not be moved: God shall help her, and that right early
Psalm 46:5

RIDE OUT YOUR STORM – Reading: Psalm 46:1-11

While we waited for Hurricane Beryl to make landfall on the island of Jamaica, many of us were going through different stages of emotion. With the uncertainty of the impending storm, we were unsure how we would fare.

As we go through life, different categories of storms come our way. Unlike Beryl, we were advised to make the necessary preparations. Yet, our storms don't give us warnings that they are coming; they just come, and we must adjust our lives and ride out our storm. One thing is certain: it does not matter which category of storm comes into our lives; if the Lord is with us, we can rest in Him.

Spiritually, different categories of storms require different levels of prayer and trust in God. Beryl passed through Jamaica, and many of us suffered different losses: loss of lives, homes, utilities, livestock, floods, etc. But no matter the condition of our storm, hope in the Lord, He will put the pieces of our lives back together and make us whole again.

In the natural, after a storm, we pick up the pieces and move on. However, in the spiritual, it is the Lord Jesus who picks up our pieces and puts us back together, *"It is the Lord who goes before you. He will be with you; he will not leave you or forsake you. Do not fear or be dismayed"* (Deuteronomy 31:8).

Let us persevere in prayer, praise, and trust in our Lord Jesus; He is our shelter in times of storm.

Marlene Hines
Jamaica

SUNDAY 6th

My help cometh from the LORD, which made heaven and earth
Psalm 121:2

WITH HIS HELP I CAN – Reading: Psalm 121:1-8

My help comes from the Lord, the source of all power and strength. He is my rock, my shield, my protector!

Having the privilege of a right relationship with the Almighty God, my saviour and redeemer, is one that has no comparison. I know that I can put my trust, faith and confidence fully in Him.

We can walk with a special air of confidence knowing that we are not alone – even in our darkest hour, when joy and peace seem a long way off. But yet, when we stop and take a breath, when we truly consider our situation and see that *"we are surrounded by the walls of God's salvation"* Isaiah 26:1 (NLT), we have a reason to lift our heads and praise the One who not only made heaven and earth, but cares about you and me.

Life comes with highs and lows, good days and not so good days, but never forget that you are loved and cared for. Look to the One that gave His all for you. That same power that rose Jesus from dead is the same power that will keep you.

You are an overcomer – just believe when you call on His name.

CDK

MONDAY 7th

This is the day which the LORD has made; we will rejoice and be glad in it
Psalm 118:24

CELEBRATE YOUR DAY IN GOD – Reading: Psalm 117: 1-2

This is the day that you the Almighty God has made...from the rising of the sun till it sets. When Jesus died on the cross to save humankind from sin and death, it was a special day that the Lord had made. Because of my Saviour's love for me, His saving grace, His pardon for sin and in its place His righteousness, the gift of life, the Holy Ghost and the promise of eternal life, I will rejoice and be glad.

A personal testimony:
It's been a long time now - some thirty years. I remember because of the harrowing experience, the pain, anguish and distress entailed then. It was a very sad day when myself and a family member were wrongfully accused of wrong doing. The police were involved and after weeks of providing statements, going to the police station, questionings, I received a letter exonerating me/us from the false allegations.

David in Psalm 31, stated that he cried unto the Lord in his distress and He heard him. God serves as a refuge of goodness for those who trust Him. This day, though there are many, was the day that the Lord gave me the victory from the schemes of Satan. Over the years, I've looked back and seen the goodness and mercies of the Lord and how He rescued us from evil. I do believe that those who serve the Lord will always be rescued from evil.

I observed how the Lord has cleared mine and my family members names, and the relief that brought from the pain and anguish that engulfed our minds. I can relate with the various psalmists when they expressed despair, anxiety, depression and fear because of their enemies. Other times they shout from heights of joy for God's goodness towards them.

I was able to shout praises to God for His deliverance, for setting me/us free. The day I can recall how sad and frightful it was to be persecuted and accused by our very own church sister. Then, and even today, it is the day that the Lord has made when he brought deliverance to our lives from the enemy. I will rejoice and be glad in it. I was able to move on and have a life with a career rather than spend a life of hell behind bars and experience the stigma attached. My family member was also able to move on, grow up, have a life, a career and a family.

I can testify that my blessings are many. I have a lot to rejoice about...in the day that God has made me glad. I claimed the day and will rejoice in it for he has made me glad.

Minister ML Fraser

TUESDAY 8th

I remain confident of this: I will see the goodness of the LORD in the land of the living
Psalm 27:13 (NIV)

I HAD FAINTED UNLESS… – Reading: Psalm 142:1-7

Stagnant, that's how life felt, or in a circle from disappointment to despair and back round again. My mind had become a constant battlefield each thought diverse in its thinking. So many unanswered questions, like, *"Why do the shadows of darkness appear so real and the pain in my heart cut so deep?"*

Lost within my own reasoning, which tried to justify the fatal steps I had taken. Indeed, I had remained trapped within the barrier of these darkening thoughts, ripped between the whispering cry of my spirit and the lusts of my flesh, literally torn between the forces not knowing how long this torment would last.

Denial had become my constant drive and so I had learned and mastered the art of pretence yet, beneath the façade my soul it cried out like a prey captured by its predator. The turmoil was unbearable, feeling like I had lost my mind and forced to cry out, *"Is there no remedy for this hurt?"*

His barrier was no longer encamped around me, open to the vicious wiles of my enemy and my cry for help seemed in vain. Self-destruction had set in and the words *"Why me?"* had become my endless bellow. My heart was full, full of pain and guilt and my spirit imprisoned. Even my tears had become tiresome and the burden finally seemed too much to bear.

I had for too long subconsciously allowed the dreaded mockery, and consciously heard the audible laughter of my enemy. Buried deep within, I had secretly yearned for God's peace to erase this inward turmoil, and for His perfect love to rescue my wandering soul. The hurt rushed back when my mind began to think – so I tried not to. My heart cried, *"No!"*, but my flesh ruled, *"Yes!"*. Trapped in the path of unrighteousness, the vicious cycle seemed unstoppable. I had to somehow draw the line between the present and the future but without vision it was doubtful, without faith it was impossible.

This anguish I now called 'my world' left no room for hope, no room for happiness, only rejoiced in my misery. I had (almost) fainted, my strength was no longer. I was removed from any erg or drive to 'get up'.

BUT, deep within there was a fight, a fight that I seemed to have no power over. It willed me to look past my dreadful state, past the sorrow and emptiness that consumed my being. It eliminated the wicked thought of ultimate defeat. It somehow promised peace and whispered love; it wiped away my tears and comforted my lonely soul.

Surely, I began to find faith - faith that I would survive, faith *that, "I shall not die but live"*. I was broken and wounded, so many hurts. My mind had been open to self-defeat but His promises were sure. Helpless and feeble, I agreed to the operation. Every wound, every infected area, was about to be operated on and healing was in store, peace was in store, strength, restoration, joy was in store.

Name withheld

WEDNESDAY 9th

If it had not been the LORD who was on our side, now may Israel say
Psalm 124:1

IF IT HAD NOT BEEN THE LORD… – Reading: Psalm 124:1-8

The psalmist of Psalm 124 addresses the question, *"Who is the God we bless?"* He is the One who has *"not given us as prey to our enemies' teeth"*. He did not allow the enemy to devour us, but we escaped the traps they set for us, *"as a bird from the snare of the fowlers"*. So after reflecting on all of the Lord's mercies, he repeats the refrain, *"If it had not been the LORD who was on our side…"*.

Like the psalmist, you've no doubt said this yourself, or heard someone say, *"If it wasn't for God…I don't know what or how …"*. Each time we utter, or hear those words, we are drawing from this Pilgrim Psalm of Psalm 124. It is a psalm of victory. Every child of God has a victory praise and a shout of triumph which boasts of the protection, preservation and deliverance made possible through our Lord and Saviour, Jesus Christ.

For every crisis that the Lord has seen us through, let there be a shout of, *"Hallelujah, thank you Jesus"!* Every time He carried us through the flood of troubles, when it felt like we were about to drown as Satan's minions threatened to overwhelm us, let our cries of victory ring out loud and clear. For every storm we went through, despite our sails becoming battered and torn, we were not destroyed on the rocks because our Protector led us to a safe harbour onto firm, dry ground. So let us not forget to do the victory dance as we give Him a shout of praise and sing that song, *"If it had not been for the Lord on my side, tell me where would I be?"*.

Just as the psalmist took a series of psalms to proclaim God's goodness as Israel walked through the streets of Jerusalem up to the sanctuary of the Lord, this psalm reflected on the greatness of Israel's God. He had been their shelter, defender and deliverer. Israel's enemies came to recognise and fear their God. We read how Rahab of Jericho, confessed that the inhabitants of her city were enveloped in fear of Israel's approach because they had heard about the power of Israel's God, and that no king could stand against Him. Just as the God of Israel had repeatedly proven that He would fight for His people, He is no less concerned about the lives of His people today.

Zion still sings, *"Through many dangers, toils and snares, I have already come. It was grace that brought me safe thus far and grace will lead me home"*. It is all because of His love and grace towards us. We receive His grace, unmerited favour, every moment of every day and so He deserves our praise. He deserves our worship. The Lord our God bows down His ear and hears our cry and having heard our requests, He steps into our situations and He does what only God can do! Therefore, we joyfully sing and declare with a loud affirmation, *"Had it not been for the LORD on our side, tell me where would I be, where would I be?"*.

"Experience teaches wisdom" and the wisdom gained, compounded with the assurance coming from the inerrancy of His Word, with the authority of who He is, means that we can face every crisis, with unwavering confidence that He will never leave us nor forsake us. We may walk through the fire and the floods, through loss and pain, but as Job said, *"He knows the way that we take"* and His protection is over us.

No problem leaves him puzzled; no circumstance wearies Him. He is not pressed down by the weight of any burden we may carry and through every trial, He offers us a way of escape. He may allow His children to walk through some unexpected places we never imagined for ourselves, but we have learnt from Job, *'Though He slay me, yet will I trust Him'*, and when the time of testing is over, we will come forth as pure gold.

Name withheld
USA

THURSDAY 10th

For I will not trust in my bow, neither shall my sword save me
Psalm 44:6

HOLD YOUR PEACE - Reading: Psalm 44:1-26

Think about this question deeply before you answer: *"In whom do you put your trust?"* The question may not be as simple as it seems!

May I emphasise this point, i.e., that God does not set us up to fail, He is on our side. We sometimes get ourselves worked up into a knot of worry because life is not going our way, nothing seems to be going according to plan. God is on slow, or worse, He's on mute, we therefore mentally create our own solutions, i.e., Plan A, B, C.

Stop! Do not trust in your own bow or your sword when God wants to fight for you, *"Stand still and see… the LORD will fight for you, and you shall hold your peace"* (Exodus 14:13-14).

I wonder how many battles we have lost because we could not hold our peace! We spoke too soon, said the wrong thing, said too much! At the conquest of Jericho, Joshua commanded the people, *"Ye shall not shout, not make any noise with your voice, neither shall any word proceed out of your mouth until the day I bid you!"* (Joshua 6:10). Well, I'm having a private laugh with myself whilst typing this because silence for some of us is work – hard work!

Can you please hold your peace for a bit longer? Instead, save your voice for the victory!

JEJ

FRIDAY 11th

Except the LORD build the house, they labour in vain that build it: except the LORD keep the city, the watchman waketh but in vain - Psalm 127:1

CO-LABOUR WITH CHRIST - Reading: Psalm 127:1-5

In the life of every believer, there comes a moment when God asks you to do something that you simply don't want to do. We often say that we want God's will for our life, but when faced with the reality of this, it's another thing entirely!

I remember a time when God told me to stay put at a church that I wanted to leave. I was in charge of a department and had been hurt in ministry, and I struggled to forgive. I was upset with God and fought Him constantly. But then God said something to me that completely changed my attitude. He said, *"Who is leading this mission?"*.

In that moment, I came to the realisation that the answer was *me* when it should be *God*! The Holy Spirit should have been who was guiding me but my emotions became the driving force behind my actions. My failure to include Him in the details while building up this department led me to the point of frustration that I was now at. As a result, I almost missed out on the lessons that God was teaching me because I didn't like where His will was leading me.

Anything that we attempt to build without Christ will simply not last. Whether this be our lives, our careers, our marriage, our families or our friendships.

Coming to this point in your walk with God is inevitable. But I encourage you to ask yourself, *"Who is leading the mission, me or God?"*

When I resubmitted myself to God's will, He immediately began to instruct me on how to handle the situation with grace, love and compassion. If I handled it on my own, I would have reacted out of anger and hurt, then doing emotional damage to someone's soul that God placed me in care of.

Sophia Pierre

SATURDAY 12th

But it is good for me to draw near to God: I have put my trust in the Lord GOD, that I may declare all thy works
Psalm 73:28

CLOSE TO GOD: A JOURNEY OF TRUST – Reading: Psalm 73:1-28

Life can feel like a constant battle between our desires and God's will.

Psalm 73 reveals the psalmist's struggle as he compares his life to others, wrestling with envy and doubt. Yet, he finds his answer, not in worldly pursuits, but in drawing near to God.

Psalm 73:28 speaks directly to our need for a deep and intimate relationship with God. When the psalmist says, *"It is good to draw near to God",* he is reminding us that closeness to God is not just beneficial but essential. In a world full of distractions, drawing near to God helps us to shelter our hearts and minds in His truth.

Making God our refuge means trusting Him with our fears, anxieties, and uncertainties. It's about surrendering our desires and allowing Him to guide us. This trust doesn't just change our perspective, it transforms our entire being. As we dwell in His presence, we find peace that doesn't make sense! We find strength and clarity.

In these 31 days in the Psalms, let Psalm 73:28 be your guide. Draw near to God daily. Seek His presence, and let Him be your refuge. Share your testimony of His goodness with others, just like the psalmist did. In doing so, you'll be building on an unshakable foundation that only comes from a life with Jesus at the centre.

Let this be a month of transformation, as you walk closer with Him each day. You'll be amazed at how your life changes for the better!

Latoya J. Foster

SUNDAY 13th

Wait for and confidently expect the LORD; Be strong, and let your heart take courage; Yes, wait for and confidently expect the LORD
Psalm 27:14 (AMP)

WAITING PAYS DIVIDENDS – Reading: Psalm 27:14

Wait? Now there's a novel idea for the post-modern individual. Instant gratification is what it's all about these days! Buy now pay later.

However, that phrase *"pay later"* is loaded with implications. Imagine this scenario: you take out a loan to purchase that car you've always wanted. You've just had an increase in salary and your calculations show you can easily afford the repayments. What you can't plan for, is losing your job. Suddenly job security is gone. The company has gone bankrupt, employees weren't even warned that there was trouble ahead. Now they are down-sizing the workforce. Buying that car, it seemed like a good idea then, but doesn't look so sensible now!

The experience of Abraham and Sarah is a case-in-point. God made a promise that they would give birth to an heir. First Sarah decides she is too old, then she decides the promise is taking too long, and maybe God didn't mean she personally would give birth, so she decides to help God keep his promise. What was the outcome? Disaster!

Five lives were impacted negatively by the *"buy now pay later"* syndrome. Hagar, Ishmael, Sarah, Abraham and Isaac. It's not such a modern idea after all. It was Peter who said we ought to obey God rather than man. Whatever God promises He will do, He will do! He is not a man that he should lie.

Today's scripture text begins and ends with the admonition to wait. This repetition is there to emphasise the point, with a caveat, that God will strengthen the heart of those who wait on Him. There are 116 instances in Scripture where the reader is urged to wait. We may not like the idea, but His Word tells us that, *"Eye hath not seen, not ear heard, neither have entered into the heart of man, the things which God hath prepared for them that love him"* (1 Corinthians 2:9).

Waiting on God is always going to be worth it.

Cheryl Lowe
Guyana

MONDAY 14th

Thy word have I hid in mine heart, that I might not sin against thee
Psalm 119:11

THE WORD IN MY HEART – Reading: Psalm 119:9-16

The Word of God is precious. What do we do with precious things? We put them in a safe place so that we can easily find them when needed.

Our heart is the best place to hide God's Word because it's from the heart that flows the issues of life (Proverbs 4:23). It is the heart that stores bitterness; it is the heart which is described as being *"desperately wicked"* (Jeremiah 17:9).

The Word within therefore acts as the cleansing agent and a source of keeping our conscience alive, letting the Spirit-filled believer know when they have sinned, or are about to sin.

No wonder an unknown writer said:

Lord, write thy name all over my soul
That I sin not, that I sin not
Lord, write thy name all over my soul
And I shall be whiter than the snow!

JEJ

TUESDAY 15th

Thou art my God and I will praise thee: thou art my God, I will exalt thee
Psalm 118:28

PRAISE IS COMELY – Reading: Psalm 118:1-29

The writer of Psalm 118 is anonymous, although the psalm has been attributed to King David by many theologians.

The psalm expresses the psalmist's gratitude towards the LORD for His goodness, mercy and kindness towards him. The writer also gives praise for the hope of the Messiah and encourages the house of Israel and all who fear God to be thankful and trust God.

The Word of God says that, *"(the LORD) inhabits the praises of His people"* (Psalm 22:3), so *"It is a good thing to give thanks unto the LORD"* (Psalm 92:1), for His mercies endure forever. Let all who read this, praise Him. *"Let everything that has breath praise Him"* (Psalm 150:6)! For praise is comely.

So magnify the Lord with me and praise Him for the great things He has done. He deserves all the glory and honour. Praise Him for who He is. Praise Him for keeping us day and night. Praise Him for the healing of the body, soul and spirit. May all that is within me, praise the Lord. Oh, my soul, praise Him for shedding His blood for us to allow all who believe on Him and on His saving name 'Jesus', to be reconciled unto God and have everlasting life (John 3:16-18). Oh, what a mighty God we serve.

Lord, let every moment of my life flow with ceaseless praise of you; for *"Praise is comely for the upright"* (Psalm 33:1).

Dr Anna Crouch

WEDNESDAY 16th

Blessed is the man who walks not in the counsel of the wicked
Psalm 1:1 (ESV)

WE ARE BLESSED TO BE BLESSED – Reading: Psalm 1: 1-6

Psalm 1 presents us with a choice of two ways; one way leads to blessings and the other leads to destruction.

In verse 1, we are invited to partake of the blessed life that God offers. This is the all-wise and all-knowing God, who knows our end from our beginning. As presented here, it is better to obey God rather than follow the advice of the wicked which would lead to an unfortunate end. God's ways lead to everlasting life, in a place void of pain and suffering which is all some of us here on earth know.

What does it mean to be blessed? Not that everything is perfect but that we are able to withstand the onslaught of the enemy because we have God on our side. We are blessed because we benefit from God's benevolence.

Ungodly friends may wield an influence to which we yield if we are weak in the faith. This influence will cause us to lose out on our godly inheritance thereby missing out on our blessing. Proverbs 3:5 encourages us to trust in the Lord…Depending on our own council or even that of friends and others will surely cause us to go astray.

How do we receive counsel from God? We have to meditate in his law, day and night. This law encompasses all of scripture. Consistent and diligent study of God's word is vital for believers. 2 Timothy 2:15 encourages this pathway when it says, *"Study to show thyself approved…rightly dividing the word of truth"*.

Rather than focusing on unfounded truths, we are to let the Word of God dwell in us richly and it will sustain us daily. This is what keeps us blessed. This daily saturation in the Word of God keeps us from going down the paths of unrighteous living, for, *"(the) Word of God is a lamp unto my feet and a light unto my path"* (Psalm 119-105). As we delight ourselves in God's law and obey His commands, we become more like Him, our faith grows stronger and we are not easily moved.

The advice of those who do not trust in God, who are labelled as the scorners and the mockers, cannot stand against or replace godly counsel. I challenge us as women of God who know we are blessed to hold the fort and encourage others by being blessings ourselves.

Sister Barbara Hendrickson
Nevis

THURSDAY 17th

LORD, who shall abide in thy tabernacle? Who shall dwell in thy holy hill?
Psalm 15:1

WALK STRAIGHT, ACT RIGHT, TELL THE TRUTH: Psalm 15:1-5

Many years ago, I worked my way through the ranks of a particular career, gaining experience along the way, until I reached the highest level for the role.

However, from leaving school, no significant further education was studied which, when faced with redundancy from this role, put me at a disadvantage.

I spent many hours applying for an external job, before I was offered a unique role with the deputy chief executive at my then current workplace. My qualifications did not matter to him, just that I was willing and available. That's a good starting attitude, but it took more for me to establish and develop my knowledge, skills and experience.

I am encouraged to know that when we are willing and available, we qualify to praise and worship our creator. However, for to have an ongoing deep fellowship and relationship with God, He requires more.

The psalms, sacred songs and poems used throughout the Bible, provide a base to praise and worship God and to walk deeply with our Heavenly Father. The psalmist asked, *"Who shall **abide** in thy tabernacle? Who shall **dwell** in thy holy hill?".* He answered with this criterion: *"He that walks uprightly, and works righteousness, and speaks the truth in his heart".*

I encourage you to use the psalms as a daily springboard to propel you to remain connected, stay in His house, stay in His presence, obedient to His will and His way.

Today, walk straight, act right, tell the truth.

Sister Dorcas (nee Simmonds)

FRIDAY 18th

Preserve me, O God, for in thee do I put my trust
Psalm 16:1

TO KNOW HIM, LEADS TO TRUST – Reading: Psalm 16:1-11

When I was in my late teens/early twenties, I really struggled with my Christian Walk. I had a lot of anxiety, low self-esteem and an inferiority complex. I always felt that everyone was better than me, and I allowed myself to be treated that way.

My mother saw what was happening and one day, while I was helping her in the kitchen, she asked me a question, *"Would you trust someone that you don't know?"*. I answered, *"No, mom!"*. Then she told me that I needed to know Jesus, and when I get to know Him, I'll begin to trust Him.

The impact of that statement blew my mind! She quoted Philippians 3:10 to me, *"That I may know him, and the power of his resurrection, and the fellowship of his sufferings…"*. Her advice was, *"Get to know Jesus and see your life change"*.

I began to read the gospels more, i.e., Matthew, Mark, Luke, John, which highlighted the life of Christ. I also took David's example and prayed like he did in the psalms and, bit by bit, I began to really know my Lord.

My mindset changed and I saw myself as God sees me. I began to make declarations like:

- I AM THE RIGHTEOUSNESS OF GOD IN CHRIST!

- I AM FEARFULLY AND WONDERFULLY MADE!

When we get to know Jesus Christ, then we will have the confidence to ask Him to preserve (keep and protect), with faith and confidence because we TRUST HIM!

Evangelist Patricia Pierre

SATURDAY 19th

Surely goodness and mercy shall follow me all the days of my life...
Psalm 23:6

MY GOOD SHEPHERD – Reading: Psalm 23:1-6

Greetings in the holy name of Jesus, our soon coming King and Saviour.

Jesus is my shepherd, supplying my daily needs. I learned to trust Him because I have faith in Him. As St John 10:11 says, *"I am the good shepherd, the good shepherd giveth his life for the sheep"*. Whenever I lay down in green pastures, He surrounds me with many blessings. Besides the still waters, He comforts my soul with the Holy Ghost, and I am walking in the Spirit as He is. He restores my soul by giving me strength in my weakness and leads me in the path of righteousness for His name's sake.

I'll obey His will as I listen to His voice and keep praying and fasting. *"Yea, though I walk through the valley of the shadow of death, I will fear no evil, for thou art with me. Thy rod and thy staff comfort me"*. The Lord will keep my soul and deliver me. I will not be ashamed, for I put my trust in Him. *"Let integrity and righteousness preserve me; for I wait on thee. Redeem Israel, oh God, out of all his troubles"* (Psalm 25:21-22).

"Thou prepared a table before me in the presence of my enemies. Thou anointest my head with oil, and my cup runneth over" (Psalm 23:5). The Lord said, *"No weapon formed against thee shall prosper, and every tongue that shall rise against thee in judgment you shall condemn. This is the heritage of the servants of the LORD, and their righteousness is of me, said the LORD"* (Isaiah 54:17).

"Surely goodness and mercy shall follow me all the days of my life, and I will dwell in the house of the Lord forever" (Psalm 23:6). Psalm 1:3 says, *"And he shall be like a tree, planted by the rivers of water, that bringeth forth his fruit in his season; his leaf shall also not wither; and whatsoever he doeth shall prosper"*.

God is a good God and will always be a good God. He will make a way for His people out of no way. I was happy the day that Jesus found me, and I will continue to hold on to Him. He comforts my soul whenever I need Him. I love the Lord deep down in my soul. Amen.

Mother Joycelin Griffiths

SUNDAY 20th

He that dwelleth in the secret place of the most High shall abide under the shadow of the Almighty
Psalm 91:1

ABSOLUTE TRUST IN GOD OUR REFUGE & FORTRESS – Reading: Psalm 91:1-16

I have always found comfort and strength in this passage of scripture, as it reminds me of God's supreme power as Sovereign and King.

To dwell in the secret place of the Most High, is to live daily in the presence of the Lord. The psalmist also found solace under the shadow of the Almighty and declares that, *"Thou wilt shew me the path of life: in thy presence is fulness of joy; at thy right hand there are pleasures for evermore"* (Psalm 16:11).

Dwelling daily in that secret place gives confidence though being persecuted or surrounded by danger. There we are empowered for such a time as this, as our inner man is renewed daily. The Shekinah presence of God makes you feel thoroughly protected and safe, despite the many darts the enemy throws at us, because we trust in Him.

The children of Israel lived this experience, they were protected by a pillar of cloud by day and a pillar of fire by night, indicating the visible presence of the Almighty God for forty years in the wilderness (Exodus 13:21-22).

This is the same God today; He's never changed and cannot change. The Word of God is powerful, therefore if we follow His instructions (Psalm 91:1), we will experience His complete protection and declare with confidence that, *"I will say of the LORD, He is my refuge and my fortress: my God; in him will I trust"* (Psalm 91:2).

So, when the enemy comes in like a flood, I know that I have refuge in Jesus. Sometimes we feel like the pressures and uncertainties of life are about to overflow us. But in Isaiah 43:2, we see the rewards of those that dwell in the secret place. The Lord is ever present, we are never alone, He's got our backs, He covers us with His feathers from dangers seen and unseen, *"When thou passest through the waters, I will be with thee; and through the rivers, they shall not overflow thee: when thou walkest through the fire, thou shalt not be burned; neither shall the flame kindle upon thee" (Isaiah 43:2)*.

Let us continue to dwell daily in the secret place where God promises to protect and preserve His people from all harm.

Minister KJ

MONDAY 21ˢᵗ

I will meditate also of all thy work, and talk of thy doings
Psalm 77:12

REFLECT & TALK – Reading: Psalm 77:1-20

The psalmist, Asaph, is here reminding us to look back and consider all of God's work in our lives, and meditate on all the mighty deeds He has done.

We all will agree that God has been faithful. His works are numerous; a multitude of His tender mercies should not only come to mind, but we ought to dwell upon them in our hearts, meditate upon them in order to gain relief and hope from the past in our present circumstances.

This is for our good and the good of others who don't yet understand why we keep praying in good and bad times. But most importantly, the glory goes to God, He deserves it all. Psalm 77:12 confirms and says, *"I will meditate… and talk of thy doings…"*.

Sisters, let us remember where God has brought us from, from generation to generation He has been faithful. So, praise God in the valley, praise Him on the mountain, and keep praising until our help comes.

Sis Esther Miller

TUESDAY 22nd

He that dwelleth in the secret place of the most High shall abide under the shadow of the Almighty
Psalm 91:1

THE SECRET PLACE – Reading: Psalm 91:1-16

There was a time in my life, where I didn't see the need to trust in God nor did I see the need for intimacy with Him.

I believed that our relationship with God was transactional. As long as I did what He wanted me to do, then and only then would He grant me the desires of my heart. Yet somehow, it would seem that no matter how hard I worked for God, He didn't give me the things that I wanted.

This changed my perception of who God was.

I started to believe that God was a liar and that He wasn't true to His Word...and this broke me! I lost all hope and I didn't know where to turn. But the God who leaves the ninety-nine for the one, found me in this pit and showed me the truth of who He was.

Even though I was lost, hopeless and confused, I knew what a life without God looked like and I didn't want to go back to that. I found myself at an all-night prayer, without expectation, but knowing that I still needed God. I encountered Him in that prayer, and found myself being drawn into the SECRET PLACE where He revealed Himself to me.

In the secret place, is where we can learn to trust God. This is the place where His strength can be made perfect in our weakness.

In the words of Hayley Mulenda, *"The secret is the secret place!"*.

Sis Sophia Pierre

WEDNESDAY 23rd

You are my hiding place and my shield; I hope in your word
Psalm 119:114 (NKJV)

A GUARANTEED ASSURANCE – Reading: Psalm 119:113-120

In the journey of life, we all encounter challenges and moments of doubt. These moments can sometimes feel overwhelming as you juggle numerous responsibilities and expectations. However, Psalm 119:114 offers a profound source of encouragement and strength.

Our everyday experiences seem to be synonymous with various sorrows, or challenges, with the potential to take you off track. You have been designed to rule, reign and have dominion; you are programmed with potential to achieve the things you can perceive.

A reflection on God's Word and the many things that you have achieved is an important reminder. You must intentionally reflect on your achievements, be purposeful in acknowledging steps toward your goal(s), being careful to praise God for the strength which He has given you. The practice of reflection will help you to remember where you are and how much you have grown, it will also help you remember that God gave you the strength and continues to do so.

The strength of this psalm is consistent with the character and nature of God. His presence, power, and protection are evident. Evidence summarises a series of steps that culminate in an assurance that despite what comes your way, you will stand in the face of the storm.

God's presence is with us all the time; we link presence with a feeling of safety and security, but when challenges come, our thoughts of assurance can dissipate to feelings of frustration, fear and anguish. The truth is, our emotions, especially ones which hinder our progress, must be governed by the Word. The power of this psalm is a reminder that God has you!

As you navigate your path, remember that you possess an incredible inner strength, bolstered by your faith. Embrace your unique gifts and talents, knowing that God has equipped you with everything you need to thrive. Your resilience and grace are a testament to His work in you.

Psalm 119:114 is a powerful reminder of God's unwavering presence and protection. Draw on your strength, knowing that God is your refuge and shield, and His Word is a source of enduring hope. Stand tall in this knowledge, and let it empower you to live with boldness and grace each day.

Georgina Walker

THURSDAY 24th

...it was my closest friend, the one I trusted
Psalm 55:13

WHAT KIND OF FRIEND ARE YOU? – Reading: Psalm 55:1-23

Friendship is one of life's most precious gifts. True friendship is built on love, trust and loyalty. We sing the words, *"There's not a friend like the lowly Jesus. No not one..."* and truly there's none. We also know that no man is an island, so we form friendly relations with other persons out of a need for physical interactions.

A true friend will stand by us despite the circumstances. When we celebrate, our friend will be there and when life brings challenges, there is nothing better than a friend by our side. We have that friend in Jesus.

The pain of betrayal by a friend is unbearable. In this passage, David is deeply hurt by someone he trusted. His pain is palpable, and is especially so because this was a companion whose fellowship he had once enjoyed. If it had been an enemy, it would have been understandable, perhaps even expected. But a friend? How can someone whom I trust turn on me like this? David was dumbfounded.

But David had his Forever Friend to turn to. He was always cognizant that he could turn to God no matter what. So he poured out his angst to God who is the only one who could appease his hurt, *"As for me, I call to God, and the LORD saves me"* (Psalm 55:16).

"What a friend we have in Jesus……..what a privilege to carry everything to God in prayer" (Joseph M. Scriven, 1855)

What comfort, what peace, that when our earthly companions forsake us, we have a God who is able to help us to overcome. We can pour out our heartbrokenness, and have confidence that God's shoulder is always available to us, just as He was there for David in his time of need.

Sister Barbara Hendrickson
Nevis

FRIDAY 25th

You will do everything you have promised; Lord, your love is eternal. Complete the work that you have begun
Psalm 138:8 (GNT)

NEVER ALONE – Reading: Psalm 138:1-8

Have you ever felt as if you are failing at most things that you attempt? Do you feel at times as if the enemy has the upper hand? How confident are you that you are not forsaken or rejected by God and that He does care, even about the seemingly insignificant things in your life?

In today's Scripture, David seeks to remind us that we are not alone, neither are we forgotten by God. What are those things that you feel incapable of doing? What are those circumstances that you have been facing that seem insurmountable? Have you been feeling insufficient in some areas of your life? Are you faced with extreme opposition from the enemy? This is a reminder to you today that God is with you, His mercy endures forever, and that He is working it out. Everything is made perfect through Christ, and we must trust His work. He is continuously acting on our behalf, putting all the pieces in the right places that ensure our victory.

There are times when we may not see Him at work but that's because He is fixing things behind the scenes that will cause everything to fall into its rightful place. Let us not cast any doubt on His omnipotence, omnipresence or omniscience.

Can we think of someone who we really love and care for? How concerned are we about their wellbeing and making sure that everything is alright with them? Well, how much more our heavenly Father in caring about all that pertains to us!

Cherely S.
USA

SATURDAY 26th

As the deer pants for the water brooks, so pants my soul for You, O God
Psalm 42:1 (NKJV)

THE SUSTAINER – Reading: Psalm 42:1-11

Today's psalm begins with an ode to the true lover of David's heart.

The one David acknowledges through every season in what was a life with many highs, and equally many lows. David would seek the face of the Lord with an intensity and thirst that he describes so passionately as the thirsting of a deer panting, longing for the water brook. David seeks after an intimate relationship with God knowing that the God of creation is the only one that can fulfil him.

David is probably one of the first to truly recognise the spiritual art of meditation. In other chapters the reader is instructed to not only thirst for God but to pause and spend time with God and meditate on His word. Meditation on the Word is more powerful than many of us may even realise today. Meditating on the Word of God is the only way to obtain greater depth and increased longing for God, who also longs for you to be in His presence. In His presence is peace.

We see David often yielding to his desires but, even in these moments, David runs back to the Father because he understood that he could do nothing without Him. There is a humility which David experiences that even when he succumbs and makes improper decisions, yet his desire for God stays true and God's love for David was evident. David reminds us of human fragility.

This desire, like the deer panting for the water, expresses an insight for us to thirst but also to drink from the life source - the true living water that is Christ Jesus our Lord.

Georgina Walker

SUNDAY 27th

For in the time of trouble shall He shall hide me in His pavilion: in the secret of His tabernacle shall He hide me: He shall set me up upon a rock
Psalm 27:5

WE HAVE A BLESSED HOPE – Reading: Psalm 27:1-7

Life is full of peaks and troughs. We tend to be joyful when all is going well. However, when things are not going as well as we would like, there is a tendency for one to become anxious and sometimes depressed. This coupled with ongoing world events and news, which currently reflect troubling times, can be and is proving challenging to many.

In times like this, however, it is good to remember certain promises of God. Psalm 27: 5 assures us that the Lord *"will hide us in His pavilion in the time of trouble, in the secret of His tabernacle"*. This is similar to Daniel's prophecy of the last days that says concerning the nation of Israel: *"...there shall be a time of trouble, such as never was since there was a nation even to that same time: and at that time thy people shall be delivered, every one that shall be found written in the book".* (Daniel 12:1). We are therefore not to fret: *"For God has not appointed us to wrath, but to obtain salvation by our Lord Jesus Christ"* (1 Thessalonians 5:9).

God is a promise keeper and shall fulfil all His word. He is not a man that He should lie (Numbers 23:19); so watch, pray and look up, for our redemption draweth nigh. He is at the door!

Dr Anna Crouch

MONDAY 28th

Create in me a new, clean heart, O God, filled with clean thoughts and right desires
Psalm 51:10 (TLB)

SEARCH ME, O GOD – Reading: Psalm 51:1-19

Jeremiah 17:9 says, *"The heart is deceitful above all things, and desperately wicked: who can know it?"*

David acknowledged his sin. He knew that he had messed up and therefore surrendered to God. He cried out to God for mercy!

We can only receive help, cleansing, purging and forgiveness, when we are honest with ourselves that we are in need of it.

There must be a surrendering, a daily dying to self and sin. Self-righteousness and sin separate us from God.

A *"die-to-self-daily"* kind of life leads to a Spirit-filled life. That's the abundant life which the Word of God speaks about!

One songwriter penned the words, *"This is my desire, to honour you. Lord with all my heart, I worship you. All I have within me - I give you praise. All that I adore is in you. Lord, I give you my heart, I give you my soul, I live for you alone. Every breath that I take, every moment I'm awake; Lord, have your way in me"*.

Give Him the RIGHT OF WAY to do with us as He wills!

May we cry out, *"Have mercy upon me, O God!"* and, *"Create in me a clean heart!"*.

Evangelist Patricia Pierre

TUESDAY 29th

When the LORD turned again the captivity of Zion we were like then that dream
Psalm 126:1

EUPHORIA – Reading: Psalm 126:1-6

This is one of my favourite psalms.

We have a familiar expression: "Walking on air". It describes that feeling of euphoria that comes when something wonderful happens and it's better than you ever imagined. Passing that driving test, opening those exam results that were better than expected; getting that job! That marriage proposal; I could go on and on. Even now when I think about those moments I get "butterflies in my tummy". At times like these, all is well with the world, you can't stop smiling and as we all know, smiles and laughter are infectious.

I remember a day when I was giggling about something that had happened. My eleven-year-old son at the time saw my amusement and without knowing what I was laughing about, began laughing himself so hard he was beside himself with laughter, still not knowing why I was laughing.

Imagine what it was like when slavery in the US was abolished. This was the experience of Israel. They had been in captivity for 400 years. In Genesis 15:13; God told Abraham, *"...thy seed shall be a stranger in a land that is not theirs and they shall afflict them four hundred years"* The night of the exodus, after the first born had been killed, was surreal. Israel was prepared and ready to go at midnight. Then they came up against the Red Sea, more heart-pounding consternation, how will they get across?

The sea rolled back and they walked through on dry ground. What is more, they had a fiery cloud that gave them light at night and shade from the heat by day. Not only that, they saw the whole Egyptian army that had followed them with evil intent dead on the sea shore. Best of all, the nations around heard their story and were amazed. What a witness (Joshua 2:10; Joshua 5:1). For forty years they had cried because of their bondage (Exodus 2:23). They wept for their sons - all boys around the age of Moses died at Pharaoh's decree. *"Every son that is born, you shall cast into the river"* (Exodus 1:22).

Now they were reaping in joy, led out of Egypt by the only surviving male from that era, i.e., Moses. Emancipation/freedom came like a dream. Laughter followed, and singing was the overflowing of the joy that filled their souls. This is a psalm relevant for past, present and future. The redeemed at Christ's return shall sing the song of Moses and the Lamb celebrating ultimate emancipation from the bondage of sin (Revelation 15:3).

Today our crucibles are temporary! Praise God for deliverance; we must laugh for it doth good like a medicine (Proverbs 17:22). We must sing, we must be joyful. Practice for when Jesus Christ returns and the sheaves are brought into His kingdom, there will be rejoicing such as we have never known.

"He that goeth forth and weepeth, bearing precious seed, shall doubtless come again with rejoicing, bringing his sheaves with him" (Psalm 126:6).

Cheryl Lowe
Guyana

WEDNESDAY 30th

I laid me down and slept; I awaked for the LORD sustained me
Psalm 3:5

LET GOD FIX IT – Reading: Psalm 3:1-8

Psalm 3 is a passionate writing of David who is on the run from his palace and Jerusalem. He is fleeing because of his son Absalom who has staged a rebellion against his father, seeking to take the throne.

Unfortunately, this uprising is partly God's chastisement for David's past sins which, although he had been forgiven, David still had to bear. God's word cannot return to Him void – that means blessings and also curses.

Notwithstanding, God was with David, and we see that He dealt with Absalom for his rebellion against his father (2 Samuel 18:9-17) who was God's choice servant.

Whilst fleeing, and contemplating the complexity of his circumstance, David marvels at the speed at which enemies had risen up against him. People whom he had served, those who once applauded him, who danced and said, *"Saul has slain his thousands and David his ten thousands"* (1 Samuel 18:7), had been charmed and won by Absalom.

Running but communing with the only one that he could, David started to remind himself of who God is, *"But thou, O LORD art a shield for me; my glory, and the lifter of my head"* (Psalm 3:3). Not feeling like a King, now a fugitive because of his own son, the prestige and honour of his kingship in tatters, a feeling of utter shame and embarrassment, but you O LORD, you continue to be faithful, nobody can take you from me. Your glory, O God, continues to cover me.

You too may be hanging your head down today in shame. Somebody has done something wicked to you, they hit you where they knew that it would hurt, and you wonder how you will ever recover and clear your name. But for sure, God is the lifter of your head. David in the same chapter says that the teeth of his enemies are broken (v7), meaning that in God's time, they would no longer be able to bite and cause him pain.

Waiting for God to clear your name may seem like it's taking forever, but God stands true to His Word, *"Vengeance is mine, I will repay"* (Deuteronomy 32:35; Romans 12:19).

Don't stay awake at night thinking about it. Let God fix what's gone wrong as you learn and allow this painful season to draw you nearer to Him.

JEJ

THURSDAY 31st

For thou, LORD, wilt bless the righteous; with favour wilt thou compass him as with a shield
Psalm 5:12

HE IS OUR SHIELD – Reading: Psalm 5:1-12

A shield is described as a piece of defensive armour carried on the arm. It protects as a barrier to deflect any attacking force.

God first told Abram in Genesis 15:1, *"Fear not Abram, I am thy shield and thy exceeding great reward"*. God assures him of protection.

There are some fifteen mentions of God being our shield in the psalms - this is fighting talk!

Abram was called to leave his home and everything that he knew to go to a new land where God will sustain him. He will face difficulties however God will protect him.

When we respond to God's call on our lives everything changes for us as well, and the same God of Abram/Abraham will protect us.

In Psalm 5, David also joins the chorus of thanksgiving for God's protection. From the time that he awakes (v3), he will make his voice heard - he will pray to his God and King!

In verse 8, David asks the LORD to lead him in righteousness because of his enemies. He is asking for a straight path. The words of an enemy may well be hurtful; however, God will deflect the intended aim.

Verse 11's encouragement is to all those that put their trust in God to rejoice; *"let them ever shout for joy, because (God) defendest them; let them also that love thy name be joyful in thee"*.

When David reaches verse 12, he is able to say that, *"the LORD will bless the righteous; with favour wilt thou compass him as with a shield"*.

When we consider men like Abraham and David who are heroes of faith, we must also remember that they are not exceptions but examples for us! If they and others mentioned in the Word were exceptions, we'd have no reason to have faith or believe that our God is a shield for us too.

BVG

August
Women of Purpose

FRIDAY 1st

But the queen Vashti refused to come at the king's commandment...
Esther 1:12

BEAUTIFUL CHARACTER: VASHTI THE QUEEN
Reading: Esther 1:1-22

Little is mentioned about Queen Vashti in the Bible, and it's very tempting to use what is known about her to give an unfair portrayal of who she actually was.

The name *"Vashti"* is a Persian name which means *"beautiful woman"*. Vashti has been linked to being the daughter of King Alyattes (King of Lydia); or the daughter of Belteshazzar, or the daughter of Otanes an Achaemenid judge during the reign of Darius the Great.

In ancient Persian culture, Vashti, as the principle queen (known as the 'King's Lady'), could travel on her own, have her own entourage and staff, sign agreements and have her own seal as well as have places to hold banquets as demonstrated in Esther 1:9.

King Ahasuerus flaunted his wealth and power for 180 days, followed by a 7-day feast for his princes and servants and powerful leaders of Persia and Media. Intoxicated with wine, he demanded his wife to appear naked only wearing the royal crown to display her beauty before his guests.

Ahasuerus' request was a direct breach of Persian law regarding modesty, and an insult towards his most prized possession who was prohibited from presenting herself before a group of men clothed in her royal robes, yet alone naked. In Persian custom, the queen was secluded during feasts where wine flowed freely, and the wives of inferior ranks or concubines were called.

Vashti was placed in an unfavourable situation; obedience to the command would bring disgrace and dishonour, and disobedience would lead to disrepute and dismissal. Vashti valued her self-respect and acted with integrity and courage in her refusal to exhibit herself. The thought of entertaining such an act before a group of drunken men is repulsive and indecent.

Vashti stood strong and bold in the face of severe punishment for her refusal to obey, leading to her being dethroned. She maintained her dignity and was willing to endure humiliation as she was degraded from the lavish lifestyle she enjoyed as a member of the royal household.

In our modern world, modest dressing has become a way to empower women to be known for who they are, and not be judged by their beauty or how they look. It can be utilised to help women to be taken seriously and demand respect.

Vashti's real beauty was her inner strength and bravery to stand up for what was right. As godly women, we may face situations that challenge what we know to be right. Be prepared to take a stand for what is right, even if it means humiliation, rejection or loss. As John P. Kee wrote in his song, *"Stand"*:

"Stand for holiness, stand for righteousness
And be counted among them that shall reign with Him
You stand, when friends are gone
Stand when you're all alone, and believe He shall receive His own".

Name withheld

SATURDAY 2nd

And the maiden pleased him, and she obtained kindness of him; and he speedily gave her her things for purification, with such things as belonged to her, and seven maidens, which were meet to be given her, out of the king's house: and he preferred her and her maids unto the best place of the house of the women
Esther 2:9

POSITIONED FOR PURPOSE - Reading: Esther 2:7-9; 1 Corinthians 1:27

Today we look at Queen Esther and note that her story is a powerful testament to living with purpose. Her journey from being an orphan to becoming a queen was marked by divine purpose, and the favour she found with key individuals like Mordecai and Hegai.

Mordecai, adopted his cousin Esther after her parents died (Esther 2:7). He raised her as his own daughter, providing her with guidance and protection. This relationship was crucial as Mordecai's wisdom and faith played a significant role in shaping Esther's character and decisions. This chapter reminds us that our God is a God who sees beyond our limitations and has a divine plan for our lives. He uses the ordinary to achieve the extraordinary (1 Corinthians 1:27).

Hegai's (the eunuch in charge of the women) favour toward Esther was not just about her physical beauty, but also about positioning Esther in the best possible way to win the king's favour. Her favourable treatment by Hegai also demonstrated how God's favour can lead to preferential treatment and blessings in unlikely places! This favour was part of a divine plan to place Esther in a position where she could influence the king and ultimately save her people.

I want to encourage you, my sisters, who may not know their purpose. I'm sure that Esther didn't either but God positioned her for a purpose. He strategically guided her step by step to put her in a position to be used by Him, and He'll do the same for you as you submit yourself as Esther did to Mordecai and Hegai.

CP

SUNDAY 3rd

Mary said, Behold the handmaid of the Lord; be it unto me according to thy word
Luke 1:38

TELL ME AGAIN WHO I AM – Reading: Luke 1:26-38

Mary is a young lady, new at life, but by now clear on who she is and where she fits. Yet unwed, she knows fully well that she is physically incapable of mothering a baby, let alone the Messiah! She describes herself in other texts as "lowly". Was this in status only? Age? Ability? Who knows the degree to which she was convinced of her own unworthiness, but it was all there in this woman who loved God.

And often it is all there in us too!

But what do we learn about our own prescribed identity by watching Mary? It is that whilst her self-description was true, it was not all the truth in the eyes of God. The truth was that she was blessed and to be the mother of Jesus. She may well have been lowly and unconsidered, but she was simultaneously favoured and God's chosen. Do we think of ourselves in such a humbling way?

The kingdom of this world will sell us yet another lie that we are to deny our own flaws in order to feel fulfilled. To dispute that we have any weakness, regret or un-glossed realities. And whilst we live in denial, we are to simultaneously 'slay' at life and live in success, love and ministry. Well, I for one am a Christian woman who ticks the 'opt out' box to that narrative! Rather discerning the truth about godliness and purpose through this discourse.

Whilst we work on our realities, speak and share about them with intention, we are shown that we as women of GODLY purpose, lean in again to the narrative of heaven and ask God, *"Who am I again?"*. Because, like Mary, if we agree with heaven to say, *"Be it unto me as you have said, God"*, His truth will surge through the veins of our tomorrow, shaping the yet unknown of our story in tiny increments.

We don't know the fullness of who we are through the mirror of this world. But we're praying, *"God, be it unto me as You have said"*, and therein we will find our identity.

Joy Lear-Bernard

MONDAY 4th

Come, see a man, which told me all things that ever I did: is not this the Christ?
John 4:29

THE APPOINTMENT – Reading: John 4:4-29

Jesus had an appointment to keep, and He couldn't be late!

His disciples had gone on an errand while Jesus sat at Jacob's well in Sychar (John 4:5-6), and waited patiently. It was quiet now. The early morning rush when all the women draw their water, had long gone. Now, the temperature was too hot to draw water. Or was it?

As Jesus looked up, He saw her: the woman of Samaria. We never heard her name. All we know is that she had had several husbands. Yet, right there at the well, in the heat of the sun, despite her past, instead of condemnation she received compassion. Instead of judgment was joy. Instead of rejection was revelation. Her purpose was unlocked. Her past was forgiven, and all was made new. This sinner woman's eyes were opened and she realised, even before Jesus' disciples knew, that this indeed was the Christ, the Anointed One.

When you keep your appointment with Jesus, (He has an appointment booked with each of us), and you meet Him face to face; when He sees your past, yet still loves you, at last – like that Samaritan woman - your purpose too will be unlocked! Your past will be forgiven, and all things made new.

Min Jo Earle

TUESDAY 5th

Adam named his wife Eve, because she would become the mother of all the living
Genesis 3:20 (NIV)

PURPOSE & COURAGE – Reading: Ephesians 4:7-16

From the very beginning, God infused purpose into the life of Eve. In Genesis 3:20, Adam names her *"Eve"* meaning *"life"* or *"living"*, recognising her as the mother of all humanity. This simple yet profound act highlights a divine truth: we are all created with an exclusive purpose, intricately woven into the fabric of God's plan.

Eve's purpose extended far beyond her role as the first mother. She was a partner, a nurturer, and a bearer of life; both physically and spiritually. Her life serves as a reminder that we carry the potential to influence and nurture life in countless ways. Imagine being a collaborator in bringing forth the Seed of the woman, Jesus Christ Himself! Now that's purpose!

As women of purpose today, we are called to embrace our God-given roles with faith and intentionality. Our purpose may manifest in different ways; whether through our family life, career, ministry, or community service. However, the common thread remains: we are designed to bring life, hope, and love into the world.

Let us reflect on the legacy of Eve and recognise that our purpose is not defined by our circumstances but by the Creator who named and called us. As we walk in our divine purpose, let us be encouraged that we, too, can be bearers of life, contributing to God's kingdom in ways uniquely orchestrated by Him.

Prayer: Lord, help me to embrace my purpose with courage and grace. May I bring life and hope to those around me, fulfilling the calling You have placed on my life. Amen.

Latoya J. Foster

WEDNESDAY 6th

But (Rahab) had brought (the spies) up to the roof of the house, and hid them...
Joshua 2:6

DESTINED FOR GREATNESS – Reading: Joshua 2:1-6

The people, a chosen people by God,
Neither to be despised nor forsaken,
For a woman of God might face challenges,
But it must be her faith in God that is never taken.

For the trust we have in God is comforting,
A reassuring feeling of belonging,
So even if you have gone astray,
God provides you with the refuge you've been longing,
For the past is set in stone and today brings a new.

Concealed in the hearts of every woman is purpose sent from God,
So let what God has sown in you, the purpose of today,
Be the drive of your life without hesitation or delay,
For God's promise is assured, the covenant of His creation.

To change your life for the better through complete transformation,
For the confession of faith to God and God alone,
Is the confession to work according to His will,
Through God's grace and mercy he allows us to atone.

Even in worry remember what Jesus said, peace be still,
For God will calm the storm whether you are aware or not,
So woman of God, hold on to the journey that God has pathed for you,
For there is greatness in your purpose, know that God will see you through.

Name withheld

THURSDAY 7th

...when she saw that he was a goodly child, she hid him...
Exodus 2:2

FAITH & LOVE – Reading: Exodus 2:1-10; Numbers 26:59

Long before William Ross Wallace coined the phrase: *"The hand that rocks the cradle rules the world"*, a little slave woman, Jochebed, living in the great Egyptian metropolis, recognised that God had empowered her as a mother to determine the future of her child.

In the midst of the calamity that was going on with the genocide decreed by principalities and powers of Egypt, she realised that she had been blessed with a 'goodly' child. And so, against all odds, she determined to save his life and be instrumental in helping him achieve his destiny.

This seemingly insignificant housewife, under godly inspiration, became somebody and taught her children to partake of her divine inspiration. She would exercise faith by 'watching and praying'; she would show her children how. Her daughter Miriam was an astute learner. She watched and waited for the right opportunity and instinctively knew when the time was right and what to say to clench the deal (Exodus 2:4&7).

When the miracle came, Jochebed would raise her son Moses whilst being paid. She would homeschool him, train him, and by the age of accountability - 12, he would be ready to face the world. By the time he became a man, he was an independent spirit. He had learnt to resist the temptations of modern Egyptian society, to the point where it was said of him, *"...by faith he forsook Egypt, not fearing the wrath of the king"* (Hebrews 11:24-26).

Like Jochebed, every woman must be aware of her power and how to use it in the right way. It's your God-given unchallengeable right. It makes you co-worker together with God (1 Cor. 3:9) to shape the future in your children. Faith and love in action made Jochebed strong and successful in achieving her goals. It can do the same for you.

Cheryl Lowe
Guyana

FRIDAY 8th

...before I had done speaking in my heart, behold, Rebekah came forth
Genesis 24:45

REBEKAH – Reading: Genesis 24:1-67

Rebekah was a woman of purpose, we do not know her age, but we can see in the Word that she married to Isaac when he was 40 years old (Genesis 25:20).

Rebekah had unknown divine purpose. Unwittingly, her actions and responses when she went to draw water from the well one day would take her away from everything that she knew and propel her into a whole new life.

Her father-in-law, Abraham, desired in his heart that his son, Isaac, would marry someone from his own people and not somebody from the land in which they were living (Genesis 24:7). Eliezer, the faithful servant of Abraham, was sent to seek a wife for Isaac. He prayed by the well that God would provide, and as we know, God cannot fail (Genesis 24:11-15). Rebekah confirmed her identity as the God-prepared spouse for Isaac, by a generous act. Eliezer had asked in his prayer that she carry out a specific task and Rebekah did it exactly, word-for-word (Genesis 24:19)!

Women of God, our actions, attitude and words are powerful; they show whose we are. When Eliezer saw the hand of God on this young woman's life, he bowed down and worshipped the Lord (Genesis 24:26-27).

Rebekah's family agreed to the marriage, but they wanted to give her at least ten days to spend with them before she left for Canaan. Eliezer had other plans; he wanted to leave straightaway. Rebekah was given the choice; she chose to go immediately and so her family sent her off with a blessing!

Rebekah and Isaac meet at the end of the journey; he takes her into his mother's tent and she becomes his wife, and he loves her. All is well but for the fact that Rebekah is barren. Our destiny is assured however we must reach it in relationship with God by prayer and fasting.

When Rebekah conceived, there were problems for her - the children struggled within her womb. She went to enquire of the Lord. He told her that two nations were in her womb, and one would be stronger than the other and the elder would serve the younger.

At her delivery the first twin was named Esau, his brother was called Jacob. Isaac was by now 60 years old. As the boys grew, Esau was a good hunter and Jacob was a homely man. Isaac loved Esau because he liked eating his venison but Rebekah loved Jacob. We may look at their parenting with surprise yet the Word of God was fulfilled in this family, despite their preferences. God uses us despite of us.

As we read on, we see the words of God lived out in this family with some challenging results. Rebekah and Isaac in Genesis 27:5-6 are referred to as parents in the singular; it's as if they have one son each! Rebekah continues to help Jacob obtain all that was Esau's by any means that she can, even deceiving the husband that loves her.

She has changed from that carefree girl at the well!

Rebekah a woman of purpose…

BVG

SATURDAY 9th

Bathsheba bowed, and paid homage to the king, and the king said, What do you desire?
1 Kings 1:16 (ESV)

BATSHEBA: A WOMAN OF PURPOSE – Reading: 1 Kings 1:1-53

"Even when bad things happen you have to try to use those bad things in a positive manner and really just take the positive out of it." (Natalie du Toit)

The story of Bathsheba reminds us that God has a plan and can work even through difficult situations with imperfect people to bring about something good. Despite the unsavory events surrounding her life coming to the palace, Queen Bathsheba became the mother of the wisest and most successful king ever to grace the throne.

Let's examine both the positive and negative aspects of Queen Bathsheba's life.

Bathsheba (which means *"daughter of abundance"*) was the daughter of Eliam and the wife of Uriah the Hittite, a soldier in King David's army.

Initially, we are introduced to the passive side of Bathsheba in her first appearance before the King:

- ❖ King David commanded his servant to have her brought to him in the palace (2 Samuel 11:4)
- ❖ She was silent and
- ❖ without agency
- ❖ a victim of sorrow, loss, and grief

Following the tragic passing of Bathsheba's first son, her role in the story gradually diminishes. Nevertheless, in 2 Samuel 12:24, she is identified as David's wife and the mother of Solomon. It is estimated that twenty years have elapsed since Solomon's birth when Bathsheba re-emerges in the narrative, nearing the end of David's life. At this point, she is portrayed as:

- ❖ a woman of great strength and determination, symbolizing resilience during challenging times (1 Kings 1:28).

- ❖ a teacher
- ❖ A woman of action who embraced good council (1 Kings 1: 11-35)
- ❖ A woman of faith
- ❖ A survivor
- ❖ Compassionate (2 Samuel 11:26)
- ❖ Trusting and helpful (1 Kings 2: 13-21)
- ❖ Bathsheba played a key role in securing her son's royal future (1 Kings 1:30-31)

Reflecting on both the negative and positive aspects of Bathsheba's life, we acknowledge that, regardless of the situation we find ourselves in, God's plan for our lives will be fulfilled. We find reassurance in the belief that no sin is too great for God to forgive, and no grief is too profound for God to comfort, *"But as for you, you meant evil against me; but God meant it for good, in order to bring it about as it is this day, to save many people alive" (Genesis 50:20).*

Marlene Hines
Jamaica

SUNDAY 10th

...yea I will bless her, and she shall be a mother of nations; kings of people shall be of her
Genesis 17:16b

CHOSEN TO SERVE – Reading: Genesis 17: 1-27

When God made His promise to Sarah that she would become the mother of many nations, she was in disbelief. Barren for all these years and being well past the time of motherhood, Sarah only saw the impossibility of it all. But with God, all things are possible.

Sarah had been granted the wonderful opportunity to be part of the lineage of Jesus Christ the Saviour. As the first matriarch, she was abundantly blessed by God. As Sarah's daughters, God's blessings continue to be harvested by us. How do we translate these blessings? We become women of purpose, chosen to serve. As part of that mandate, women must also tell the Good News. What an awesome responsibility and opportunity to share the love of God!

Wherever there is work to be done for the Kingdom, women are at the forefront. Jesus himself demonstrated that service is important. As His followers, women pattern their lives after Him. Our purpose is to declare that Jesus Christ is Lord, that He came to remove the sting of death and reward us with abundant life. Women serve as Pastors, Teachers, Missionaries and much more and we are endowed with the ability to bring others to Christ.

We must be intentional as befits women of purpose so that all with whom we interact will be impacted by our way of life. As women of purpose, we are the conduits through whom God works. We serve because we love. We love, because we are loved.

We are light bearers and as such our light must shine through our service while we point souls to the Light - Jesus the Christ. Sarah's faith and obedience made her a vessel of honour and worthy of a mention in the Hebrews' Hall of Faith (Hebrews 11:11), *"Through faith also Sarah herself received strength to conceive seed, and was delivered of a child when she was past age..."*. That is an excellent example for women of purpose.

Let us embrace our purpose especially in these troublesome times, serve faithfully, and put the enemy to flight.

Sister Barbara Hendrickson
Nevis

MONDAY 11th

And the angel answered and said unto the women, Fear not ye: for I know that ye seek Jesus which was crucified...go quickly, and tell his disciples...behold, he goeth before you...
Matthew 28:5 & 7

CALLED FOR PURPOSE – Reading: Matthew 28:1-20

This passage is a profound reminder of the power of God and fulfilment of His promises.

The resurrection of Jesus Christ is not just a historical event; it is the cornerstone of our faith, the proof of God's ultimate victory over sin and death. It is a message of hope, renewal, and the assurance that God's promises are true and steadfast. The empty tomb is a symbol of the new life available to all who believe in Christ.

As believers, we are called to live in the light of the resurrection. Just as the angel instructed the women to go quickly and tell the disciples that Jesus had risen, we too are called to share the good news with others. The resurrection is not only a message of victory, but also a mission. It compels us to proclaim the life-changing power of Christ's resurrection, to offer hope to a world in desperate need of it.

For women of purpose, this illustrates that they are called to be bold and courageous messengers of God's truth, entrusted with carrying and sharing the transformative message of Christ's resurrection. The women at the tomb were commissioned to share the good news of the resurrection, women today are called to step into their purpose and make a transformative impact in the world for Christ.

Name withheld

TUESDAY 12th

...your sincere faith...dwelt first in your grandmother Lois and your mother Eunice and now, I am sure, dwells in you as well
2 Timothy 1:5 (ESV)

PASS IT ON! – Reading: 2 Timothy 1:1-6

Many of us reading this page did not know our grandparents. I used to be so jealous of friends at school when they spoke about their grandparents; how I wish I knew my grandmother!

Timothy was so blessed to have been jointly raised by two women who had a mutual interest in his spiritual growth; his mother, Eunice, and grandmother, Lois. This is the only scripture where these ladies are mentioned; their faith was so strong and the way they taught Timothy is an example to us all.

Scripture says in Proverbs 22:6 that we must, *"train up a child in the way he should go: and when he is old, he will not depart from it".* This is exactly what Lois and Eunice jointly did, and Timothy didn't depart from the truth. They may not have known it at the time, but their purpose was to prepare young Timothy for ministry.

Let us continue, or begin, to be like Lois and Eunice. Allow our faith to penetrate the hearts of the next generation because our purpose is to spread the gospel, and this starts from home; they may be an upcoming Timothy. Let's pass on what we know not just in words but actions also.

"...Faith cometh by hearing..." (Romans 10:17)

Lady Pam Lewin

WEDNESDAY 13th

Favour is deceitful and beauty is vain, but a woman that feareth the LORD, she shall be praised. Give her of the fruit of her hands; and let her own works praise her in the gates.
Proverbs 31:30-31

WOMAN OF SUBSTANCE – Reading: Proverbs 31:30-31

"I am beautiful, I am valuable, I am God's peculiar treasure". *"Affirm yourselves through God's Word"* - Overseer Joy Henry

These powerful words express the importance of speaking, declaring and believing who we are in God. The journey then to becoming a woman of substance and purpose is often one of brokenness, growth, fortitude, transparency, determination, grace and beauty.

There is a saying that states, *"Beauty is skin deep"*, meaning that a person's appearance does not necessarily determine who that person is. Often times the external beauty does not reflect the inner person. But the beauty that is mentioned in Proverbs 31 speaks of the inner qualities of a virtuous woman such as faith, integrity, character, which are far more valuable than external beauty… This virtuous woman has a deep awe and reverence for God which is worthy of praise and adoration.

She exemplifies four different character traits of a virtuous woman; she has a balanced work, home life. This woman knows how to take care of her personal life, meet both the physical and emotional needs of her husband and children, she is diligent in work and business and, because she can be trusted, her husband is respected and she is recognised, loved and appreciated in her community.

This aligns with biblical principles that we too can strive to do good whether in our home, church or the local community, by treating others with respect and kindness so God will be glorified in all.

Name withheld

THURSDAY 14th

The inhabitants of the villages ceased, they ceased in Israel, until that I Deborah arose, That I arose a mother in Israel
Judges 5:7

ONE ACTION – Reading: Judges 5:1-31

Deborah was a prophetess, yet she is remembered and marked by one action.

She gave herself credit as a *"Mother in Israel"* (Judges 5:7) who rose up and reminded Barak of God's instruction which enabled Israel to conqueror Canaan.

Mothers, i.e., stay-at-home mothers, spiritual mothers, biological mothers, 'like a mother' and adopted mothers. Whichever label you accept, **all** have a purpose.

Sometimes the Woman of Purpose is recognised at the end of life when the impact of one action is voiced during the eulogy, or memorial, wake or repast. That one action made a difference and fulfilled the purpose for someone or in the lives of many people.

We can be Women of Purpose every day:
Seeing when no one sees,
Hearing when no one hears,
Listening when no one listens,
Encouraging when no one encourages,
And caring when no one cares.

We are Women of Purpose when we break the silence of pain for the down-trodden, change the norm of complacency and apathy, doing what is needed, unnoticed behind the scenes, bridging the gap, creating hope in relationships, and befriending the isolated. The list goes on!

One action in obedience to God's command. One action reminding each other of the calling to be overcomers.

Today, let's arise with one 'mother-like' action, that reflects Christ in us as Women of Purpose!

Sister Dorcas (nee Simmonds)

FRIDAY 15th

Blessed above women shall Jael the wife of Heber the Kenite be, blessed shall she be above women in the tent
Judges 5:24

JAEL – Reading: Judges 4:1-24; 5:24-27

In a time of war and bloodshed, the wife of Heber the Kenite, lived with her husband in a tent pitched in the plain Zaanaim. Her name was Jael, a woman with no fancy titles, no special designation, and no credentials, but her name was about to become part of history.

King Jabin of Canaan and Heber were at peace, so it was not surprising for Sisera, the captain of Jabin's host, to seek refuge at Heber's house when he was being chased by the Israelites – Deborah and Barak. Like an excellent hostess, Jael went out to meet Sisera and invited him to enter her home. She covered him and instead of the water which he requested, she 'kindly' gave him a bottle of milk and made sure he was comfortable. She also listened to his instructions to guard the door and not let anyone know that he was there. We can imagine her smile as she nodded, *"Yes"!*

While he slept, Jael went softly to Sisera, and with her hammer and a large tent nail, she drove the nail through his temples and into the ground. She disobeyed his instructions and showed his dead body to Barak and Sisera when they arrived. Her purpose in God went beyond even her husband's peaceful relations with a king. A woman with no credentials brought deliverance to Israel.

Zahra H. Oliphant
Jamaica

SATURDAY 16th

...a certain woman named Lydia...whose heart the Lord opened...was baptised, and her household ...
Acts 16:14-15

TRUST IN HIS WORD – Reading: Acts 16:11-15

Lydia was a worshipper of God, yet it was not until she heard Paul's message that her heart was fully opened to the gospel. This pivotal moment led to her immediate baptism and the baptism of her household, marking a significant turning point in her life.

Lydia's response to the gospel was characterised by openness, faith, and immediate action. She didn't merely listen to the words; she received them with a heart ready to embrace the truth. Her willingness to accept the message of Christ, and her subsequent actions, reflect the importance of having an open heart when it comes to matters of faith.

I remember a time when I was struggling with my faith in God. I wasn't as close to Him as I wanted to be, and I was going through a difficult period in my life, constantly bombarded with negative and destructive thoughts that affected my mood. I found myself believing these thoughts, doubting myself, and thinking badly about who I was.

It was then that I realised I needed the Word of God to fight back against these negative thoughts. So, I began to recite the scriptures I knew, speaking them into my life. With every negative thought, I countered it with God's Word, encouraging myself, and I would immediately feel a sense of joy and relief! I understood that I needed more of God and needed to trust in His Word and what **He** says about me. This time, I believed in His promises so that I could truly receive them.

Reflecting on Lydia's story, I realised how crucial it is to receive the truth, act on it, and desire a deeper relationship with God to grow in Him.

Name withheld

SUNDAY 17th

For if you remain silent at this time, relief and deliverance for the Jews will arise from another place, but you and your father's family will perish. And who knows but that you have come to your royal position for such a time as this?
Esther 4:14 (NIV)

PURPOSE TO SAVE YOUR PEOPLE – Reading: Esther 4:1-17

Esther's story is testament to the significance of purpose our lives. As queen, Esther faced a daunting dilemma, risk her life by approaching the king without being summoned or stay silent and watch her people perish. Mordecai's words, found in Esther 4:14, reveal a profound truth: every woman has a divine purpose, and the stakes are usually incredibly high…

This is because God places us in specific positions, not by accident, but by design and most of the time, these situations present a great test of faith. Just as Esther was strategically positioned to save her people, you, too, are placed in your family, community, workplace and church for a reason. The challenges you face may seem overwhelming, but remember, God equips those He calls. Your courage, wisdom, and faith can change the course of history for those around you.

When you encounter moments of doubt or fear, reflect on Esther's story. Ask yourself, *"What is my 'such a time as this'?"* God is calling you to step into your purpose with boldness and trust. Your obedience can be the key to unlocking blessings, not just for yourself, but for generations to come. You better believe it!

Join me in embracing purpose, knowing that you are part of God's plan; a woman of influence, designed for a unique mission that only you can fulfil.

Latoya J. Foster

MONDAY 18th

...the angel said unto her...the LORD has heard your affliction
Genesis 16:11

FORSAKEN BUT NOT FORGOTTEN – Reading: Genesis 16:1-16

The story of Hagar is surrounded by negativity. She was disliked by her mistress who made her life so difficult that the only way out for Hagar was to run away. But God had not forsaken her. Hagar was found in the wilderness by an angel at a fountain of water and, after telling the angel why she was there, she was told to go back to the very place she'd ran away from. Imagine, being told to go back to your nemesis!

The name Hagar means *"flight"* or *"forsaken"*; very apt for the situation Hagar found herself in. However, the reality was although she fled, she was not forsaken.

So, what can we learn from Hagar or what was her purpose?

Her purpose was to teach us that running away is not always the answer. No matter what situation you find yourself in, whether you have been disliked, rejected, or mistreated, the Word said, *"...he will never fail thee, nor forsake thee"* (Deuteronomy 31:6 KJV). Hagar was not forgotten by God. Her situation was dire, but there was hope in God.

Your situation may also be dire - don't run away. Seek God. Even if His answer isn't what you want to hear, be obedient like Hagar, and have confidence that God is with you in all situations.

Lady Pam Lewin

TUESDAY 19th

And the LORD God formed man of the dust of the ground, and breathed into his nostrils the breath of life; and man became a living soul
Genesis 2:7

UP CLOSE & PERSONAL – Reading: Isaiah 25:1-12

How much closer can you get than being given the 'kiss of life' by the Creator Himself? When Adam saw Eve, his exclamation was *"this is bone of my bone, flesh of my flesh"* Genesis 2:22,23. By the same token, we could say that when God breathed his breath into Adam and Eve, they were breath of His breath, because only then did they (man and woman) become a *"living soul".*

God has always been 'up close and personal'. At no time was the human race left to their own devices to mutate in a way other than God purposed. We were made in His image, (Genesis 1:26,27); formed by His hands, then He breathed life into them (Genesis 2:7). Next, He socialised with them, for the Scriptures tell us that they heard the voice of the LORD God walking in the garden in the cool of day. He was clearly coming to meet with them and they hid from him (Genesis 3:8).

There are endless accounts in the Old Testament telling of His interaction with human beings; Moses, Joshua, Gideon... until His condescension as a babe, born of a woman, and spent thirty-three years living as a man amongst men. God has always intended to be up close and personal.

His final promise is to come again that where he is there we may be also (John 14:1,2). So my sisters, when we realise that God is always and has always been with us, that He knows everything about us, up to the hairs of our head (Matthew 10:30), when we know that He cares so much, that He sent His Son to give His life so that we could be cleaned up for an "up close and personal" everlasting life with him in heaven, what have we to fear or worry about?

God has it all covered. We just need to accept that He knows what He is talking about and what he has planned will come into being because He says so (Isaiah 55:11).

"For ye are the temple of the living God; as God hath said, I will dwell in them, and walk in them; and I will be their God and they shall be my people" (2 Corinthians 6:16).

Cheryl Lowe
Guyana

WEDNESDAY 20th

They reached Bethlehem, and... the women who lived there asked, "Can this really be Naomi?"
Ruth 1:19 (CEV)

DETECTING THE BIGGER PICTURE – Reading: Ruth 1:15-22

Nothing was as I expected it to be. I had planned, prayed and prepared for every event that could arise - or so I thought! My mission, to give my dependant a new start and assist waiting youngsters with their education. My retirement years would be a time of giving back. Guyana was my first project.

Ever wondered how it was for Naomi and her family when they left a famine-stricken Bethlehem for Moab? No doubt they were in anticipation of a life that offered something better. I wanted self-sufficiency, but before that could happen, I would have to deal with *'nature raw in tooth and claw'*. Pests of every kind dogged my endeavours to grow my own produce. I faced one disappointment after another.

The tragic outcomes for Naomi were not the end of her story. She suffered undeniably, losing her whole family save one daughter-in-law; but who would have thought that living the godly life that she did, would gain her a place in the lineage of the Messiah; making her a grandmother; a coveted position?

On return to Bethlehem, Naomi expressed bitterness, but she was not overcome by it. Soon she was supporting her daughter-in-law Ruth, looking out for her happiness, as mothers often do, and in doing so, she secured her own beyond her wildest dreams.

Naomi's story gives hope. Life is often beset by disappointments and tragedy; how we deal with these two imposters determines our success or happiness. God promises never to leave nor forsake us. Repeating this in Old and New Testament, tells us that God is unchangeable; the same yesterday, today and tomorrow (Deut. 31:3; Heb. 13:5). We can rest assured that His plan for us is bigger than our dreams for ourselves!

Cheryl Lowe
Guyana

THURSDAY 21st

Sarah laughed within herself, saying, after I am waxed old shall I have pleasure, my lord being old also?
Genesis 18:12

DO YOU NOT SEE WHAT I SEE? – Reading: Genesis 18:1-15

There's a stark contrast between young Mary being told the impossible for her life, and the more mature Sarah who, in old age and beyond child bearing years, laughing at the prospect of a promised child through her womb.

Mary had a sense of fear at the appearance of the angel, not knowing what he might say. She then collapsed her own logic for the greater wisdom that she perceived to be of God and somehow was still simple-minded enough to accept it as truth, beyond the odds.

There are so many nuances tucked away in this text that fuel (or challenge) our faith. The promise spoken to Abraham meant his faith would carry his dubious wife to purpose. She laughed at the illogical, he grabbed at it! Aren't you glad that God speaks to those of faith to believe for us, when we as women are laughing in the wings at the idea that the miraculous can happen to us! I'm glad that God and Abraham both let Sarah have her moment!

Women, sometimes we laugh too quickly at the good spoken over us. We shy away from the compliment, we run from the purposes that don't make sense often because we feel incapable, past the time of possibilities or just simply unworthy. We brush off the impossible that is held and offered from the hand of God!

What is further true is that Sarah, this famous woman of purpose, denied that she lacked of faith. Can we admit that we may live below the faith line? Can we be honest in saying that we may have ejected ourselves out of the seat of purpose because it's been too long and continuing to believe no longer makes sense.

I have heard myself say, *"I just don't feel like I can",* but let's not laugh away the promise. To leave our story there is not comely for the purposed. It is okay to say, God I laughed because I don't feel I can. It is okay to lean on those one or two that will believe for you, until you believe too.

I believe more than ever that God is breaking open the reality of what a Woman of Purpose means through the eyes of these beautiful ordinary women - too old, too young, too many errors, too unqualified, too qualified, too shy, too bold. But also too purposed not to make the pages of scripture our example!

One thing that nurtures purpose is process and pruning. Can we together pray?

"God, I quietly laugh because I see me, I know my story and I'm sorry that I haven't been able to grab with both hands the possibility of your fulfilled promises yet to come in me. Help my unbelief. Grant me faithful people who please you and will help me to grow. I will not ask you to see what I see. I'm here and willing to see what you see in me. In Jesus' name. Amen".

Joy Lear-Bernard

FRIDAY 22nd

She girdeth her loins with strength, and strengtheneth her arms
Proverbs 31:17

FOLLOWING GOD'S DIRECTION – Reading: Proverbs 31: 16-24

Proverbs 31 is a testament to a phenomenal woman, the quintessential woman and most definitely a woman of purpose.

This is a woman who, on the one hand, can inspire other women, or discourage them, depending on their perspective. On the surface it may seem a daunting task to emulate this woman, but taken in small practical steps the heights are not insurmountable. The secret is to follow God's direction.

Verses 16-18 points us to a woman with foresight, and one who plans for the future. She considers the field, then purchases it because she has a vision of its potential. She is a woman of industry. Having bought the field, she proceeds to make it work for her by planting a vineyard. Vineyards were, and still are, profit-making businesses.

This is a strong woman who is not fearful of hard work. She is resourceful and diligent so that her work is profitable. She trusts her intuition, and is confident about her performance. She is prepared to go the extra mile to ensure that her goals are achieved, because she is a shrewd and purposeful woman.

We see these traits in women all around us. We admire them for their tenacity and their abilities as movers and shakers. These are women of purpose. Within all of it though, God needs to be part of the equation. It is He who gives us the strength and capabilities to accomplish our aspirations. We must not think that we can subvert His authority. We achieve so much more when we follow as He leads. It is not about equality, or being superior, but allowing God to work out His purpose in us, as women.

We can be all that we can be as Women of Purpose if we just hand the reins to God, trusting Him with our lives. Proverbs 3:5-6 says, *"Trust in the LORD with all thine heart; and lean not unto thine own understanding. In all thy ways acknowledge him, and he shall direct thy paths"*. When we seek God's help in our various undertakings, He never lets us down but points us in the right direction every time!

Sister Barbara Hendrickson
Nevis

SATURDAY 23rd

And Leah said, Happy am I for the daughters will call me blessed...
Genesis 30:13

A PROFILE OF LEAH – Reading: Genesis 29:17, 23-27, 31-35; 30:9-13, 17-21

Leah was described as *"tender eyed"* in Genesis 29:17, and her six sons eventually became fathers of six tribes in Israel. However, Leah's start as a mother of six tribes was not a particular happy one.

"I know that I'm not the one he loves", was likely her thought on a dark Honeymoon night as she lay with a husband who thought she was someone else. In the morning, the shock and distress on her husband's face when he realised that she was not his 'dear Rachel', must have cut through her like a knife. *"I knew I was unloved, but it still hurts"*, may have been her thought at that moment. Yet, the Bible shows us that the Lord saw Leah's pain, and because He saw that she was hated, He opened her womb while her sister remained barren (Genesis 29:31).

As she started to bear children, she anticipated that her husband would grow to love her and undoubtedly, she hoped for him to favour her more than Rachel. However, by her fourth child, Judah, she declared that she will now praise the LORD, and by her sixth child, she declared, *"Happy am I, for the daughters will call me blessed"* (Genesis 30:13).

Her start was full of hurt but the LORD loved her, showed her favour and eventually, from the lineage of the wife not loved by her husband, the Messiah would come. The latter for Leah was greater than her former and indeed, a generation now considers her blessed.

Zahra H. Oliphant
Jamaica

SUNDAY 24th

We are therefore Christ's ambassadors, as though God were making an appeal through us. We implore you on Christ's behalf...
2 Corinthians 5:20 (NIV)

WOMEN, WHAT DOES GOD THINK OF US?
Reading: Ephesians 2:1-10

As women, what does God think about us? This is one of the many questions on the lips of numerous Christian women. The answer is found in God's written Word. We are valuable, Spirit-filled, constantly being transformed, and are representatives of Him.

In Jesus Christ, we are no longer in darkness but in light. We are encouraged to walk as children of light (Matthew 5:14; Ephesians 5:8). Through Jesus we are victorious (1 Corinthians 15:57). We are Citizens of Heaven (Philippians 3:20). We are a Kingdom of Ambassadors (2 Corinthians 5:20).

As we travel along life's journey in pursuit of Christ, He will help us to recognise our true reflection through our daily passion for His Word. The Bible is the living Word of God. There is no short cut to wisdom. God purposely places people in our lives to help us fulfil our spiritual aspirations. Others can learn a lot about who they see when they look at us, by who He has surrounded our lives with.

We are not the mistakes we've made - at times our mistakes threaten to define us - but biblical truths prove our actual worth. We are created by love to love, and walk with love. We exist to make His name known. His desire is to walk along the way with us, blessing us, and fulfilling our lives with more than we can ask or imagine. Only by drawing close to Him, with our life's priority to put Him first, will we witness the layers of who we are as God sees us.

God's limitless resources are behind every promise that He has ever made, and He has not left us to our own devices or cleverness to journey through life. We are reminded by the word of Zechariah, that it is, *"Not by might, nor by power, but by my Spirit, says the Lord of hosts"* (Zechariah 4:6).

G. K. Chesterton (1874-1936) in his article about the paradox of self-sufficient pride, wrote: *"What we suffer from today is humility in the wrong place. Modesty has moved from the organ of ambition and settled upon the organ of conviction, where it was never meant to be. A man was meant to be doubtful about himself, but undoubting about the truth; this has been exactly reversed".*

The devil will want us to depend upon our own abilities to be successful in our spirit's pursuit, but we are not ignorant of his devices. Martin Luther, in the hymn, A Mighty Fortress is Our God, wrote, *"And though this world with devils filled, should threaten to undo us, we will not fear, for God has willed His truth to triumph through us".*

In closing, happiness is linked with self-esteem. Work on spiritual self-awareness to improve your self-image and ultimately your confidence.

Dr Una Davis

*MONDAY 25th

...but David encouraged himself in the LORD his God
1 Samuel 30:6

A WOMAN OF PURPOSE - Reading: Ecclesiastes 3:1-22

Do you talk out loud to yourself? I do!

I've started to do it more as I get older, partly because some of those who used to speak with me and into me are no longer here. I therefore sometimes tell myself what I know they would say; I recall their counsel and encouragement and encourage myself. I tell myself to rise above how I sometimes feel and carry on.

A Woman of Purpose doesn't have a life of ease, she is pressed, and pressed regularly, on purpose for Purpose, just like olives and grapes go through a distressing process. You can't get olive oil or wine without some squeezing going on.

A Woman of Purpose must also know her purpose! There's no point claiming to be a WOP, yet when asked do you know your purpose, you cannot reply.

I recognise that I've already lived most of my life; if I double my age, I will no longer be here. Neither will you, probably. If this thought does not spur you into action, or cause a feeling of, *"Lord, show me my purpose"*, nothing will. I'm not talking about being famous, I mean purposeful. Famous does not necessarily mean purposeful. How is my life making a positive difference? Will anybody notice when I'm gone? How will I be (or will I be) remembered?

The Woman of Purpose has no time to covet another woman's purpose, she's too focused on her own! She recognises that she is an original and has no carbon copy. She is not perfect but perfection is not needed to complete Purpose. She nurtures her God-given gift(s) to keep it/them healthy, vibrant and 'palatable' for the Kingdom.

Am I the only one who has done some mental arithmetic and almost panicked that I may have wasted time granted to me only for Purpose?

Now I pray on purpose, fast on purpose, read the Word on purpose, review my career on purpose, save money on purpose. I even go to bed on purpose! I've learned to praise God on purpose. When my heart is broken and in pieces, I cry on purpose to give my heart a purposeful release. On rare occasions, I will decide to do absolutely nothing, on purpose. I choose my conversations and my friends on purpose. I'm careful where I go, on purpose. I ask God some deep questions, which only He can answer, on purpose for Purpose.

Saul on the Damascus Road when he fell to the ground, after asking the Lord for an introduction, his next question was, *"Lord, what do you want me to do?"* (Acts 9:6). In other words, tell me my purpose!

There is no more time to lose, O Woman of God, Woman of Purpose.

JEJ

Summer Bank Holiday (UK)

TUESDAY 26th

...and the twelve were with him...and...Mary called Magdalene, out of whom went seven devils
Luke 8:2

TRANSFORMATION, FAITH & DEVOTION - Reading: Matthew 27:45-56; Luke 8:1-3

Luke 8:2 introduces Mary Magdalene as a woman from whom Jesus cast out seven demons. This great act of deliverance and healing marked a remarkable transformation in her life.

From her freedom of affliction by demons, Mary Magdalene became a devoted follower of Jesus Christ and maintained her support of His ministry. Her support was not just spiritual but practical (St Luke 8:2-3).

Mary Magdalene's significance is further highlighted by her presence at the most crucial times of Jesus' life. She was a witness amongst other women at the crucifixion of Jesus, standing near the cross when most of His disciples had fled (St John 19:25).

Her devotion did not end there as she was also the first to witness the empty tomb and see Jesus as the risen Saviour (St John 20:1-18). Jesus entrusted Mary to take the resurrection message to His disciples. Mary Magdalene's journey from a woman delivered and healed from demons, to a devoted disciple of Jesus reminds us that no one is beyond help and the reach of God's power to heal and set free.

Mary Magdalene's steadfast faith, loyalty and devotion, even with the challenges she faced, embellished the depths of true discipleship. Her endeavour to share the gospel encourages us to be bold in our witness with sharing with others the message of redemption (ref. Christine Schenek 2017).

Mary Magdalene remains a beacon of hope and inspiration to Christians everywhere, and reminds us of the impact that one person's faith can have on others.

Minister ML Fraser

WEDNESDAY 27th

And Jacob loved Rachel; and said, I will serve thee seven years for Rachel thy younger daughter
Genesis 29:18

A PROFILE OF RACHEL – Reading: Genesis 29:1-18; 30:1-8; 15-20

"Give me children, or else I die", Rachel bitterly told her husband, Jacob (Genesis 30:1).

The Bible describes Rachel as being beautiful and well favoured (Genesis 29:17), and indeed Jacob loved her dearly. A wife loved by her husband would make any woman happy, yet Rachel mourned her lack of fertility and hence her husband's favour meant less to her. She wanted children…desperately.

One…two…three…four…five…six…seven. Rachel watched as her sister give birth to seven children one after another over the years, and each child Leah bore was a reminder that her womb was 'useless'. After the passing of years, Rachel no doubt felt like less of a woman, and death would be a welcome exchange for a childless life. Then, when Rachel had reached breaking point, the Bible says that, *"God remembered Rachel…and opened her womb".* After she gave birth to Joseph, she declared that the LORD had taken away her reproach.

From Rachel's life, we learn that even when it seems like God has favoured others over us, that is not the case because He will deliver at the appointed time. Rachel died in childbirth delivering her second child, whom she named Benoni, but Jacob called him Benjamin (Genesis 35:17-19).

Who knows…but perhaps her delayed childbearing was for the intent of preserving her life and saving Jacob from being plunged into grief early. That is one school of thought. However, for whatever the reason, God did as He did in His timing, and out of Rachel came Joseph who the LORD used to save His people during the seven years of famine.

Zahra H. Oliphant
Jamaica

THURSDAY 28th

...I am the LORD that healeth thee
Exodus 15:26

PURPOSE IN MY PAIN – Reading: Psalm 107:1-21

So at one point, I felt that my life was about the worst anyone could live through. I mean literally nothing that happened 'next' actually made a difference to anything. I had reached the end as far as I was concerned, nothing mattered anymore not even my own existence. In fact, to live was pain, to live was heartache, to live was torture. Nobody's words were enough, nobody's encouragements made it better, nothing and no-one could change my circumstances and this devastating outcome that I faced.

I was doomed. I felt used, abused, made to feel like a failure. Unloved. Damaged goods are what they would call the remains of my being. So many wounds, so many pain-filled areas. My trust, my honesty, my love, had been mistreated and left me in a state of self-destruction.

If anybody had felt pain - I mean real heart-wrenching pain, it was me. I mean the kind of pain that leaves you helpless, lying in a corner somewhere blinded by tears while holding your stomach trying to stop the deep-seated agony that began to rip through your insides from the pit of your stomach. Oh yes! This pain was as real as it gets.

If anybody had been betrayed and mocked, it was me; like my whole world had taken my goodness and affection that was as pure and real as any human's can get and cunningly taunted its genuineness. It had been on display for all to see before being viciously ridiculed and thrown back in my face, as if this was my dedicated reward for giving my all.

If anyone had felt ashamed and guilty as hell it was me. I had done the most heartless thing so alone and oblivious to the resurfacing pain and guilt that overshadowed my heart, as if the fact that it was broken wasn't enough. I couldn't possibly as a human being take anymore.

I had been there. I had done it all to say the least; I had experienced it like never before and now I was flat on my face and wasn't getting back up from the final blow. It had (almost) killed me and there was no way out of this deep, dark, lonely pit.

BUT (and this was a big 'but') amidst the million trillion tears that I cried, and amidst the deep pain that was buried within my heart; amongst the feeling of worthlessness, and the feeling of wanting to die as this was the only thing left, the only thing that would end the torment and torture that rocked every bone in my body, I heard a small voice say, *"Your search, my child, has come to an end and I have been with you through every single tear you have shed"*.

I wept as the story began to unfold. God had patiently waited, He had watched and allowed every blow, every single onslaught of my enemy, every cunning plan they had in wait, but just as the final blow was about to be unleashed, the blow that would literally wipe me out for good, He stepped in and said, *"Enough!"*. It was then that I realised God hadn't left me, in fact He was with me all along, although I'd felt so alone.

I began to acknowledge that He was the only one that could fulfil all that I wanted, and all that I would ever need, and NOW He was the only one that could heal all the open wounds and all the hurt and deep filled pain in my heart. He was the only one that could take the pain away and make my broken and shattered heart whole again.

And so, NOW I have hope, I have hope in my Father that He will mend this broken vessel and prove that, somehow, as brutal and as evil as it all seemed, there is divine purpose in my pain…

"Thou tellest my wanderings: put thou my tears in a bottle: are they not in thy book?" (Psalm 56:8)

Name withheld

FRIDAY 29th

And Deborah said unto Barak, Up; for this is the day in which the LORD has delivered Sisera into thine hand...
Judges 4:14

WOMEN ARE IMPORTANT TO GOD – Reading: Judges 4:1-24

This writer can think of several women in the Bible who fit the category, *'Women of Purpose':*

Esther - a Jew, niece of Mordecai, a virgin and chosen by King Ahasuerus to be his queen. After a while, her nation was threatened by Haman with annihilation. In order to get help for the Jews, she asked the Jews to fast with her for three days and three nights. This request was to enable her to approach the king uninvited (for it was forbidden to appear before him without his formal invitation). Esther was definitely a woman of purpose; she was phenomenal in the deliverance of the Jews. Mordecai, when he first heard about the decree of destruction to his people, sent a message to Esther, imploring her to help the Jews, *"...and who knoweth whether thou art come to the kingdom for such a time as this?"* (Esther 4:14). She was indeed placed in the kingdom at the right time to deliver the Jews.

Deborah – a prophetess and female judge who was given a prophetic Word from the LORD to give to Barak that Israel would get the victory in the battle against their oppressor, King Jabin of Canaan. The Word was clear and precise that the honour and victory would be by a woman (Judges 4: 9).

Jael - the woman that got the honour and recognition for killing Sisera, commander of the Canaanite army of King Jabin

Eunice and Lois – mother and grandmother of Timothy, both were significant in his spiritual nurturing long before he became Paul's son in the gospel.

Each woman in the LORD is a woman of purpose, whether they are young like The Little Maid, or Mary (Jesus' mother), or they may be in their old age like Sarah and Elisabeth. All are highly significant to God if their calling is an outward service seen by everyone, or in the background, e.g., nurturing their family, Sunday school, etc. There are many more women in the Bible who were strategically placed to fulfil God's purpose. We know that the LORD does not make mistakes, He called and chose His vessels before the foundation of the world.

Women play an important part in the will of God.

Minister MB

SATURDAY 30th

...Abigail was a woman of good understanding, and of a beautiful countenance: but (her husband) was churlish and evil in his doings...
1 Samuel 25:3

ABIGAIL – Reading: 1 Samuel 25:1-44

In 1 Samuel 25:3, Abigail was described as a beautiful woman of good understanding. The Hebrew word for *"understanding"* is *"śekel"* which means good sense, intelligence that goes beyond book knowledge and insight. In other scriptures, the same word is used to describe insight as a gift from God and the person with this level of insight exhibits patience and wins praise from others.

How aptly that word describes Abigail. She was married to a harsh and evil man; a real scoundrel who did not know how to appreciate or show respect for others. We wonder what Abigail's days were like – patiently tending to her husband and doing the business of the house. Undoubtedly, she must have prayed that he would change, while likely wondering when she will get her change.

Such are some of us – patiently waiting and praying through a difficult marriage, or praying for a change to come to a hopeless situation. Abigail is an example that we can emulate. Abigail could have stayed inside her home when she learned of what her husband did but instead, she exhibited courage to chase down a man that could easily destroy her.

That insight from God led her to mount her donkey and plead the cause for not only herself, but the entire household. The situation is difficult but there is a God who will grant us a way of escape so we pray for our 'sight' to dim so His insight can light our way.

Zahra H. Oliphant
Jamaica

SUNDAY 31st

By faith the harlot Rahab perished not with them that believed not, when she had received the spies with peace
Hebrews 11:31

RAHAB THE HEROINE – Reading: Joshua 2:1-24

In the Shalvi/Hyman Encyclopedia of Jewish Women, Rahab is described as *"a prostitute who is also a biblical heroine"*.

The same person, a prostitute and a heroine? …in the Bible? How can that be? This monumental achievement was possible in a woman of ill repute because she was on the side of a God whose specialty is redemption and who is not daunted by the darkness in one's life.

Indeed, Rahab's story is one of hope. Her dark history was not her destiny, just as my history is not my destiny, and neither is yours. Rahab rose to the challenge to answer a call higher than her debase behaviour. She was more than her circumstances. Rahab's career choice did not define her. She had abilities, talents, and capacity beyond the bedroom and when the situation arose, she jumped into action, putting her problem-solving skills to good use.

Rahab had a purpose to be fulfilled that required heroic action. Yes, it required looking beyond disappointments with self and one's own burdens to help others deal with their situation. Rahab was an MVP (Most Valuable Player) in the spy hiding contest.

If you were in Rahab's position, would you have answered the call or would you have disqualified yourself by pointing to your faults? Do you feel unqualified to do somethings that you are called to do? Do you face some seemingly insurmountable tasks? Like Rahab, you can be more than a conqueror through Christ Jesus who loves you (Romans 8:37) and in whom is all power to do even the impossible. Indeed, whatever your circumstance, no matter how tainted, a hero lies in you! As you seek to fulfil your purpose, trust in God's strength and wisdom to work out what he desires through you.

Let your faith rise to carry out that task. You will be numbered among God's heroines.

Keshawna Salmon-Ferguson
Jamaica

September
Fearfully & Wonderfully Made

MONDAY 1st

...and they knew that they were naked; and they sewed fig leaves together, and made themselves aprons
Genesis 3:7

WALK IN YOUR GOD-GIVEN AUTHORITY – Reading: Genesis 3:1-24

God made Adam in His own likeness, placed Adam in the Garden of Eden, a paradise where Adam did not have to work or labour, and gave Adam one rule to live by:
"And the Lord God commanded the man, saying, Of every tree of the garden thou mayest freely eat: But of the tree of the knowledge of good and evil, thou shalt not eat of it: for in the day that thou eatest thereof thou shalt surely die" (Genesis 2:16-17).

All Adam had to do was to listen and obey the voice of God. We can only do this if we TRUST Him. Even when we cannot see Him and feel Him. This is how we walk in our God-given authority.

The enemy's goal is to sow a seed of deception and rebellion. Right from the beginning of time, he challenged the Word of God. Disguised as a subtle serpent, the enemy spoke to Eve, with whom Adam had shared the command: *"…Yea, hath God said, Ye shall not eat of every tree of the garden?"* (Genesis 3:1).

And ever since then, those are his tag lines: *"Has God said?"* In other words, *"Did God really mean that?"*! The enemy constantly tries to challenge and undermine the Word of God to cause doubt and fear.

We are fearfully and wonderfully made, but we can only experience what that means if we value and obey the Word of God, above the word of the enemy. Dispel every doubt and fear by honouring the Word of God above everything else.

Don't lose your privileges as a child of God by failing to believe: believe and obey the Word of God, even if it brings you challenge and pain, and thereby, walk in your God-given authority.

Min Jo Earle

TUESDAY 2nd

...I...saw the holy city, new Jerusalem, coming down from God out of heaven, prepared as a bride adorned for her husband –
Revelation 21:2

OUR NEW HOME – Reading: Revelation 21:1-27

The main reason that some of us are running in this race and going through trials and tribulations is because Jesus promised, *"...I go to prepare a place for you. And if I go and prepare a place for you, I will come again, and receive you unto myself; that where I am, there ye may be also"* (John 14:2-3). We desire to go to that special place that is fearfully and wonderfully made by our Lord.

How wonderful it is to know that we will have a perfect home prepared and ready to receive us. We will not need to do any decorating, furniture buying, etc., everything we need will already be there. By that I mean our LORD will be there; this makes everything we go through on earth worth going through.

So, when John saw the holy city, he could only liken it to *"a bride adorned for her husband"*. Brides look beautiful and so will our heavenly home be beautiful. However, we can only claim that home if we are a child of God. If you are reading this and are not yet a child of God, then use today to consider where you would like your future to be.

Lady Pam Lewin

WEDNESDAY 3rd

And (God)… took one of (Adam's) ribs and closed up the flesh…
Genesis 2:21

I AM A MASTERPIECE – Reading: Genesis 2:21-23

In Genesis 2:21-23, we witness the profound moment when God created woman. After causing Adam to fall into a deep sleep, God took one of his ribs and fashioned it into a woman. When Adam first laid eyes on her, he recognised her as *"bone of my bones and flesh of my flesh".* This scripture reminds us of the intimate care and intention with which God created women.

To be *"fearfully and wonderfully made"* (Psalm 139:14) means that every detail of our being was crafted with purpose and love. God didn't create us haphazardly, or without thought, but with awe-inspiring intention. Our physical bodies, minds, and spirits were uniquely designed to reflect His glory. Every strength, every gift, and I believe even every challenge we face, God uses as part of His divine plan.

I don't have to listen to a world that tells me I need to be more or less of something, and neither do you! In fact, I completely ignore anything in this world that attempts to make me doubt who God has made me to be. We don't need to strive to fit into society's mould because we are already perfectly designed by our Creator. We are valued, cherished, and deeply loved just as we are. This should be the basis that anchors everything we do.

Let this be a reminder today: You are not an accident. You are a masterpiece, created in the image of God with infinite worth and purpose. Embrace your uniqueness, knowing that you are fearfully and wonderfully made by the One who knows you completely and loves you unconditionally.

Latoya J. Foster

THURSDAY 4th

For he commandeth, and raiseth the stormy wind, which lifteth up the waves thereof
Psalm 107:25

MASTER OF THE STORMS – Reading: Psalm 107:23-32

Imagine setting sail on a sea as smooth as glass on a beautiful summer day, with bright sunshine and a cloudless sky. Imagine this same sea with mountainous, white crested, crashing waves rushing headlong to the shore on a path of destruction.

This is God's creation, over which He has total control. The same can be said of the wind - that invisible force which can appear as a gentle, cooling breeze, or as a shrieking, howling monster, capable of uprooting huge trees and reducing structures to rubble in a storm of categorical devastation! Yet, God also controls the wind. What a mighty God, we serve!

In Psalm 107, the sailors who were out plying their trade experienced the turbulence of wind and waves in a majestic display of God's power. Imagine their terror! But when they cried out, verse 29 says, *"He calmed the storm to a whisper and stilled the waves"* (NLT).

We can recall Mark 4:35-41, when the disciples were subject to great consternation as a storm raged and Jesus slept peacefully and unperturbed. When He awoke, He calmed the storm by simply saying, *"Peace be still"*, and the wind and the sea obeyed.

As children of God, we are not exempt from the storms of life. Our storms take different forms. They wreak mental, physical, emotional and spiritual havoc, but we too can cry out as the sailors did, *"Lord help!"*. We too, can call out like blind Bartimaeus, *"Jesus, thou Son of David, have mercy on me"* (Mark 10:47).

God is the Master of every storm. At any time, He can give the command, *"Peace be still"*, and the tumult will cease. Lord, give us the faith to trust that, as you are in control of everything you created, seen and unseen, we can leave our lives and troubles in your hands. You are the Master and no matter the storm, you will always see us through.

Sister Barbara Hendrickson
Nevis

FRIDAY 5th

Yet God made everything beautiful for its own time
Ecclesiastes 3:11 (NLT)

SEEING BEAUTY – Reading: 2 Corinthians 10:1-18

I was on a lovely getaway. The skies were bright, the gardens were luxurious, birds were singing, the lush greenery on the mountains was magnificent, and there was a gentle breeze. What a beautiful day it was!

Later in the day the sky began to turn grey foretelling the coming rain. I began to say to myself, *"Oh, how sad that it will no longer be lovely day"*. In that moment the Lord said to me, *"So, is the day no longer beautiful when the rain is falling? Is it only beautiful when the sun is shining?"*

I was jolted into consciousness. The limitation of my perspective was glaring. I was seeing beauty only in things that met certain criteria which excluded things that were seemingly bad or negative. This encounter caused me to have a different perspective of beauty. Yes, I had to change my posture. I have learned to appreciate the beauty in every day, in both the sunshine and the rain, in gladness and in pain.

Indeed, God continues to make things beautiful for its time and in its time. The sun has its place and is beautiful in its time. The rain also has its place and is beautiful in its time. It is important to recognise and acknowledge the pleasing or attractive features of the things one encounters. This might require reframing to see the pleasant aspects instead of just bad. I have found that such a perspective makes life more enjoyable.

Life is framed by one's thoughts. (*Proverbs 23:7 "For as he thinketh in his heart so is he")*. The more one sees bad in things the more negative effect it has on one's mood and general experience. The opposite is also true. I pray that you will find beauty in all of God's creation, in what is considered good and also the seemingly bad. This posture will add more pleasantness to life.

Pray today for new eyes to see and experience God's beauty in the things you encounter.

Keshawna Salmon-Ferguson
Jamaica

SATURDAY 6th

My beloved spake and said unto me, Rise up, my love, my fair one, and come away
Song of Songs 2:10

WHAT DOES SELF-CARE MEAN TO YOU? – Reading: Song of Songs 2:1-17

The World Health Organisation (WHO) defines self-care as *"the ability of individuals, families and communities to promote health, prevent disease, maintain health, and to cope with illness and disability with or without the support of a healthcare provider"* (Sept 2021)

The scope of self-care as described in this definition includes health promotion; disease prevention and control; self-medication; providing care to dependent persons; seeking hospital/specialist care if necessary; and rehabilitation including palliative care. Inherent in the concept is the recognition that whatever factors and processes may determine behaviour, and whether or not self-care is effective and interfaces appropriately with professional care, it is the individual person who acts (or does not act) to preserve health or respond to symptoms.

Self-care is a broad concept which also encompasses **hygiene** (general and personal); **nutrition** (type and quality of food eaten); **lifestyle** (sporting activities, leisure, etc.); **environmental factors** (living conditions, social habits, etc.); **socioeconomic factors** (income level, cultural beliefs, etc.); and **self-medication**.

Core principles: Fundamental principles for self-care include aspects of the individual (e.g., self-reliance, empowerment, personal responsibility) as well as the greater community (e.g., community participation, community involvement, community empowerment).

Stewardship of the body: We are to be good stewards of money but also of ourselves, i.e., the whole being: body; environment; our time; our talents/gifts and our relationships. Stewardship is defined as the conducting, supervising or managing of something. The careful and responsible management of something entrusted to one's care.

Matthew 11:28-30, *"Come unto me, all ye that labour and are heavy laden, and I will give you rest. Take my yoke upon you, and learn of me; for I am meek and lowly in heart: and ye shall find rest unto your souls. For my yoke is easy, and my burden is light".*

Matthew 22:39, *"... Thou shalt love thy neighbour as thyself".*

If you do not take care of yourself, nor love yourself, how can you love your neighbour? Lack of self-confidence or hate of yourself can take our mind off God and cause us to negatively focus too much on ourselves. The reverse is also true, i.e., loving ourselves too much and above God is dangerous!

In closing, let's reflect on the Word:

Psalm 139:14 says, *"I will praise thee; for I am fearfully and wonderfully made: marvellous are thy works; and that my soul knoweth right well".*

1 Thessalonians 5:23, *"And the very God of peace sanctify you wholly; and I pray God your whole spirit and soul and body be preserved blameless unto the coming of our Lord Jesus Christ".*

1 Corinthians 3:16, *"Know ye not that ye are the temple of God, and that the Spirit of God dwelleth in you?"*

Philippians 4:6-7, *"Be careful for nothing; but in every thing by prayer and supplication with thanksgiving let your requests be made known unto God. And the peace of God, which passeth all understanding, shall keep your hearts and minds through Christ Jesus".*

When you meditate as part of self-care/ good stewardship, what are you meditating on?

Psalm 1:2, *"But his delight is in the law of the LORD; and in his law (God's Law) doth he meditate day and night".*

Name withheld

SUNDAY 7th

The earth is the LORD's and the fulness thereof; the world and they that dwell therein
Psalm 24:1

OUR CREATIVE GOD – Reading: Psalm 8:1-9; 24:1-10

As a small child, I used to love the song, *"He's got the whole world in His hand"*. I didn't really understand what I was singing then, but I now link it with Psalm 24:1.

There isn't a corner of the universe that does not belong to the mighty God, and we all also belong to Him, even those who say that there is no God. Everything in this world was either made by God, or He gave us the wisdom of how to make it.

Sometimes I try to slow down to absorb the beauty of God's handiwork and I am blown away by His 'creative skills', and how creation works in such order! For instance - the four seasons, night and day, the earth continually turning on its axis without us feeling anything. God spoke all of these things into existence. He had no need of a hammer or nails to hang the sun, moon or stars in place. He needed no paint brush to dye the grass green or the sky blue. And what a beautiful choice of colours for the flowers in our gardens!

God needed no needle and thread to embroider the pretty peacock's feathers. There was no need for a team of surgeons to assist Him with making Adam and Eve – He did it all by Himself and said it was good! How great is our God!

No wonder Paul said in Philippians 2:10-11: *"That at the name of Jesus, every knee should bow: of things in heaven, and under the heaven, and things in earth and under the earth. And that every tongue should confess that Jesus Christ is Lord…"*. He is Lord of Creation, can't you see?

(From me to You, 90 Days in the Psalms – Jackie Jacobs)

JEJ

MONDAY 8th

...the mountains and the hills shall break forth into singing, and all the trees shall clap their hands
Isaiah 55:12

IF THE TREES CAN PRAISE GOD... – Reading: Isaiah 55:1-13

If the trees can praise God
Then why can't I!
I am praising you, Jesus.
Because of the many
Answers you give me when I cry.

The trees were waving energetically at you God
They did not care who was staring at them
They were applauding the Great I AM that I AM.

Their branches were moving to the right, and to the left
They were moving to God's rhythm and His beat
Their leaves praised God as they did not want to be left out
They were coming with their own praise so look out!

If all of creation can praise its Maker
What can I say?
Despite what comes
I must praise God now, not later
God who created man on the sixth day.

God is worthy
For none is like our Great God
There is nothing God can't do for us
If we praise and give Him.
Our total trust.

God be praised!

Sister Jennifer Henry

TUESDAY 9th

And God said, Let the earth bring forth grass, the herb yielding seed, and the fruit tree...and God saw that it was good
Genesis 1:11-12

SPECIAL IN THE EYES OF GOD – Reading: Genesis 1:6-13

When I look at the natural beauty of the world around me, I am in awe of God and His handiwork. Everything in nature works together so perfectly, creating beautiful landscape, that I wonder, *"How can you see this and not believe that there is a God?"* (Psalm 14:1a).

God created the heaven and the earth and perfectly aligned every aspect, every detail. Our Almighty Creator looked at His own work declared it good - He does all things well.

He is a God of order and precision and is worthy of appreciation and praise. As creation falls in line with the pattern that God has set in place, we can trust him and know that following His lead will never take us down the wrong path. This doesn't mean that everything will be easy or without challenge, but there is an assurance that we do not have to walk this road alone. Hold on to God and He will guide you through this journey that we call life.

We can praise Him every step of the way, with the assurance that He will provide everything that we need to make it through, making us more than conquerors.

Let your confidence be in all that God has spoken into and over you – you are loved, you are chosen, you are called, you are special, He calls you friend.

CDK

WEDNESDAY 10th

And he showed me a pure river of water of life, clear as crystal...
Revelation 22:1

A VISION OF BEAUTY – Reading: Revelation 22:1-6

God is faithful, showing the Apostle John what is to come as a pure river of the water of life, crystal clear flowing from the throne of God.

As Born Again believers, in that heavenly city, there will be no more curse, but we shall serve the Lord Jesus, we shall see His face and we shall be like Him and His name shall be written in our foreheads (Revelation 21: 3-4). We shall be like Him (1 John 3:2).

This is the Word of the Lord, written by one of His apostles. Now we either believe this or we don't. We live by the Word of God, or we don't, or we believe some of it depending on our circumstances.

I believe what God says in His Word. His Word goes beyond defining, beyond time and space, and sometimes goes beyond understanding to the human mind. We are called to believe in Him, what He said, and to walk faithfully according to His Word.

In Revelation 7:9-10, the apostle describes an innumerable great multitude of nations, race and people (more than the nation of Israel mentioned in the earlier part of the chapter), clothed in white robes, they stood before God's throne worshipping Him with a loud voice saying: *"Salvation to our God which sitteth upon the throne, and unto the Lamb..."*. Indeed, in verse 12, the angels fell before the throne on their faces and worshipped God, saying, *"Blessing and glory, and wisdom, and thanksgiving, and honour, and power, and might, be unto our God for ever and ever. Amen"*.

This is the worship Jesus taught us in Matthew 6:13 (b): *"For thine is the kingdom, and the power, and the glory, for ever. Amen"*. So as the angels are constantly doing this, so should we.

Let the Holy Ghost teach us these things, bringing the different parts of His Word together within our minds, our souls and our spirits. Amen.

SSP

THURSDAY 11th

For we are God's handiwork, created in Christ Jesus to do good works, which God prepared in advance for us to do
Ephesians 2:10 (NIV)

I AM GOD'S HANDIWORK – Psalm 19:1; Ephesians 2:1-10

In this era of mass production, it is heartening to know that there are still some unique things around. Human beings have been meticulously designed by God, the Creator, who has a deliberate intent for every design. Indeed, God's handiwork is seen in the heavens but also in the aspects of creation made in His image - humankind. Of approximately eight billion people on earth, no two persons are the same. What a mighty God!

It is amazing to know that God took the time to fashion each of us. He was in every detail such that He knows even each hair on our heads (Matthew 10:30). What a caring God! How amazing it is to know that we are not here by happenstance. Whatever the circumstance that brought our parents together, each individual was specifically conceived and brought into existence by God's design. No person came into this world by mistake.

There are times, however, when this truth becomes obscured. Comparison with others, and tough situations, can sometimes lead to misgivings about one's uniqueness, worth, and favoured position in God's eyes.

As you look on yourself today, rejoice in God's handiwork in you. Yes, you were fearfully and wonderfully made. No, you were not a mistake. Let this positive posture guide your reflections. You are a unique and worthy human being, no matter what others say or how you may sometimes feel.

Thank God today for that person in the mirror - His handiwork – YOU!

Lord, God, I thank you that I am your handiwork.

Keshawna Salmon-Ferguson
Jamaica

FRIDAY 12th

I praise you because I am fearfully and wonderfully made; your works are wonderful, I know that full well
Psalm 139:14 (NIV)

GOD'S MASTERPIECE: WORTH BEYOND MEASURE
Reading: Psalm 139:1-16

In a world that constantly tells us to strive for perfection, it's easy to forget the truth of Psalm 139:14. This verse reminds us that we are not a mistake, nor are we defined by society's standards. Instead, we are the intentional creations of a loving God.

To be *"fearfully"* made means we were crafted with reverence and awe. God, in His infinite wisdom, intricately designed every part of us, from our physical features to the depths of our souls. To be *"wonderfully"* made highlights the beauty and uniqueness in each of us: - there is literally no one else like you!

When self-doubt creeps in, or when the world tries to tell us that we're not enough, we can cling to this truth: God Himself, the Creator of the universe, took the time to create us, with all our quirks and imperfections, exactly as He intended. This makes our value too high to measure!

So, let's celebrate who we are: - God's masterpiece, dependent totally on Him. When we start to see ourselves as He does, we can walk in confidence, knowing we are fearfully and wonderfully made by the One who loves us more than we can ever imagine.

Latoya J. Foster

SATURDAY 13th

Come...enter thou into thy chambers, and shut thy doors about thee: hide thyself as it were for a little moment...
Isaiah 26:20

EDEN PRINCIPLES OF CARE & BALANCE – Reading: Isaiah 26:1-21

At a time of need and private study, God helped me to develop a personal practice that has become my lifeline in the past twelve years to support self-care and balance.

Consider that, with all the blessings of Eden which humankind was given, dominion over time was not one of them. God made the evening and the morning and orchestrated their function, and those functions have not changed. Honouring time wisely with His guidance is still a God honouring act of worship. When overwhelm bleeds into my schedule, I prioritise the most personal needs for me: Word, food, rest, study, meditation, productivity. I then order the prominent responsibilities that are pressing. Care and connection of loved ones, (i.e., God, neighbours, family, loved ones, parents) care of surroundings, care of my body, considering meals to prepare, and of course work and ministry commitments. For me this includes writing, music, etc.

I write REST as a valid **diarised commitment**.

I note these particularly after a busy weekend or pressing appointment. This way I look through my diary and can see clearly where I am given liberty to say yes to the use of the gift God has given me, the gift of time. And am reminded at a glance when to say no.

Often "Yes" comes so easily when we **are** in hectic days and busy conversations. Agreeing to things after a pause to consult that diary helps us not to overbook and omit rest when it is already written down. With only crucial exceptions to the rule, this still allows to hold balance!

The basics of food, rest, connection and Word are still the essentials for living well, and yet they're often the first we forfeit when it gets busy. Write them down and honour the use of time as simply as Eden intended.

Above all, let peace be our referee, not our earthly changeable peace, but the peace that comes from connection and obedience to God and His Word in the simple solace.

Joy Lear-Bernard

SUNDAY 14th

The word which came to Jeremiah from the LORD, saying, Arise, and go down to the potter's house, and there I will cause thee to hear my words
Jeremiah 18:1

IN THE MASTER'S HANDS – Reading: Jeremiah 18:1-23

God in His sovereignty and love shows Jeremiah, the weeping prophet, how He is able to restore His people even after they had become marred in His hands.

God can speak to us in various ways, including direct communications, through circumstances and the people around us. When our ears and eyes are attentive, God can speak to us through a billboard, through a work colleague, through a family member.

Jeremiah had to be attentive and open to hearing from God in different ways. As Christians, it is important that we too cultivate a listening ear and an attentive heart to what God is saying and doing around us. Sometimes we become stuck in the traditional way of how God is moving in our lives that we miss pivotal moments of changes, breakthroughs in our circumstances.

God wanted to use the analogy of the potter and the clay to bring out a spiritual meaning for the prophet and His people to see that, although the clay had become marred in His hands, disfigured, damaged, spoiled, at no point did the clay leave the potter's hands. Throughout the moulding, the disfiguring, the potter's hand remained consistent in the 'life' of the clay.

We too can be reassured today that no matter how things look, we might have lost our way, we might have stopped praying, stopped reading the Word, stopped going to church, just know that you are still in the potter's hands. His love for you has not changed and it is the will of the Father to reshape you again so that you can be the vessel of honour He has always intended you to be.

Name withheld

MONDAY 15th

To him that by wisdom made the heavens: for his mercy endureth for ever
Psalm 136:5

HE'S STILL WORKING ON ME – Reading: Psalm 136:1-9

"*I can understand why they say the world is flat"!* These words came from my co-traveller as they watched the sea through the cabin portal of the cruise liner. The water rippling to and fro reached an endless to the skyline.

"If the world is round", they said, *"how comes the water doesn't fall off the edge?"*

Their question I could not answer. The vast sea stretched meeting the sky, with the silver line of sun in between. The earth, sea and sky created by God's wisdom without human intervention, suspended in the universe for His glory.

It reminded me of a song I learnt as a child:

"I marvel at the wisdom of my God
I marvel at the wisdom of my God
When I see the little lily pushing up the great big clod,
Then I marvel at the wisdom of my God".

Today, I arise and not just wonder and question God's greatness around me, but praise and thank God that, that same wisdom made me.

"He continues to work on me, to make me what I ought to be.
It took Him just a week to make the moon and stars,
The earth and moon, Jupiter and Mars
How lovely and patient He must really be
For He's still working on me".

Sis Dorcas (nee Simmonds)

TUESDAY 16th

He maketh me to lie down in green pastures: he leadeth me beside the still waters
Psalm 23:2

SELF CARE FOR BEAUTIFUL WOMEN - Reading: Psalm 23:1-6

*Choose a space in your home, big or small. That is your place of solace. Place there a candle, a book, a scripture, a lovely smelling hand lotion or spray, and commit regular pockets of time there, even 10 minutes. Keep a note pad there to always pour out a simple prayer and commit it to God.

*Keep three books to hand in your home, bag or car. One for the well-being of the heart, one for the renewing of the mind, one for health of the body. Often, we struggle to read a stealthy piece of literature but having these books to hand means that we can absorb a page or two in response to our present need.

*Checking that it's appropriate for your health, keep a foot spa nearby with suitable oils. Many a Zoom meeting where we're unusually still can allow you to enjoy a foot soak as you log on! Keep a towel handy before you start, keep the space safe and clear. Enjoy!

*If possible, meditate on a Word that resonates as you travel to and from work. Rest, exhale, cleansing, joy, imagine a fragrance from the Word and ponder on what that Word really means. You'll be amazed at where that Word might take you by association.

*Connect with three friends and agree to send a voice note of life, inspiration and care. In the busy-ness of the day, those notes can be listened to build one another up and be responded to when you have a quiet moment.

*Plan a simple place to visit once a month. Plan ahead of time and keep it attainable - a simple evening or morning breakfast - alone, with a friend, a podcast, Bible audio or silence. As soon as you leave, book the next.

*Practice breathing slowly, and exhaling with intentional thought on the vastness of God's presence and His Word

*We are fearfully and wonderfully made. Specifically consider one feature that you have. It could be your smile, your voice, your hands or heart. Ponder the intricacy of that unique part of you.

What gifts you have enjoyed by the blessing of your wellness!

Joy Lear-Bernard

WEDNESDAY 17th

Who by God's power are being guarded through faith for a salvation ready to be revealed in the last time
1 Peter 1:5 (ESV)

THE SUSTAINING GOD – Reading: Psalm 16:1-11

God will sustain me
I believe He will take me through
God will sustain me.
In whatever I am going through
God will sustain me
For God is there guiding me too.

God will sustain me
He is in my thoughts
God will sustain me
He sees me afar off.

God will sustain me
When I feel I cannot pray
God will sustain me
For He sustained me
Yes! just yesterday.

God will sustain me
Today I am sure
He tells me to never give up
On Him, but to be full of faith.

For He will sustain me
Every day of my life
I am sure.

Thank you Jesus!

Sister Jennifer Henry

THURSDAY 18th

...the LORD God formed the man of dust from the ground and breathed into his nostrils the breath of life, and the man became a living creature
Genesis 2:7 (ESV)

TRULY AMAZING – Reading: Genesis 1:6-8; 2:1-7

How often do we hear the preacher expounding the Word of God? We read that the angel of the Lord appeared unto Abraham, Moses, Israel, and David. But do we realise, or have we ever taken note, that the first time the angel of the Lord appeared to a human being was to a runaway single mother-to-be?

The only way that she thought she could survive was to escape from her environment, as she was mistreated by the woman who put her into the whole mess in the first place! A servant girl by the name of Hagar was struggling with the issue of pride, which resulted in strife (Proverbs: 13:10). Despite this sinful issue, she had an encounter with El Roi (the God who sees). God's love extends to this unlikely servant girl, whom He instructed to return home. God assured her of His promise to protect her, and further supports her with an action plan for the future (of the Arab nation).

God's divine protection is upon all of His children. When God created the first man, the care and attention to detail were impeccable. It is awesome how He made man in His image and blew into man the breath of life and man became a living soul. The intricate workings of the human body are truly amazing in structure and design. King David, once a shepherd boy, shouts God's praises, *"I am fearfully and wonderfully made"* (Psalm 139:14).

What are we saying today when knowledge has increased and God has given us the wisdom, knowledge and understanding to know much more about the human body? Yes, every child of the most, high God should be shouting a Hallelujah praise, *"I am fearfully and wonderfully made"*, body, soul and spirit!

Missionary Audrey Simpson

FRIDAY 19th

I no longer call you servants, because a servant does not know his master's business. Instead I have called you friends, for everything…I have made known to you
John 15:15 (NIV)

SELF CARE & GOOD COMPANY – Reading: Proverbs 17:17; John 15:10-17

It's important that we look inward and upwards to God in developing good self care. But one other important consideration is our company.

Given that we are positioned to serve others, we can sometimes neglect that we too must have healthy relationships that pour well into us. Here are a few connections to consider:

✻ Which circle or person offers clear biblical navigation where you are able to learn and listen as much or more than you share?

✻ Who amongst your friends or company considers physical health as being important – with who can you walk or a swim, exercise, discuss eating well and gain wisdom on new things to try?

✻ Where is your safe space to truly offload and 'hash' through ideas, hurts or challenges?

✻ Where or with whom do you laugh heartily and enjoy downtime?

✻ Who nurtures you and sees your pain, fears and burdens?

✻ Who truly enjoys your wins, believes in your success and is not bogged down with competition or comparison?

✻ Which group or persons share your experiences of motherhood, grief, travel, singleness, business, ministry, marriage, adoption, illness, etc.

One relationship may encompass more than one need, and you may mutually pour into one person as they also pour into you. Some of the points listed may yield no answers for you right now. Your heart's response may show you the direction of your next prayers to God, to open doors to deeper relationship for this season. Some may be in your church, 'across the pond' or within an organised group to which you subscribe.

Be prayerful in your self care, guard your heart with wisdom, but truly be trusting of God's desire for you to have good companions.

Joy Lear-Bernard

SATURDAY 20th

...speak the word only, and my servant shall be healed
Matthew 8:8

MADE THROUGH WORDS – Reading: Proverbs 18:21; Matthew 8:5-13

The creation story opens with God declaring, *"Let there be light, and there was light"* (Genesis 1:3). For everything else that God desired to come into existence, He spoke a word and it was so. There was creative power in God's words. Indeed, what an awesome wonder is our God. A being so powerful that even the winds and the waves obey His voice.

It is important to note that, as humans, we were created in God's image. Indeed, we have been fearfully and wonderfully made. As humans, we are not just another creature. We were designed to be a reflection of God's characteristics and abilities as His image-bearers. Some of the ways in which we reflect God's image are the ability to create, reason, think rationally, and experience emotions.

Humanity's creative power through words was seen from the beginning. After God formed the animals, He brought them to Adam and whatever name Adam called every living creature, that was the name thereof (Genesis 2:19). Can you imagine, the name we now know an animal by was something that the first man spoke into existence! A lion is a lion and will never be a fly, and vice versa.

This ability is often not taken seriously enough - whatever you call something, that's what it becomes. That's what it is. As God's image-bearers, we have the ability to create through our words as death and life are in the power of the tongue (Proverbs 18:21).

Seek today to use your words wisely to speak life into situations as you declare God-breathed words. Ask for God's wisdom and guidance to renounce words that might have been spoken which have led to some kind of death. And pledge to be conscious and deliberate about creating positive things through the life-infused words that you will speak.

Lord, please help me to facilitate life and not death through my words.

Keshawna Salmon-Ferguson
Jamaica

SUNDAY 21st

To another the working of miracles; to another prophecy; to another discerning of spirits; to another divers kinds of tongues; to another the interpretation of tongues
1 Corinthians 12: 10

UNIFIED FOR VICTORY – Reading:1 Corinthians 12:4-12

Have you ever imagined what the world would be like if everyone was a lawyer or a doctor? This means that we would never need to go on waiting list for a doctor's appointment. Everyone would have a brother, or a sister, or an uncle who is a lawyer, leaving us with no need to worry about saving to pay for expensive legal fees if ever this service was required.

This may sound great, until we ask ourself the next questions: *"Who will teach them the information needed to become a lawyer or a doctor?" "Who will build the hospitals and courts where they will work?" "Who will clean the floors and make sure the hospital beds are sanitised for patients to use?"* We can see very quickly the great difficulties that would arise if being a doctor or a lawyer were the only two professions! There would be many tasks left undone, thus hindering the work of the lawyer and the doctor.

For these evident reasons, when Jesus called us, He called us as many members not all with the same functions, but many members with diverse gifts, diverse talents, so that we may compliment each other in the purpose of fulfilling His mission on earth. Therefore, let's not boast about what the gift which God gave to us, or murmur about the part that we were not given. Instead, seek to understand the role we must play that we can grow together in Christ, lacking nothing but becoming as a puzzle solved and a body restored as brand new in strength, love, and power.

Shanique Graham

MONDAY 22nd

...the body is not made up of one part but of many...As it is, there are many parts, but one body
1 Corinthians 12:14 & 20 (NIV)

KINGDOM MEMBERS OF HIS BODY – Reading: 1 Cor. 12:14-26

Take a look at your hand.

Manicured or with rough callouses, do you notice that one digit - removed from the others – is shorter, stubbier and just a little lower in position, it seems? I'm talking about the thumb, it's anatomically different to your other fingers on the same hand, isn't it?! But imagine a moment without it! Yes, it's all of a sudden more esteemed than we gave it credit for!

We are members of one body; digits on one hand. It doesn't matter the name or function of each part, we know that it is one single hand. We never shake a thumb or a finger, that would be incomplete and frankly awkward! And so should it be in our thinking when we adopt division based on importance of roles.

Paul referenced the singularity of the body when speaking to individuals who still held on to their cultures, learning and status. Such thinking is illegal in His kingdom. It's akin to driving on the wrong side of the road, i.e., dangerous and lacking in understanding or submission to a higher law.

In 1 Corinthians 12, Paul reminds me of a weary parent reminding the children that they are to take care of one another as one family. What this speaks to is our somewhat unregenerated mindset, rooted in comparison and status. Words like feeble, honourable and comeliness are words that decipher who is more worthy.

But God, in His wisdom, made even the tiny members of the body great in weight and relevance so that by being needed, there could be no superiority order in the body of Christ where the Spirit moves through mutual servitude and the gracious meeting of needs.

God has made us to drink of the same Spirit and birthed in us gifts meant to edify this same body. Oh, to be a servant glorying in the grace of God who has made us a part of His body. What a resound of worship God would see in the earth when the hand clasped together grips the image of heaven and reflects on a His nail-pierced palm.

If we are to truly be a member in His body it will take relearning, crucifying of flesh, and taking our value from the cross of Jesus Christ. Learning to drive on the correct side of the road and giving way to other members so that we all hail the King and give flesh no space to glory in His presence.

Joy Lear-Bernard

TUESDAY 23ʳᵈ

Now ye are the body of Christ, and members in particular
1 Corinthians 12:27

YOU MATTER IN THE BODY OF CHRIST – Reading: 1 Corinthians 12:27-31

I am reminded of the song, *"I'm Available to You"* by Milton Brunson penned below:

You gave me my hands to reach out to man
To show him Your love and Your perfect plan
You gave me my ears, I can hear Your voice so clear
I can hear the cries of sinners
But can I wipe away their tears?

You gave me my voice to speak Your word
To sing all Your praises to those who never heard
But with my eyes I see a need for more availability
I've seen the hearts that have been broken
So many people to be free

Now I'm giving back to You all the tools You gave to me
My hands, my ears, my voice, my eyes
So You can use me as You please
I have emptied out my cup so that You can fill it up
Now I am free, I just want to be more available to You

Lord, I'm available to You
My will I give to You
I'll do what You say do
Use me Lord to show someone the way and enable me to say
My storage is empty and I am available to You

As the members of our body are to be used for God's glory, so are members of the body of Christ; we must function for God's glory. All the parts of the body are important and have a purpose. Have you identified your role and purpose in the body of Christ?

If you have identified your function in the body and are dutifully carrying out your role(s), pray today for continued direction and strength to be effective in your area(s) of ministry. If you are not functioning as you ought to, seek God's forgiveness for your omission and take the necessary steps to fulfil your call, aided by God's grace.

If you have not yet pinned down your place and function in the body of Christ, seek to understand your call and where you fit, and do accordingly. Don't be comfortable just being a Church Goer! What you do or don't do matters! You are an important member of the body of Christ.

Keshawna Salmon-Ferguson
Jamaica

WEDNESDAY 24th

…God will bless you with peace that no one can completely understand. And this peace will control the way you think and feel
Philippians 4:7

SELF CARE: MISS THAT BUS! – Reading: Philippians 4:1-9

Where does your self care begin?

A luxury day in the Spa? Reservation for a beautiful meal with a friend, or in quiet place of solace? A quiet corner with a Bible or good book? A run in the fresh air, or a hike through the countryside?

All of these are powerful, especially a moment in God's Word. But in every effort that we make, even Bible reading, real self care begins in the invisible corners of our mind.

Have you, like me, acquired a quiet intentional hour but realised that your mind has not slowed down? It's not as easy as pressing 'stop' on a treadmill. If our mind cannot be still, and keep on driving us, then this can be likened to a passenger getting on every bus that passes! Not all of them (buses or our thoughts!) arrive where we want them to take us. Eventually, experience causes us to take a step back and let the 'bus' pass by. That's not easy when we have habits of racing or negative thoughts, but it is possible when we take our thinking captive.

Today, truly make a note of whatsoever things pass your mind, and consider which thoughts you 'get on'. We have power over the greatest self care tucked away in the corner of our minds.

Joy Lear-Bernard

THURSDAY 25th

Did any of you measure the ocean by yourself or stretch out the sky with your own hands?
Isaiah 40:12 (CEV)

WHO DID THAT? – Reading: Isaiah 40:12-18

The prophet asked a rhetorical question, i.e., *"Who had meticulously created the universe, ordered and put in place all its intricate elements with perfect balances and coordination?"*

For of course, only God commanded creation into existence by the word of His mouth. Who Himself was and is, before the heavens were made and the earth was formed, and in eternity He divided time. It is God who challenged Job with the same sentiment – *"Where were you…?"* (Job 38:4).

Yet, for humankind, God got down in the dust and manipulated it with the working of His fingers to form and fashion us into His own image. So David proclaimed in one place, *'I'm compelled to praise you for reasons of your marvellous actions'*. And is convinced to the core of his inner being that, *"I am fearfully and wonderfully made" (Psalm 139:14)*.

When all was completed, God with the entire host of heaven agreed, *"it was good"* (Genesis 1:25). But after humankind, God was especially pleased with His masterpiece so declared it all *"very good"* (Genesis 1:31).

Sis Jx

FRIDAY 26th

Casting all your care upon him; for he careth for you
1 Peter 5:7

I SEE – Reading: 1 Peter 5:6-11

I see the dark clouds
But God's sunshine is still there
I see the blue sky
Peeping through.

And I realise God
Is watching over me
My God, He is taking care
Of you.

I see the tall buildings
But I do not see
The people
That live therein.

Only God knows
Their situation
Behind that closed door.

In fact, God knows us all
The good and the bad
He knows the unloved
And lonely
The ones who struggle
For they are sad.

Our God, He sees it all
So I will leave every person
At His feet.

Praying God
Will grant deliverance
The enemy He will defeat.

For it's better
If Jesus sees
Because He knows all
That is hidden
That I cannot see.

God be praised.

Sister Jennifer Henry

SATURDAY 27th

I thank you, High God -you're breathtaking! Body and soul, I am marvellously made! I worship in adoration - what a creation! You know me inside and out, you know every bone in my body; You know exactly how I was made, bit by bit, how I was sculpted from nothing into something. Like an open book, you watched me grow from conception to birth; all the stages of my life were spread out before you. The days of my life all prepared before I'd even lived one day
Psalm 139:14-16

HOW DO I LOOK? – Reading: Proverbs 31:30-31

Self-image is a major concern for many of us – how do I look? Our appearance matters much and most of us women will have at least one compact mirror in our handbag to take a quick glance at ourselves during the course of the day. We must accept though that our external features will not remain as we'd like them to forever, *"Beauty is vain"* (Proverbs 31:30).

In Psalm 139:14, David does not declare that he will praise God because he is handsome, but makes a declaration, *"I will praise thee because I am fearfully and wonderfully made"*. What do we mean by handsome, pretty, good looking, beautiful? We would all give different answers if asked for our opinion. Nevertheless, who can disagree that we are all awesomely made?

Let's interrogate this, just a little bit (please note that I am not a nurse or doctor, I'm trying to recall from Biology lessons at school!):

- The pupils in our eyes automatically constrict when we enter a bright space, and then dilate when we are in the dark. This constriction and dilation regulate the amount of light which reaches the retina
- Our ears are not only to hear but they give us balance
- Our kidneys filter our blood and excrete wastes and fluid
- Our lungs move oxygen into the bloodstream

- Our heart acts as a pump for blood and oxygen around the body and removes waste carbon dioxide. The heart works in conjunction with our lungs
- Our eyelashes act as a protective barrier to our eyes, keeping out dust, insects and other things which would cause irritation
- Our salivary glands are there to help us swallow our food and keep our mouth lubricated
- All those taste buds on our tongue tell us when we're eating something sweet or sour, salty or bitter, hot or cold
- Our bones and internal organs are covered with skin which has three layers, i.e., epidermis, dermis and hypodermis

Isn't God amazing! So, make some time each day to praise Him for **how you are made**, and **not** for how you look!

JEJ

SUNDAY 28th

The heavens keep telling the wonders of God, and the skies declare what he has done
Psalm 19:1 (CEV)

THE VOICE OF CREATION – Reading: Psalm 19:1-4; 74:13-17

There's a saying that every picture tells a story. How true! Creation is the most beautiful picture ever painted and it tells the story of the glory and wonder of God.

The lifestyle of many of us these days is at such a pace that we can scarcely slow down long enough to notice the handiwork of God. But today, let's pledge that we won't spend our spare time with our heads hanging down reading and sending messages on or phones/devices. Look up at the skies, up to the heavens. Observe the clouds as they move along and the sun if it is shining. Tonight, see if there are any stars, or if the moon appears.

I still remember as a young child bringing my paintings home from school. I would be so excited with my work; to me it was not just a mix of lines and smudges. Every colourful line and dark smudge were for my audience whom I loved. When I got home, I wanted my family and visitors to look and 'coo' with admiration (as infants still do) even if they didn't know exactly what I had drawn!

I believe that God is waiting for some of us to actually notice what He did in the beginning. Teachers know that there is great benefit to their students in the use of visual aids; it helps them to absorb what is being said. The greatest teacher of all set the first example by putting visual aids everywhere in places where we cannot miss them! God really is the Wonderful in Wisdom!

The heavens and firmament in picture-form still display and make known the glory of God. They are permanent reminders of what happened in the beginning, i.e., *"In the beginning God…"* (Genesis 1:1).

I told you that every picture tells a story. The Wonder of Creation is still being told!

(Adapted from: From Me to You – 90 Days in the Psalms – Jackie Jacobs)

JEJ

MONDAY 29th

And the rib, which the LORD God had taken from man, made he a woman, and brought her unto the man
Genesis 2:22 KJV

HELLO, BEAUTIFUL WOMAN OF GOD! – Reading: Genesis 1:19-23, 26-28

God was intentional when He created you.

He formed you with such precise measure, detail, accuracy, and features, so that you can only be you. A woman so fearfully and wonderfully made, it is not a surprise that you are made in the image and likeness of God.

Do not be persuaded by others and society of who you are, be persuaded by God. He was the one that made both, you, and I. Woman, take charge, lift your head up high and know that God was not unsure or doubtful when he made you - the wonderfully you.

Be courageous, be strong, as He has purposed you from before the foundations of the world for great victory to be won. Woman, I say, be you, again be the fearfully and wonderfully made you. Our Lord Jesus sees you, oh yes, He knows you, and there is nothing more important than understanding the love He has bestowed upon you when He created you.

So, walk in love, in faith, and trust that He was deliberate when He created you. There is no need to be like your sister, your mother, or the girl next door, just be the best version of the beautiful woman that God has purposefully created and nurtured in you.

Shanique Graham

TUESDAY 30th

I have the strength to face all conditions by the power that Christ gives me
Philippians 4:13 (GNT)

BE A TRYER – Reading: Philippians 4:10-20

Never say you can't
Never say it's impossible
But always try.

Try when you are weak
Try talking to the Lord
When you feel you can't speak
Try to listen instead
To the Lord.

Never give up
Always be a tryer
For a tryer is strong
They keep trying.

They believe
And try hard to trust God
He sees this
And He knows
Did you know?
God will not despise a tryer
But He can work with
A tryer
He can bless a tryer.
God can forgive
A tryer.

So continue
To live for Him
And keep trying
And love Jesus
And Christian live.

Sister Jennifer Henry

October
Parables of Jesus

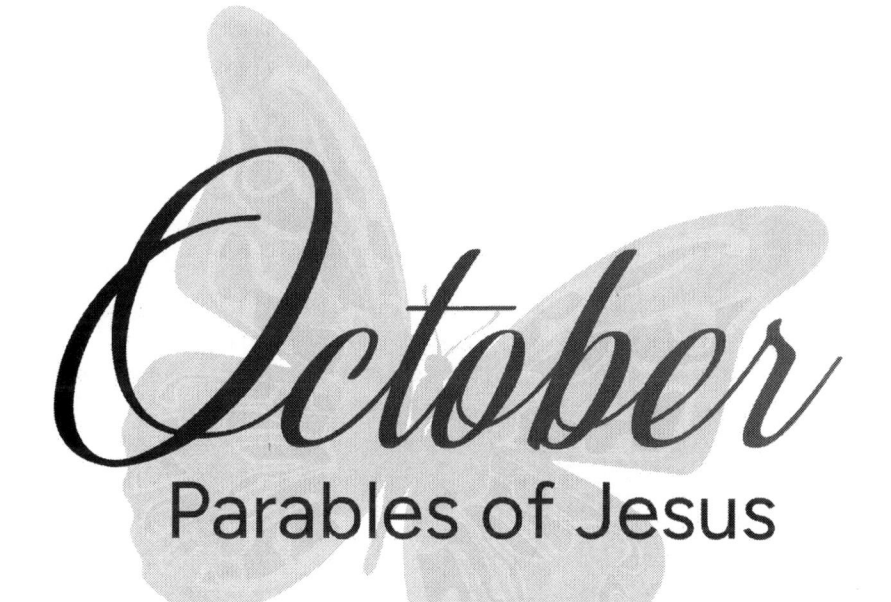

WEDNESDAY 1st

...Rejoice with me; for I have found the piece that was lost
Luke 15:9

THE LOST COIN – Reading: Luke 15:8-10

Jesus taught and conveyed His messages through parables. This format used expressed and instilled His thoughts to the many multitudes He ministered to. Why, you may ask?

These were ordinary people and often not wealthy or established in their communities. Therefore, Jesus spoke to them in ways that they could identify with and understand.

"A parable: an earthly story with a heavenly meaning" (n.d)

In the parable of the 'lost coin', Jesus teaches of the woman having ten silver coins. The monetary coin was known as a denarius (Roman coin). The coins in the form of a garland were worn by married women, and considered to be a fashion statement.

The loss of one coin could create disturbance and anxiety for the women. In this parable that Jesus shared, the woman noted she had lost a coin and searched with diligence for it. With fervency she lights a lamp, and sweeps the room to find it. The room was probably one room, with no windows and very dark.

The light symbolises an action to search thoroughly, in earnest to find it. She seeks diligently until she finds it! With exhilaration and happiness at finding the coin she shares the good news with her friends and neighbours, *"Rejoice with me, for I have found the piece that was lost"* (Luke 15:9).

And so, this parable demonstrates to the multitude Jesus' mission to earth as the Son of God. He came *"to seek and to save those who are lost"* (Luke 19:10). We, who are created in God's image have been given the gift of His Son, that through the act of salvation we may be redeemed. No longer lost but found to become part of His garland (Kingdom) established by our Sovereign God.

Hedy C Edmund

THURSDAY 2ⁿᵈ

And unto one he gave five talents, to another two, and to another one, to every man according to his several ability, and straightway took his journey.
Matthew 25:15

THE ABILITY IN THE HAND – Reading: Matt. 25:14-15; 1 Peter 4:10

In today's scripture reading, Jesus is comparing the Kingdom of Heaven to a wealthy man who gave his servants different amounts of talents (a form of currency) according to their abilities before going on a journey.

Notice that the servants were not all given the same amount but *"according to their several ability"*. Five talents would be too much of a burden with someone who has a one-talent ability, and a five-talent individual would be unchallenged by a gift of only one.

Let's consider this metaphorically by looking at the function of our hand. Each finger has a unique and crucial role, even the smallest finger is valuable and necessary. Look at your thumb. Your thumb is versatile and used for many tasks, symbolizing the highest responsibility and capability. Similarly, the servant with five talents, the thumb has the ability to achieve a lot and support the other fingers. The two talents could be the index finger which is essential for direction, representing a slightly lesser responsibility compared to the thumb. The servant with the two talents also had important duties and made good use of their abilities.

The one talent could be the little finger which may seem less significant. However, the little finger is vital for the hand's overall function and dexterity. The servant with one talent had a small role but their contribution was still important.

Jesus' distribution of talents according to our abilities is a reflection of His wisdom and understanding of our nature. He know what we can handle and gives us accordingly. It encourages us to use our talents to their fullest potential, fostering growth, responsibility, and faithfulness all for His glory.

1 Peter 4:10 says, *"…each of you should use whatever gift you have received to serve one another as good stewards of the manifold grace of God".*

CP

FRIDAY 3rd

(the house) fell not: for it was founded upon a rock
Matthew 7:25

HEARING & DOING – Reading: Matthew 7: 24-27; James 1:22-27

Many people think this parable is saying that Jesus is our rock. Well, yes, He is our rock, but Jesus is saying something else here. He is saying that the person who hears His teachings and puts them into action is wise *like* the man who built his house on a rock. Anyone can say Jesus is my rock, but not everyone can take heed, obey and put into action the teachings of Christ.

The natural storm, tornado, tsunami, hits everyone and everything in its way. However, some buildings are still standing when the storm has passed; others crumble falling to the ground. One can assume the buildings built with a deep solid foundation, and have care taken regarding its structure, are the buildings that remain standing.

The parable speaks of our spiritual house. Being a Christian doesn't mean we won't be hit by the storms and trials of life; these hit both the believer and unbeliever, just like the natural storm. The difference is we have an assurance that, as long as we live by the Word of God, then our spiritual houses are built on a solid foundation and able to withstand all things.

As long as we are doing what Jesus says, then we are building our spiritual homes on the rock, which will give us strength, peace and an assurance that we will stand and not fall.

"On Christ the solid rock I stand, all other ground is sinking sand ..."
(Rev Edward Mote)

Lady Pam Lewin

SATURDAY 4th

They that were foolish took their lamps, and took no oil with them: but the wise took oil in their vessels with their lamps
Matthew 25:3-4

BATTEN DOWN THE HATCHES! – Reading: Matthew 25:1-4; 2 Peter 3:1-18

In some parts of the world, the idea of always being in a state of preparedness is an integral part of life. One common thing we hear about COVID 19, is how it took everyone by surprise.

Blackouts and water shortages are a frequent occurrence where I live, so it's important that sources of light are accessible and a couple of five-gallon bottles of water are close to hand so daily life can continue. The reality is, no one knows when the lights will go out.

In the parable of the ten virgins, no one expected delays, but five of them thought ahead. Determined not to miss the wedding, they made certain that they were in a state of readiness. They decided to make sure that they could relight their lamps if they went out. The foolish, on the other hand, didn't give it a thought.

Perhaps the foolish virgins didn't want the inconvenience of having another vessel to carry. All dressed up with somewhere to go, they didn't want any cumbersome items cramping their style. The wise made the sacrifice though and they were rewarded.

So, what does this mean for today's Christian woman? It's that little extra time spent in communing with God (1 Thessalonians 5:16). It's that time devoted to reading and studying God's Word (2 Timothy 2:15) so that you can answer for the hope which is in you (1 Peter 3:15). It's making the effort to commit another scripture to memory (Psalm 119:11) so that when you're called to stand, you can, fully clothed in the armour of God (Ephesians 6:10).

We have been warned that times will become perilous as we get closer to Christ's return. Are you, am I ready to rekindle those lamps, or will we be found frantically trying to get oil at the last minute to do what we should have done when we had the opportunity?

Cheryl Lowe
Guyana

SUNDAY 5th

...how many hired servants of my father's have bread enough and to spare, and I perish with hunger!
Luke 15:17

HARD LESSONS – Reading: Luke 15:11-32

It's unlikely that there's anyone reading this page who, at some stage in their life, has not learned a truth by a hard lesson.

You may have been warned by a parent or guardian, a pastor or friend, a teacher, or even in a dream, but you chose to do the opposite of what you were told.

Such lessons are painful, and whilst we may never admit to anyone the full consequences of our errant behaviour, or our regret for not listening, we will never forget the lesson and yes, that we learned the hard way.

In the parable of The Prodigal Son, we don't read that the father cautioned his son regarding his request for his portion of inheritance. However, the son would have known that this was a premature demand. His father may not have challenged him because of events leading up to that conversation. There are times when parents, pastors, and other people of counsel, and even God, will cease to speak resigned to the fact that, *"If you can't hear, you will feel"!*

If the prodigal son's father had said, *"Don't go!"*, would he have listened? If his father said, *"Be careful of who you make friends with!"*, would it have made a difference? If his father had said, *"Don't stray too far from home!"*, would he have not gone to a *"far country"*? If his father had said, *"I dreamt that I saw you feeding pigs and eating the husks that the swine did eat!"*, the son would surely have dismissed this as nonsense – *"You just don't want me to have a life!"*.

But there are a few things which I admire about the son in this parable. One of them is, *"I will arise and go back..."* (Luke 15:18), he eventually acknowledged his mistake; he did not let pride keep him where he was until he died in the far country. Luke also pens, *"And he arose"* (v20), he followed through his decision. As well as these points, I love that the son did not return with excuses, nor did he blame anybody for his leaving home, for his folly, or his sin. He was totally contrite, *"Father, I have sinned against heaven and in thy sight, and am no more worthy to be called thy son"* (Luke 15:21). For if we are not repentant of our errors and sins, and will not take responsibility for our wrong, we have not learned and it's just a matter of time before we will do the same or similar again. Also, if the son had returned with a wrong attitude, we can be sure there would have been no 'Welcome Home' party!

When we sin, when we grieve the heart of God, when we bring shame upon His name, let's not come before God reminding Him of our rights as a son! Start the dialogue with, *"Father, I have sinned…"*. Of course, it's not possible to stop being a son; once a son, always a son! But what the son wanted more than anything else, was to be back in his father's house – even as a servant, I'm still in the house, under my father's covering and in his presence.

The prophet Hosea said to the Kingdom of Israel: *"Take with you words, and turn to the LORD: say unto him, Take away all iniquity, and receive us graciously: so will we render the calves of our lips"* (Hosea 14:2).

JEJ

MONDAY 6th

But the wise answered, saying, Not so; lest there be not enough for us and you
Matthew 25:9a

ARE YOU A 'YES' PERSON? – Reading: Matthew 25:1-9

Some people struggle to say, *"No"*. It makes them feel very uncomfortable, and gives a feeling of letting down the one who has made the request. Whilst I'm not suggesting that we cancel *"Yes"* from our vocabulary, the inability to say *"No"* can prove very expensive, not just financially, but in other ways.

If your diary is already full and someone asks you to do something for them on that day, why say yes, if it's not an emergency? O, they'll love it if you squeeze them in, and will of course report to others, *"God bless Sister Jane! She **never** tells me no!"*. Sister Jane also doesn't tell the others *"No"* who call wanting her (on the same day) to do an airport pickup, take them to the market, plait their hair before church tomorrow. They too all report to somebody else, *"God bless Sister Jane! She **never** tells me no!"*.

But generous Sister Jane is digging her own grave by saying yes to every appointment and every request. She has her own growing pile of things to do which never gets done, while she accommodates everybody else's wishes! She becomes known as the most faithful member of the church (she is also the most exhausted!).

In today's focus parable, there are ten bridesmaids, all of them were waiting for the wedding of a mutual friend to begin. No doubt they looked very beautiful in their special dresses and lovely hair-do. Maybe the ten of them were friends, perhaps some of the bridesmaids were even related to each other.

If you've ever been a bridesmaid, you'll know that it's an honour to be asked to be part of the bridal party. The day of the wedding is a flurry of excitement, giggling and laughing, as the long-awaited day is now here. You help each other to get dressed, pull up the zip on the dress of another, help to style the hair, share each other's body lotion and perfume, compliment one another, *"You look good, girl!"*. It's a time of camaraderie. All those involved want the day to be a success and nothing to spoil it for the bride and groom.

Unfortunately, this wedding did not have a happy ending! Five of the women were unprepared for a long wait for the bridegroom to come to where they were, at the home of the bride, to start the procession back to his father's house for the wedding feast (the feast would last for about one week). Although these ladies had all things common when getting ready, although earlier Rebekah had brushed Mary's hair, and Martha had helped Sarah to strap up her shoes, there was now a clear change in the atmosphere! Mary and Sarah, and three others, realised that their lamps to help lighten the pathway of the bridegroom to the feast had gone out. No one was laughing now. *"Please can I have some of your oil"* was met with a blunt refusal of, *"Not so"*.

How seriously are you taking your salvation at this time in the church's history, when it is evident that time is winding up? Have you yet learned how to say, *"Not so!"*? *"My son, if sinners entice thee, consent thou not"* (Proverbs 1:10), meaning, say, *"Not so"*. If you're present when certain conversations are taking place and you're asked to give your opinion, say, *"Not so"*. If those around you try and dilute the Word of God and compromise and you feel alone and 'stand out like a sore thumb', it's still, *"Not so"*! If 'everybody's doing it', still say, *"Not so"*!

Ladies, if you're on your own with a man that is not your husband, and he turns into an octopus with arms all over the place, do like Joseph had to do with Potiphar's wife (Genesis 39:15), leave your coat (and the expensive bag), you run for your life, while shouting, *"Not so!"*.

JEJ

TUESDAY 7th

...Go ye rather to them that sell, and buy for yourselves
Matthew 25:9b

LATE NIGHT SHOPPING – Reading: Matthew 25:9b-13; 1 Thessalonians 4:13-18

If you knew that today was going to be your last day alive, what are some of the things that you would/would not do?

If you knew that Jesus was coming today, what are some of the things that you would/would not do?

How do you know that today is not your last day on earth, for either reason?

In yesterday's lesson, we looked at the moment of realisation for half of the bridesmaids when, although they looked the part, they discovered that, but for a last-minute miracle, they would not be part of the bridal procession nor wedding feast. In their desperation, they took the 'advice' of their wise colleagues who suggested, *"Go ye rather to them that sell, and buy for yourselves"* (Matthew 25:9b).

When you think that things can't get worse, sometimes they do! Panic can cause clouded-thinking, it can interrupt your normal logical thought-flow. It's midnight, the bridegroom was already in view for the proclamation was made, *"Behold, the bridegroom cometh, go ye out to meet him"* (v6). Is midnight a time to go to the shop? Would not most places that sell oil now be closed? How far and how fast would these bridesmaids have to run to find a shop open? It's now past midnight. Instead of running out to meet him with joy, they had gone to do some emergency late night shopping!

Now is the time to do some spiritual checks. It's more than singing, *"A little more oil in my lamp, to keep it burning 'til the break of day"*. Fast! Pray! Read the Word! Forgive! Live holy! Focus! We've heard for so many years that Jesus is coming, that it's almost just a story. But what is it that may prevent me not from going out to meet him (Matthew 25:6), but going up to meet Him (1 Thessalonians 4:17)?

*"My bridegroom is coming, I hear his sweet voice
Make ready! I soon shall be there
It thrills through my spirit and makes me rejoice
To know we shall meet in the air.*

*I hear speeding nearer His blessed chariot wheels
So softly they turn in the skies
This world cannot hear them, He only reveals
His truth to the Spirit-touched eyes!*

*He's coming so soon, He's coming so soon
O, watch for it may be today
He is coming so soon, He's coming so soon
To take His beloved away".
(My Bridegroom is Coming – LC Hall)*

JEJ

WEDNESDAY 8th

Some (seeds) fell by the way side, and the fowls of the air came and devoured them up
Mark 4:4

HOW IS MY HEART? – Reading: Proverbs 4:23; Mark 4:1-4, 14-15

What is a parable one may ask? A parable is an earthly story with a heavenly meaning. Often in the Bible, we see Jesus using parables to relay a story of spiritual truth. He uses a natural example, to bring out a spiritual truth.

In the book of Mark, we observe the daily duty of a farmer sowing his seeds which was a familiar sight to Jewish people who were farmers. Thus, the parable was used to enable understanding. The farmer was strategic in sowing consistently. The seeds fell on three types of soil which were not suitable for growth.

Farmers generally ploughed after sowing their seed. The issue for the farmer being he is unaware of where rocks and thorns might be growing. It is often said that this lesson should be named the Parable of the Soil.

As believers in Christ, we know that, *"the seed is the Word of God"* (Luke 8:11). When the word of God goes forth, and is received in the heart, it must bear fruit. The disciples 'of the day' were seeking to know about the kingdom of God. Despite Jesus sharing the mystery of God, they could not understand unless God revealed this to them. Today, *"without controversy, great is the mystery of godliness…"* (1 Timothy 3:16) there is no confusion with revelation, believers in Christ with gratitude in the heart, thank the most, high God for revealing the mystery through His son, Jesus Christ.

Today we must routinely carry out the introspection of our hearts, the condition of it matters where God is concerned. Evil can live in the heart and will be exposed when we open our mouths (Matthew 12:34). That is why it is important to ask God to create in us a clean heart and renew a right spirit. Worshipping the true and living God means that we must meet his Terms and Conditions.

Missionary Audrey Simpson

THURSDAY 9th

...when he comes home, he calls together his friends and neighbours, saying unto them, Rejoice with me; for I have found my sheep which was lost
Luke 15:6

RESCUED, RECEIVED & REJOICING – Reading: Luke 15:1-7; 19:10

Have you ever met a person that had an *"anything you can do I can do better"* attitude? The type that says if you've been to Tenerife, they've been to 'Eleven-erife'! Everything you say or do, they're always trying to one-up you; they can be so annoying, right?

Well, this parable is the response of Jesus speaking to the self-righteous and obnoxious Pharisees and Scribes after they accused Him of receiving and eating with sinners. However, Jesus took it one step further, He righteously 'one-upped' them in the most beautiful, wise, and non-annoying way, by declaring that not only does He receive and eat with the sinners, the lowest and outcasts of society, but that He rescues, receives, and rejoices over these lost sinners!

Jesus, in His wisdom, includes the element of repentance in the equation to highlight the fact that a truly righteous God still holds the standard high, and expects all people everywhere to repent. Therefore, the Pharisees and Scribes 'didn't have a leg to stand on'.

Jesus graciously highlights HIS value system that displays so well that:

He will go to any lengths to rescue a wandering, erring, wounded sinner. He'll leave all to rescue one.

Lost sheep don't find their way home, the Good Shepherd begins the 'search and rescue' mission to find and rescue them!

Not only does He receive them, but carries them back to the fold; oh, the gentle merciful Saviour doing what He does best – loving us.

Jesus rejoices, and heaven rejoices, when repentance restores relationship. Rejoice in the Lord always, and again I say, rejoice!

Thank you, Jesus, for all the rescuing, receiving, and rejoicing you have done for us.

MinK / Minister Kay

FRIDAY 10th

No one tears a piece of cloth from a new garment and puts it on an old one; otherwise he will both tear the new, and the piece from the new will not match the old
Luke 5:36 (AMP)

COMPLETE TRANSFORMATION – Reading: Luke 5:33-39; Acts 9:20-21

Often, there's a temptation to patch a damaged, cherished piece of clothing, to give it an extra lease of life. This is a false economy; the patch ends up being unsightly and the original garment, from where patch was taken, is rendered useless.

In today's verse, the *"new garment"* represents a new way which Jesus was bringing to the world based around grace, faith, and His Word. The *"old garment"*, symbolised old ways, of Jewish laws/traditions. Jesus emphasises His new doctrine can't be patched onto old ways of living.

2 Corinthians 5:17 explains that in Christ Jesus, we are new creations, *"Old things are passed away; behold, all things are become new"*. Further, Romans 12:2 admonishes us, to *"be transformed by the renewing of your mind"*. Today, we're encouraged to be open to the transformative power of Jesus. Clinging to outdated beliefs or practices will hinder spiritual growth. Putting a band aid on a serious wound will not help it to heal. We need all of what Jesus has to offer!

Mixing fundamentally different principles/lifestyles causes conflict and dissatisfaction. We must fully commit to new, healthy ways rather than trying to blend them with old, ineffective habits. Transformation might require leaving behind old behaviours and traditions which no longer serve our growth. Embracing innovative ideas often means letting go of outdated methods, being open to change.

True renewal and transformation require a complete embrace of the new, not a compromise, which will dilute their intended efficacy. This principle should guide us, encouraging us to fully adopt positive changes and new directions, through Jesus Christ.

Marie Nicol

SATURDAY 11th

And no man putteth new wine into old bottles; else the new wine will burst the bottles; and be spilled, and the bottles shall perish. But new wine must be put into new bottles; and both are preserved
Luke 5:37-38

RENEWED MINDSET – Reading: Romans 12:1-2; Colossians 3:1-3

I'm sure you've heard the adage, *"You can't teach an old dog new tricks"*. People generally do not like change. They like to feel that what they do, is being done their way. But here's the thing, the world might applaud, but is your way actually working? Doing things our way is precisely why the world is in the state it is today. And, to do things my way, is by default to reject God's way.

Change takes effort; it means accepting that your way of seeing and doing things might not be right, and we all know how we love to be told that we are wrong! The parable about putting old wine into new bottles and vice versa, was a direct challenge to the thinkers of His day. Jesus was the author of the message that had been given to save the world, but somewhere along the way, the message got polluted with 'my way' philosophy.

This quickly advanced into 'my truth' and 'your truth' ideology to the point where, one, not of the faith had to ask Jesus the question, *"What is truth?"*. You see, doing things our way confuses the issue for the very people with whom we are supposed to share the truth. Jesus had to cancel the idea that there were hundreds of different truths. He said: *"I am the way the truth and the life"* (John 14:6). There's no wavering here, no hesitation or consideration that he may have overlooked another way of seeing truth. There was only one way.

Today's text also examines the idea of 'new wine' suggesting that Jesus was introducing new doctrines into Jewish theology. In Matthew 22: 37,39, answering a lawyer's question about the greatest commandment, Jesus responds: to love God with all the heart soul and mind and love your neighbour as yourself. Was this a new concept? Leviticus 19:18 and Deuteronomy 6:5, two books in the Old Testament, says the same thing word for word!

The reality was that the chosen people had neglected to follow God's standards for so long, that when Jesus came and reinstated the principles of the law, it sounded like something new. So what is the essential message in the wine and bottles scenario? The wine and bottles have to match. We have to change, if we are to accept the truth of God. Paul puts it this way, *Put off...the old man which is corrupt according to the deceitful lusts and be renewed in the spirit of your mind, and that ye put on the new man..."* (Ephesians 4:22).

When our mindset changes, we are ready for the Holy Spirit and the truth of God to do its work.

Cheryl Lowe
Guyana

SUNDAY 12th

...thy brother is come...and he was angry, and would not go in
Luke 15:27-28

WHY WAS HE ANGRY? – Reading: Luke 15: 25-32; Romans 12:15

When the prodigal son returned home, his father who was still looking out for him, rejoiced.

But his elder brother was angry. Verses 25-32 tell us:

1. He had been out working in the field all day.
2. He did not want to go into the celebrations.
3. When his father came out to persuade him to join in, he released all his pent-up emotions.
4. He had served for many years.
5. He had never broken a commandment of his father.
6. He had never been given a kid to have a celebration with his friends.
7. He had never spent his father's money frivolously.
8. He had never had any acknowledgment for his years of service.
9. His father explained that as he was always with him, everything that he had was his.
10. The father said: *"It is meet that we should make merry – and that **we** include **you**, the **elder brother**"*!

Hallelujah!

BVG

MONDAY 13th

But he that had received one went and digged in the earth, and hid his lord's money

Matthew 25:18

WHAT ARE TALENTS? – Reading: Prov. 31:13-19; Luke 19:11-28

Years ago, a well-known celebrity, Steve Harvey, interviewed a 3-year-old Mayor of Dorset in the US (Little Big Shot).

When asked what he did as Mayor, he replied, *"I shake hands"*. That was his talent and, in developing it, he took advice from his 6-year-old brother, Robert. Robert had been Mayor twice and advised to, *"shake with your right hand and look people in the eye when you talk to them"*. Here is a valuable lesson. His simple talent could be improved, and he was willing to take advice on how to do that.

I was here reminded of Jesus saying, *"Unless you become as little children, you cannot enter the kingdom of heaven"* (Matthew 18:3). This child's responses were simple and direct. No one expects a 3-year-old to do more than shake hands, but as the interview progressed, viewers learnt that he *"liked people"*. His polite interaction with Mr Harvey, and childlike acknowledgement that he thought Mr Harvey was *"the best man in the world",* showed that he possessed far more than the one talent he had identified earlier.

Talents are not given for vain glory, but for God's glory. They are the Lord's 'goods' (Matthew 25:14), and we are accountable to Him how we use them. Often talents are showcased to exhibit abilities, thus overshadowing the less talented to the point where they fail to value what they have received, *"burying it in the sand"* (v25).

As women, we tend to do much self-abnegation: *"I'm only a housewife"*; *"I don't really do anything"*; *"I'm just a domestic help…"*. In Proverbs 31, the talents of the virtuous woman are listed. God wants each of us to recognise and improve on the talents He gives to us so that we can glorify Him, and have positive impact on the lives of others.

**Cheryl Lowe
Guyana**

TUESDAY 14th

After a long time the lord of those servants cometh and reckoneth with them
Matthew 25:19

KEEP WORKING – Reading: Matthew 25:14-19; Hebrews 10:35-39

Something in today's parable stood out to me a few years ago whilst looking at it from a different angle.

It was this: The two servants who traded on the talents given to them by their lord, doubled on the original amount that they were given. This was of course very commendable - a 100% increase is excellent work.

What I pondered on though was, after making a profit (Matthew 25:16-18), why did they stop working? Matthew records (v19) that, *"after a long time, their master returned from his trip and called them to give an account of how they had used his money"* (NLT).

I guess that I was curious to know why they did not just keep on working until their lord returned, and keep on doubling.

Keep on working, even when you feel that you've done enough! Carry on until Jesus comes.

JEJ

WEDNESDAY 15th

…Whosoever shall not receive the kingdom of God as a little child shall in no wise enter therein
Luke 18:17

THE HUMBLE HEART WINS! – Reading: Mark 10:13-16; Luke 18:15-17

Luke 18:15-16 says, *"People were also bringing babies to Jesus for him to place his hands on them. When the disciples saw this, they rebuked them. But Jesus called them unto him, and said, Suffer little children to come unto me, and forbid them not: for of such is the kingdom of God".*

These verses may seem simple, but they carry profound meaning, especially when considered alongside the parables of Luke 18.

Jesus welcomed the children, despite the disciples' objections. In a culture where children were often overlooked, Jesus emphasised their value, showing that the kingdom of God belongs to those who approach Him with childlike faith and humility. This act of welcoming the children underscores a key message in the parables: God's kingdom is for the humble, the overlooked, and those who recognise their need for Him.

For us as women, this passage is a reminder that we are all valued by God, no matter our status or situation. The Luke 18 parables - about the persistent widow, the pharisee and the tax collector - further illustrate the power of consistent prayer and the importance of humility before God.

We often juggle many roles and responsibilities, and it's easy to feel unnoticed or unimportant. But Jesus sees us, values us, and invites us to come to Him just as we are. Let's approach God with the same childlike faith, knowing that we are precious in His sight, and that His kingdom is open to those who seek Him with humble hearts.

Latoya J. Foster

THURSDAY 16th

Then he which had received the one talent came and said, Lord, I knew thee that thou art an hard man...
Matthew 25:24

DISSATISFIED & CONTENTIOUS – Reading: Matthew 25:24-25; Philippians 2:13-16

Bitter and twisted are apt descriptions of the servant with the one talent. He is belligerent and contemptuous. His accusations against his master sound rehearsed and contrived. He says he was afraid, suggesting his master's behaviour has placed him in harm's way, yet he is not fearful to show his contempt for his master by subjecting him to a tirade of abuse and insult.

Unlike his fellow counterparts, this servant's time is used, not to improve but investigate and indict his master. He counts his master as being unworthy of his time or effort. Little does he know that wasted talents can be very costly; in fact, waste of a talent cost him his job!

Are this servant's actions beset by covetousness and jealousy? His beliefs about his master are misconstrued. He thinks that the master has been hard. This begs the question, to whom? It may be that he believes he should have been given as much as his counterparts, but his mismanagement of one talent disqualifies him for more. He questions his master's methods of gaining wealth, yet he is still working for him. He feigns fear, but it's unclear why he believes he will be held accountable for his master's failings.

In Philippians 4:11-13. Paul declares, *"I have learned in whatever state I find myself, there to be content"*. Dissatisfaction with our lot can make us bitter and twisted. Women of God should cultivate habits of gratitude; we can always find someone whose situation is better or worse than ours. Paul further admonishes us that, *"in everything, we should give thanks and rejoice"* (1 Thessalonians 5:18). Not an easy thing to do when the storms of life are raging, but God's Word is never wrong. Psalm 119:165

says: *"Great peace have they who love thy law: and nothing shall offend them".*

Cheryl Lowe
Guyana

FRIDAY 17th

I was afraid, and went and hid thy talent in the earth: lo, there thou hast what is thine
Matthew 25:25

THE FIVE TALENTS – Reading: Matthew 25:19-30; Revelation 22:12

The just and good master
Bid his slaves to come
For he was going away
On a journey
And he would not be at home.

Whilst away his investments
Still had to made
By his slaves
He thought.

He was a businessman
One day
This was what he decided.

To distribute
The many talents
According to
Each slave's capabilities.

To his slaves
Who were the ones
Who he could confide
And who saw the possessions
Had he.

The many talents were these
Five, two and one
Which he distributed freely.

But he gave specific instructions
That he was expecting
A return a profit you see.

Then was the slave
Who given so much
He did not sit on his talents.

Five talents were great
But by trading them
He gained five more talents
Remembering the words of his master
He more than took heed.

The 2nd slave
His master's words
Ever ringing in his ears
He did not ignore
But worked with the two talents
So that he gained two more.

Then there was the 3rd slave
One talent had he
But his attitude was all wrong
For he dug a hole
Hiding the one talent
So easily.

The master returned
From his journey
And honoured
The slave who had added
To his five talents.

The master was so glad
At his slave's obedience
That he blessed him the more.

For his attitude and faithfulness
Was why he gained his rewards.

Again the master
Spoke to the 2nd slave
Who had added to his talents
Two more.

In which again
The master commended
And gave his grateful rewards.

But the 3rd slave
Criticised the master
About his character
He made excuses too
And he did not take heed
Of his Master's commands.

To make a good profit
He could have put
His one talent in a bank
So that his master's talent
Would prosper and succeed.

The master
Spoke judgment
To the 3rd slave
And took what he had.

And distributed
To the one who had ten talents
An added one bonus to him.

The 3rd slave
He told him that he was lazy
And was ungrateful for
The one talent he had
Been given
To grow and do so much more.

That was not the end of that slave
For he could no longer stand

In the presence of his master
Whose life was in his hands.

That ungrateful servant
We must not be
We must work with
Our God given talents
And not be ungrateful or lazy.

The good Lord, gives to all
What should be
So let us work
And be a blessing
Adding to what
God has given you and me.

For if we are mean
For if we are lazy
For if we are unfaithful.

We won't get another chance
But we would have lived
Our Christian lives in vain.

And we will face
God's eternal damnation
For we squandered
All that we should have gained.

God be praised.

Sister Jennifer Henry

SATURDAY 18th

Rejoice with me; for I have found my sheep which was lost
Luke 15:6

YOU ARE PRECIOUS – Reading: Isaiah 53:6; Luke 15:1-6

In this parable, Jesus teaches us about the value of one soul. Today's lesson shows how precious we are to Christ as individuals in an age where low self-esteem is endemic.

Jesus is at the peak of His earthly ministry; He is popular with some and yet so misunderstood by others. His proximity to sinners and publicans, i.e., tax collectors, does not go unnoticed by the Scribes and Pharisees. There seems to be much division in the community, each group appears to have its own little lifestyle.

Still, Jesus came to seek and save that which was lost, regardless of background or social group. Whilst everybody may want to hear Jesus for different reasons, yet His plan is the same for all. He loves humankind and wants to save the world from their sins.

"All we like sheep have gone astray, each of us has turned to our own way" (Isaiah 53:6). Some sins are public, and some seem to be private, but they will be revealed. Somehow, sheep sometimes stray away from the sound of their master's voice, perhaps seeking something better in another field - who knows what goes through the mind of a sheep! Their lives are simple, their needs are few, yet they are still prone to wander! They wander and soon get themselves into problems although they have a caring shepherd whose job is to provide and protect them. Sheep are vulnerable, they cannot defend themselves, they need a good shepherd's care. A sheep in isolation is in danger; they could be hurt or destroyed and this is why the shepherd will leave ninety-nine in the fold to find the one which is missing.

We have a Shepherd who cares and loves us. Wandering starts when our minds move away from our beloved Shepherd's Word for, He is His Word. He is also our deliverer and hiding place. He knows our cry and where to find us. We are all of great value to Him!

BVG

SUNDAY 19th

...Seek and you shall find...
Matthew 7:7

WHAT HAVE YOU LOST? – Reading: Luke 15:1-32

In Luke 15, we read of three people losing something of importance to them.

What is noteworthy to me is that in the parables of The Lost Sheep and The Lost Coin, the owner did not write-off what was missing and decide just to get another one. A diligent search was carried out until what was lost was found.

Both the coin and the sheep were replaceable, plus that sheep would be sold soon (or eaten for dinner anyway!), but a replacement would not have been the same. I guess it depends on the value that you place on your loss which will determine the level of diligence you employ for it to be recovered.

However, the parable of The Prodigal Son is very different. The father dearly loved his son, yet he did not go out to find him, although he was not replaceable. The father had to wait for his son to come home.

There are some things over which we have no control, there isn't always something that we can do to change our circumstance. We just have to 'wait it out' with a Word, and pray for a desirable outcome.

JEJ

MONDAY 20th

Whoever cometh to me, and heareth my sayings, and doeth them, I will shew you to whom he is like
Luke 6:47

WHAT ARE YOU BUILDING ON? – Reading: Matthew 7:21-29; 1 Corinthians 3:1-11

You'll never know how solid your foundation is until the storms of life begin to rage, and your feet feel entrapped in a *"slough of despond"* (Pilgrim's Progress).

Life was challenging until those teenage years began to rise about the parapet of life, and then it seemed as though the formative years were not that bad after all. *"Lord. I'm not ready for this..."*! And the Spirit said, *"Pray on...My grace is sufficient for you"*.

I questioned my parenting skills. Was I cut out for this? I was reminded, *"You are not alone. The battle is not yours, but mine, I will contend with those who contend with thee and I will save your children. Fight on"*. Those words brought peace to my soul.

Then, another confrontation, greater than the one before! All my resolves were dissolving one by one. My achilles heel was having the law at my door, endless fabrications, violent outburst, wilful damage to property, vindictiveness, and it began to feel like every day. Every week there was a misdemeanour for me to deal with and, finally, the school announced that there was nothing more they could do for this youngster; take him somewhere else - and I did.

We flew to pastures green in search of a new start, but things got worse. Then I cried to the Lord in my trouble, and He delivered me out of my distress. Nothing was as I expected. I had planned meticulously, prepared for every event of this journey but it wasn't enough.

You see, God brought me face to face with experiences I had really only heard about. Now I was living amongst the poverty stricken, the helpless, the hopeless. People, young people, were busy building their lives on shifting sand. Their only ambition was to obtain what they needed, to purchase a few moments of sweet oblivion. Could it be that in refocusing my attention on Him, on them, that I could alleviate my stresses in my home? Our world is fractured but nothing can separate us from the love of God (Romans 8:38).

I can see now that for every problem, He had provided a solution. My support came in the form of praying family, friends, helpful strangers. His still small voice reminding of the reliability and power of His Word. I knew that God was there, immoveable, solid as a rock. I had nothing to fear unless I forget the way He led me. His plan for me and mine is solid as a rock. His support is solid as a rock. His love is solid as a rock. He is the rock.

Things are calming down now. God has illumined our way to the end of the tunnel.

"The LORD is my rock and my fortress…my God…in whom I will trust…" (Psalm 18:2).

Cheryl Lowe
Guyana

TUESDAY 21st

Why call ye me, Lord, Lord, and do not the things which I say?
Luke 6:46

BUILD ON THE ROCK – Reading: Luke 6:46-49; John 14:15

We are exposed to sound all day long. As I write, my neighbour is teaching his son to ride a bicycle. He keeps saying, *"Keep going, trust me, I have got you"*, as he walks beside his child.

It made me think about our Heavenly Father. He wants us to succeed as we navigate life's experiences, and helps us by His Spirit comforting us, encouraging us, and walking not just beside us but within. If we listen, we will hear Him and will not stop at just listening but, as He spurs us on, we will be enabled to do exploits.

Our verse today comes at the end of one of Jesus' parables. In it He shows us, by the analogy of construction, a basic principle for life. Many of us have built sandcastles on the beach; we collect water in our buckets, mix it with sand, and then turn our buckets over to make a turret for our castle. We then continue the process until we have completed our castles. As the day goes by, our castles disintegrate because they have no foundation - they are built of sand on sand! Added to that, the tide comes in and washes away our constructions!

We must build on a sure foundation in every area of our lives – education, careers, relationships, etc. Listening to Jesus and doing what his Word says will ensure our success (Joshua 1;8). Yes, we have options in life, yet the tried and trusted way of God is best (Proverbs 14:12). Sometimes it's the hardest option, but it will be fruitful (Psalm 126:6).

My sisters, keep listening and doing. God is always speaking.

BVG

WEDNESDAY 22nd

*...a man ... sowed good seed in his field:
but while men slept, his enemy came and sowed tares among the
wheat, and went his way
Matthew 13:24-25*

WHILST MEN SLEPT – Reading: Matthew 13:24-30

Although I'd overslept and drove in the rain, I was on time for the 7:53am train.

I chattered to the ticket master, recognising him from the previous day's purchase. I brought my train ticket to work. I glanced at the train schedule, noted it was delayed by 20 minutes. I settled down, like the other potential passengers waiting. Why not? I have time. Hmm... WhatsApp, Trainline, Google.

Suddenly, I looked up. Where did the time go? Outside stood the train, ready to leave the platform. Yes - I missed it! How careless of me! I'm reminded of the parable of the wheat and tares.

As Christians, we can't afford to daydream, sleep, or become complacent of the truth. Distracted, whilst the enemy creeps in, to stunt and stifle our spiritual growth. Arise from spiritual sleep today, beloved. Watch and be alert, there's no time to waste. The enemy comes to sow seeds of discord, deceit, and doubt - diluting the truth.

Lord, today, help me to shine your light. Help me be savoured. Help me to be ready with my spiritual ticket, working earnestly and waiting expectantly. Let my fruit be ripe, affecting those around me. Ready any time to be taken to my Heavenly Father's kingdom.

Sis Dorcas (nee Simmonds)

THURSDAY 23rd

...thou wicked and slothful servant...thou oughtest...to have put my money to the exchangers...
Matthew 25:26-27

THE PARABLE OF PREPARATION – Reading: Matthew 25: 24-30

Cast your mind back to parents' evenings and the obligatory school reports with character assessments like, *"Talks too much"*, *"Conscientious"* *"Needs to engage more"* *"Could do well if he/she applied themselves"* or *"Has a bright future ahead".*

Nothing would be a more crushing blow than being described as *"wicked"* or *"lazy"*. The slothfulness of the ill-prepared student is akin to the servant making no effort to prepare for the master's return in Matthew 25.

Firstly, the master's disappointment was because **he knew them** and their capabilities, and that upon his return what they lacked was not ability, but willingness and heart. To him who knows to do good and does it nor, is sin (James 4:17) God doesn't take kindly to a response of apathy and laziness to His enduring love and sacrifice.

Secondly, we could ask, was the master in the text upset that his talents were wasted? Perhaps, but what ignited his anger was that **they knew him**! Much like that reporting teacher knows what they have painstakingly instilled in the student who just didn't bother to revise.

The greatest resource God has given us is Himself, His passion, His life on earth, His Word in the heart and His own Spirit, His own character to empower us. What a spurn towards Him that we would have the treasure of the very character of God at our disposal, and deflect to our own way. To not be Christ-like nor take account of the preparation He began for His own second coming. Rather, burying our talents in the ground, is to minimise the weight of salvation we have known through Him.

As believers is it possible that we have been equipped with every resource to follow but what we have given God back is slothfulness instead of passion, conviction and preparation? We are simply to have the mind and character of Christ and to do as He would do. Our undeterrable aim should be to reflect Jesus. To be good and to be faithful to Him and to His work until He returns.

Joy Lear-Bernard

FRIDAY 24th

...Take care of him; and...I will repay thee
Luke 10:35

WHO IS MY NEIGHBOUR? – Reading: Luke 10:30-37

We often meet unexpected people as we travel, they can help us while on a long journey. You never know who you might meet.

I am reminded of the time when I moved back home after a long period living in London. I settled into my seat on the train, took out my Bible and began to read. From time-to-time, I looked up to reflect and noticed a man across the carriage, also reading his Bible. He nodded at me and went back to his reading.

As the train pulled into the station, I went to collect my suitcase - it was large and quite heavy - thankfully it was on wheels! I made it to the exit after a struggle on the stairs. It was late, and although my parents' home was nearby, I knew that I should take a taxi. It was cold and dark, there were no taxis in sight, so I waited. The man that I had seen on the train came towards me, he asked if I was alright, and I told him that I was fine. He asked if he could help; I told him that I could manage.

I made it home and the following Sunday went to my new church. Even though it was my hometown, I was more than a little anxious. I opened the door and was met by a familiar face that I had not seen since my Sunday school days. What a relief! We talked for a while, and I was at ease again. She said, *"Let me introduce you to our pastor"*. I waited and had to smile when she came back with the man I had seen on the train! He looked at me, smiled and said, *"I think I have seen you somewhere before!"*. We both laughed. The service was wonderful and I felt so at home and welcome.

Over the years, I was so thankful for the way that we met. It turned out that that suitcase was synonymous with the number of burdens I was carrying. My new pastor guided me, taught and trained me, counselled me. We celebrated the good days and worked through the challenging ones. Year after year he was faithfully serving God's people, and I am one of them that will never forget him. You may have known him as

Bishop Martin Howard Simmonds; I was privileged to know him as 'Pastor'.

Life may batter us and bruise us, but God has a way of sending good souls to help us heal and develop as we grow as Christians. Our churches are like hospitals where we can find refuge and peace. Let us never forget that there are others just like us who are on the Jericho Road and need our help. Everybody is our neighbour.

BVG

SATURDAY 25th

And he shall set the sheep on his right hand, but the goats on the left
Matthew 25:33

ON THE RIGHT OR SINISTER? – Reading: Matthew 25:31-46

The Latin word for *'left'* is *'sinister'*. In the Bible, Old and New Testament, the positions of right and left play an important role. e.g., when a heavenly messenger, stands on the right of the altar, he brings good news. The story of Zachariah, the father of John the Baptist, is a case-in-point; the angel stood on the right of the altar denoting the good news of John's conception (Luke 1:11).

The allegory of sheep and goats, takes up this idea of good on the right and bad on the left. God is portrayed sitting in the final judgment, separating sheep and goats, righteous and unrighteous.

The goats have earned their accursed position on the left. They, although exposed to similar experiences as the sheep, fail to administer Christian charity to the needy. But even in this act of His displeasure, God's love is manifested. He informs them that everlasting fire - that from which they will never return - was not prepared for them, but *"for the devil and his angels"* (Matthew 25:41) The goats are defensive, they don't recall any encounter with the Lord, but He informs them that they had many opportunities to give aid, but did nothing. Denying help to such need was the same as denying assistance to Christ.

Christ maintains that we have a duty to the poor that is with us always (Matthew 26:11). Whatever we do, we do as unto Him. The term *'poor'* covers every aspect of need, i.e., spiritual, physical and mental. Many of the parables Jesus told centre around this theme of helping others and serves as a warning to His church, highlighting that there will be a day of reckoning.

Women have a unique place in this work as we can impact families in ways men may not be able to. This is especially true within diverse cultures within modern communities.

Cheryl Lowe
Guyana

SUNDAY 26th

Let both grow together until the harvest...
Matthew 13:30

BLOOM REGARDLESS – Reading: Matthew 13:24-30

"A flower does not think of competing to the flower next to it. It just blooms" – Zen Shin

I had the privilege of visiting a rice field and noticed, on very close inspection, that not all the plants were rice. Among them was a weed that looked convincingly like rice.

In Matthew 13:24-30, Jesus tells the parable of the wheat and tares. These tares likely refer to a weed called darnel, which looks like wheat in its early stages. The roots of the tares (darnel) can intertwine with the wheat, making it difficult to pull them out without damaging the wheat. The tares also compete for water, sunlight and nutrients, affecting the wheat's yield.

In the parable, the farmer wisely waits until harvest time, because at maturity, the wheat is distinguishable by its fruit.

Like wheat among tares, we may feel surrounded by situations in this secular world that try to choke out our faith. Despite the enemy's attempt to steal our joy and darken our days by robbing our sunlight, we will bloom and bear fruit. We are assured that when we live boldly in our God-given purpose, rooted in His Word, we will flourish. The wheat doesn't strive to be like the tares; it grows in its unique identity.

We, too, should not conform to the world's patterns but trust God's process. When we truly live for God, trusting His wisdom, we can rest knowing that, at the right time, He will separate us unto Himself. Until then, trust His timing and let the challenges push you to grow deeper in Him.

Shani Oliphant
Jamaica

MONDAY 27th

...the kingdom of heaven is like to a grain of mustard seed, which a man took, and sowed in his field
Matthew 13:31

BEING DELIBERATE – Reading: Matthew 13:31-32

It is a sad fact of life that, too many of us who are called by the name of Christ, have yet to learn what it means to *"build for others and not for self"*.

Here we have an analogy of one man planting a little seed, aware that it may never grow and flourish in his lifetime, but planting it anyway. He did this knowing that, as a servant of God, he needed to care for the kingdom of God. If we are going to be concerned for the kingdom of God, we cannot be concerned with advancing our own agenda.

The smallest effort that we make today, the smallest task that we accomplish today, the smallest word that we utter today, the smallest smile that we share today, **all** have the potential of reaping rewards for generations to come. This is not for our praise but for the glory of God! The heavens and the earth declare His wondrous works through this smallest of seeds growing into a giant of a tree.

How many generations and families of birds were able to build their nests in this tree and nurture their young? How many weary and heartsick travellers were able to find shade under the branches of this tree while harnessing the energy and fortitude to go on?

Like this man, we must be deliberate in making these small efforts knowing that the tree that grows will build relationships for eternity. No one would ever know but the Father who sees all things.

Reflect - How can you be deliberate in your service for God today?

Pastor Londy Esdaille
Nevis

TUESDAY 28th

...a woman took (leaven), and hid in three measures of meal, till the whole was leavened
Matthew 13:33

YOU CANNOT HIDE – Reading: Matthew 13:33-35; Acts 4:13-21

For anyone who has had an encounter with God, these words will always be true – you cannot hide! The presence of God, the love of God, the peace of God, the joy of God, they will all overflow in your life and perfume the atmosphere around you.

The smallest amount of leaven, or yeast as many of us call it today, will forever change the balance of the largest amount of flour in which it has been placed. This is how we need to see our relationship with God. Any encounter that we have with God will forever change the way we think, believe, and behave.

Unbelief may cause us to deny it. Fear may cause us to reject it. Doubt may cause us to refuse it. The reality is that we will never be able to hide from it. Our lives would forever be changed by it.

Just as the leaven has no control over when it is placed into a position to be activated, so too we have been placed in our families, our communities, our places of work, as agents of change without having any say in the matter! Until it is placed in the flour, yeast remains inactive and unable to effect a change.

Let us be the leaven that changes the world around us, rather than the flour that is changed by the leaven of the world! Whatever way the change happens, it cannot be hidden.

Are you willing to be activated as God's leaven in this dark world to effect a positive change for Him?

Pastor Londy Esdaille
Nevis

WEDNESDAY 29th

...because this widow troubles me I will avenge her, lest by her continual coming she weary me
Luke 18:5 (NKJV)

NOT PLAYING BY THE RULES? – Reading: Luke 18:1-8

Have you ever felt that somehow life is just not fair? That some people are playing the game but not abiding by the rules like the rest of us? Isn't it just so frustrating that the lawmakers are often the ones who are the biggest lawbreakers and somehow, they bypass the consequences for law breaking? If you have ever felt this way trust me, you are not alone!

We see that the judge in this parable has a reputation for not fearing God or regarding man. He feels that he is above the law and rules, he is not answerable to anyone, and nothing stops him from doing what he wants to do.

We see that he persists with this attitude when the widow comes to him making her request for justice. However, there's a shift and this judge's supercilious and obstinate attitude gives way to the widow's importunate pleas. The unjust judge changes his mind and grants her request, just to stop bothering him.

Jesus began this parable by saying, *"men ought always to pray and not to faint"* to explain that prayer is meant to be a consistent and fervent spiritual discipline which should continue in spite of challenges faced. Persistent prayer is the key that unlocks doors to endless possibilities. With persistent prayer you step out of the realm of *"No"* from the unjust judges in life and into the realm of *"Yes"* from the judge of all justice and righteousness - Jesus Christ; remember you are praying to the God who makes all things possible according to His will.

The judge said that he had to give the widow what she wanted lest she weary him by her persistence. The word *"weary"* in the original language of Greek that the New Testament was written in is the word *'Hypōpiazō'* (pronounced Hoo – Pope – Pee – Ard – Zo) which means to beat black and blue, to attack, to cause bruises, to buffet and knock out like a boxer. When you pray persistent fervent prayers, you deliver a knockout punch to any and every obstacle, trial, or issue. It has to bow in defeat. Get excited!

It doesn't matter who isn't playing by the rules or thinks they're above the law, because when you pray persistent fervent prayers by faith, you appeal to the righteous God of Justice which means that the game is rigged and you win!

MinK / Minister Kay

THURSDAY 30th

...even though he will not get up and give you bread because of friendship, yet because of your shameless audacity he will surely get up and give you as much as you need
Luke 11:8 (NIV)

UNASHAMED PERSISTENCE – Reading: Luke 11:5-13

In the early years of starting our family, life dealt us an unexpected blow. My husband and I were laid off our jobs at a time that we had a young child to care for. The surmounting financial obligations forced me to work as a credit card sales representative; a fully-commissioned mobile job.

I must admit that my first days on the road were filled with shame, especially as a university graduate. To make matters worse, my inquiries and proposals were met with many, *"No's"*. But as the bills piled up and our supplies dwindled, pride, shame and fear vanished from my mind. I began to persistently pursue strategies to meet monthly targets, irrespective of initial rejections. Slowly, *"No"* turned into *"Yes"* and things started to look up.

This experience taught me the power of unashamed persistence; the kind needed in our walk with the Lord to turn closed doors into open doors, asking into receiving and seeking into finding.

Persistence is what gets us the answers as demonstrated in Luke 11:5-13. It's not that our Lord Jesus is waiting for us to beg and cry before He gives us what we need, but the persistence required is for us! Persistent prayers bring us to a place of total dependence and reliance upon our Savior. It is the catalyst for unwavering faith and spiritual growth in the life of a believer.

Women of God, keep persevering; keep pushing - even in the midst of unanswered prayers because, as James wrote, *"...the effectual fervent prayer of a righteous man availeth much"* (James 5:16*).*

Evangelist Sherrina Richards
Antigua & Barbuda

FRIDAY 31st

...a man...went out early in the morning to hire labourers into his vineyard
Matthew 20:1

THE CALL IS OUR REWARD – Reading: Matthew 20:1-16

The labourers in Matthew 20 remind me of the sibling who remained in the house when his prodigal brother wandered. I tend to think that there were two prodigals in that story, one whose mind wandered and the other who let his body follow!

Both the labourer and the son in the house had this in common: they had forgotten the measure of grace they had received to even be considered to be part of the work.

We see the parable describes the householder going out at different times of the day to put those not yet employed to work. It is he that turned each one into a labourer, from the early workers to the last.

He graciously gave each person a role to work in his vineyard and, from the start, told them their wage. And yet, just like the brother of the prodigal, they assumed themselves better and deserving of a more noble receipt of pay although they were not deserving of anything.

It is God who ignited us and made us workers, labourers and citizens of His Kingdom - He has called us into service. It is because of His justness that He rewards. Ultimately, the greatest reward is this glorious salvation. Christ owes us nothing but we owe him everything, whether we are stalwarts in the faith or have just begun the journey.

Joy Lear-Bernard

November
The Goodness of God

SATURDAY 1st

That you may love the LORD your God, and that you may obey His voice, and that you may cleave unto Him: for He is your life, and the length of your days...
Deuteronomy 30:20

FOR I AM YOUR LIFE & THE LENGTH OF YOUR DAYS
Reading: Deuteronomy 30:1-20

On Wednesday 13 March 2024, I opened my Bible, and was led by the Holy Spirit to read Deuteronomy 30. This scripture speaks about the curses of disobedience, the blessings gained for obediently returning to God and receiving His great restoration, and the plea to choose life with all its benefits.

As I read the words, one line jumped out at me: *"for He is your life, and the length of your days..."*. These words were constantly ringing in my spirit, they blessed me to the depths of my soul, so I immediately updated my social media display picture with the quote.

On Friday 15 March 2024, I joined my regular Zoom service at 8pm. We were running a health presentation on this particular evening, and I was asked to read the doctor's biography. It was only a couple of paragraphs long and I had around two sentences left to read, when something happened. The only way I can describe it; is to say it was like a bomb went off in my head! It was like the quick snap of an elastic band breaking. I felt an overwhelming, sudden excruciating pain in my head, I was seeing stars, and the room was spinning. I remember gripping the table and saying to myself; *"Dear God what is that!?"*

Somehow, I managed to finish the last two sentences; I switched off my camera and pressed the mute button. That's when I started screaming! The pain was intensifying by the second. My mum came rushing in from the kitchen, asking, *"What's wrong, what's wrong!?"* Because one moment she heard me reading the biography, then in the next moment I was screaming. I replied, *"My head, my head. Call the ambulance!"*. Mum grabbed the phone and dialled 999. She had the phone in one hand and me in the other trying to help and comfort me while talking to the emergency services. By this point I'd lost all power in my body, I couldn't open my eyes because of the pain, I couldn't hold my arms up, I couldn't hold my neck up, and I was just limp and lifeless in the sofa.

My mum went across the road to our neighbours for help. As I was fading, I felt the cold hand of death try and grab hold of me. I remember saying to God – *"God, I don't want to die now, and I don't believe it's your will to take me either"*. God's Word assured and reassured me that He indeed is my life and the length of my days. Then I passed out.

Slowly I remember realising that I could hear voices in the living room, but I couldn't figure out who they were; it was the longest time before I recognised it was my two neighbours talking to my Mum. One neighbour was a retired nurse, and she began to do my observations, etc., while Mum spoke to the emergency services again.

I was declining rapidly, couldn't hold my head up, and couldn't string a sentence together, I was just groaning. I began vomiting and the pain was unbearable and getting worse.

The ambulance took almost two hours to come. I don't remember what happened after that until I arrived at the hospital. I was seen by several doctors and nurses, and they sent me for a CT scan, because the symptoms I displayed fell outside the usual pattern of a Sickle Cell crisis (i.e., I suffer with Sickle Cell Anaemia).

A doctor saw me after the CT scan and said, *"Miss Dawkins, unfortunately you've got a bleed on your brain (a brain aneurysm/ a subarachnoid brain haemorrhage)"*. He told me that he'd sent the scan pictures to a specialist hospital in Central London, and I would need to be transferred there at once, and more than likely I'd need brain surgery.

I was transferred in the early hours of Saturday morning to the specialist hospital. Originally, surgery was scheduled for Monday morning. However, the surgeon and team arrived suddenly on Sunday and told me I must go into surgery that morning. I was mentally prepared for surgery on Monday and told my Mum and family, but they insisted I must go in now, because the seriousness of my condition meant they had to bring the surgery forward. I had no one with me, it was too late for my mum to make it in time, and I began to feel desperately alone and anxious. That was when the words, **"I am your life and the length of your days"** came forcefully into my spirit, and a wave of peace swept over me as they wheeled me into surgery.

News of the situation had spread rapidly around my family, church community and friends. Everybody who knew me here and overseas seemed to be praying for me. Believe me when I say I felt that 'prayer wheel turning'.

Needless to say, the surgery was successful. But I don't remember anything immediately after the surgery until they woke me up hours later in the High Dependency Unit, where Mum greeted me in my groggy, incoherent state.

I couldn't use my mobile phone as I was extremely light-sensitive, and I couldn't open my eyes due to pain. It was so hard to see and focus on anything for more than 10 seconds, but I later found out that I had way over 500 individual messages of prayer and support, with multiple missed calls and voicemail messages. The outpour of love was just amazing, I am truly blessed.

The neurology doctors and nurses were amazed at my recovery and that I didn't present with any of the lasting speech and cognitive impairments most patients typically show from this condition.

Remorsefully, I recalled how my dentist suddenly passed-away the year before with the same condition. Another patient later told me about a young Sports Journalist who died from a brain aneurysm the week before I was admitted. I recognised that people younger, fitter, and healthier than me without any underlying illnesses had died from what I lived through!

As the psalmist said in Psalm 4:4, *"I communed with my own heart upon my bed and was still"*. I spent a lot of time reflecting on the goodness of God as I began to process what I had been through, and I was so utterly assured of His faithfulness.

I also thought about how uncanny the whole thing was because the health presentation title was 'Strokes and BRAIN BLEEDS' – the online audience had no clue that at the time they were learning about this subject I was going through it in real-time! Of all the Friday evening services, and of all the health presentations, THIS was the Friday that I had a brain bleed! This will forever be a strange, inexplicable occurrence for me.

During the three weeks I spent at that hospital, I was still having severe headaches and other symptoms. They looked after me very well and as I desired, I was able to be home in time for my 43rd birthday. I'm still recovering as it will take time for the headaches to subside completely and be back to full health and strength.

I could say with all certainty that because God is the length of my days, He wasn't going to allow me to die before I was 43, as that would not be length of days for me.

This experience has taught me that the goodness of God to me is unquantifiable. God has been graciously good, kind, and merciful to me, more than I feel I give Him reason to be. God has been better to me than I've been to myself.

I thought about how I walked through the valley of the shadow of death, but God told death NO! and sent His rod and staff – His Word, to prepare me for what I was about to face. It's absolutely amazing how God works. He gives you a Word for the season, a Word you can stand on, and a Word you can take back into the courts of heaven and remind God of His Word and promise to you.

Truly, God is my life, and the length of my days, HALLELUJAH!

MinK / Minister Kay Dawkins

SUNDAY 2nd

The grass withereth, the flower fadeth: but the word of our God shall stand for ever
Isaiah 40:8

I TRUST IN GOD (HE BLOCKED IT!) – Reading: Isaiah 40:1-9

At the end of July 2023, I noticed a pin spot, literally tiny, on my right leg.

By the end of August, it had not only grown into half a penny size, it was no longer smooth but raised and changed colour. My family was bothering me but I remained calm, finally getting it checked.

My GP saw me on 31 August. She appeared worried, far more than I was, to be honest. But I was referred urgently to the hospital for tests. I procrastinated to ask others to pray; I told myself that once I had results, I would share it, as I really wanted to use my faith in God first.

Anyhow, we were in September and about to travel to New York. I tried to put it out of my mind, but somehow knew that the results would be at home the moment I returned. I had not asked God for His will, but asked boldly for His hand stating I was not going through this, but out of this, because He's my Daddy!

All of the messages during the New York Convocation, especially Bishop Cawley's, struck that chord of, *"Claim your Healing"*. Upon our return, I noticed a very obvious NHS envelope on the mat. I opened it with a bit of fear that had crept in, but on opening I saw one word stand out in bold: **Benign**. Oh, hallelujah Jesus! I then read the rest, i.e., to keep an eye on the lesion.

Since that letter, I have noticed a decrease in the lesion's size and its texture has become smoother.

Who could it be but JESUS! We never expect certain things to happen to us but let's remember that our God dwelling in us is able to do more than we can ask or THINK.

Lady Coronet Landell

MONDAY 3rd

Oh that men would praise the LORD for his goodness, and for his wonderful works to the children of men
Psalm 107:8

GOD IS TRULY GOOD – Reading: Psalm 107:1-15

As believers of Jesus Christ, we all love to say, *"God is good"*, because this is the truth.

When we are given an opportunity to share what we believe is the goodness of God, we all share our many different experiences. Like you, I have had many experiences of the goodness of God, but today will share a most recent one.

In Isaiah 11:1-3, the prophet reveals beautiful characteristics of the Messiah. In particular, the last clause or verse 3 says of Him, *"...he shall not judge after the sight of his eyes, neither reprove after the hearing of his ears".* The writer was given this chapter and verse 3 whilst travelling to church one morning, and meditated on the last clause for days after.

Jesus does not judge by appearances, by what He sees, or even by what He hears. He judges the heart which houses our true intentions. Often, we judge each other by outward actions, by what we think we see, by what we hear or by what we are told and then we come to a negative or a positive conclusion. Many times, our judgment is incorrect.

The Holy Spirit is never wrong, He is Truth. He chose young David to be King and what a great king he was. The LORD knew David's heart. This same David experienced so much pain in his life, and confessed that he would have fainted had he not believed to see the goodness of the LORD. David chose the LORD to judge him on a serious matter (1 Chronicles 21:7-13). Why choose God? Because His mercy is great. He is a good God.

The LORD chose you, Dear Believer, and He does not make mistakes. You can trust that He will never judge you incorrectly. He knows your heart and as such you can safely submit your all into His hands.

Don't be discouraged when others judge you, call you names, tell you that you are weak and have no substance. May I remind you, it is the weak things of the world that the LORD uses to confound the mighty (1 Corinthians 1:27). You are important to Him.

Wow! God is good.

Of all the things on earth that God could choose
Of all the many people that God could call
Of all the many places where God could dwell
Of all the many vessels that God could use
What did He do? He chose me
Jesus chose me, my Jesus chose me.
(MJB)

Dearly Beloved, the goodness of God is a beautiful attribute that exemplifies who He is. There's so much more to His goodness that we could talk about.

God's beautiful character, 'Goodness', is produced in us as we walk daily with Him.

The Goodness of God:

    a. Does not judge after the sight of His eyes
    b. Does not reprove after the hearing of His ears
    c. Judges the heart
    d.
    e.
    f.

Can you add to the list?

Minister MB

TUESDAY 4th

O taste and see that the LORD is good…
Psalm 34:8

TASTE & SEE – Reading: Psalm 34:1-8

God's goodness is not merely who He is but what He does.
He loves, He nurtures, He directs.
Your sorrow He detects, making all things better,
Breaking every chain and every fetter.

His Word is a love letter,
For every time you indulge,
From Genesis to Revelation
There are golden nuggets and hidden treasure.

God is the only one who can give lasting joy and peace,
In your latter years, He will give increase.
His goodness and mercy will never cease
Oh, come taste and see that the LORD our God is good.

He showers us with blessings, like no other could.
His wisdom is beyond human comprehension,
All things He hath understood.

God sees us, even from afar,
His goodness is not dependent on who we are.
It's who He is, oh, this is music
To one's ears this is sheer bliss.

God is good all the time,
He is awesome and truly divine.
Come taste and see, feast on the Lord,
For He is most heavenly and sublime.

Excellent is He in all of His ways,
He will keep and sustain us for the rest of our days.
There is soul sustaining goodness that cometh from the Lord
Let us therefore be in sync and with Him on one accord.

For His mighty great works,
May our hands applaud.
He alone is our just reward,
So unto His holy temple may we look toward.

Let us, Sweet One, draw nearer and nearer unto thee,
With spiritual wisdom and eyes to see.
Others shall come to feed off thee,
This I declare and this I decree.

Thou art Sovereign over all things,
And lasting joy to the hearts of thy children only you alone brings.
May we savour every moment spent with thee,
Recognising thy goodness is a sure guarantee.

Sister Pru

WEDNESDAY 5th

Thou hast delivered my soul from death, mine eyes from tears, and my feet from falling
Psalm 116:8

MY CONSTANT HELP - Reading: Psalm 116:1-19

The writer of the hymn, "The Mercies of God" would have related well to today's psalm:

The mercies of God, what a theme for my song
I never could number them o'er
They're more than the stars in the heavenly dome
Or the sand on the wave-beaten shore.
(T O Chisolm)

The psalmist has named just three things from which the LORD had delivered him but, without a doubt, it is not the end of the list.

But, on this occasion he remembered near-death experiences, the many tears he had shed over personal sorrow and pain, and traps that had been set by his enemies for his destruction. Another word for *"delivered"* in this context is to *"rescue"*. In my mind, the word *rescue* implies that a need is urgent or time-critical. Just when the snare would have entangled our feet and cast us down, there came the LORD to our rescue!

Psalm 34:19 says, *"Many are the afflictions of the righteous, but the LORD delivereth him out of them all"*. We see then that deliverance is not a one-off rescue mission because, whenever a word ends with 'eth', we're speaking in the continuous tense. How reassuring to know that no matter how ravaged we feel during or after our storm, God is constantly there to revive us, always dry our eyes, and by His strength keep us standing tall.

JEJ

THURSDAY 6th

Now to him who is able to do immeasurably more than all we ask or imagine, according to his power that is at work within us, to him be glory in the church and in Christ Jesus throughout all generations, for ever and ever! Amen
Ephesians 3:20-21 (NIV)

THE GOODNESS OF GOD: IT'S IMMEASURABLE
Reading: Ephesians 3:14-21

In today's focus scripture, the Apostle Paul writes to remind us of the vastness of God's goodness, a goodness so profound that it exceeds our wildest dreams.

Often, we limit God by our expectations, asking only for what we think is possible or practical. Yet, God's goodness is not confined by our earthly limitations. He delights in surprising us, blessing us beyond what we could ever hope for. His plans for us are not just good, they are immeasurably better than anything we could design for ourselves. I think you should read this paragraph again before going to the next, and really let what you're reading sink in!

When life feels overwhelming, and our prayers seem small in the face of our struggles, we have to remember that God's goodness is always at work within us. His power is capable of transforming our circumstances in ways we cannot fathom. Our role is to trust in His goodness, believing that He will do more than we can ask or imagine. Why wouldn't He? He is the King of Kings and I choose to walk in my Royal Heritage each day than to accept anything other than the goodness of God.

Let's live with the confident assurance that God's goodness will always prevail. His goodness is not just a part of who He is; it is the essence of His nature, and will guide us through every season of life. To God be the glory, now and forever. Amen.

Latoya J. Foster

FRIDAY 7th

I would have despaired had I not believed that I would see the goodness of the LORD in the land of the living
Psalm 27:13 (AMP)

LOOK UP WHEN THINGS LOOK DOWN - Reading: Psalm 27:1-14

Look up, Beloved
When things look down for you,
Press on through your problems
For the LORD **will** carry you through.

You may face fiery trials
But hold fast, for there's a reason,
If Jesus has plans for you
You'll soon pass on through this season.

He'll rescue you from your dark pit
Into a much brighter day,
He'll bind up all your wounds
And chase your darkest fears away.

So look up, Beloved
When things look down for you,
Just keep on believing
The LORD will see you through!

Name withheld

SATURDAY 8th

Praise ye the LORD. Praise God in his sanctuary: praise him in the firmament of his power
Psalm 150:1.

HE KEEPS GETTING BETTER - Reading: Psalm 150:1-6

"O Sovereign LORD, you have only begun to show your greatness and the strength of your hand to me... Is there any god in heaven or on earth who can perform such great and mighty deeds as you do'"
(Deuteronomy 3:24 NLT)

I will sing of Your goodness, I will sing of Your love
Though the seasons come quickly, You have always been enough
Though the night may get darker, though the waiting seems long
You have always been faithful, to remind me of Your love.

You are good, in the morning I'll sing
You are good, in the evening I'll sing
You are good, You are good to me.
You have always been patient, You have always been kind
You're consistent through the ages, Oh, what a friend of mine
So I'll remind my soul to bless You, Standing firm upon Your truth
Knowing You cannot be shaken, 'cause I've seen what You can do…
(Lyrics by Majesty Rose & Maverick City)

"People will speak of the power of Your awesome acts, And (with gratitude and submissive wonder) I will tell of Your greatness" (Psalm 145:6). When you think about all the wonders of God's goodness, and His unfailing love towards you, it's hard not to praise Him. He has never failed you yet, why would He start now?

Sis D. Tucker Cuthbert

SUNDAY 9th

This is the day which the LORD hath made; we will rejoice and be glad in it
Psalm 118:24

REJOICE! - Reading: Psalm 118:1-29

Today's key verse is a bold declaration! *"This is the day which the LORD has made, we will rejoice and be glad in it".*

This sounds a bit like Psalm 34:1 where David says, *"I will bless the LORD at all times"*. Sometimes we have to command ourselves to do what we don't actually feel like doing. We find ourselves in situations which would rob our joy and silence our praise. It's true - life can be so challenging at times. In moments of severe testing and distress, we will wonder, what is there to rejoice about? I've learned though that when I feel like I cannot be thankful for my present, I can at least give God thanks for my past; I can go through my archives and reflect on His faithfulness up until now.

We cry at times because troubles come but they will not last forever. 1 Peter 1:6 says, *"Wherein now ye greatly rejoice, though now for a season, if need be, ye are in heaviness through manifold temptations"*. Certain words here seem to contradict each other, i.e., how can Peter speak of *"greatly rejoice"* and *"manifold temptations"* at the same time?

We can rejoice because we are assured that God is with us, and rejoice also that these trials are just temporary. Rejoice too knowing that if we suffer with Him, we shall also reign with Him (2 Timothy 2:12), and be glad that your name is written in heaven (Luke 10:20).

JEJ

MONDAY 10th

…My grace is sufficient for thee: for my strength is made perfect in weakness
2 Corinthians 12:9

OUT OF GOODNESS CAME A THORN - Reading: 2 Corinthians 12:1-10

When we think of a thorn, it is sharp and pointed. Something that represents pain and suffering if you were to get pricked by it.

Nobody likes to feel pain and discomfort, this can often cause us to fail to see God's goodness in the situation that we are in.

When we choose to adjust our perspectives, we can see His goodness, even in life's difficult circumstances. Although we may not see how the thorn is benefitting us, we must believe that God has a plan. Three times Paul sought the Lord regarding the thorn in his flesh. God's reply, *"My grace is sufficient to keep you"* (2 Corinthians 12:9).

Thorns are to humble us in case we should rise above our measure, i.e., become proud by our achievements. God gave Paul revelations which were so great that, in order for him not to rise up in arrogance which would hinder his usefulness, Paul was given a thorn to humble him. God's goodness towards Paul is seen in this - God wanted to use Paul but all that we do must bring glory to God only!

You may be bearing a thorn in your flesh but remember, *"God resists the proud but gives grace to the humble"* (James 4:6; 1 Peter 5:5). The thorn you have in your flesh is to keep you humbled so that God can use you greatly and He alone gets the glory.

Minister Faith Groves

TUESDAY 11th

Behold, the LORD'S hand is not shortened, that he cannot save, or his ear dull, that he cannot hear
Isaiah 59:1

I HEARD YOU THE FIRST TIME: Reading: Isaiah 59:1-16

Daniel I heard
You the first time
I listened to your prayer.

I sent help from heaven
Before you knew it
The archangel Michael
He was there.

Michael had a mighty
Battle on his hands
But he could not be defeated
For God was
At the forefront
Of all his plans.

I heard you the first time.
Whoever is reading this poem
I know it's hard
But hold on a little longer.
And hold on and use the sword.

God knows all of the devil's cards
Hold on my brother
Sister too
Neighbour and friend.
Yes! I mean you.

November 2025
Theme: The Goodness of God

God has shone
His miraculous light
It shines bright
On me.

But wait
I now can see the manifestation
Of His promises He has bestowed
Can you rejoice with me?

Sister Jennifer Henry

WEDNESDAY 12th

In every thing give thanks: for this is the will of God in Christ Jesus concerning you
1 Thessalonians 5:18

GIVE THANKS! - Reading: 1 Thessalonians 5:12-28

The journey of faith with the Lord has many curves, hills, valleys, ups and downs. Some may take us by surprise, but we can be assured that God is always in control. Like the song says, *"For the God of the mountain, is still God in the valley"*.

Paul commended the Thessalonians for their faithfulness in the face of persecution and false teachings. He encouraged them to be joyful, keep on praying and moreover, always be thankful in everything. Not thankful **for** everything but **in** everything. Whatever our season, circumstances change but God never changes. The same encouragement is extended to us today.

It may even seem that God is asking too much of us, especially in times of great challenges. That is why we cannot do this in our own strength or abilities. Because it is the will of God to be thankful, show gratitude, He supplies all that we need to be able to face and deal with our present-day trials.

Let's focus on His goodness and who He is – He's Sovereign Saviour, our faithful Father. We give thanks and rejoice that He is a covenant keeping God. He is able to keep body, soul and spirit. We give thanks for His goodness that is constantly pursuing us.

"Oh how great is thy goodness, which thou hast laid up for them that fear thee; which thou hast wrought for them that trust in thee before the sons of men!" (Psalm 31:19)

Evangelist Marjorie Burgess

THURSDAY 13th

Blessed be the LORD, who hath not given us as a prey to their teeth
Psalm 124:6

BLESSED BE THE LORD – Reading: Psalm 124:1-8

The goodness of God talks about God's kindness, His love, His forgiveness, His mercy, His grace – the list goes on.

On 7th - 8th July 2024, I found myself in the A&E Department of my local hospital after being driven there by ambulance. The diagnosis was two TIAs (mini-strokes) within just over 24 hours.

I laid in the ambulance thinking, *"Lord, not again!"* – I was here in the same hospital with the same diagnosis in 2013. Then I thought of the goodness of God and it gave me hope.

As I write this, I'm home resting, waiting to see the TIA specialist at the end of July, until then, no driving and plenty of rest. Isn't God good? Whatever the final diagnosis, God is good because I can speak, hear, move, and type this testimony of His goodness to encourage those who are going through a season of sickness.

Let's join with the songwriter who said:

"I love your voice
You have led me through the fire
And in darkest night you are close like no other
I've known you as a Father
I've known you as a Friend
And I have lived in the goodness of God..."

So, I give God all the glory for His goodness towards me because He did not give me as a prey to sickness (v6).

Lady Pam Lewin

FRIDAY 14th

But Jesus beheld them, and said unto them, With men this is impossible; but with God all things are possible
Matthew 19:26

FAITH HOPED FOR - Reading: Matthew 19:16-30

Lord give me faith
But not just faith that can move mountains
God give me faith
But not just faith that heals all wounds
Father give me faith
But not just faith that grows from desperation
Give me faith that can sustain me day to day.

A faith that speaks life as each day begins anew,
A faith that knows I am always protected by you,
A faith where I stand on your Word daily,
A faith that never falters,
A faith where I enter every trial bravely,
Where my life is laid at your altar.

A faith that never questions if you are by my side,
A faith that knows that I am yours and you are mine.
A faith that trusts you with all my burdens and pains,
Where you take the reigns - maintain and remain.

A faith that truly believes that for me you died,
For my sins were crucified.
That believes in your resurrection - from death to life you rose again,
Believes that without you, life would lose all meaning.
Faith to believe that all is possible with You by my side,
Faith to know that because You called me I am qualified.

Faith that won't be swayed by money or a lack of,
Faith that praises in times of abundance and times of drought.
Let my faith be unshakeable and portray your grace,
Above all, my faith unbreakable, as I continually seek your face.

Sophia Pierre

SATURDAY 15th

***I will sing of the mercy and loving kindness of the LORD forever:
with my mouth will I make known Your faithfulness to all
generations
Psalm 89:1***

I WILL SING – Reading: Psalm 89:1-18

Thanks be to God, for His forever-ness,
His eternal compassion, and His faithfulness.
So while we breathe, we will sing from this breath,
Sending up praises for eternal happiness.

By choice, I will sound harmonies of gratitude
To the Lord with my voice.
By one accord of my heart, will I express in song,
His loving kindness that has been there all along.

By the breath of God loaned to me,
Let His praises rise from my mouth, with testimonies free.
The generations will hear, many will come to know
Of the mercies by which you love us so.

Your mercy and kindness repeats,
Each day it renews, though it never sleeps.
As we reflect on His goodness that we have come to know,
We will celebrate our Lord Jesus for His glory to show!

CDP

SUNDAY 16th

...His compassions fail not. They are new every morning: great is thy faithfulness
Lamentations 3:22-23

HE MADE IT PASS OVER – Reading: Lamentations 3:1-23

I was not worshipping with my home church one particular Sunday morning because of personal challenges, but was led to attend another church in close proximity. I was able to enjoy the service as the worship songs were familiar from my youth and I was able to converse with persons I had not seen for a while. I left church buoyed up in spirit, happy that I had obeyed the Spirit.

While walking home, I could feel the portent of rain in the atmosphere. Seeing that there wasn't much hope of finding shelter, I hastened my footsteps. As I felt the first few drops, I pulled out my umbrella. Down came a flurry of heavy raindrops and I thought, *"This is it. There's no escape!"*. But miraculously, the raindrops ceased. I gave God thanks. However, within the next few moments, I heard the loud sound of the approaching downpour and immediately I thought of Pharoah's army in the Red Sea. I was about to be drenched.

I looked in the direction of the sound, prepared now to take to my heels, which would have been more detrimental to me. Yet the miracle kept right on being that, i.e., a miracle, for the Lord in His mercies had caused the rain to change direction! The impending downpour, which would have made short work of my feeble umbrella, had been diverted! He had made the rain to pass over me! I walked home in sunshine, singing His praises.

My gratitude knew no bounds. I spoke of His goodness towards me in all my conversations for the remainder of the day. God had shown me compassion by protecting me from the elements.

Sister Barbara Hendrickson
Nevis

MONDAY 17th

Then Samuel took a stone, and set it between Mizpeh and Shen, and called the name of it Ebenezer, saying, Hitherto hath the LORD helped us
1 Samuel 7:12

MARK THEM – Reading: 1 Samuel 7:1-17

Jehovah had done it again! He had given an unfaithful and undeserving Israel a spectacular victory over their Philistine enemies.

Samuel understood the magnitude of this victory; it was only by the goodness, mercy and faithfulness of God. In response, Samuel raised an Ebenezer, a monument, a visual and perpetual reminder for Israel, that, *"Up until now hath the LORD helped us"*.

If it wasn't for the Lord who was on our side, where would we be? It is only through these victories, that we understand and experience the goodness of God in our lives: making us Victors instead of Victims; we are only kept by the power of God! Every triumph and every trial that you've overcome, deserves its own Ebenezer!

So Beloved, raise your stones of help! Raise them for yourself; raise them for your children; raise them for your children's children. Mark those victories! You can be strengthened by them. They must NEVER be forgotten; they not only tell your story but they give God His Glory!

Remember! God has never lost a battle. He's been your help until now and the next time that you need Him will be NO different.

Keisha Fearon

TUESDAY 18th

Ask, and it shall be given…
Matthew 7:7

MY PERFECT FATHER - Reading: Matthew 7:7-12

In the natural, there are good fathers, but there are no perfect earthly fathers. Most fathers have good intentions and want only the very best for their children but they will always have some limitations on what they can provide.

Not so with God, our Heavenly Father. Something unique about Him is that before we ask Him or even realise that we have a need, He already knows and has the means to deliver.

Romans 8:26 says, *"for we know not what we should pray for as we ought…"*. I don't always know the full extent of what it is I am praying about, and then sometimes when I do, I don't know how to pray about it. Thank God for divine translation. I'm always amazed how parents can understand what their baby is trying to say in baby-language, when it makes no sense to anybody else.

Our earthly father would not give us a stone instead of bread, nor a serpent if we asked for fish. How much more our perfect Father – will He not give more than we could think or ask? Has He not already given to us more than our mind could have ever conceived to ask?

"But my God shall supply all of your need according to His riches in glory by Christ Jesus" (Philippians 4:19).

JEJ

WEDNESDAY 19th

Get thee out of thy country…
Genesis 12:1

MY JOURNEY THAT LED TO JESUS - Reading: Genesis 12:1-20

A few years ago, I was given the opportunity to leave my country with my cousin/sister and her children; I had refused in the beginning. Why? Fear.

But the strangest thing happened. One day, I woke up with this urge or deep feeling in my heart that I should and needed to take the chance; I didn't know how it would work out. Now I know that it was divine intervention. Hallelujah! Before leaving there were a lot of setbacks, disappointments, discouragements, and moments of fear and doubt.

Finally arriving in this country, I thought, I can breathe now the worst is over. Little did I know! The string of challenges and disappointments I would face were yet to come. I would say, *"The Lord knows what He is doing"*, but not believing it. Shortly after, Covid started. Though isolated, everything seemed to be working out just fine, but after lockdown, that's when the bad news and challenges started and seemed to be arriving in waves, one after the other. I felt I could not breathe most of the time, I was stressed, anxious and weary beyond reason, all I could think was, *"What's next?"* and *"What if?"* Most nights when alone all I did was cry and ask God, *"Why?"*. I thought, well, maybe it's punishment for the life I've had up until that point, as I didn't see anything wrong with the way I was living my life. I thought, *"I am a good person, I help people when I can, and I am kind and compassionate, so there is nothing wrong with my life"*. How wrong was I!

Again, the Lord showed up in the most miraculous and amazing way. One day at a local supermarket, one of cousins/nieces, curious as she normally is, saw Bishop Lance Dinnall and for some reason, she felt the need to ask if he was a Pastor. Wow! God is truly amazing! After this is where our life, my life, started to change.

We were invited to church, and every time that I went to a service I would be convicted. I knew it was time to surrender. Hallelujah! I realised

November 2025
Theme: The Goodness of God

my life needed a change. I discovered the real reason that I was led to this country - it was not to escape the oppression and danger in my country, it wasn't even for better opportunities, at least not the materialistic opportunities I thought I wanted or needed. No, it was to find my way to Christ, Glory to God! My soul was seeking that which the flesh does not want or recognise.

Looking back to that day now, I believe without a doubt that I too was told by the Lord to, *"...Get thee out of thy country..."* (Genesis 12:1). I just did not recognise the voice of the Lord then like I do now. It was divine intervention, one I did not understand that I needed until it happened.

If I am honest, finding Jesus was the last thing on my mind. But I thank Him every day that He found me, *"Oh, how sweet to rest in the arms of Jesus"* (Unknown writer). I have now given my life to Christ (baptised in His name and filled with His spirit); it's the best choice I've ever made.

But I won't say I don't have really difficult days. The enemy tries to deceive and tempt me, and some days I feel like it's too much, too difficult and I feel like giving up. But then I remember the goodness of Jesus and all He has done for me; where I was, and where He has brought me from. I am reminded of all the times I felt my back against the wall, everything the enemy intended for evil but the Lord in all of His grace and mercy has turned it around for my good, time and time again.

I have seen miracles in my life that has proven His love, compassion, kindness, mercy, and grace. So, I have decided to follow Jesus, and come what may, I am living for Jesus, I know without a doubt that, *"All things work together for the good of those who love God..."* (Romans 8:28). I love Him because He first loved me (1 John 4:19) and while I was yet a sinner Christ died for me (Romans 5:8). I may not have all I want but praise God I have all I need.

I am learning daily to trust in Jesus and cast my burdens at His feet. Now I walk by faith and not by sight (2 Corinthians 5:7). As long as I'm breathing, I have a reason to praise the Lord.

Sis D. Tucker Cuthbert

THURSDAY 20th

Many are the afflictions of the righteous: but the LORD delivereth him out of them all
Psalm 34:19

GOD IS IN YOUR CORNER – Reading: Psalm 34:1-22

It is a fact of life in this world that circumstances, both bad and good, will happen upon us. The Lord will not save us *from* all untoward events, but He will certainly save us *in them*.

Consider the three Hebrew boys refusing to forsake the One True God; they were not prevented from the furnace, neither was the heat turned down for them, but Jesus meets them right in the middle of the raging fire delivering them from its ravages! Daniel was thrown into the Lion's Den, a genuine lion with very real teeth, but the Lord shut the Lion's mouth, thus preserving Daniel right in the midst of trouble!

Even more awesome is that no experience is a waste! God can, and does, turn around the most horrendous events to bring good in our lives, building our faith and perfecting us (Romans 8:28; James 1:2-4).

Years ago, an incident at work involving a theft occurred. It was the perpetrator's word against mine. Police were involved and the situation was extremely difficult. Because I was the far more junior member of staff, fingers were pointing firmly at me. All I could do was believe that if God's eye is on the sparrow, surely He has all things in His sight. The truth will always prevail. It certainly took time but at the end vindication came!

Reticence in grasping this scripture is that we feel unworthy, as indeed we are! The realisation that our righteousness is by virtue of our relationship with the Saviour, and not of our own making, sets us free to appropriate Psalm 34:19 wholeheartedly (2 Corinthians 5:21; Philippians 3:9). Truly God is in your corner!

Gudrun Witt
Zimbabwe

FRIDAY 21st

God will do this, for he is faithful to do what he says...
1 Corinthians 1:9a

TRUST GOD'S WORDS – Reading: Numbers 23:1-30

Have you been angry with God because He did not do something you expected Him to do after much prayer and extended faith? Well, it has happened to me. In one such encounter I bewailed how God was not good to me. God responded to my lament. He said, *"That thing you expected, I did not tell you that your expectations were based on what others said and thought should be the outcome. Did you ask me what my desires were in this situation?"*

I was jolted to another level of consciousness by this interaction. My faith was in something God did not say. Yes, I was extending faith and that's a good thing, but it was based on faulty assumptions. It was on the wrong object.

Have you ever, like me, become despondent because of bruised feelings or dashed hope based on the words of others, which were not God's words? I have come to recognise the importance of knowing what God has to say on a matter, and not what man thinks about the matter. Man's thoughts are not God's thoughts, and man's ways are not God's ways (Isaiah 55:8-9).

Lest we question God's goodness, we are reminded in today's scripture that God is faithful to do what He says. We have a responsibility, therefore, to find out what God has to say on a matter. Once **God** says it, it can be trusted. What God says will stand and be accomplished, no matter how long it takes, and no matter how challenging the process. We can be assured that it will come to pass because God is faithful and does not lie (Hebrew 6:18).

In your prayer today, ask God to open your ears and your heart to hear and understand what He is saying on a matter. Ask God to speak to you and help you to know His voice, and not settle for any other voice, not even your own. Trust only that Word from God.

May God's goodness be revealed in the fulfilment of His Word in your life.

Keshawna Salmon-Ferguson
Jamaica

SATURDAY 22nd

It is a good thing to give thanks unto the LORD, and to sing praises unto thy name, O most High
Psalm 92:1

LORD, I GIVE YOU THANKS – Reading: Psalm 92:1-15

Lord when I was weak,
Then you were strong.
When I had doubts,
You constantly told me
To hold on.

When situations
Wanted to overcome me,
Your Spirit
It did the work for me.

So Lord today
I give you thanks.
I am forever grateful to you.

For your words
They never fall to the ground.
It does not matter
What it looks like,
It is what you say.

So I give you thanks,
Not just for today.
But thank you
For having your way.

I am not waiting
I am thanking you now
For making the way
When I did not know how.

My Father
My Friend
My Redeemer
Who knows.

My beginning
Also my end.
Dear Lord
I give you thanks
For I love you my Lord.

Sister Jennifer Henry

SUNDAY 23rd

I know that your goodness and love will be with me all my life; and your house will be my home as long as I live
Psalm 23:6 (GNT)

ALWAYS WITH ME – Reading: Psalm 23:1-6

A well-known beloved psalm - a song of David.

Psalm 23 is an expression of David's assured confidence in the goodness of God towards him. Having experienced and being a recipient of God's provisions and sustenance, David had insight of God as a good shepherd at times when he'd been vulnerable, totally dependent and reliant on Him to lead, direct and guide him throughout all his endeavours.

God had protected David and fought for him in his many battles so that he had no need to fear, not even death. He was convinced that the Higher Power was with him, on his side. David was certainly familiar with God's generosity and affection for him such that he's overwhelmed and renewed, and his soul is satisfied. David had been a beneficiary of God's loving kindness as a friend in good relationship with the Almighty. David acknowledges that even his desires to do and live what's right was through God's motivation and inspiration compelling him.

And so, with all the benefits that he had come to know and had enjoyed, David concluded his song and testimony of the goodness of God. He re-emphasised his unwavering trust, believing that God's favours, loving kindness and blessings would pursue him the rest of his life. He therefore vowed to always abide in God's presence for it was David who also proclaimed that the goodness of God brings much joy and pleasures for evermore (Psalm 16:11).

Sis Jx

MONDAY 24th

For he gives his sunlight to both the evil and the good, and he sends rain on the just and the unjust alike
Matthew 5:45 (b) NLT

BECAUSE OF WHO HE IS, NOT WHO WE ARE – Reading: Matthew 5:37-45

'*They don't deserve it!'* is sometimes a phrase that comes from one's mouth.

You may use this phrase to justify metrics like giving someone a reward, praise or even when seeing what others have. It hints that for them to receive, then something must be done first to deem it logical and reasonable. According to today's focus verse, this isn't how God operates.

Typically, good parents wouldn't feed and clothe their children based on the chores they have done on that day, or what it is they'll be receiving from them in return. It's not something that needs to be earned or worked for. In the same way, God doesn't bless us, or the rest of the world (His children), based on our titles, accomplishments or our behaviour. Rather, He blesses us because of who He is - which is good, God and Father. He does not show favouritism (Romans 2:11), He blesses based on who He is, rather than who we are or what we've done.

One of the great ways that God showed His grace is when He gave His only begotten son, Jesus Christ, to die on the cross for our sins. He gave Himself without thinking about what He would receive back in return and knowing we 'didn't deserve it'.

Today, we too should strive to do something good for someone. Something that, even if they give nothing back in return, our heart stays the same. In this way we will truly be behaving like Jesus and imitating the 'Goodness of God'!

Elessamé

TUESDAY 25th

The LORD is good unto them that wait for him, to the soul that seeketh him
Lamentations 3:25

GOD'S ENDURING GOODNESS – Reading: Lamentations 3:24-40

Lamentations 3 is set in the context of an individual sufferer who starts off bemoaning his plight. The troubles left him in a dark and bitter place, almost hopeless. His soul was sinking.

Eventually however, light dawned, a spark was lit as the writer recalled some things. He realised that, amidst the circumstances, God remained faithful. Indeed, they were deserving of being cast aside completely, but God extended mercy. It was because of God's mercies why he and others were not consumed. Like a loving father, the God who chastised His children was also waiting to do them good if they would come to Him.

Often in life we are faced with situations that are daunting, which can leave us in a state of despair. It is however important to call to mind, yes, to remember other realities in such times. One such reality is that God remains good despite our experiences. God always desires to do us good and therefore acts to bring out good, in fact, the best in our lives. Because goodness is His nature, God responds to those who reach out to Him by extending His goodness in different ways.

Whatever your circumstance, seek after God. He is good and his mercies endureth forever. Resist the temptation to focus only on the negative aspects of life. As my partner in life and ministry advises, *"Count your blessings not your problems"!* Indeed, give space for the light of God's love to shine through the dark places in your life as His goodness is unfolded.

Rest in God's enduring goodness today despite the gloominess of any circumstance you might face.

Keshawna Salmon-Ferguson
Jamaica

WEDNESDAY 26th

Having therefore obtained help of God, I continue unto this day, witnessing both to small and great…
Acts 26:22

OUR HELP – Reading: Acts 26:1-32

Today's reading serves as a powerful declaration of the apostle Paul's faith in the goodness of God.

He is recounting his journey to King Agrippa while he is in chains. Note that Paul's focus is more about sharing the gospel of Jesus Christ than his own personal freedom. Despite numerous trials, imprisonments and persecutions (2 Corinthians 22:5), Paul recognises that it was God's intervention that sustained him. He testifies that it was the *"help obtained of God"* that gave him the opportunity and ability to stand and testify.

This underscores God's faithfulness and goodness throughout Paul's ministry. Paul was not selective with his audience either in sharing the gospel, *"witnessing both to small and great";* he shared the gospel with everyone, regardless of their social status or position.

We give God thanks for the inclusive nature of God's goodness and the widespread reach of this glorious gospel. Paul also asserts that his teachings are consistent with what the prophets and Moses said would happen. This highlights the continuity between the Old Testament prophecies and the New Testament fulfilment in Jesus Christ. Praise the Lord for the good news, the gospel is based upon the Word of God, not on the traditions or experiences of man.

Paul's statement in today's reading reflects Paul's unwavering commitment to his mission and his reliance on God's strength. It's an encouragement to me of the faithfulness and goodness of God as we, like Paul, rely on our "Help" that comes from the Lord alone.

CP

*THURSDAY 27th

If the Son therefore shall make you free, you shall be free indeed
John 8:36

FREEDOM – Reading: John 8:31-47

Two hundred and fifty thousand slaves (250,000) were FREED two years after President Abraham Lincoln had signed the Emancipation Proclamation. General Gordon Granger led troops in Galveston, Texas, to ensure informant of the proclamation. Prior to the Civil War, the thirteen original colonies fought Revolutionary War against England for Independence.

Freedom. Africans brought to the New World were enslaved, and wanted to be **free**.

"I see another law in my members warring against the law of my mind, and bringing me into captivity to the to the law of sin which is in my members" (Romans 7:23)

I'm free. *"For the Law of the Spirit in Christ Jesus has made me free from the law of sin and death" (Romans 8:2)*

We are **free**. Jesus paid it all by His blood.

THANK YOU, JESUS

"In everything give THANKS for this is the will of God in Christ Jesus concerning You" (1 Thessalonians 5:18).

There's A War Going On
Walter Hawkins, Love Alive 3

There's a war going on
And if you're gonna win
So you better make sure that you have Jesus deep down within
This battle cannot be won with bullets and guns
For the enemy you cannot see with human faculties.

For we wrestle (not against flesh and blood)
But against (principalities)
Against the rulers of darkness (against the rulers of darkness)
Against spiritual wickedness (against spiritual wickedness)
In high places
It's a fact (it's a fact)
That Satan's on your track (Satan's on your track)
And suddenly, without any warning, he'll launch his attack.

So you better make sure that you know
That wherever you may go
That you have the sword, which is the word of God
Deep down in your soul.

Oh, this is what you have to know
You can't fight this battle on your own
You need the power of God rooted and grounded in your life
This is what the Bible says...

We need the armour
We need the armour of the Lord

So we can walk right (walk right)
Talk right (talk right)
Live right (live right

First Lady Yolanda Edmund

*Thanksgiving Day (USA)

FRIDAY 28th

Do good, O LORD, unto those that be good, and to them that are upright in their heart
Psalm 125:4

WHAT CAN I SAY? – Reading: Psalm 125:1-5

What can I say?
My God is for me
Though my enemies
Are against me.

What can I say?
God's light
Is always stronger
Than the devil's darkness.

What can I say?
I will believe
In my God
He is my Lord.

What can I say?
In this world
That shuns him.

I will be a true soldier
For in His army
I am sure to win.

Praise God!

Sister Jennifer Henry

SATURDAY 29th

If thou, LORD, shouldest mark iniquities, O Lord, who shall stand?
Psalm 130:3

JUST AS I AM – Reading: Psalm 130:1-8

Sometimes we are wronged by others, and we hold it against them for a long time. But what an example we have in our Lord who showed us that no matter what we've done in the past and, in the current, if we are repentant, He will forgive and not hold us in judgment.

The song, *"Just As I Am"* comes to mind because it reminds me that the Lord called us just as we were with all our sins and unworthiness. If it wasn't for the goodness of God, none of us would be here!

Imagine if God were to deal with us like the natural judge, and give us what we deserve, not one of us would be able to stand before him, but God who is rich in mercy looks beyond our faults and sees our needs – that's the Goodness of God.

Oh, for the Goodness of God, when Jesus died on Calvary, all our sins were forgiven, and he does not hold our past against us. Thank God for the blood and thank God for salvation.

"Just as I am, thou wilt receive
Wilt welcome, pardon, cleanse, relieve;
Because thy promise I believe,
O Lamb of God, I come! I come!"
(Charlotte Elliott)

Lady Pam Lewin

SUNDAY 30ᵗʰ

...now for a season...ye are in heaviness through manifold temptations
1 Peter 1:6

BEING A WITNESS IN A WILDERNESS – Reading: 1 Peter 1:1-12

I spent seven-and-a-half weeks between two hospitals in London, roughly 100 miles away from my home.

Time became a blur as days slipped into nights without warning, and the boundaries between them dissolved. I found myself grasping for something - anything - a clock, a calendar, to constantly anchor me. But no matter how many times the sun rose and set; it was the chorus of anguished groaning on the ward that became my timepiece.

I witnessed things that will be etched in my memory forever: unsettled doctors breaking the news to a patient that she had only months left to live; the unrelenting cries for help from nurses at 3am when they found a patient unresponsive, and the sighs of relief when she awoke; the relentless clatter of medical aids, blood test trolleys, and IV drips echoing through the halls. Then there were my own terrifying moments, including hurried trips to emergency scans, being strapped to a bed, or transferred by stretcher. Those nights were among the loneliest and most terrifying of my life. Yet, it was in those moments of darkness that I found myself desperately searching for the light. And with each desperate attempt, God revealed Himself.

A burden to share the goodness of God began to surge forcefully. I found myself singing outside of my mental voice until heard by others, painfully shuffling over to the bedside of patients to tell them about Jesus, to tell them they are loved, that God cares about their suffering. I remember the morning when things became clear, dare I say, a spiritual revelation that my suffering was in part an opportunity to carry out a divine assignment. I no longer saw myself as a mere 28-year-old patient on a hospital bed - I was an evangelist on a life-saving mission.

I quickly evolved from a bedside number ("E3") to "Ren" among numerous patients, nurses, students, and health assistants, all of whom became family, while far away from my own. I noticed the clear signs of favour I was being blessed with. From extra food-and-drink treats to a particular nurse who would often come to my bedside, unashamedly binding the enemy, crying with me, and feeling indebted to me - something she said she had not experienced in her entire 20-year career.

I recall three patients in particular crying at their time of discharge. All three lamented at the possibility of never seeing me again - the feeling was mutual. One became a dear friend despite our observable age difference. For a few weeks, she was my 'bed-neighbour', growing more intrigued by the God I spoke about. She would ask questions, request that I, *"sing another song"*, and pray for her. This was the same woman who had been told, *"There's nothing more we can do"*, because *"you're beyond a cure"*. I bore witness as she transitioned from a state of crippling sorrow to incomprehensible peace. I wrote her a letter, and then we shared in our tears as she was being wheeled out to start her next journey at a hospice.

Suffering offered me an opportunity to make life-changing connections with people for just a short, fleeting time. But most importantly, it was an opportunity for me to invite people to encounter Jesus for an eternity.

Suffering is also an opportunity to prove God in your own life. Around week two of seven, my PhD graduation day arrived. The days leading up to the event were filled with tears and uncertainty, as it looked increasingly difficult for the doctors to release me to attend. *"We're so sorry, we just do not see how it will be possible!"* they said. Upon hearing that, I was devastated. Until... I wasn't.

Suddenly, I...

- Went online and bought a dress
- Got friends to help me get to a nearby hair salon
- Contacted my university to inform them of my disability requirements

Time passed and then just three days before the event: *"We've thought of a plan, you can go!"*, the doctors said, *"but you will have to return to the ward straight after"*. Faith is not just about believing in something you cannot yet see, but also acting on it. To others, that may sound risky and irrational, but to me, those 'faith actions' set in motion hearing that *"Yes"* to go.

Truly, I would have wasted an opportunity if I told you about the prognoses, diagnoses, doctor's reports, and findings - for I do not yet have the words to describe just what I have been through. But I can encourage you to see your suffering, not as a setback, but as an opportunity to both reveal God to others and to allow Him to reveal His power to you.

1 Peter 4:13: *"But rejoice, inasmuch as ye are partakers of Christ's sufferings; that, when his glory shall be revealed, ye may be glad also with exceeding joy"*.

Evangelist Renée Landell

December
Salt & Light

MONDAY 1st

You are the salt for everyone on earth. But if salt no longer tastes like salt, how can it make food salty? All it is good for is to be thrown out and walked on
Matthew 5:13 (CEV)

SHINE & PRESERVE – Reading: Matthew 5:13-16

When we walk into a room at night, our instinct is to switch the light on to see what is in the room.

Jesus said, *"As long as I am in the world, I am the light of the world"* (John 9:5). He also said, *"You are the light of the world"* (Matthew 5:14). Therefore, all believers in Christ have a dual purpose, receiving and shining our light.

The child of God is the light that illuminates and exposes, we are at our best when we focus our attention on the word of God. Believers in Christ are encouraged to live their inner qualities out as witnesses to others, to enable them to see our good works and glorify God. It is only by His spirit, that a child of God can do His work.

It is mandatory to share our light with someone we meet. We will be hiding our light if we never share the good news of salvation. If someone did not share this with you, how would you know of God's love and tender mercies?

Salt is a mineral known as sodium chloride in its granulated form, which is used in cooking - commonly known as Table Salt. It is in generous supply and essential for the body. Salt must keep its saltiness to be of value, once the taste of saltiness is lost, it is no good as salt.

In Jesus' day, this commodity was precious and was sometimes used as wages to pay Roman soldiers. Today, we who are the Ecclesia, must have the preserving influence of salt. This is why Jesus states in Matthew 5:14 that disciples are like salt. The lifestyle of a child of God must be a testimony to a dying world. We are commissioned to spread the good news of salvation. When we shine our light, it's not about showing how good we are, or allowing someone to focus on us, but about seeing God's grace and mercy in our life and crying out to know some more about our heavenly Father.

Salt is a preserver thus it is the opposite of corruption. When we have the Light/Word, it guides us through our Christian journey and also helps those who are lost to get back home (Psalm 119:105).

Missionary Audrey Simpson

TUESDAY 2nd

For unto us a child is born, unto us a son is given...
Isaiah 9:6

A MESSAGE OF HOPE – Reading: Isaiah 9:1-7

When there is a sudden power outage and we are plunged into deep, impenetrable darkness, it can be stifling. Once the light returns and pierces the darkness, there is an immediate sense of relief.

In the passage we focus on today, the people of Israel were in despair and darkness brought on by their disobedience and rejection of God. But since, *"The Lord will not cast off forever..."* (Lamentations 3:31), the prophet Isaiah begins this chapter with an immediate shift from what was, to what is coming. He writes, *"Nevertheless that time of darkness will not go on forever"* (NLT). He continues in verse 2a: *"The people who walk in darkness will see a great light"*.

How comforting to know that the tunnel experience will end, and the light will no longer be a faint and distant glimmer. The light would come in the form of a child, but this would be no ordinary child. This would be *"Emmanuel...God with us"* (Matthew 1:23). This is the light of hope that dispels the darkness of sin and despair.

The accolades given in verse 6 point to the special nature of this child, destined to rule before the foundation of the earth. It speaks to the ability to lead – the government will rest on His shoulders. It foretells that He will be full of knowledge and wisdom with the ability to make advocacy for His subjects/children. It indicates how powerful and awe-inspiring He will be, that He is immortal and that He, alone, can bring true peace. This was the prophecy to the children of Israel as to the kind of King their Messiah would be. This was the great light that would shine in the darkness and draw men to Himself, justifying and sanctifying them.

Thankfully, He is also our great light and we remain grateful that, in time, we, ourselves, became children of light. Moreover, we point others to this light so that they too can be saved.

Isaiah's message of hope has resounded through the ages - and remains relevant today - that is, the Messiah came as a child to be the Saviour of the world.

Sister Barbara Hendrickson
Nevis

WEDNESDAY 3rd

Be ye kind one to another, (compassionate), forgiving one another…
Ephesians 4:32

PRESERVATION & INFLUENCE – Reading: Ephesians 4:17-32

As children of Light we ought to live a higher standard. We are the called-out ones, the Ecclesia. Those who are set apart, elect and chosen of God, are partakers of His heavenly calling.

Jesus likens us to salt of the earth and light of the world. And as salt we have properties to preserve, to bring change, make distinction and be effective. Light on the other hand influences, leads, guides. Light also makes a difference by keeping back darkness, it gives clarity and reveals right perspective.

That's the purpose of children of God in the earth. As long as the church is in the world, there is light. To make impact where ever we go, causing darkness to flee as we influence righteousness and truths in the earth.

Our relationship with The Light influences our relationship with each other. One of the qualities of God's light is love. God's love compelled Him to manifest Himself in flesh to die for the whole world so that those who accept Him would be forgiven. Likewise, as Christ loves and forgives us, we must also live that lifestyle of love and forgiveness to each other, seeing that Christ declares, *"I am the light of the world"* (John 8:12) and then proclaims, *"Ye are the light of the world"* (Matthew 5:14).

He is the source of Light which generates rays that beam into our soul which empower us to live in love and togetherness in order to reflect that Light.

Sis Jx

THURSDAY 4th

Bear ye one another's burdens, and so fulfil the law of Christ.
Galatians 6:2

LOVE FULFILS THE LAW – Reading: Romans 13:8-10; Galatians 6:2

When I think of a burden, I think of a weight. For every one of us, there will come a time where we are overwhelmed by the weight of life.

I am so thankful for those who cared enough to help me carry a particular burden in my life. These individuals didn't just talk about faith and love but by demonstration, i.e., through prayer, listening, encouraging and support. I heard someone once say that to be a burden bearer, you first have to be a burden carer! In other words, see the weight and care enough to help to carry it. Even Jesus, after being whipped and beaten, had His cross carried by Simon of Cyrene. The bottom line is that we need each other.

As we bear one another's burdens, we are fulfilling the simple law of Christ: *"A new commandment I give to you, that you love one another; as I have loved you, that you also love one another. By this all will know that you are My disciples, if you have love for one another* (John 13:34-35).

In this letter to the Galatians, Paul is essentially saying, *"Do you want to fulfil the law? Here is your law to fulfil. Bear one another's burden and so fulfil the law of Christ. Love fulfils the law"* (Roman 13:8-10).

CP

FRIDAY 5th

If you love only someone who loves you, will God praise you for that? Even sinners love people who love them
Luke 6:32 (CEV)

SALTY FLAVOUR & SHINING LIGHT – Reading: Luke 6:27-36

As children of God, we are called, *"the salt of the earth and the light of the world"* (Matthew 5:13-16). We should maintain our saltiness and be Christlike in the way that we treat people, especially our enemies. We should practice forgiveness and pray for them, so that God will change them.

If we love only those who love us, we will not get credit for that, as even sinners love those who love them (Luke 6:32). Grant your enemies the same respect and rights as you desire for yourself, as tasteless salt and hidden light are good for nothing!

Jesus used the metaphor of salt and light so that His followers could relate to the properties and benefits of salt. Salt seasons and flavours food, just as Christians should enhance and favourably influence their society.

Salt is also a preservative. Therefore, Christians should resist corruption and preserve godly influence in the community. Salt has healing properties and is used medically when replacing loss of fluids. As Christians, we should help to bring healing to people who are hurting physically, mentally and spiritually.

Jesus is the supreme Light of the World, so His followers should not walk in darkness, but must show His light in their lifestyle and actions (Colossians 3:12-14).

We can serve people through simple acts of kindness and by meeting practical needs. Thereby we can open the door to share the good news of salvation and true message of Christ.

Evg. D.G.

SATURDAY 6th

In him was life; and the life was the light of men
John 1:4

FOOD FOR THOUGHT…SALTED BY FIRE – Reading: St John 1:1-5

I had the great honour and privilege the other day, of listening to one of our seasoned mothers' testimonies. Mother was passing through what one could only describe as a *"fiery trial"* (1 Peter 4:12).

What she said that evening, which for some was a lovely thought, instantaneously catapulted my spirit out of the prolonged spiritual siege, yes, the strategic onslaught of the enemy, right into the Throne Room of Grace. Worship flooded out of my soul!

During her testimony she barely mentioned the enemy, she gave him little airtime. Mother just kept on praising God and encouraging us, repeatedly.

I was struck by how her spirit and soul were so transformed by what she was going through. **Oh, her spirit was so pure, no bitterness at all and FULL of gratitude**.

I pondered within myself and marvelled at her. Then all of sudden (PAUSE - Are you ready for this?) she said: *"I have the RISEN SAVIOUR with ME"*.

Even now, as I reflect, the tears flow down my eyes. Here, right before me was a living example of someone who was salted by FIRE. What she had gone through immersed her into the experiential knowledge of Christ's resurrection power and its significance. As an adopted son, she was conforming to His image.

THE SALT was evident, as it wrought in her such beauty and grace. Even her *very speech was seasoned with SALT!*

"For everyone shall be salted with fire…" (Mark 9:49).

Name withheld

SUNDAY 7th

Now when they saw the boldness of Peter and John, and perceived that they were unlearned and ignorant men, they marvelled; and they took knowledge of them, that they had been with Jesus
Acts 4:13

VALUE, SUBSTANCE & TASTE – Reading: Psalm 34:5-10; Acts 4:8-14

It is said that if there is a counterfeit, then there must be a true article.

Counterfeits by nature try to blend in and not bring attention to themselves, hoping that no one will notice! This is the case, until you have experienced the detail...then it is clear there is no substance, no value and sometimes no taste.

Imagine going to buy something of value (with cash) and you discover your money is fake, or you thought your gold ring was real until you needed to pawn it to get funds to survive!

Can those around us be confident that the label, 'Christlike' written on 'the tin' is what's inside when life brings challenges?

Our Heavenly Father holds the world in His hand yet knows the number of hairs on my head. Yes, He cares about every detail. I marvel, that although insignificant to some, I know I have a life of real value, substance and taste, empowered by the Holy Spirit.

Healed of a stroke eight years ago, and all faculties in working order; there is no doubt that Jesus continues to use me to be His salt and light!

"Oh, taste and see today that the LORD is good"; He is the genuine article!

Sis Dorcas (nee Simmonds)

MONDAY 8th

Blessed are the peacemakers: for they shall be called the children of God
Matthew 5:9

PEACE – Reading: Matthew 5:1-12

Today as I write, there is a great need for peace - there are so many difficult situations locally, nationally, and internationally.

We need peace, not merely the absence of war, but the deep settled peace to rule our hearts.

Galatians 5:22 teaches us that peace is part of the fruit of the Spirit. The Spirit is given to us to empower us to witness Acts 1:8. Peace is not about ignoring whatever is happening around us, but it enables us to continue to cast our cares upon the Lord and have Him sustain us (1 Peter 5:7). We can also comfort others and assure them that God is in control.

Our focus scripture verse says, *"Blessed are the peacemakers; for they shall be called the children of God"* Matthew 5:9. Two other Bible verses say, *"Great peace have they which love thy law; and nothing shall offend them"* Psalm 119:165; *"Follow peace with all men and holiness without which no man shall see the Lord"* (Hebrews 12:14).

The scriptures above show us the importance of relationships - you can't have peace and keep it to yourself. Peace needs to be shared with others, just like you would not keep anything good in your cupboard and not share it with those in need. Likewise, we have the light of the world within us, we just can't help but shine!

Let us continue to allow the Lord to use us! We are the children of God.

BVG

TUESDAY 9th

Let the words of my mouth and the meditation of my heart be acceptable in Your sight, O Lord, my strength and my redeemer
Psalm 19:14

THE POWER OF WORDS – Reading: Psalm 19:1-14

When I read Psalm 19:14, Luke 6:45 came to mind, *"Good people do good things because of the good in their hearts, but bad people do bad things because of the evil in their hearts. Your words show what is in your heart"* (CEV).

Psalm 19:14 closes in a prayer desiring that the words, thought and spoken by the psalmist, are pleasing to the Lord. When we as women share positive, encouraging and pleasing words from our heart, within our sphere of influence, the impact can be life changing!

The mother of Thomas Edison, inventor and businessman, changed his destiny by her words. This story circulating around is somewhat sensationalised, but mostly true. It began with the 'teacher's note', and serves as a valuable lesson.

Edison came home from school and gave a paper to his mother. He said, *"My teacher gave me this paper. What does it say?"*. Her eyes welling with tears, she read out loud, *"Your son is a genius. This school is too small for him and doesn't have good enough teachers to train him. Please teach him yourself"*.

After his mother died, Edison became one of the greatest inventors of the century. He found the letter that his teacher wrote. It said, *"Your son is mentally deficient. We cannot let him attend our school any more. He is expelled"*.

Edison, becoming emotional, wrote in his diary, *"Thomas A. Edison was a mentally deficient child whose mother turned him into the genius of the century"*. Such is the power of words! So, ladies, make the Lord your *"Rock"* your *"Strong Redeemer"*, and your meditative words will become life changing. This is our acceptable service.

Annette Johnson

WEDNESDAY 10th

Therefore if any man be in Christ, he is a new creature: old things are passed away; behold, all things are become new
2 Corinthians 5:17

A NEW CREATURE IN CHRIST – Reading: 2 Cor 5: 15-18

I was preparing to teach a lesson based on 1 Corinthians 1:18-31, when I heard the song, printed below, on the radio. As I pondered the question in line 4 of the first verse, *"What is that to me?"*, I understood better why 1 Cor.1:18 states, *"For the message of the cross is foolishness to those who are perishing but to us who are being saved it is the power of God"*:

In the stars His handiwork I see,
On the wind He speaks with majesty,
'Though He ruleth over land and sea,
What is that to me?

I will celebrate nativity,
For it has a place in history,
Sure, He came to set His people free,
What is that to me?

'Til by faith I met Him face to face,
And I felt the wonder of His grace,
Then I knew that He was (not)
A God who didn't care, that lived a way out there

And now He walks beside me day by day,
Ever watching o'er me lest I stray,
Helping me to find that narrow way,
He's everything to me
(Author unknown but sung by various artists)

When we were in ignorance and walking after our own ways, fulfilling every evil desire of our hearts, Christ meant nothing to us. What was that to us indeed? But, things changed. As the song says, *"until by faith I met him face to face..."*. Now it is not the old man who lives but according to 2 Corinthians 5:17, *"...he is a new creature, the old things are passed away; behold all things are become new"*.

The lifestyle, the mindset, the attitude, have all been changed. In their place is a new beginning, with new possibilities and new opportunities in Christ. There is now a chance to live a life that pleases God, and ensure that the eternal inheritance can be claimed.

As believers, and the salt of the earth, let us continue to flavour our world with the love of God. As lights in this corrupt world, let us continue to point souls to the greater light so that lives can be changed and souls saved to become new creatures in Christ.

**Sister Barbara Hendrickson,
Nevis**

THURSDAY 11th

...Abraham believed God, and it was imputed unto him for righteousness: and he was called the Friend of God
James 2:23

A FAITHFUL FRIEND OF GOD – Reading: James 2:14-26

Obedience is better than sacrifice
Submission a precious thing
A loving heart offered up in thanks
To Jesus our King.
A life of sweet devotion
Determined to succeed
To do the very best for all
And win the lost indeed.

Who will stand in the gap?' says God
'Who will work for me?
There are but few that I can trust
To do this work for me'.

Who are they? What are their names?
'The Faithful Ones', says He
'Those who do not wander
Whose lives are rooted and grounded in me.

These are my precious friends
For even in times of trouble
When they feel like they can't go on
They labour while it is still day
For soon the night comes
And then it will be too late.

So, keep on working, do not faint
You are so very dear to me
And your labour is not in vain
For great is your reward
You are my son, dear faithful Friend of God'!

Rena P. Grzeszczyk

FRIDAY 12th

So (David) changed his behaviour before them and pretended to be insane in their hands...
1 Samuel 21:13 (ESV)

TOO PREDICTABLE – Reading: 1 Samuel 21:1-15

There's a saying, *"I can read you like a book!"*. Meaning, nothing that that individual does takes the person who knows them intimately by surprise.

As we close-off this year, I'm wondering whether Satan has learnt us too well because of our predictable responses to the same traps that he's been setting for us for years!

Over the past few weeks, I've become very sensitive to this thought and have deliberately done the opposite of what I'd usually do (well, most of the time!).

When it's time to pray and Satan says, leave it for a minute and just do 'this' first, I stop what I'm doing and pray.

When he says, you're too tired now to read your Bible, I sit up straight and find a Scripture.

When someone sends me a message with an 'off' tone or a disappointing reply, I give a cheerful response.

When he tells me to ignore somebody, I talk to them.

When I'm feeling low and like I just can't go on, I find a song to lift my spirit.

When he tells me that I can't, I prove to him that I can.

Throughout our Christian Walk, the devil has been pressing the same buttons and getting the same reactions from some of us – can't you see? He knows who to send to wind us up, what to let somebody do to distract us, how to make sure we hear the negative things that people are saying about us.

He's reading us like a book!

Dear Woman of God, it's time to change your book's cover and the pages. Confuse the devil with 'a new you', and shake him off!

JEJ

SATURDAY 13th

...he hath chosen us in him before the foundation of the world...
Ephesians 1:4

THE GIFT OF SALVATION – Reading: Ephesians 1:3-14

Since the fall of Adam, we were born and shapen in iniquity,
Yet God loved us in a way that no other could.
He is so good, for He left His heavenly abode, clothed Himself in flesh,
And upon the earthly realm for the sinner He stood.

He deserves the glory, adulation, and utmost respect,
The heart of man, only He can detect.
Through the slaying of Him, that is Jesus Christ, the only begotten,
With God we can now connect.

Coming boldly before the throne of grace, where we obtain mercy,
For we are called and chosen, we are God's Elect.
Whom He doth sustain and keep, whom He doth protect.
For we are those He did select.

We are Born Again believers,
Held in the palm of God's hand,
That united we may stand.

God hath paved the way,
For He swooped in and saved the day,
When He rescued us
From the jaws of the enemy.

No longer are we bound by sin,
Because we walk in complete freedom,
With the mindset and ability to win.

When we are free,
We are truly free indeed.
As we are born of God's heavenly seed,
And it is on the Divine Word that we now feed.

The Gift of Salvation is free to one and all
I pray that the masses will heed to the call.
There is no better gift than the Gift of Salvation,
So let us sing and shout, and show our appreciation.

Our Lord and Saviour, and soon coming King,
We give thanks unto thee,
For you opened our blinded eyes that now we may see.
By grace we are saved, for by thy shed blood on Calvary,
The way to Eternal life has been paved.

Sis Prudence Mcewan

SUNDAY 14th

And when (Manasseh) was in affliction, he besought the LORD his God...
2 Chronicles 33:12

THE POWER OF REDEMPTION – Reading: 2 Chronicles 33:1-20

In speaking of repentance and forgiveness, we often speak of Paul who persecuted the church.

However, I think of King Manasseh in the Bible whose deeds were so wicked that the Bible references his evil works as being the reason for Judah being taken into captivity by Babylon. If this were a movie script, Manasseh would undoubtedly be the token villain. He established altars for Baal, practiced witchcraft and soothsaying, worshipped idols and committed the most abominable deed – child sacrifice! We can sum up Manasseh as 'evil personified'.

It is therefore remarkable that we find one of the greatest stories of repentance and forgiveness in 2 Chronicles 33:11-13. After being taken captive, Manasseh sought the Lord through prayer and humbled himself. Condemnation would be clear to us as humans, but the Lord heard the prayer of Manasseh, forgave him and restored him to Jerusalem. Manasseh thereafter sought to undo all the evil that he had done from a heart that had truly repented of his sins.

From King Manasseh's story, we learn that there is no place too dark, dirty or evil that the Lord cannot pull us out of. The same grace and mercy that was extended to an evil king, is available to all of us today in this Dispensation of Grace. All we need to do is seek the Lord, humble ourselves and pray, and like King Manasseh, truly repent and turn away from sin. His redemptive power is able to save.

Zahra H. Oliphant
Jamaica

MONDAY 15th

By this shall all men know that ye are my disciples, if ye have love one to another
John 13:35

LOVE IS THE SIGN – Reading: John 13:31-38; Romans 5:5

How do you know if someone is following Jesus, is like saying how do you know a bus is a bus! There are certain characteristics that make a bus different from a car. A bus carries significantly more passengers than the average car, for example. Similarly in today's scripture reading there are certain characteristics that every follower of Jesus Christ should have and as a result these set us apart.

Jesus has set the standard that the way we love and treat each other should reflect His love and serve as a testimony to our faith. In other words, when we show genuine love, selfless and unconditional love, it makes it evident that we are followers of Jesus.

It wasn't that love for the outside world was not important or relevant, but it wasn't first. There are other measures of discipleship, but they come after this commandment.

Jesus judges us by our love for one another. We can judge ourselves as His disciples by our love for one another. The world can judge us as His disciples by our love for one another. Jesus is emphasising that there should be a special presence of love among those who follow Him.

Charles Spurgeon, a 19th century preacher said, *"We are to love our neighbour as ourselves, but we are to love our fellow-Christians as Christ loved us, and that is far more than we love ourselves".*

Examine your love tank today, sisters. Are you allowing God's love to shine through you? Are you open and ready for opportunities to love one another? *"The love of God has been poured out in our hearts by the Holy Ghost who was given to us"* (Roman 5:5). This is how God's love is communicated…through His Spirit!

CP

TUESDAY 16th

The unfolding of your words gives light; it imparts understanding to the simple
Psalm 119:130 (ESV)

HE IS THE LIGHT – Reading: Psalm 119:129-136

Jesus said I am the light of the world; he that followeth me shall not walk in darkness, but shall have the light of life (John 8:12).

This is not just any light, this is spiritual light. We all need it so let's keep in His Word as we see the day approaching, *"The entrance of thy words giveth light; it giveth understanding unto the simple"* (Psalm 119:130).

He is the living Word. God's Word has not changed, because He has not changed, *"For I am the LORD, I change not"* (Malachi 3:6). The Word is versatile; what I mean is that we can read it, listen to it, have it preached or taught. However, we must let the Word in - there has to be entrance.

How then shall they call on Him in whom they have not believed? And how shall they believe in Him of whom they have not heard? And how shall they hear without a preacher? (Romans 10:14) Once we hear the Word, there is the potential for us to change and, having changed, to witness to others and so the Word is spread. So then faith cometh by hearing, and hearing by the word of God (Romans 10:17).

Let's continue lighting up this world, one soul at a time, with God's Word.

BVG

WEDNESDAY 17th

...when Jesus was born...there came wise men from the east to Jerusalem
Matthew 2:1

FOLLOW THE LIGHT – Reading: Matthew 2:1-12

Matthew 2:1-2 tells of the wise men who, upon seeing the star, set out on a journey to find the newborn King: *"Where is the one who has been born king of the Jews? We saw his star when it rose and have come to worship him"*. Their journey was guided by a divine light, leading them to the Savior.

In our own spiritual journey, we are often called to step out in faith, following the Light of God's guidance. The wise men serve as an example of diligence and devotion, seeking the presence of Jesus above all else. They recognised the significance of the star; a symbol of divine revelation, and responded with worship.

As women of faith, we are encouraged to seek God's Light in our daily lives. This Light is the Holy Spirit! Whether through prayer, the Holy Scriptures, or the encouragement of fellow believers, His Light is always available to guide us. Like the wise men, we have to be intentional in our pursuit of Jesus, allowing His Light to lead us in every aspect of our lives. In doing so, we not only find direction for ourselves, but also become a reflection of His Light to others.

Ask yourself the question, what/who am I a reflection of? The answer should indicate any changes needed. Don't forget, it's a daily pursuit. Let the Holy Spirit lead you!

Latoya J. Foster

THURSDAY 18th

Now then we are ambassadors for Christ…
2 Corinthians 5:20

SHINE YOUR LIGHT – Reading: 2 Corinthians 5:16-21

Recently, I came across a poem by Jacqueline Schiff and have extracted a section that I feel is in line with our theme 'Salt & Light':

"You are an Authentic Woman

…Be true to the light that is deep within you. Hold on to your joy for life. Keep good thoughts in your mind and good feelings in your heart. Keep love in your life, and you will find the love and light in everyone … Most of all, never forget that there is no brighter light than the one with you. Keep on being true to yourself. Keep shining your light on others so they will have a reason to smile. Follow your inner light to your own personal greatness and remember that you are admired and loved just as you are".

The scripture says we are ambassadors for Christ. So, if we are ambassadors, we must represent Him by making our light shine from our inner self to our outer self. When light shines, it lights up the room; we should light up every room we enter, every place we go, and every road we walk.

Be confident in who you are and walk tall because we are His ambassadors.

Lady Pam Lewin

FRIDAY 19th

The entrance of thy words giveth light; it giveth understanding to the simple
Psalm 119:130

BEAUTIFUL LIGHT – Reading: Psalm 119:129-136

A songwriter penned:

Walk in the light
Beautiful light
Come where the dewdrops of mercy shine bright
Shine all around us by day and by night
Jesus, the Light of the world.
(Unknown)

Light gives us a sense of safety and security. Walking up a road during the day has a completely different feeling to when you walk along the same place in the night.

As we interact with people who do not yet know Christ, may they be drawn to the light in us. May we be outstanding and change the atmosphere in our places of work, at our places of education, the streets on which we live.

Pledge to be a lighthouse, do not blend in with your dark surroundings so that you are not seen. Jesus said, *"…a city set on a hill cannot be hid"* (Matthew 5:14).

It's not only Jesus who is a 'beautiful light' as the song above says. If Christ is living in us, we will be a 'beautiful light' too.

JEJ

SATURDAY 20th

The thief cometh not but for to steal and to kill and to destroy: I am come that they might have life, and that they might have it more abundantly
John 10:10

---◆●◆---

HOPE OF EARTH – Reading: John 10:1-15

I don't think that I'm the only one who has a feeling of dismay when I watch or listen to the news. Our world is in a terrible state!

Sin has reached its peak just as it had in Noah's day and in the time of the destruction of Sodom and Gomorrah. Unfortunately, we have almost become hardened to the climate – what I mean is that shocking news does not shock us in the same way it would have done 20 years ago. Criminals have become innovatively wicked in their thinking – every imagination of the thoughts of their heart is only to do evil continually (Genesis 6:5).

A songwriter asked, *"Is there any hope for tomorrow? Is there any hope for love, hope for peace? What's the world going to be like, tomorrow?".*

Yes, there is hope. And hope is never more important than in times of despair. Likewise, light is most welcome when in pitch darkness. Light is so powerful that, in a large dark room if there is just one lit candle, the flicker of that flame will stand out.

Be aware that you are someone's conduit of light and hope today:

Frustrated brother
See how he's tried to
Light his own candle
Some other way
See now your sister
She's been robbed and lied to
Still holds a candle without a flame!

So carry your candle
Run to the shadows
Seek out the lonely
The tired and worn
Hold out your candle
For all to see it
Take your candle and go light your world!

We are a family
Whose hearts are blazing
So let's raise our candles
And light up the sky
Praying to our Father
In the name of Jesus
Make us a beacon in darkest times!

So carry your candle
Run to the darkness
Seek out the helpless
Deceived and poor
Hold out your candle
For all to see it
Take your candle and go light your world!

So carry your candle
Run to the darkness
Seek out the hopeless
Confused and torn
Hold out your candle
For all to see it
Take your candle
And go light your world!
(Go Light Your World - Unknown)

JEJ

SUNDAY 21st

...and thou shalt call his name JESUS: for he shall save his people from their sins
Matthew 1:21

THE LIGHT OF REDEMPTION – Reading: Matthew 1:18-25

In Matthew 1:20-21, the angel's words to Joseph are a beacon of hope: *"Do not be afraid... for what is conceived in her is from the Holy Spirit. She will give birth to a son, and you are to give him the name Jesus, because he will save his people from their sins".* In a moment of uncertainty and fear, Joseph received the assurance that God's plan was in motion: - a plan to bring the light of redemption to the world through Jesus Christ.

As women of faith, we are called to reflect this light in our lives. Just as Joseph's obedience paved the way for God's redemptive work, our actions and words can make a huge positive difference to the path of others. We are the salt that preserves and the light that guides, called to live in a way that reflects the love and grace of Jesus.

In a world often overshadowed by darkness, our role is to be beacons of hope, just as Christ is our source of light. Never dim your light. Shine brightly, sharing the message of salvation with those around you, so that they too may experience the never-ending joy and peace that come from knowing Jesus.

Latoya J. Foster

MONDAY 22nd

...Go quickly, and tell...
Matthew 28:7

TELL THE STORY – Reading: Matthew 28:5-20

Tell the story of how He was born in a manger
Tell the story of how He was nailed to the cross
Tell the story of His pain and suffering for you and me
Tell the story of how He died and rose again.

Tell the story of how He died that we might live
Tell the story of His love for you and me
Tell the story of His grace and mercy toward us
Tell the story of how He forgives our sins.

Tell the story of His mighty power
Tell the story of our Saviour, Jesus Christ our Lord!

Audrey Carletha Davis
USA

TUESDAY 23rd

...there went out a decree from Caesar Augustus, that all the world should be taxed
Luke 2:1

INSIDE THE WILL OF GOD – Reading: Luke 2:1-6

We are in the midst of the Christmas season, a time in which many people think more than usual about the nativity of Jesus Christ.

The Roman emperor of that time, Caesar Augustus, had introduced a worldwide census. This meant that all males had to return to their place of birth to be taxed (Luke 2:1-3). Since Joseph was from the lineage of King David (Matthew 1:1; Luke 2:4), his place of registration was Bethlehem.

God can do a parliamentary cabinet reshuffle, He can allow new legislation to be passed, just to get you where He needs you to be at a particular time. His Word cannot return to Him void; it had already been prophesied that Jesus would be born in Bethlehem Ephratah (Micah 5:2), and a divine plan was therefore in place to ensure that it came to pass.

I can only imagine the backache that Mary must have experienced as she journeyed with Joseph from Nazareth to Bethlehem to obey the law. She must have been in a lot of physical pain. Have you ever been pregnant? How do you think you would have managed riding on a donkey for such a long distance?

Often, the journey into the will of God is painful and long. You wonder, as I'm sure that Mary did, how much longer until I get there? Then labour pains, and nowhere comfortable to give birth – only a stable. Mary must have had to remind herself of the visitation from the angel Gabriel, and that with favour can also come pain. She gave birth far away from home, separated from family and friends, and any kind of comfort or things familiar, because the fulness of the time had come (Galatians 4:4-5). That was the will of God.

At times we may wonder whether we are truly in the will of God and, if we are in His will, how comes there are so many bumps in the road! In those moments, we have to hold on to His promise. Remember that being in the will of God does not always mean plain sailing. My mom told me of a preacher who once said, *"It's better to be in the will of God in a wilderness, than out of His will in a city"*.

Sometimes the choice is: "Comfort or The Will of God". Which one is best?

JEJ

*WEDNESDAY 24th

This shall be a sign…you shall find the babe…lying in a manger
Luke 2:12

THE KING IN A MANGER – Reading: Luke 2:8-20

There are many rich people who live in ordinary houses in non-exclusive areas. They don't all drive the most expensive of cars, neither do they always wear exclusive clothes. They are rich and recognise that their affluence is not based on their location or having costly possessions. They are confident and secure to live way below their means because they know who they are.

The birth of Jesus was like that. The maternity ward for Mary was a stable, and Jesus' Moses basket was a manger. A manger is a trough or box from which horses or cattle feed. We can understand why the angel of the Lord would explain to the shepherds that, despite the place and surroundings, when you see a baby lying in a manger (Luke 2:10-12), that's Him!

What do I mean by, *"Him"*? Well, this is Him of whom Isaiah spoke in 7:14 and 9:6-7. This is *"A light to lighten the Gentiles, and the glory of His people Israel"* (Luke 2:32). In the trough is *"God clothed in flesh"* (St John 1:14) dressed in His working clothes/overalls, come to minister and die to save humankind from our sins.

You've heard of Daniel's prophecy concerning, *"The Ancient of days whose hair was white as snow, with a throne like the fiery flame"* (Daniel 7:9-10)? Well, although He's just been born, this is Him. In that feeding box, *"He made himself of no reputation"* yet, one day, *"Every knee shall bow and every tongue confess that He is Lord"* (Philippians 2:6-11). The baby in the smelly stable is Jesus Christ who, *"Although he was rich, for our sake became poor"* (2 Corinthians 8:9).

Shepherds, don't be confused by the stable, the manger, or that the baby is wrapped in strips of cloth. It's definitely Him!

JEJ
(Adapted from "I Arise!" 2023)
*Christmas Eve

*THURSDAY 25th

For the Lord himself shall descend from heaven with a shout, with the voice of the archangel, and with the trump of God...Wherefore comfort one another with these words
1 Thessalonians 4:16, 18

JESUS' SECOND COMING – Reading: John 14:1-3; 1 Thessalonians 4:13-18

"Soon", was the response that my son texted me when asked, *"When will I see You, again?"* Okay, we do not live in the same city, but we live 90 minutes' drive from each other. My expectations under these conditions are high. We were 3,000-plus miles before I moved from 'Across cross The Pond' to England from Maryland, USA.

The other son is currently residing on another continent. The expectations to see him *"soon"* are not as high! Disappointment occurs when expectations are not met. The son within driving distance is held more liable to visitation, and to honour his word, so says his Mother (smile).

Yes, *"soon"* is relative. Jesus said, *"He has gone to prepare a place for (us)*, John 14:3-4, *"I will come again and receive you unto myself"*. You may ask, *"When?"*! **Soon and very soon**, as Andre Crouch recorded in 1976, *"It Won't Be Long"*.

Paul Revere gave the midnight call, *"The British are Coming, The British are Coming"* to the residents in Boston, Massachusetts. And later to other places in the 'new world'. The word spread. Paul was employed as express rider to carry news, messages and copies of important documents, by horseback. He was later 'horse jacked' and had to walk back home. However, he arrived early enough to witness the battle.

JESUS IS Coming!!

He's arriving on a cloud, not a horse like Paul Revere. And the message has been sounding for days. Any day now, we'll be going home; *"...beloved, be not ignorant of this one thing, that one day is with the*

Lord as thousand years, and a thousand years as one day" (2 Peter 3:8).

Any day now, JESUS is COMING!

The Question Is
(Song by The Winans)

The question is will I ever leave you?
The answer is no, no, no, no, no, no

The question is will I ever leave you?
The answer is no, no, no, no, no, no

Oh, I love the Lord for He's so dear to me
Oh, He died that I might be free
I was asked, this question is and the answer is still no

Now the question is, will I do His will?
And the answer is yes, yes, yes, yes, yes, yes
I was at home late one night
The Lord asked me would I do His will
I told Him yes, yes, yes, yes, yes, yes

I'm presenting my body, a living sacrifice
All I'm gonna do is the will of Christ
I was asked this question and the answer is yes
Now the question is when will Jesus return?

I want you to know soon, soon
Look at the trouble all over the world
I'm telling every man, woman, boy and girl He's coming soon
Soon, soon, soon, soon, soon, soon

Oh, but I can hardly wait for Jesus to return
For His returning my heart does yearn

I was asked this question and the answer is real soon

Now the questions are, will I ever leave you?
Will I do Your will and when will Jesus return?

No and yes and soon, soon, soon, soon
Will I ever leave you, will I do Your will
When will Jesus return
And the answer is no and yes and soon, soon, soon, soon

Oh, if you've questioned when Christ is coming
The answer is SOON.

First Lady Yolanda Edmund

*Christmas Day

FRIDAY 26th

A light to lighten the Gentiles, and the glory of thy people Israel
Luke 2:32

LET JESUS LIGHT THE WAY – Reading: Luke 2:21-33

A minister advised my high school mates and I to be conscious about looking always to Jesus Christ in conducting our lives, as the world is in confusion. Decades later, the situation is even more dismal. A person convicted of crimes being considered for leadership of a country, fluidity in sexuality, the commonality of divorce and many other happenings in our world and communities speak to the muddle we are in.

It is however encouraging to know that, as was true decades ago, it remains true today that Jesus Christ is the answer. He is the way, the truth, the life (John 14:6) and is also the light of the world (John 8:12). The darkness that has led to the confusion can be dispelled when the light shines in, and people will stop stumbling when the way illuminated by that light is found.

Unfortunately, too many for one reason or another are not being guided by the light and not walking in the life-giving way. Don't be among those who are stumbling along a dark path that is leading to destruction of one sort or another. Don't be among those who are leaning unto their own limited understanding. Seek after the way, the truth, the life, and the light in all aspects of your life. Whatever dark situation you may face, reach out to Jesus Christ, the light of the world. He will show you the way.

Whatever you need to deal with, whatever you have to do, pray today that Jesus Christ will light your way.

Excerpt from a song by Hezekiah Walker
Jesus is the light, light of the world
Light of the world, light of the world
He's the road out of darkness - the brightest way out
Jesus is the light of the world!

Keshawna Salmon-Ferguson
Jamaica

SATURDAY 27th

...restore such a one in the spirit of meekness...
Galatians 6:1

THE LIGHT WITHIN – Reading: Galatians 6:1-18

Another year is drawing to a close already. Is your light still shining as brightly, or even brighter, than when the year began, or is it waning dim?

We sometimes observe circumstances which befall others and think that such a thing could never or would never happen to us! Just thinking that way can make us vulnerable and a prime target for Satan at a later date. I've learned that, anything that can happen, could in the right/wrong environment, happen to me. It only takes a momentary lapse of focus to fall.

Let's reflect on Noah for a little bit, he found grace in the eyes of God (Genesis 6:8). A builder and faithful preacher, Noah did not deviate from his God-given assignment to build an ark, as specified in God's pattern. We've learned through studies that Noah built and warned of rain for 120 years, all by faith. Before the flood (the antediluvian world), there had never been rain, only a mist watered the ground, but Noah carried on building nonetheless.

Noah completed this mammoth task, then having survived the flood and challenges of living in the ark, he built an altar and offered sacrifices to God as soon as he came out (Genesis 8:20-21). Noah dotted every "I" and crossed every "T". How then do we later read of this exemplary figure in a drunken stupor, naked, and needing to be covered by his sons (Genesis 9:19-29)?

Paul writes to the Christians in Galatia to advise, *"...you who are spiritual restore such a one (who has fallen) in the spirit of meekness; considering thyself, lest thou also be tempted"* (Galatians 6:1). O, it's true! The man chosen by God to build himself an ark so that life could continue after the flood, was now a laughingstock to his son, Canaan. Thankfully Shem and Japheth protected themselves and their father's name, and instead of leaving him exposed, they covered his nakedness.

There is often only a thin line to cross to leave light and enter into darkness. But thanks be to God that His light, when we allow it, eliminates darkness such that John, the apostle, said, *"the Light shines in the darkness, and the darkness has not overcome it (comprehended it not)"* (John 1:5). So Noah's mistake, which landed him into a dark place temporarily, is not how his story ends. His name is included in the Gallery of Faith in Hebrews 11. He's not referred to as an alcoholic, or as the man who embarrassed himself, but is commended as a man of great faith:

"By faith Noah, being warned of God of things not seen as yet, moved with fear, prepared an ark to the saving of his house; by the which he condemned the world, and became an heir of the righteousness which is by faith" (Hebrews 11:7).

Right now, let's glorify God that even when our lights have at times become dim, they have not completely gone out. God granted a little mercy to bring us back to consciousness and shine again as we ought. His light within us ousted the darkness of each temptation and every bleak situation that we faced during this year.

Yes! We have the victory through our Lord Jesus Christ.

JEJ

SUNDAY 28th

...no matter what I do, I'm bankrupt without love
1 Corinthians 13:3 (MSG)

GENUINE LOVE – Reading: 1 Corinthians 13:1-13

*T*hough I speak with the tongues of men and of angels, but have not love, I have become sounding brass or a clanging cymbal. And though I have the gift of prophecy, and understand mysteries and all knowledge, and though I have all faith, so that I could remove mountains, but have not love, I am nothing. And though I bestow all my goods to feed the poor, and though I give my body to be burned but have not love, it profits me nothing. Love suffers long and is kind; love does not envy; love does not parade itself, is not puffed up; does not behave rudely, does not seek its own, is not provoked, thinks no evil; does not rejoice in iniquity, but rejoices in the truth; bears all things, believes all things, hopes all things, endures all things (1 Corinthians 13:1-7 NKJV)

Ladies, may our words and actions be seasoned with salt and full of light; not boastful, arrogant nor keeping account of evil.

Whatever our services for Christ, whatever gift we have been endowed with, it should be motivated and manifested with the spirit and attitude of true agapé love, as displayed through the fruit of the Spirit.

For this to happen, our Saviour Jesus Christ - through the workings of the indwelling Holy Spirit - must change and fill us from the inside so that what people see on the outside is God-driven.

Someone once said, *"You can give without loving, but you can't love without giving"*. Or as Gene Barron wrote, *"The world will not care what we know until they know what we care"*.

So, at every opportunity, let us be kind. Let us think no evil. Let us rejoice in truth. We must dare to love in a world that does not know how to love. This is our Christian witness.

Annette Johnson

MONDAY 29th

If you love only the people who love you, why should you receive a blessing? Even sinners love those who love them!
Luke 6:32 (GNT)

LOVE – Reading: Romans 12:1-21

The focus verse for today is part of Jesus' sermon as He stood in the plain; He had just spent a night in prayer on a mountain. He called his followers together, and from them He chose twelve to be His apostles (Luke 6:12-17a).

Amongst the twelve is Judas, the one who would betray Him, yet Jesus treats him just like the others! This is the love He wants us to show in this dark world. In order to love like this, we need to look a little deeper into the heart of our God who loves us, even though we sin.

He looks past our faults and sees that we need a Saviour and so He forgives. He forgave those who failed to heed the messages sent through His prophets, and sent His only Son to take the punishment that we deserved. Such love.

Jesus could have come to live a life of luxury, but instead the King of kings came quietly, born to a virgin in a stable. Nearby were shepherds who heard the announcement of the Saviour's birth from the angel of the Lord, then they saw a multitude of the heavenly hosts praising God and saying, *"Glory to God in the highest, and on earth peace, good will toward men"* (Luke 2:14). Such love.

Like other children, Jesus grows. We hear that He went to the temple when He was twelve years old and sat with the doctors hearing them and asking them questions. He came with such humility although He is the living Word. Such love.

Jesus starts His ministry when He is thirty years old, turning water into wine at a wedding in Cana of Galilee. He came so discreetly, not wanting to draw attention to Himself. Such love.

In ministry, He continued to show Himself as the promised Messiah, teaching, healing, delivering, but most noticeable of all was the compassion with which He ministered. He knew that he came to die, His time on earth was limited, so He focused on the purpose of reaching the lost.

He asks us to do the opposite of the world, to swim upstream, to turn the other cheek, to give and not to ask for any reward. To love when we are faced with hatred.

This is how to be salt and light.

BVG

TUESDAY 30th

Salt is good. But if it no longer tastes like salt, how can it be made salty again? Have salt among you and live at peace with each other
Mark 9:50 (CEV)

YOU ARE THE SALT OF THE EARTH – Reading: Mark 9:43-50

I answered a telephone call at work recently.

I said hello, announced my department, my name and waited for a response from the caller (a member of the general public). *"Ohhhhh, I was having lots of thoughts…lots of them"*, the caller said and then fell silent for a few seconds. I waited for her to continue. *"Now they're gone. The moment you spoke, they stopped. It's peaceful".* She sounded surprised. My calls are monitored by my employers, and religious responses are not allowed so I said gently, *"How can I help you today?"* The caller answered but this time her tone was professional.

I began to process her request and interacted with her sometimes. The call took a while and I apologised for keeping her waiting. *"It's okay; I can listen to your voice all day"*, she responded.

After the call was over, I thought about what she had said. Her mind was being bombarded with *"lots of thoughts"* that she could not control but suddenly these thoughts disappeared when she heard the voice of the Holy Spirit in me. Yes, the Holy Spirit speaks through us, Dear Believers. Why? Because He lives in us. Jesus Christ in me touched the caller in her moment of need. How many times have we read in the Bible that *"We are the salt of the earth"* and truly not considered that we really are the salt. We really make a huge difference, helping others knowingly and unknowingly.

Jesus Christ lives in us and is the Light of the World. He said that we too are the light of the world (Matthew 5:14) therefore we should impact every person that we come into contact with. The caller heard the voice of Jesus in me that day and instantly felt His peace.

December 2025
Theme: Salt & Light

The storm is loud and raging
Its wind blows hard at me
Its many voices roaring
Words to make me weak.

God speaks His peace
The storm…has ceased
Oh, the sweet voice of Jesus
Speaks peace, peace to me.
(verse 1 & chorus of song by MJB)

Be assured, dear child of God, that He lives within you. Continue to trust Him.

Have a beautiful day knowing that Jesus Christ in you will touch others.

Minister MB

*WEDNESDAY 31st

You're here to be the light...God is not a secret to be kept. We're going public with this, as public as a city on a hill
Matthew 5:16 (MSG)

LET IT SHINE! – Reading: John 15:17-27

Could it be that we have become too quiet when others are being very loud? Could it be that the darkness we see in this world is rapidly extinguishing the light?

While I think it's time to *"Arise"*, it is also a time to *"Awake"*! Look at what has happened this year, and no doubt will continue to happen in the year to come. Daily we wake to devastating news in the world and in the weather. Not only are these perilous times, but they are also perverse times.

The darkness of the culture is invading even the most sacred spaces of our lives challenging our doctrine, our traditions and our worship. I came into the new year determined not to be quiet anymore, to own fully who I am as a person of faith, celebrating the fact that I have firm convictions about what and why I believe.

The LBGTQ+ communities are not hiding, those who support binary and non-binary lifestyles are not hiding. The Conservatives and Labour parties, along with others on both side of the Atlantic, are propagating their political agendas, they are not hiding.

We are and always MUST be the light of the world and the salt of the earth! While preaching a message from John 14:6, *"I am the way, the truth and the life",* I spoke of the need for the church to stop apologising for being who we are. During the message I shared that, *"The drug dealers, and drug users are not apologising for their behaviour, neither are the homosexuals".*

Soon after, a few people walked out. Even while preaching I noticed, but immediately I was encouraged that when the Word is being preached, it is going to make people uncomfortable, and yes some will walk out, but that is what should happen when sin is being confronted!

December 2025
Theme: Salt & Light

Don't stop living with and for the truth, don't ever be ashamed of your faith, walk and stand tall! The Light of the World has come and now we are the light. Keep shining, keep being the salt that savours the world.

The year has gone, and a new year will hopefully soon begin, but I exhort us all, *"Let us not be weary in well doing: for in due season we shall reap if we faint not"* (Galatians 6:9).

This little light of mine, I'm going to let it shine, let it shine, let is shine, let it shine!

Dexter E. Edmund
Presiding Bishop, BUCJC Apostolic UK & Europe

*New Year's Eve

They said:

- *God is a bridge over troubled waters! Mother Chloe Dunn*
- *Always let your failures be your teacher, not your undertaker! Mother Margaret Brown*
- *Go down in prayer, and rise to meet your day! Mother Sweedie Edmund*
- *The LORD is my shepherd. Mother Pearline Miller*
- *Believe and receive. Doubt and do without! Mother Ethlyn Simmonds*
- *Walk in your calling with confidence, with power, with the cloak of Christ's anointing, and excellence! Mother Alberta Saunders*
- *Keep walking in victory! Dr Una Davis*
- *Don't wait to be discovered, discover yourself! Overseer Joy Henry*
- *Keep your faith in Jesus. Keep believing because He never fails. Mother Marian Bell*
- *Don't cut it! Don't Trim it! Mother Alvera Landell*
- *Avoid unnecessary temptation! Mother Gloria Fearon*
- *Hold on to your faith and don't be fearful. Pastor Verna Wynter*
- *We are going through rough rivers, but God is with us! Mother Cherry Redman*
- *Mercy is not getting what you deserve. Pastor Hazel Jacobs*
- *The world's system of parenting has taken over, but stand for God in your home. Mother Icilda Hall*
- *Church is my life! Mother Beverley Donaldson*
- *If in doubt, check it out! Dr Una Davis*
- *Are you wearing a petticoat? Mother Maudeline Laird*
- *Do what you can, when you can! Mother Beverley Donaldson*
- *The Lord continue to bless you richly! Pastor Hazel Jacobs*
- *No matter how you feel, pick yourself up, wash your face, fix your hair, and face your day! Mother Sweedie Edmund*
- *A friend that can be bought is not worth anything! Overseer Joy Henry*
- *In all things give thanks. Mother Victoria Nicely*
- *The whole Word of God is my favourite! Mother Vivelyn Sheppey*
- *O thank you, Jesus! Mother Gloria Brooks*
- *God is not a microwave God - He's not a push button God either! Whatever we want from Him, we have to wait! Mother Ethlyn Simmonds*
- *If you don't have anything good to say about anyone, say nothing! Mother Gloria Fearon*
- *Make sure you have the Holy Ghost! Pastor Hazel Jacobs*

SUPPORT DIRECTORY

Please contact one of our professionally qualified Bethel UK Counsellors if you have been emotionally affected by any of the subjects covered in *"I Arise"* 2025: **Bethel Counselling Initiative 07783 046250.**

Alternatively, please see the list below which includes independent agencies in the UK who will be able to offer you support:

Child Bereavement UK
https://www.childbereavementuk.org/
Helpline: 0800 02 888 40
Email:helpline@childbereavementuk.org

Provides support for children and young people up to the age of 25 who are facing bereavement, and anyone impacted by the death of a child of any age. They offer support sessions for individuals, couples, families and children and groups for families, parents and young people. Also provides a helpline and guidance for professionals.

Cruse
https://www.cruse.org.uk/
Helpline: 0808 808 1677 (Monday to Friday 9am to 9pm)
Email:helpline@cruse.org.uk
Cruse Chat live online chat also available

A national charity offering bereavement support, information and campaigning. Cruse offers up to six sessions of one-to-one counselling support, usually on the phone / online, as well as a free helpline and chat support. The website includes guides to understanding grief that are written by bereavement specialists, and information about what to do after someone dies.

Dementia UK
Tel: 0800 888 6678
Carers Direct - helpline for Carers: 0300 123 1053
John's Campaign: 01245 231898 (support to be able to sit with /support loved ones whilst in hospital). Contact Julia Jones julia-jones@talk21.com or Nicci Gerrard nicci.gerrard@icloud.com
Admiral Nurse Dementia Helpline 0800 888 6678
Age UK National Helpline 0800 6781602

Hope Again (Cruse)
https://www.hopeagain.org.uk/
Tel: 0808 808 1677 (Monday to Friday 9.30am to 5pm)
Email:hopeagain@cruse.org.uk

Trained volunteers are available to speak on the free helpline or by email. The website includes parental / guardian advice, videos and resources for families on how to support a child or young person who is grieving.

MIND
http://www.mind.org.uk/
Info line (Tel.): 0300 123 3393 (open 9am to 6pm, Monday to Friday)
Legal line (Tel.): 0300 4666463 (open 9am to 6pm, Monday to Friday)
Mind's Info line provides information and signposting about mental health problems, where to get help, treatment options and advocacy services. Legal Line is a telephone service offering legal information and general advice on mental health related law e.g., on being detained under the Mental Health Act ('sectioned'), mental capacity, community care, discrimination and equality.

National Association for People Abused in Childhood (NAPAC)
https://napac.org.uk/
Tel: 0808 801 0331 (helpline open Monday to Thursday: 10am to 9pm, Friday: 10am to 6pm)

Email:support@napac.org.uk

A registered charity providing support and information for adult survivors of any form of child abuse.

National Domestic Abuse Hotline
https://www.nationaldahelpline.org.uk/

Tel: 0808 2000 247 (free and 24/7)
Live chat also available through the website Monday to Friday, 3pm to 10pm.

Run by Refuge, this national helpline provides emotional and practical support, including helping individuals to find a refuge or other place of safety and access specialist services in their locality.

National Stalking Helpline
Tel: 0808 802 0300
https://www.suzylamplugh.org/am-i-being-stalked-tool

The National Stalking Helpline is run by Suzy Lamplugh Trust. They provide information and guidance on topics including:
•The law in relation to stalking and harassment in the United Kingdom
•Reporting stalking or harassment
•Effective gathering of evidence
•Ensuring your personal safety

Rape Crisis
https://rapecrisis.org.uk
Tel: 0808 802 9999
Live chat available through the website.

Rape crisis is a charity working hard to end sexual violence and abuse. They provide support after rape, sexual assault, sexual abuse or any form of sexual violence.

Relate
https://www.relate.org.uk
A national charity offering support for marriages in crisis

Shelter
https://england.shelter.org.uk/
Helpline: 0808 800 4444
Live chat available through the website.
National charity providing one-to-one, personalised help with housing issues and homelessness, a free emergency helpline and free legal advice for people who have lost their homes or who are facing eviction.

Silverline
www.thesilverline.org.uk
Helpline Tel: 0800 470 80 90

Silverline is a national, free, confidential helpline for older people offering friendship, advice and information. It is open 24 hours a day for anyone who feels alone or wants to talk about something. As well as the helpline, they offer telephone friendship (a weekly 30-minute call between an older person and a Silver Line Friend volunteer), Silver Letters (a fortnightly exchange of a letter between an older person and a volunteer), Silver Circles (a call between a group of older people on a shared interest or topic, taking place each week for 60 minutes) and Silver Line Connects (help with informing and connecting an older person with national and local services).

The Daisy Chain Project: Domestic Abuse Legal Advice Charity
https://www.thedaisychainproject.com
Email: info@thedaisychainproject.com

A charity based in Worthing with a UK-wide reach that aims to help fight domestic violence by providing pro bono legal advice, educating people about what constitutes domestic abuse. The Daisy Chain Project legal team consists of qualified and regulated barristers and solicitors who offer free legal support to men and women experiencing, or fleeing, domestic abuse. All barristers and solicitors are regulated by the Bar Standards Board and Solicitors Regulation Authority respectively.

Victim Support
https://www.victimsupport.org.uk/
Helpline: 0808 1689 111 (24/7)
Webchat available through the website

Provides free and confidential support for people affected by crime and traumatic events, regardless of whether they have reported the crime to the police. Services include information and advice, immediate emotional and practical help, longer term emotional and practical help, advocacy, peer support and group work, restorative justice, personal safety services, help in navigating the criminal justice system.

Young Minds Crisis Messenger
https://www.kooth.com/
For urgent help text YM to 85258

Provides free, 24/7 crisis support across the UK if you are experiencing a mental health crisis. All texts are answered by trained volunteers, with support from experienced clinical supervisors. Texts are free from EE, O2, Vodafone, 3, Virgin Mobile, BT Mobile, GiffGaff, Tesco Mobile and Telecom Plus.

Contact us at: bethelwomen@betheluniteduk.org.uk

Printed in Great Britain
by Amazon